Healing for the Heart

Encouragement and Truth
for the Chronically Ill

Peggy Holt

WESTBOW
PRESS
A DIVISION OF THOMAS NELSON

WestBow Press books may be ordered through booksellers or by contacting:

WestBow Press
A Division of Thomas Nelson
1663 Liberty Drive
Bloomington, IN 47403
www.westbowpress.com
1-(866) 928-1240

Because of the dynamic nature of the Internet, any web addresses or links contained in this book may have changed since publication and may no longer be valid. The views expressed in this work are solely those of the author and do not necessarily reflect the views of the publisher, and the publisher hereby disclaims any responsibility for them.

Any people depicted in stock imagery provided by Thinkstock are models, and such images are being used for illustrative purposes only.

Certain stock imagery © Thinkstock.

ISBN: 978-1-4497-4613-1 (sc)
ISBN: 978-1-4497-4615-5 (hc)
ISBN: 978-1-4497-4614-8 (e)

Library of Congress Control Number: 2012906485

Printed in the United States of America

WestBow Press rev. date: 5/25/2012

To Tammy Baldwin

If I were to express my thanks over and over again, I could still never really communicate it enough. To say that I couldn't have made it back without you would be to deny the power of God, but I am so grateful that He chose to have our paths cross for a brief but critical period of time. He knew I needed your patient love, your firm but gentle guidance, and your God-directed counsel. If some of the entries sound familiar to you, it's probably either because you've shared them with me or because I've shared them with you. Thank you for being a true friend who has helped to sharpen me. I love you.

And to Jack and June Palmer

Thanks for supporting me in the continuation of the recovery process. Your love and prayers meant so much to me. Thank you for understanding with me that this project was God's plan for my life during a time that He closed all other doors. My life didn't seem to make too much sense, and I couldn't reveal to others what I was really doing in those long months of waiting and trusting, so I appreciated your understanding. Thanks for believing in me and for encouraging me as I tackled this project. I am so grateful for the opportunity to get to know you. I love you both.

Acknowledgments

First and foremost, I must give credit to God, the one who made this project possible. From beginning to end, He was in control. I would never have chosen the years of illness that God used to teach me His truth. I could never have learned the lessons without God's grace, patience, and help. I would not have tackled such a huge project without God's prompting. Neither would I have chosen the time of unemployment that God gave me in which to write the book. Each of these factors was brought about by God's hand.

God has given me the sobering opportunity to share His truth with others. Although many ill people have learned the same lessons that God taught me during my illness, various factors have prevented them from writing those lessons down to share with others. Some never regained their health, some didn't formulate the lessons clearly, some returned to busy lives and numerous responsibilities, and some lacked the skill or ability to write.

By His grace God has blessed me in all four areas. He restored my health and mental ability so that I was capable of working on the project. He left me unemployed at the end of my illness, giving me time to spend in His Word in order to solidify the lessons He had taught. After a series of what looked like certain job opportunities, God unexpectedly gave me an extra year of unemployment in which to write the book. Finally, through my many years of teaching English and studying the Bible, God gave me the skills to write a book of this nature.

Ultimately, all of the insights contained in this book are God's truths, which is the only reason they are effective. These truths represent the accumulation of life-long study of the Bible. Most of the entries come from personal Bible study or from meditation on specific verses. That being the case, there are some sources that I recognize as having contributed to my understanding of Biblical truth, thereby having specific impact on this book.

I would first like to express my appreciation for several individuals who helped me to learn some of the lessons contained in this book. Through sermons, conversations, and counsel, they guided me toward truth. Most significant was Tammy Baldwin, my former pastor's wife, who spent many hours with me at a critical point in the learning process. Her husband, Jared Baldwin, preached some helpful sermons. Several of the lessons were learned through sermons preached by Mark Minnick, who additionally taught me valuable skills for studying the Word of God. I also recognize the impact of Pastor Jack Palmer. Some of his sermons guided me, and conversations with him and his wife June were also very helpful. Finally, I am grateful for the input of missionary friends Kristi Colas and Jane Gibb.

In addition to these individuals, there are some books that have influenced me along the way. The books listed here provided specific springboards for thought and encouraged me toward deeper Bible study in areas they discussed. *Streams in the Desert* by Mrs. L. B. Cowman brought many helpful verses to my attention. Other impacting books include *Lies Women Believe* by Nancy Leigh DeMoss, *Disciplines of a Godly Woman* by Barbara Hughes, *Humility* by Andrew Murray, and *Not By Chance* by Layton Talbert.

A small group of people was aware of this project from the beginning, or at least for most of the process. These individuals were valuable as they provided both prayer support and encouragement. I thank God for Luke Holt, Kristi Colas, and Deborah Steel, who have consistently been willing to pray for me in various needs, as they gladly prayed with me on this project. Tammy Baldwin was aware and prayed with me from the beginning. Pastor and Mrs. Jack Palmer and missionary friend Jennifer Mitchell also prayed throughout a significant portion of the project.

I must express my appreciation for my parents, Lee and Betty Holt. When I was unemployed, they readily opened their home to me, which certainly played an important role throughout the process. Though they were not aware of all that was going on, they patiently allowed me to have many quiet hours in which I retreated to "the dungeon." Their support allowed me to spend many months both in critical communion with God and also in incorporating God's truth into manuscript form.

I am very grateful for Jennifer Mitchell, Leslie Rheinheimer, and Shawn Chisholm. These three wonderful ladies very willingly agreed to read through my manuscript for me. In spite of the challenges of their busy lives, they read, evaluated, identified errors, and offered suggestions. Most importantly, they offered words of encouragement and support, providing the wonderful reassurance that I had been able to record God's truth in an effective way.

Finally, I want to mention Cliff Jenkin. Though he never knew of my project, I had hoped that he also would read through my manuscript. In the providence of God, Cliff went home to heaven several months before I reached that point in the project. Cliff was a man who learned many of the lessons contained in this book. He was a friend and encouragement to me in my illness and a challenge to many through his own illness. While his body was weak, his heart was healthy, as God healed it with His wonderful truth.

Introduction

I've been there. I hope you'll realize that as you read these pages. Early in 2007 I was diagnosed with chronic Lyme disease. The disease, exhibiting only isolated and random symptoms, had gone undiagnosed for perhaps close to twenty years. In 2006 it went very active, leading to the diagnosis and four years of treatment. I know about aches and pains, debilitating fatigue, limited mobility, sleepless nights, emotional challenges, mental limitations, and all kinds of other strange things happening in the body. I certainly don't claim that my illness was the worst ever; you may have numerous symptoms and areas of challenge that I can't relate to. I do know what it is like to spend months barely moving and years isolated from normal life. I understand physical limitations, a brain bound by fog, thoughts and emotions gone crazy, and the uncertainty of unanswered questions.

Although you may be glad for someone to understand you (finally!), it is not primarily my experience that allows me to help you. The help comes from the Word of God – from what God has taught me and from what He has used to comfort me. All I can do is to pass on the lessons and truths that God used to help me through the trying years. The Word of God was what I needed. My words are not magic; God's words, however, are supernaturally potent. They are comforting, enlightening, and powerful. Only the Bible has the help you need. It is not my understanding or sympathy that is most helpful, but God's understanding and sympathy. God does indeed understand, and He does have sympathy. He cares about you, and because He cares, He wants to help. Unlike mere humans, God has the ability to fulfill His sympathetic desire; He can actually give you help.

As you can tell simply from the number of entries, this devotional is not intended for someone who has the flu for a few weeks, has a broken leg, or is recovering from surgery. Those are real illnesses and have their challenges. While I don't intend to minimize their difficulty, a long-term illness presents an increased level of challenge that does not exist in a short-term illness. These entries are designed for people with extended, perhaps life-long, illnesses. It is for those who are significantly debilitated month after month and year after year. Perhaps as you begin to read, your illness has already lasted for weeks, months, or even years. You have been longing for someone to share encouraging truth with you. My prayer and desire is that this book will do that over and over again.

When you are dealing with the symptoms of a serious illness, it can be hard to get spiritual input. You barely have the energy to try, and your brain has trouble processing what you do read. You're not even sure you know how to think right any more. You may not be able to attend church, and you are isolated from Christian friends. The barriers to spiritual nourishment are real, while the need for it is greater than ever. You must have that critical input from God's Word. To go without it is devastating. Your need is so great that you need truth tailored specifically for your situation. Unfortunately, there are two significant factors working against you. Not only is your strength too low to allow you to seek out pertinent truth, but the timing is also so critical that you can't afford to wait until you stumble across those truths. You need focused truth, and you need it now. My desire is to give you truth that is especially designed for the precarious situation you are in.

Far more than just an occasional lesson, you need frequent and constant reminders of God's truth. I hope that these short entries will give you those reminders, and that they will be something for you to sink your thoughts into each day. May they be nuggets that you can hang on to and remind yourself of on a daily, or even hourly, basis. God's Word can help you to be victorious through the trial. In the midst of your affliction, you don't have to turn from God with a heart grown cold. You don't even have to stagnate, merely muddling through until the trial is over. Instead, you should actually have spiritual progress through the illness. You should have a relationship that is constantly closer to God and a fellowship that is increasingly sweeter.

The various entries have three purposes: they are designed to bring comfort, clarification, and challenge. The majority are intended to bring comfort, because that is what you most crave when you are hurting and needy. Life is hard, and you want encouragement. Life is oppressive, and you want to hear words of hope. Life hurts, and you want to know that someone cares. You just need something that will help you to keep going. Many of these comforting entries are based on verses from the Psalms, though there is a lot of comfort throughout the Bible. These entries share God's promises and reassurances. They present His care for you. Some of them examine God's names and characteristics, which are wonderful sources of unchanging comfort.

The second intended purpose is that of clarification. You need to know what to think regarding troubles and trials. In the midst of illness, you are assaulted in a heightened way with expectations. You have your own expectations of how you think you ought to respond in your trial. Perhaps just as troubling, you have the stated and implied expectations of others. Both sets of expectations contribute to an overwhelming burden to be sure you are "handling it right." When it comes down to it, you don't need to know how others think you should act. You don't need your own perceptions of how you should act. You need to know what God says and what He expects from you in the midst of trouble. Many of these entries come from a thorough study of what the epistles have to say about trials. Seeing God's truth about trials can provide a great deal of help and clarity.

The third purpose is to challenge, because being ill does not exempt you from being a Christian. You still need to please God and follow His Word. Illness does not give you a free pass or an excuse to act and think any way you want to. There are some specific temptations that come along with illness, areas in which you must be especially alert. When you are ill and suffering, there are some temptations that are ever so much stronger and ever so much harder to combat. You must be challenged with the truth of God's Word. If you allow sin to build up for months or years without confronting it, there is little hope for you to be a fit servant of God. There is little opportunity for you to minister to others through your trial. You must unflinchingly face the areas that God wants to address. You must confess sins and keep the pathway clear so that God can effectively speak to you. A careless and permissive view of sin will hamper your walk with God and will make what is already a challenging ordeal that much harder.

Interestingly, the areas of clarification and challenge also bring comfort. There is peace in knowing what God has to say about trials, because it removes some of the uncertainties from your markedly uncertain situation. As you understand clearly what God wants from you, you are freed from the unrealistic expectations of others. It is comforting to know that God is the only one you need to please and that He instructs you about how to please Him. As you are challenged and rebuked by God's Word and as you make the appropriate changes in your life, you enjoy restoration and sweet fellowship with God; this restoration also brings comfort. There is comfort in knowing that God is still working in your life and that He has not given up on you. A lesson learned is simply confirmation that you really are His beloved child. So, whether an entry is designed primarily for comfort, for clarification, or for challenge, my desire is that God's words will strengthen your soul. Whether or not God grants you physical healing, I trust that He will give you healing for your heart.

I have sometimes been frustrated with devotional books. Too frequently I have read entries which had as their foundations an illustration or a mere snatch of a verse. The brief phrase or selected words from the verse were often out of context, and the entries ended up having nothing to do with what the verse was actually about. It is not my intent to criticize the labors of others, nor do I wish to deny the help they have given to many. It is my belief, however, that for something to provide the best help and the most benefit, it must be based on what God actually says. It must reflect what God intended to teach. Each entry in this devotional is therefore based on a verse or passage of Scripture, and I have attempted by God's grace to accurately examine the truth that God intended to share. An apt illustration or a life parallel might provide momentary encouragement. Man's words semi-supported by a phrase of Scripture might inspire someone for a short while. By contrast, God's enduring and eternal Word is the only source of answers and hope that really last. The Bible is filled with truths that can be returned to over and over again, and it will always have the same message. God's Word must be the source of help.

I have kept the entries short and relatively simple. I know how challenged your brain can be and how hard it can be to think. For the same reason, I have used the New American Standard Bible. If you prefer a different translation, please feel free to look up the verses and read them in the translation with which you are most familiar. I have ended each entry with a brief prayer, not as a substitute for your talking to God and not as a complete way of doing so, but more as a reminder to talk to God and as a prompt to direct your thoughts.

Illnesses don't come at convenient times or fit into neat, confined spaces. They don't start on January 1, and neither does this devotional. The entries are simply numbered consecutively so that you can pick it up and start at any time of the year. If you miss a day, you won't be thrown off schedule, and if you want to spend more than one day on an entry, you can do that as well. If you need additional encouragement throughout the course of a day, you can read additional entries. If you finish the devotional and are still sick, you can go back to the beginning and start over again.

Finally, I need to clarify that this book is written for Christians. God cares about the unsaved who are ill because He is a God of love and compassion, but the real answers to any problem, including the challenges of illness, can be found only through God and a relationship with Him. That relationship is the starting point for real understanding of God's truth.

A Christian is one who believes the following:

1. That he is a sinner both by nature and by action and does things that are displeasing to God.
    As it is written, "There is none righteous, not even one." (Romans 3:10)
    For all have sinned and fall short of the glory of God. (Romans 3:23)

2. That his sin puts a barrier between him and a holy God, condemning him to spend eternity in hell.
    For the wages of sin is death. (Romans 6:23a)
    And if anyone's name was not found written in the book of life, he was thrown into the lake of fire. (Revelation 20:15)

"He who believes in the Son has eternal life; but he who does not obey the Son will not see life, but the wrath of God abides on him." (John 3:36)

3. That he cannot do anything to save himself or make peace with God.

   For by grace you have been saved through faith; and that not of yourselves, it is the gift of God; not as a result of works, so that no one may boast. (Ephesians 2:8-9)

   He saved us, not on the basis of deeds which we have done in righteousness, but according to His mercy, by the washing of regeneration and renewing by the Holy Spirit. (Titus 3:5)

4. That God, in love, sent His perfect Son Jesus to die on the cross, paying the penalty for man's sin and thereby providing the opportunity for reconciliation with God and eternity in heaven; Jesus then rose from the dead, conquering sin and death.

   "For God so loved the world, that He gave His only begotten Son, that whoever believes in Him shall not perish, but have eternal life." (John 3:16)

   He made Him who knew no sin to be sin on our behalf, so that we might become the righteousness of God in Him. (II Corinthians 5:21)

   But God demonstrates His own love toward us, in that while we were yet sinners, Christ died for us. (Romans 5:8)

   Knowing that Christ, having been raised from the dead, is never to die again; death no longer is master over Him. (Romans 6:9)

5. That God will hear the sinner's prayer of faith as he humbly accepts the gift of salvation provided by Jesus' sacrifice and earnestly asks God to save him.

   For "Whoever will call on the name of the Lord will be saved." (Romans 10:13)

   That if you confess with your mouth Jesus as Lord, and believe in your heart that God raised Him from the dead, you will be saved; for with the heart a person believes, resulting in righteousness, and with the mouth he confesses, resulting in salvation. (Romans 10:9-10)

   But as many as received Him, to them He gave the right to become children of God, even to those who believe in His name. (John 1:12)

Only with this relationship in place can you fully understand the concepts presented in this book. Only then can you have the help of your loving heavenly

Father. The lessons learned from the Bible must be based on a relationship with God. If you have not yet received Him as your Savior, you have a more serious problem than any physical illness. More than the possibility of just physical death, you have a condition that will lead to spiritual death – permanent separation from God. The good news is that your spiritual illness has a fail-proof cure. God will receive all who come to Him seeking salvation.

Day 1

"However, put forth Your hand now, and touch his bone and his flesh; he will curse You to Your face." So the LORD said to Satan, "Behold, he is in your power, only spare his life."
Job 2:5-6

The challenge of a chronic or serious illness cannot be underestimated. You may be thinking something like this: "It's only an illness. Things like this happen to people all the time. It shouldn't be too hard to get through." Others have perhaps reinforced this casual assessment, saying something like, "Oh, is that all that's wrong? You're being treated, aren't you?"

While you may have high expectations for yourself, and while others may quickly forget that anything is wrong, the fact is that a serious illness presents a tremendous challenge. When Satan first appeared before God, God allowed him to sorely test Job, while restraining him from any attack on Job's body. Satan made some horrific and staggering attacks. Job lost his livelihood, his investments, and his wealth. In perhaps a single hour, everything he had worked for was destroyed. As if this were not enough, he then lost all ten of his children in a terrible accident. Although God allowed *these* attacks, He did *not* allow a physical attack on Job.

When Job passed the initial tests, Satan came to God again. He asked God to send a real test, an attack on Job's body. Satan insinuated by his request that a physical attack would be harder to deal with than what Job had already faced. God seemed to agree with Satan's assessment. Not only had He initially protected Job from this type of attack, but when Satan threw out this new challenge, God allowed him to move to the next level in his attack.

If the example of Job's response is a valid indication, the illness *was* more challenging to deal with than the previous trials had been. Job had handled some extremely difficult circumstances unbelievably well; it was the illness that finally put him over the edge. Illness can have a devastating effect on people's minds and spirits in addition to their bodies. Man is probably incapable of explaining the effect on the non-physical realm, but that effect is very real, very common, and very daunting. While enduring an illness is not impossible, it must be faced soberly and realistically.

"Father, help me not to face this illness too lightly. May I soberly realize that it will be tough and that I am not up to the challenge. I must have Your help."

Day 2

Our soul waits for the LORD;
He is our help and our shield.
Psalm 33:20

An illness makes us dependent, at least to some extent. Instead of being able to do everything for ourselves, we may now have to rely on someone else to do the housework and yard work. Perhaps we need someone else to drive us around or to take care of some of our responsibilities. We might have to rely on others even for our personal care. From a medical standpoint, we are dependent upon doctors to evaluate and make decisions. We need them to prescribe treatments or recommend options.

It is a relief to have support that we can count on. It is a blessing to have reliable helpers on whom we can depend. The best help of man, however, pales in comparison to the help of God. While we rely on family members, friends, and medical personnel for many things, our most important needs can be met only by God. We can wait confidently on Him, and He will be our help and shield.

The speakers of this psalm waited on God, trusting their care and lives to Him. God is a worthy and dependable source of help that can be completely relied upon. The psalmist explains God's qualifications and tells why trust in Him can be so certain. God wonderfully created the entire earth and the skies; He continues to manage every aspect of the earth. God intricately controls every aspect of world affairs, bending world leaders to conform to His wishes. God is also faithful to interact with His people and deliver them.

Because God is so great, His people fear Him. They can wait for Him and trust in Him. They can do this confidently because of who He is. He is a God who constantly watches over His own. He is a God who shows mercy. He is a God who delivers from death and gives help and protection to His children. This God can be trusted. We can depend on Him to meet our greatest needs.

"Father, thank You that You are reliable and that I can wait confidently on You to meet all my needs. Thank You for Your help that surpasses the help of all others."

Day 3

"In My Father's house are many dwelling places; if it were not so, I would have told you; for I go to prepare a place for you. If I go and prepare a place for you, I will come again and receive you to Myself, that where I am, there you may be also."
John 14:2–3

These words of Jesus were spoken for the purpose of comfort. The hearts of His disciples were troubled and fearful, and Jesus gave them truth to reassure them. Jesus' antidote for their troubled hearts was given in their time of need, but it would also be effective for troubled times in the future. Now they knew what to think about when their hearts needed comfort.

Our hearts today can be calmed and comforted by the same truth. We can be encouraged and strengthened by remembering that this world, with all of its troubles, is not the end. We have heaven to look forward to. Heaven is a place that God has made to share with all of His children. Jesus Himself has gone there to help with the preparations. He is making a place for each one of us. Some glorious day He will come and take us to be with Him. We will be united with our Savior and our God forever. No matter how bad things get on earth, we have the sure promise that we will spend eternity in heaven.

In addition to being united with God, we will also be reunited with our loved ones who have gone on before. We will be in a perfect place that is filled with the beauty and glory of God. There will be no more sin, no evil or wickedness to soil our surroundings. We will have no more pain and no more suffering. There will never again be an illness to weaken or limit our bodies. There will be no more medicines, no more doctors, no more surgeries, and no more hospitals. Our bodies will be restored and made new. Heaven will be a place of glorious perfection and complete joy. Most amazing of all, our time in heaven will never end. We will live with God forever in that wonderful place that surpasses our imaginations.

"Oh, Father, what a wonderful promise! When my days are hard and my heart is troubled, help me to remember the reality of heaven. Thank You for such an incredible hope."

Day 4

You also joining in helping us through your prayers, so that thanks may be given by many persons on our behalf for the favor bestowed on us through the prayers of many.
II Corinthians 1:11

For a variety of reasons, you may have decided not to let other people know about your illness or about its severity. You might think you are really not so important that you have to bother others with your problems. It may seem there are much more serious things for people to pray about. You may think your silence is protecting those you care about. Maybe you don't want to sound like you are complaining. You may want to handle your illness on your own, without relying on other people. You may not want to admit you are weak or have a problem. You may be embarrassed to discuss the particular type of illness you are facing. You may dread all the fussing that people would do and the free advice you would receive. You may even fear that people wouldn't really care very much, and you don't want to be disappointed if they don't.

While each of these reasons may seem to have some merit, the Bible reveals that it is not wrong to let others know that you are in a trial. You don't have to hide your needs. In fact, there is good support for sharing that information with fellow believers. In verse eight of the above chapter, Paul purposefully told the believers about his trial, not wanting them to be unaware. It was important for them to know of his struggle. The purpose of sharing his need with others was so they could join with him in prayer. The prayers of others are part of the help that supports a sufferer through his trial. Then when the trial is over, the thanks to God can also be shared by others. In God's plan many people pray together, and then many people are able to give thanks together. The trial (with its victory) is an opportunity to thank God, and that rejoicing should not be limited to just one person.

"Thank You, Father, for fellow believers who can pray with me. I look forward to the day when we can all rejoice together in what You will do through our prayers."

Day 5

"And do not suppose that you can say to yourselves, 'We have Abraham for our father'; for I say to you that from these stones God is able to raise up children to Abraham."
Matthew 3:9

Stop for a minute and think about the fact that we serve a God to whom nothing is impossible. There is no situation, health or otherwise, that is too hard for our God. He is able to give great healing, but His power is not limited to just the realm of healing. The simple fact is that God is able to do amazing things that we cannot even comprehend. In the example of this verse, He is able to produce living, breathing beings from mere stones. Impossible? Not for God. He is capable of all kinds of impossible things.

God can produce food in the middle of nowhere, as He did for Elijah. He can provide resources from the most unlikely places, such as providing money for Peter from the mouth of a fish. He provided enough water in the middle of the desert to sustain an entire nation of people, and He gave them shoes that lasted for dozens of years. God can make food have tremendous nourishment, as He sustained Elijah for forty days on a single day's food. He can control the weather, causing it to reach extremes or change rapidly. He can darken the sun, make it stand still, or even go backwards. He can control the earth itself, opening holes in the ground, moving mountains, causing earthquakes, and stopping rivers. God can influence the most powerful kings on earth. He can direct in their decisions and can control the events of history. He can destroy cities and even entire nations almost immediately, as He did with Sodom and with Babylon. God's hand can do anything that God's mind determines to do. There is nothing impossible for God.

"Truly, Father, what a great God You are! Thank You that I can rely on You, for whom nothing is impossible."

Day 6

And my God will supply all your needs according to His riches in glory in Christ Jesus. Philippians 4:19

Are you needy? Do you have more needs than you would have imagined possible? Are you helpless to meet those needs? Then it should be an amazing encouragement to realize that not one of those needs is beyond the resources of God. He has all the riches of glory available to meet those needs through His wonderful Son.

God can meet your practical needs. He can provide a meal, a ride to the doctor, and money for the mounting bills. God can meet your physical needs. He can give strength for the day, relief from pain, a good night's sleep, and even healing. God can meet your mental needs. He can focus your thoughts, quiet your mind, and give you wisdom for decisions. God can meet your social needs. He can provide a timely phone call, a visit from a friend, or a cheery card with words of encouragement. God can meet your emotional needs. He can give unexpected stability, a tender hug, or privacy to cry. God can meet your spiritual needs. He can supply a friend to pray with, a reminder of a precious promise, or a verse that is perfect for your current state.

It does not matter what the need is, because no need is greater than what God can supply. Although you may not see the answer until the most desperate moment, God often works behind the scenes to bring about His answers. When the need is met, you often realize that God had begun preparing the answer weeks, months, or even years in advance. God can do that because no need ever surprises Him. He knows what you need today, and He will provide. He also knows what you will need tomorrow, and He already has a plan for meeting that need too.

"Help, Father. Meet my needs, and give me the confidence to believe that You can and will." $\longrightarrow$

My Needs (Sonnet 34)
"Oh, God, I come to You and stand in need.
Are You equipped to meet needs physical?
My health and strength, a job – great needs indeed."
"Frail child, with Me these things are possible."
"But God, I must admit my needs are more.
Can You meet needs involving wisdom, too?
Give guidance for the path that lies before?"
"Yes, child confused, I'll show you what to do."
"Well, God, You see, there is another thing.
How are You with emotions of the heart?
The pain is strong; I feel its cruel sting."
"Dear hurting child, I can much grace impart.
I'll meet all needs - yes, each and every one.
To share my riches I have just begun."

Day 7

Shout for joy, O heavens! And rejoice, O earth!
Break forth into joyful shouting, O mountains!
For the LORD has comforted His people
And will have compassion on His afflicted.
Isaiah 49:13

Perhaps you don't want people to feel sorry for you or pity you. You don't want them to treat you like a defective person or like someone whose life has fallen completely apart. You don't want people to exaggerate by creating needs that don't exist, but you do want them to have compassion on the needs that do exist. What you want is someone to care.

God has compassion, and His compassion is directed toward people who are in need. God's heart desires to help afflicted, needy people. Because God is compassionate, He hears His people when they call on Him in times of distress (Deuteronomy 4:30-31). He won't fail them or turn His back on them. When the time comes to rescue His people, God will be gracious. He will have compassion on them and arise on their behalf (Psalm 102:13). God performs great wonders for His children, wonders that are worthy of being remembered (Psalm 111:4).

In Isaiah 49, God tells a story about His people at a time when they are cast out of their land. They are bound in chains and trapped in darkness. They are hungering and thirsting, and the hot sun is blazing down upon them. God responds to these needy people with His compassion (Isaiah 49:8-13). He restores them to their land and gives them an inheritance. He gives them food even in remote places. He satisfies their hunger, quenches their thirst, and protects them from the sun. He guides them to water and makes roads for them to walk on. He comforts them. God states that He personally will deliver His people because of His compassion (Hosea 1:7). God has great compassion, and He expresses it toward those who are needy.

"Father, I have hurts and needs. I know You have compassion for me in my need. Will You show it to me by acting on my behalf?"

Day 8

In the same way the Spirit also helps our weakness; for we do not know how to pray as we should, but the Spirit Himself intercedes for us, with groanings too deep for words.
Romans 8:26

As you've lain on your couch or bed, have you thought, "I don't even know how to pray for my situation"? Should you pray for complete healing or for grace to endure? Should you pray for a miraculous answer or for the effective working of medicines? Should you pray that the surgery would be approved or that there would be an alternative treatment? Should you pray that the test would come back negative or that this would finally be the answer? And how do you pray for God's work in your heart? How do you know what He is trying to teach you? How can you pray for what you do not know?

Humanly, you are weak and don't even know how to pray. You don't always pray the right way simply because you are ignorant of what you should be asking. At a time when you are in desperate need of God's help through prayer, you don't even know what to say to Him. Thankfully, you are not alone. God has given you His Spirit to help you in your weakness. Part of the Spirit's ministry is to pray on your behalf. He takes your needs to the Father, praying for you in groanings too deep for words.

No wonder you don't know how to pray. There aren't even words to express what you should be praying – just deep sighs. I'm sure you've felt that unexplainable inner compulsion to just dump your soul on God, and there were no words with which to do it. There is a deep anguish of spirit that results in the midst of your struggles. In your anguish you don't know how to pray because you don't know what God's will is, but God knows. In these times that confound the human mind, God knows exactly what to do, and the Spirit prays for you accordingly. You can rest assured that the prayers He prays for you are the right prayers and will be answered.

7

> *"Father, I don't know how to pray, so I trust the Spirit*
> *to pray for me according to Your perfect will."*

Day 9

> *Beloved, do not be surprised at the fiery ordeal among you, which comes upon you for your*
> *testing, as though some strange thing were happening to you.*
> *I Peter 4:12*

We should not be surprised when a trial comes into our lives. There is nothing strange about such a thing happening. Trials are very common occurrences. There is no reason for us to gaze incredulously and open-mouthed at someone in a trial and wonder what he did to deserve such a fate. Neither should we look at our own lives in shocked amazement and despair, assuming that we must have done something horribly wrong. Just because we are suffering, we shouldn't make the assumption that we must be very wicked, nor should we be unduly alarmed that we have in some way incurred God's wrath.

Trials are common in the lives of Christians because they are a very necessary part of our development in godliness. God must use trials in order to help His children grow. Growth and increased strength come through struggle. There is no doubt that the trial is a struggle. The above verse describes a trial as a fiery ordeal. That phrase does not picture a birthday candle, a fireplace, or even a campfire. Instead, it is the idea of a large and raging fire, like a house fire or a forest fire. Trials can indeed be very harsh. It might seem as if the raging fire would completely overwhelm or consume us, but even the severity should not surprise us. The fire must be harsh in order to do its work. It is designed for our testing, proving our faith to see if it is genuine and valuable. The fire comes from God for that purpose, and a tiny fire would not be sufficient to accomplish the same results. God carefully directs the fire so it will accomplish His intended purposes, and the fire never rages out of His control.

> *"Father, as the fire burns, may it do its intended work in my life."*

Day 10

> *Jesus came and stood in their midst and said to them, "Peace be with you."*
> *John 20:19b*

God's desire for His people to have peace is unquestionable. Jesus' interaction with the disciples is a good illustration of this desire. After Christ's death and resurrection, the disciples were gathered together behind closed doors, fearful and uncertain. They were greatly in need of peace because of their multiple concerns, troubles, and uncertainties. Christ appeared to them and immediately tried to bring them comfort. As He stood in their midst, His first words were to wish them peace. Because He is God and the source of peace, He not only desired peace for them, but was able to give it to them. His "wish" was more than just a wish; it was an imparting. Now instead of being fearful, they gladly rejoiced.

After He had already given them peace and they were now glad and encouraged, Christ repeated His wish for peace in verse twenty-one. The disciples were in such a trying situation that Jesus gave them extra peace and reassurance. One week later (v. 26), He appeared to them again. They were apparently still in a time of fear and caution, remaining together in their closed room. On this occasion, Christ started with the same greeting. He once again desired and imparted peace to them. These repeated reassurances and bestowments of peace are a wonderful illustration of God's tender care for His children and also of His understanding of them. Rather than becoming impatient when their peace quickly fades, God continues to remind His children to be peaceful. He continues to offer His peace to them.

> *"When my thoughts become troubled, Father,*
> *remind me quickly of the peace that You make available to me."*

Day 11

> *Every word of God is tested;*
> *He is a shield to those who take refuge in Him.*
> *Proverbs 30:5*

God is a shield that is capable of protecting every person who hides in Him during an attack. God cannot and will not fail. God and His Word are closely linked, because God's Word is the revelation of God, His character, and His actions. God's Word has been thoroughly tested, and it has always been found true. Not even the tiniest part of God's Word has failed. It is completely dependable and entirely trustworthy.

When God tells how the earth was created, He does so accurately. When God lists genealogies, every name is in the correct position. When God recounts history, He never messes up the facts. When God reveals something about nature, it always holds true. When God tells the story of a man's life, He does not include a single error. When God predicts judgment, every detail will happen exactly as He has described it. When God reveals something about His character, there is no exaggeration or inconsistency. When God makes a promise, He will complete it. When God gives doctrinal instruction, every tenet is correct and never needs revision. When God records the life of His Son on earth, He gives a correct representation of the God-man. When God describes His redemptive plan, it works precisely as He says it will. When God tells of a salvation open to every man, He will not exclude anyone who comes.

A God that produces such a faithful Word is a faithful God. Just as He was capable of producing a Bible without a single error or weakness, so He is capable of protecting His children. Each of them can confidently take refuge in His Word.

"Truly, Father, Your Word is a masterpiece. It will never fail, and neither will You. I can trust You to protect me."

Day 12

Jesus Christ is the same yesterday and today and forever.
Hebrews 13:8

Life changes. In the past year, your life may have taken a totally different direction than you had anticipated and planned. People change. Sometimes that change is for the better, and sometimes that change is for the worse. When it comes down to it, there is nothing in your life or circumstances that you can definitely count on, because you don't know how any of those things will change.

Jesus, on the other hand, never changes. He never has changed, and He never will change. Because He is constant, you can always depend on Him. You can know what to expect. Jesus loved the people of the world enough to suffer and die a cruel death on their behalf; His love has not changed. Jesus had wisdom to hang each planet and star in the proper place; His wisdom has not changed. Jesus had compassion for His friends that caused Him to raise Lazarus from the dead; His compassion has not changed. Jesus offered forgiveness to Saul, a great persecutor of the church, and to Peter, who denied Him; His forgiveness has not changed. Jesus gave grace to Paul that enabled him to endure a thorn in the flesh, live a demanding life, and suffer much physical abuse; His grace has not changed. Jesus had power to calm the waves and winds of a raging storm; His power has not changed.

Jesus is the same now as He always has been. He will continue to be the same. He is the same for you as He was for Lazarus, for Paul, for the disciples, and for the multitudes. Jesus will not change.

"Thank You, Father, that You will never change. With all the uncertainty around me, I can safely rely on You."

The Same (Sonnet 5)
In days gone by, the reigning King was He,
And He was righteous, merciful, and true.
His love was real, His death enough for me.
His Word endured; He stayed right with me, too.
In life today, as mighty King He reigns,
I see His mercy, truth, and righteousness.
I know His love; His death still breaks sin's chains.
His Word holds firm; His presence is no less.
In years to come, almighty King He'll be.
His mercy, truth, and righteousness He'll show.
His love will last, His death sufficient be.
His Word will stand; He'll always with me go.
So yesterday, today, forever, just
The same is He – so worthy of my trust.

Day 13

And that which was a trial to you in my bodily condition you did not despise or loathe, but you received me as an angel of God, as Christ Jesus Himself.
Galatians 4:14

Does being ill make you no longer valuable or able to contribute to the church? Does it make you an outcast in society? According to Paul's example, neither is true in reality, and neither should be true in practice. Being ill should not be a cause for disdain by others. Quite honestly, Paul's physical condition was hard for the church to deal with. It was a burden to the people, yet they did not reject or despise him because of it. In contrast, they rallied around him and readily received him. They were even willing to give sacrificially in order to help him (v. 15).

It is not right to look down on someone who is ill. Fellow church members can't assume that the person is in sin or judge that he has no value. They can't judge him as unworthy of their love, help, and support. They should, in contrast, be burdened for his need and have a desire to help him. Beyond their care for him, they should value what he has to offer. They should still respect and cherish his spiritual gifts and the contributions he is able to make.

Paul's physical condition did not preempt him from usefulness. These people received Paul as a messenger of God and were ready to receive his message. I realize you are on the other end of the equation. You can't determine the actions or attitudes of others, but it is also important for you to recognize this same truth. Your illness doesn't make you worthless. You still have gifts that God has given you, and you can still have usefulness in His service. Instead of closing yourself off in a corner, continue doing what God enables you to do. Instead of presenting a worthless, defeated picture to others, keep using the gifts that God has entrusted to you.

"Thank You, Father, that being ill doesn't make me a cause for rejection in Your sight. Help me to fulfill the usefulness that You have for me."

Day 14

The name of the LORD is a strong tower;
The righteous runs into it and is safe.
Proverbs 18:10

Everyone in trouble needs a refuge. He needs somewhere to hide where he can be safe. He needs something to protect him from the constant attacks. There is a refuge just like that available to the righteous. That refuge is the name of God.

If it seems a little puzzling to comprehend how God's name can be such a strong defense, a few minutes thinking about God's name should clarify the concept. God doesn't have just one name, because no single name for God would come close to adequately describing or identifying Him. God is complex beyond comprehension, and the human mind is incapable of understanding all of His aspects. In His Word, God has wisely revealed Himself through dozens and even hundreds of different names, such as Shepherd, Refuge, or Almighty God. Each name helps to fill in another facet of God's complexity. Each name provides greater understanding of who God is and what He can do.

The righteous man chooses a name of God and begins to think about it. What truth does that name reveal about God? What aspect of God's character is highlighted? What picture does it create? How does God demonstrate that aspect to man? How does that name present God as bigger than man and his problems? How does it show God to be capable of handling anything? What does that name mean to people in trouble?

A few minutes spent in asking and answering questions such as these can anchor the soul of man, as God is lifted up and His greatness is considered. Such meditation is a tremendous refuge against doubts, fears, and discouragement. When that particular name of God has been thoroughly examined and has given its encouragement, the rest of the Bible awaits – filled with hundreds more names to consider. There is no end to the protection given by the many names of God.

"Oh, Father, I have been fearful because my view of You has been too small. May I begin to understand how big You really are so that I can find my defense in You."

Day 15

For we do not want you to be unaware, brethren, of our affliction which came to us in Asia, that we were burdened excessively, beyond our strength, so that we despaired even of life; indeed, we had the sentence of death within ourselves so that we would not trust in ourselves, but in God who raises the dead.
II Corinthians 1:8-9

In these verses Paul describes an overwhelmingly challenging situation. He and his companions faced a very difficult scenario in Asia. It was an excessive burden that was beyond their strength and made them think they were going to die. They were hopelessly weighed down and at an utter loss. This seemed to be the situation that would finally bring about their end.

Paul doesn't stop by just describing his dire situation. He goes on to say there was a purpose for this extreme affliction: that they would trust in God and not in themselves. Like Paul, we also need to learn about God-dependence. As humans, we have a tendency to depend largely on ourselves, and for much of our lives, this strategy seems to work out okay. Then we face a major illness and things change. Suddenly we come to the point of needing to rely on God for simple things like standing up, breathing, and walking. We come to realize how much we need to depend on God daily, for the small things as well as for the large.

It is not a bad lesson for us to learn that we are incapable in ourselves. Our limitations drive us to God so that we put our hope and trust in Him for things that are too hard for us. Though impossible for us, no difficulty stops God. He is able to raise the dead, so He is able to deliver from any other affliction. Paul had seen God deliver in the past and was confident that He would deliver again in the future (v. 10). Paul's hope was set in God, the one who is able to deliver even in a life and death situation. With that kind of power, surely He can help in anything less severe.

"My situation is too hard for me. Thank You, Father, that no situation is too hard for You. May I lean on You and not on myself."

Day 16

For I consider that the sufferings of this present time are not worthy to be compared with the glory that is to be revealed to us.
Romans 8:18

This verse addresses the perspective of our hardships. Are there sufferings in our present time? Oh, yes. There is no denial of the hardships. We are living with them day after day. As we look beyond ourselves, we see many, many others who are also hurting. The sufferings are real, and they are painful. Getting out of bed each day is a chore. Preparing food to eat is a challenge. Going anywhere is nearly impossible. The pain can be intense, the weakness debilitating, and the other symptoms overwhelming.

However, no matter how extreme the level of our difficulty, it cannot compare with the glory we will receive in heaven. Some day this life will be over. When that happens, all of our suffering will end. There will be no more pain and no more weakness. In their place we will enjoy the beauties and pleasures of heaven, which will be amazing beyond words. The glories of heaven far exceed the hardships of earth. When we compare the earthly suffering with the heavenly glory, the comparison is not even worth making. It's like a child who brings a fist-sized pumpkin to a contest where it is surrounded by pumpkins that must be transported in pickup trucks. The difference is so obviously vast that the judges have no reason to actually place the pumpkins on the scale to compare them.

In the meantime, the trials are hard. They do make us groan. We sigh and pray with grief, and we eagerly long for our redemption (v. 23). Even though we have the Spirit living in us, our human response is to groan. When we find ourselves in that condition, we need to focus on eternity. We need to say, "Someday I won't care or even remember this; it will be completely overwhelmed by what God has for me." The trials make us long for that glorious day in which all of our struggles will be forgotten.

"Father, thank You for the blessed hope of heaven where Your glory will completely overshadow all earthly suffering."

Day 17

"Thus says the LORD, 'You must not go up and fight against your relatives the sons of Israel; return every man to his house, for this thing has come from Me.'"
I Kings 12:24a

What do we do when disaster strikes? Israel found itself in the midst of a national disaster. Following the death of King Solomon, the transition of leadership did not go smoothly. Israel and Judah were at odds with each other, showing loyalty to two different kings. At this critical time, they reacted by preparing to fight. God cautioned and settled the people, thereby preventing a civil war.

God's reason for stopping the armies' intended action is insightful; He revealed that the tragic division of the kingdom had come from Him. The story itself is interesting, as it reveals a truly traumatic episode in Israel's history. In a sense, however, the particular details of the occasion don't matter. In reality, all things come from God. Just as the kingdom was divided because God ordained it, so each event that enters our lives comes because God has ordained it.

When "disaster" strikes, often the first and the most persistent thing we do is ask God to change our situation. We beg God to change our circumstances, to heal us, or to work a miracle. It is certainly appropriate to pray that way, but we must also consider the reality that our illness came from God's hand. We are ill because He intended for us to be ill. God has very deliberately chosen illness for us so that He can work out some plan of His. Instead of submitting and allowing Him to work that plan, we tend to spend all of our energies fighting against the very thing that God has chosen. We want God to *react* by changing our situation when He has already *acted* by sending our situation. Can we pray for healing? Of course, we can. God may ordain healing as part of His plan. In the midst of our prayers, however, we must also consider that being ill might be the very condition God has chosen for us.

"Father, I don't want to be sick, but if you have chosen for me to remain sick, I must allow that to be Your plan. Please do what Your hand has designed."

Day 18

Every good thing given and every perfect gift is from above, coming down from the Father of lights, with whom there is no variation or shifting shadow.
James 1:17

God is called the Father of lights. He shines brightly in contrast to all others. Instead of imperfections or even dullness, God is full of radiance. He is full of light, glory, majesty, and goodness. He is, in fact, entirely good and wonderful. People might be able to give that impression of themselves for a brief space of time to those who don't know them well, but God is always full of goodness and light.

The perfect image that God presents never changes, no matter how long we look or how well we get to know Him. There is no changing in God. Not even the least imperfection or inconsistency can mar His character. He will never change even one millimeter from who He is. Shadows may move across the earth slowly, as the earth rotates or as clouds move across the sky. Those changes may be barely perceptible, yet God is even steadier. While the changes of light on the earth may be difficult to discern, changes with God are even harder to find, because with God they never happen. Before the beginning of time, God was pure and good, and He is exactly the same today.

This God gives us gifts. Everything that we receive is a gift from God. We may consider our illness and say, "If that's the kind of gift He gives, I don't want it." While we may not realize it, even our illness is a good gift from God. Other people are inconsistent; at times they might give us gifts that are quite thoughtful, while at other times their gifts are completely useless. God, on the other hand, always gives good gifts. Every good thing we ever receive comes from our good God. Because God cannot change, He and His gifts will always be good. God can never give any other kind of gift because He will never be the kind of person who gives faulty gifts. God's gifts are unchangeably good because He is unchangeably good.

"Father, You are good, and You always will be. Therefore, everything You ever give me is good. Help me to accept Your gifts as good though I don't really understand how they are."

A God to Trust (Sonnet 39)
Sometimes, dear God, You send into my life
A hardship I don't want, would never choose.
It scares me and it fills my soul with strife –
Not natural, but seeming to abuse.
In such a time, O God, how can I trust?
How can I see this gift of Yours as good?
By deeming that You're always good and just.
That fact won't change; I know it never could.
Though I don't understand, Your way is best.
Your watchful eye won't send too much for me;
In Your great love and gentle care I rest.
Oh, yes, my Lord, in You my trust can be.
Because I trust, I must submit anew,
Lay down my will, and take this gift from You.

Day 19

The God of peace will soon crush Satan under your feet.
The grace of our Lord Jesus be with you.
Romans 16:20

Conflict does not contribute to peace. Satan is the master of conflict. He constantly makes war against us and threatens our peace. We troubled humans have enough problems remaining at peace without having to face the attacks of Satan. Thankfully, we do not have to face those attacks on our own. We have God on our side. God joins us in the battle against Satan, and, in actuality, God is the one who does the fighting.

Greatly differing from Satan, God specializes in peace. God achieves peace as He triumphs over Satan. God will be victorious. The God of peace will crush Satan.

While we know this will happen ultimately when God establishes His kingdom, it also happens on a more constant basis. Paul encouraged the Roman Christians by telling them that God would bring Satan into subjection shortly. They were in the midst of a battle, one that was apparently prolonged and difficult. Paul assured them that the battle would not continue forever; God would soon give them the victory.

Whatever trials we have are under God's control. He will not allow Satan to prevail indefinitely, but will subdue him – both ultimately and also on a regular basis as we face our earthly trials. As the God of peace achieves victory, He replaces our conflict with His peace.

> *"Father, this battle is tough and I am troubled. Please fight for me.*
> *Crush Satan and give me Your peace."*

Day 20

> *"Because he has loved Me, therefore I will deliver him;*
> *I will set him securely on high, because he has known My name."*
> *Psalm 91:14*

Psalm 91 describes God as a place of secure shelter. God shelters His people from the scorching sun by giving them a place to escape its blazing rays (v. 1). God shelters His people from attacking armies by providing a trustworthy fortress (v. 2). God provides shelter from the trapper who would catch His people by surprise and from the pestilence that attacks pervasively and without mercy (v. 3). God shelters His people gently, just as a mother bird shelters her chicks under her wings (v. 4). God shelters His children from the incoming arrows that are very real, and He also shelters them from the terrors brought on by imagination, by the unknown, and by impending threats (v. 5).

God shelters His children just as well in the blackness of night as He does in the light of day (vs. 5-6). God can shelter His people in seemingly impossible situations, when danger is thick on every side (vs. 7-8). God securely shelters those who hide in Him and who choose to live under His protecting care (v. 9). God can shelter His people completely, stopping not just the largest dangers or the majority of the dangers; He is able to stop them all (v. 10).

God uses His vast resources, including angels, to give His children protection (vs. 11-12). He can give protection that seems unbelievable, with dominance and victory over even the most formidable foes (v. 13). God provides shelter to those who know and love Him, and He places them securely above any danger that threatens to destroy them (v. 14). Yes, when God's children call to Him, He answers. He is with them in their trouble, and He rescues them (v. 15). With such a source of secure shelter, how can His beloved children have any doubt or fear?

"Thank You, Father, for the security and shelter You provide. Thank You that it is so thorough that there is nothing I need to fear."

Day 21

For You are my hope;
O Lord GOD, You are my confidence from my youth.
Psalm 71:5

This verse contains two striking pictures of God. First, God is our Hope. The word's background comes from the idea of a rope. It is specifically a rope in which several cords have been twisted together for extra strength. We are familiar with the picture, because we often compare desperate times to holding on to the end of a rope. The rope provides the idea of expectancy. It is what we cling to for help and deliverance. The aspect of help comes first, as the rope keeps us from falling into the danger below. The aspect of deliverance follows, as the rope lifts us up and brings us to safety. God is that kind of hope for us. When all other helps have proven insufficient, and when one by one they have given out, we are left hanging onto one final rope. It is the only thing keeping us from falling, and that last rope is God. He is a strong rope, able to keep us from falling and ultimately pulling us out of our desperate situation.

The second picture is that of God as our Confidence, which refers to a place of refuge. There are different types of refuges, or, more aptly, different ways of approaching a refuge. A refuge might be a place that we run to frantically in a time of danger, slamming the door behind us and panting in exhaustion. That is not the type of refuge referred to in this verse. This refuge is one that is approached with calmness and confidence. It is such a well-known, well-used, and trusted refuge that we are comfortable in going to it. Our entrance to this refuge is almost automatic, rather than desperate. Instead of a bunker reserved only for extreme emergencies, it is a familiar, frequented place of security. The contrast is between a beekeeper who wears his suit confidently and without fear or alarm in the midst of a swarm of bees and someone else who frantically runs toward a pond to seek protection under the water. This confidence in God is a permanent state that we depend on so regularly that we forget the sense of danger. His consistently proven protection gives us confidence.

"Father, be my rope to cling to. I know You are so strong that You won't fail. Be my confidence that I can calmly rest in, even as the troubles clamor outside."

Day 22

Because of the surpassing greatness of the revelations, for this reason, to keep me from exalting myself, there was given me a thorn in the flesh, a messenger of Satan to torment me – to keep me from exalting myself!
II Corinthians 12:7

Paul is very clear about the reason for his affliction. He states it twice in this verse; it was to keep him from exalting himself. In Paul's case, he had lived an incredible life. He was well-known and well-respected as a leader in the church. The many experiences he listed prior to verse seven are proof of his dedication and service to Christ. On top of all those confirmations and incredible deliverances and repeated protection by God, he had seen visions that were nothing short of incredible. He had seen and heard heavenly things that he couldn't even share with others. What a unique situation he was in! What a temptation he faced to think of himself as somewhat special, an icon in the church. God knew the temptation, and to help Paul resist it, He sent an infirmity to keep him humble.

Affliction can be used for the purpose of keeping us humble. We have probably not had great experiences to the same level that Paul did, but we can still reach a point where we feel that our lives are pretty successful. We've raised a fine family, we've reached a respected position of leadership in the church, and we've dedicated many years of our lives to God's service. It's easy to rest in our accomplishments: the lessons taught, the souls saved, and the people helped. God knows that we are not so great. To remind us of the same truth (and to keep us useful for Him), He sends trials to show us our weakness and to remind us that we cannot rely on our own strength. We cannot boast in ourselves or our abilities or our own sufficiency. We are still mere men in need of help from a great God. Isn't it better to suffer while remaining useful than to be healthy but worthless to God?

"Father, I don't like the illness, but if that's what it takes for me to remain useful in Your service, thank You for sending it."

Day 23

Concerning this I implored the Lord three times that it might leave me.
II Corinthians 12:8

It is not natural to want affliction; Paul didn't want his and prayed repeatedly for God to remove it. The fact that God did not choose to remove Paul's infirmity teaches us that sometimes it is God's will for the affliction to continue for a prolonged length of time. An immediate (or even delayed) healing is not always God's plan. God's allowing the illness for a prolonged amount of time indicates that He has a prolonged purpose for it. God does not send afflictions randomly or capriciously, and neither does He extend them under those same conditions. God has a specific intent for each trial, and He also has a specific length of time for each trial. If God does not remove the trial, then He has an on-going purpose for it. He is still doing something through it.

Paul was content with his affliction because he knew it was not without reason. He states in verse ten that it was for Christ's sake. We also can be content when we recognize that our trials have purpose. When we suffer, it is for the sake of Christ. We do it because He asks it of us. There is a greater purpose than just us. While we may not be happy that we are sick, we can be content if we recognize that God has a purpose and that we are suffering because He asks it. It is not wrong to ask for healing; God invites us to do that, but we must also realize that God does not always intend healing. At some point, we must at least recognize the possibility that God has already done what He has intended to do. The reason that He has not answered our prayer for healing is that He intends for us to remain sick so that He can continue to accomplish His purposes in and through us.

"Father, I long to be healed, but if it is Your will for me to be sick for an extended time, then I submit to Your purpose and plan."

Day 24

And He has said to me, "My grace is sufficient for you, for power is perfected in weakness." Most gladly, therefore, I will rather boast about my weaknesses, so that the power of Christ may dwell in me.
II Corinthians 12:9

Bearing an affliction is hard, so in order to help us do so, God gives us His grace. No matter how challenging the affliction is, God's grace is sufficient. It is always enough. That may at times be hard for us to believe, but God doesn't lie. His grace *is* enough, whether we believe it or not. We may not have enough strength to do everything we want to do, but we have enough for everything God intends for us to do. His grace never fails us. Haven't we made it through every day so far, including all the ones we thought were impossible?

We can boast (rejoice) and be content in our affliction because along with the affliction, we also receive God's grace. The rejoicing and pleasure are not in the affliction itself, but in the accompanying grace from God and in the opportunity to receive and display God's strength. We become strong through God's grace as we are recipients of His power. Too often we live our Christian lives relying almost entirely on ourselves and only minimally on God. When illness makes our strength so low, the best effort we can give is not nearly enough to get us through the day. The amount done in our own strength necessarily decreases, and God picks up the rest. Now the effort expended is only minimally ours and almost entirely God's.

It is precisely in this situation of human weakness that God is best able to show His strength. When God takes someone who has almost nothing to give and carries him through day after day, He showcases His strength. It clearly reveals the fact that the strength is God's. It makes us see the reality of how strong God is and what He is able to do. In the course of the trial, it becomes clearly apparent to us that we are incapable of continuing. When we do continue, the only possible explanation is God.

"Father, thank You for Your sufficient grace that carries me through each day, allowing me to continue with strength that is far greater than my own."

Day 25

I can do all things through Him who strengthens me.
Philippians 4:13

Being sick changes things. A healthy person's list of difficult challenges might include a doctoral dissertation, a marathon, six foster children, or two jobs. Those are the tasks that seem next to impossible to a "normal" person. When you become seriously ill, your list of priorities drastically changes. While many of the challenges of "ordinary" life are no longer remote possibilities, you still face your own list of difficult challenges.

Your list of impossible tasks contains things most people wouldn't even think twice about. Your list might include caring for your children, teaching a Sunday school class, and cleaning the house. It might even include getting dressed by yourself, driving a car, or walking across a room. In addition to those practical things, you face more serious impossibilities: maintaining a sweet testimony before your children, refraining from yelling at your husband, and making it through another day without collapsing from the inside out.

There is no doubt that these are hard tasks for someone who is chronically ill. There is also no doubt that God is able to help you with every one of them. He says that all things are possible with His help. His strength is so abundant that it can enable you to do what would otherwise be impossible. As you strive to obediently serve God, He upholds you and gives strength for each day. God is not going to ask you to do something and then leave you powerless to obey.

Some days you may be dragging, hurting, fainting, and weeping, but you will be able to do all that God asks of you. Lean hard on Him. You need God's help more than you ever have before. Constantly rely on Him for the next thing – and focus only on the next thing. Take one day at a time, or even one hour at a time. Many times even the moment before you will seem impossible, but you can do all things through His strength.

"Father, You know all about the ordinary things of life that are impossible for me. I need Your strength. Help me to face the impossible through You."

Impossible (Sonnet 13)
To live my life in constant victory,
To give You thanks for gifts and hardships, too,
To yield myself completely unto You,
To love You more and others fervently,
To trust Your plan in peaceful certainty,
To wisdom have for knowing what to do,
To live by faith based on Your Word that's true –
Each one remains impossible for me.
These vict'ries happen by Your pow'r alone.
Your promises of help will never fail;
When I depend on You, You will prevail.
It's through Your work the victory is shown.
Impossible for me, without a doubt,
But possible for You. You'll bring me out.

Day 26

Therefore, since Christ has suffered in the flesh, arm yourselves also with the same purpose, because he who has suffered in the flesh has ceased from sin, so as to live the rest of the time in the flesh no longer for the lusts of men, but for the will of God.
I Peter 4:1-2

Christ suffered in the flesh and He did so with a purpose. We are to take that same purpose for ourselves when we suffer. Christ's purpose was to bring the unjust to God (I Peter 3:18). God was pleased with Christ's obedient sacrifice, which was designed to bring death to sin. Sinners can be made just, and ultimately sin will be completely eradicated, all because of the suffering of Christ.

This same motive should be a factor in our own lives. Suffering should be a deterrent to sin. There is something about suffering that causes us to cease from sin. Perhaps it provides a reminder that all suffering in the world is the result of sin. Perhaps it gives us a taste of Christ's suffering, which was necessary only because of our sin. Perhaps it simply puts the important and serious things of life into focus for us.

Whatever the explanation, suffering in the flesh does have a purifying effect in helping us to cease from sin. It is therefore an important foundation for achieving godly living. When we suffer, it should have the effect of adjusting our purpose in life. We should no longer have a desire to live our lives for selfish and worldly desires; instead, we should now want to dedicate ourselves to living for God. We should soberly realize that the time we have left in this world needs to be dedicated to living according to the will of God. We've spent enough time living to satisfy the flesh and to please ourselves. Our illness has provided a wakeup call and a new opportunity from God. As we are confronted with the reality of human mortality, we ought to become serious in wanting to live for God while we still have the chance.

"Father, may this time of suffering help to focus me on what is truly important. May I desire to live for You rather than for myself."

Day 27

Therefore He is able also to save forever those who draw near to God through Him, since He always lives to make intercession for them.
Hebrews 7:25

Jesus is different from earthly priests. One of the most notable differences is that all of the earthly priests died. A person was served by a variety of priests over the course of his life, because the priesthood passed from one man to another as a result of death. By contrast, Jesus never dies. He lives forever.

Jesus is an ultimately reliable source for me as I seek peace with God. Because He is eternal, Jesus can eternally maintain that relationship of peace. I have no fear that it will ever falter or lapse, because Jesus is constantly on the job, maintaining it.

In addition to being saved forever, the eternality of Christ also impacts my daily life. Jesus constantly intercedes on my behalf. My intercessor is eternal. I don't need to have any concern that He will die, retire, or even take a day off. He always lives to intercede for me – every day, every hour, and every minute of my life.

On the darkest of days, Jesus is there. When the worst news comes, Jesus is there. When I am alone, Jesus is there. When my needs threaten to topple me, Jesus is there. When my world comes crashing down around me, Jesus is there. When it comes time for me to die, Jesus is there. He intercedes for me in each of these situations. He knows my need, and He carries it to God on my behalf. Jesus will do that every day of my life, and when this life ends, my eternal Priest will be waiting to receive me to heaven.

"Father, I need someone to be on my side. I need someone that I can rely on who will never fail. Thank you for Jesus, my constant intercessor."

Day 28

For through the grace given to me I say to everyone among you not to think more highly of himself than he ought to think; but to think so as to have sound judgment, as God has allotted to each a measure of faith.
Romans 12:3

Although we tend to think of a trial as something that beats us down, there can also be a tendency to become over-confident in a trial. For example, we might consider ourselves worthy of being entrusted with a trial. We can believe that God must consider us to be pretty good Christians, because, after all, He doesn't send this kind of thing to everyone. This type of situation is reserved for people who are especially strong.

In a similar fashion, we might consider ourselves capable of handling the trial. We feel an expectation and pressure to "handle it right," and especially at the beginning of a trial, we might have a firm resolve to do so. We may be determined to shine forth in our trial with a glorious testimony. We intend to show those around us how to really trust and glorify God.

A third expression of over-confidence might be to think that we actually are living a victorious life in the midst of the trial. We may evaluate ourselves as responding successfully to the challenges. We perceive that others have handled trials marvelously, and we don't want to admit that we can't do the same. In our quest to claim victory, we easily overlook our faults and focus only on our successes.

God cautions us not to think too highly of ourselves. There actually can be a bit of excitement at the beginning of a trial, as we anticipate what God is going to do. It is right for us to long for spiritual growth and instruction from God, but we must be careful to remember how weak and needy we are. We are merely humans, greatly in need of God's grace. We can no more handle a trial perfectly than we can create the world.

It is not easy to admit weakness, but when we present ourselves as strong and unshakeable, we introduce four problems. First, we limit our ability to minister to others because we make ourselves intimidating and unapproachable. Second, we deny others the blessing of fulfilling their God-given charge to help bear our burdens. Third, we cut off the encouragement and support that we desperately need from others. Fourth, we hinder the work that God wants to do in our lives. We are far better off just to admit our weakness and accept the help of God and the help of others.

"Father, You know how much I hate to admit I'm weak. I want to be a great example to others. Please remind me often that I can never be strong enough to do that on my own."

Day 29

For if He causes grief,
Then He will have compassion
According to His abundant lovingkindness.
For He does not afflict willingly
Or grieve the sons of men.
Lamentations 3:32–33

God is not cruel, capricious, or mean-spirited. He doesn't sit in heaven looking for people to torture or seeking out people on whom to experiment. God does not want to afflict people, especially when they are His own children whom He loves. Causing them pain is not His desire. He afflicts only when He has to and when suffering is the only way to give correction, molding, or guidance. God cares about His children too much to hurt them without a very good purpose.

When God must send pain, He always accompanies it with His compassion. When He must of necessity correct or teach through pain, His abundant undying love does not disappear. Instead, it becomes very active. God always loves His children more than they can imagine, and that incredible love causes His heart to respond with compassion. God knows it is sometimes necessary for His children to suffer for a while, but His compassionate arms are right there to hold them up. His compassionate voice whispers loving and encouraging words. His compassionate heart refuses to leave them alone or without comfort. God's compassion remains with His suffering children every day, as He surrounds the hurting soul and gives the comfort and support that only God can give.

"Thank You, Father, that it is not Your desire to hurt me, but rather to love me and help me. Thank You for Your constant compassion."

Day 30

That He would grant you, according to the riches of His glory, to be strengthened
with power through His Spirit in the inner man, so that Christ may dwell in your
hearts through faith; and that you, being rooted and grounded in love, may be able to
comprehend with all the saints what is the breadth and length and height and depth,

and to know the love of Christ which surpasses knowledge,
that you may be filled up to all the fullness of God.
Ephesians 3:16-19

These verses contain one of the great prayers found in the Bible. The first request concerns internal strength. Although physically you are in great need of strength, you have a more critical weakness – that of your spirit. God is able to give strength and power to meet that inner weakness. When you are faltering and seem about to collapse, God can give strength from the inside out. His Spirit upholds and supports you.

The second request is in regards to faith. The internal strength supplied by God makes it possible for a thriving, faith-based relationship with Christ. When your inner man is strengthened and encouraged by God, it becomes easier to trust Him. It becomes easier to allow Christ to have more constant control and influence. As He dwells in your heart, your faith grows stronger, and therefore your steps are more obedient.

The third request centers around the love of God. You can be deeply and firmly established in that love. You can begin to understand the vast extent of God's great love. His love is so great that it expands in all directions, stretching beyond what you can see no matter which way you look. Man has trouble understanding even the smallest part of God's love. In truth, His love is so great that when man achieves a tiny bit of comprehension, ever so much more remains outside of his understanding. These three requests – strength on the inside, faith in the heart, and comprehension of love – can be fulfilled. Each one is possible because, as the beginning of the passage states, God grants these requests based on His great riches.

"Strengthen me, Father, in my faltering inner man. Increase my faith so that my relationship with Christ can prosper. Help me to understand something of the extent of Your love for me."

Day 31

The LORD is your keeper;
The LORD is your shade on your right hand.
Psalm 121:5

Psalm 121 provides a wonderful description of the source of our help. Our help comes from the God who powerfully created the heavens and earth. This God watches all of our steps, whether we're coming or going, and can keep our feet from slipping. This God never sleeps or dozes off; He is always alert. This God protects us both in the daytime when the sun blazes down and in the nighttime when the darkness swallows us up. He can protect us from every bit of evil and can keep every part of us, including our soul. This God who has preserved Israel through numerous dangers against impossible odds is the same God who watches over us today.

Verse five presents two pictures of this incredible, protecting God. First, God is our Keeper. He guards us and protects us by putting a hedge about us. The protective hedge described has thorns protruding from the outside to keep predators away. It is a pain-inflicting defense, like barbed wire or the spiked structures in the waters of Normandy on D-Day. The barrier is designed to be an impregnable defense that prevents any enemies from penetrating it.

The second picture is that of God as a Shade. This refers to a shadow that hovers over someone and blocks out the light. The idea is well illustrated by a person sweltering on a hot day, perhaps in the desert. At the very least he is uncomfortable, and at the worst he is in danger of dying at the hand of the elements. He can be protected by a palm tree or a booth of fronds that stretches over him and blocks the strength of the sun. The shade provided can mean the difference between life and death. Even in a less dramatic setting, the shade still provides comfort and relief. God, the best source of help, thoroughly protects us by being both a shade and a keeper.

"Father, how can I doubt? Your power is unstoppable. Your vigilance is constant. Your protection is complete. Help me to rest peacefully in Your care."

My Guard (Sonnet 15)
When for a source of trusty help I search,
Where can I look but to the Lord above?
If He from nothing made the heav'n and earth,
Then He can surely care for me in love.
He won't allow my feeble foot to slip.
He keeps me safely, right down to my soul.
He shades me gently on my earthly trip.
When facing evil, He will keep me whole.
This God who watches me will never sleep;
He gives protection through both day and night.
He watches ev'ry path, both smooth and steep.
He will forever guard me with His might.
Oh, great Protector, Watcher, heav'nly Guard,
To trust my steps to You should not be hard.

Day 32

Make sure that your character is free from the love of money, being content with what you have; for He Himself has said, "I will never desert you, nor will I ever forsake you."
Hebrews 13:5

God instructs us to be content. While the passage refers specifically to finances, the principle is that we are to be content with what we have or don't have. Contentment, in my words, is being satisfied to remain peacefully in a situation for as long as God decides to allow it. Contentment is not about liking or not liking a situation, or even about being happy regarding it. There are situations that it would be wrong to like and sadistic to be happy about. Although we do not like being ill, and we are not happy to be so, we can still be content in our illness.

Being healthy and strong is a natural human longing. Discontent comes when we place that longing in a higher position than God's plan. When we make our own desire paramount in our lives, we become discontent. Contentment comes when we yield to God's plan.

The process requires understanding that God's plan is good. God accomplishes good things through undesired circumstances. Through a serious illness, for example, we learn of God's power. Therefore we can be content in the illness because we are in a position to see God's power displayed. We also learn of God's love. We can be content in our affliction because we are in a position to receive and appreciate God's love as never before. We learn of God's faithfulness, so we can be content in knowing we will see a demonstration of God's faithfulness to stand by us like no one else can. We learn of God's grace, so we can be content because we are in a position to be sustained by His abundant grace. Our illness presents opportunities to see God's character displayed in marvelous ways.

The bottom line is that we see how very great God is. He is therefore able not only to take care of us in the trial, but also to use the situation for great benefit. If we are that confident in God's ability, then we are able to rest confidently, contentedly, and peacefully in His competent arms. We will have no worries, no arguments, and no protests, because we know God will do great things. When God becomes that big to us, it's hard for us to argue or fret.

"While I don't like my illness, Father, I know that You are doing amazing things through it. May that knowledge make me content to rest in Your care."

Day 33

He has regarded the prayer of the destitute
And has not despised their prayer.
Psalm 102:17

The unnamed author of Psalm 102 suffered from a serious illness. Verses three through seven list many of his symptoms. His days were eaten up in smoke, perhaps meaning they were foggy and indistinct and that he passed through them with little consciousness of what was going on. His bones were scorched, probably referring to pain. He was discouraged and compared his heart to withered, dried-up grass. He didn't have an appetite and didn't even remember to eat. He groaned loudly. He lost weight until he looked skeletal. He spent sleepless nights. He was lonely and neglected. Additional verses reveal that he cried frequently (v. 9). His life was fading away (v. 11). He was weak, and his lifespan was shortened (v. 23).

In the midst of his suffering, the psalmist was neglected and even abused by others. Instead of helping him, they mocked him and looked on him in derision. When he was misunderstood and neglected, the psalmist took great comfort in God's faithfulness. God didn't ignore him or turn him away. The psalmist had hope in the fact that God listens to those who are in trouble. God looks down from heaven and sees those who are groaning. He cares about their needs. He has pity on their distresses. He is compassionate and gracious.

The most wonderful thing that the psalmist focused on was not God's compassionate responses in themselves, but the fact that God performs them so faithfully. God abides forever. He never dies. He never weakens. He never changes. He never wears out or gets old. God will always be, even when the heavens are destroyed. Not only will He always be, but He will always be the same. He was the same for this psalmist as He was in the beginning of time. He is the same today as He was then. He will always be the same compassionate and reliable God.

"Father, in an unpredictable world, thank You that You are always the same. I can depend on You every day to be just the same as You always have been. You will always care."

Day 34

In this you greatly rejoice, even though now for a little while, if necessary,
you have been distressed by various trials.
I Peter 1:6

Have you ever felt pressure from others to maintain a cheerful outlook through your illness? Have they frequently encouraged you to put a smile on your face? Have you expected it of yourself? Peter acknowledges to these believers what happens when trials come. They distress us. That is what trials do. It is part of their nature. Trials cause us to be sad and sorrowful. It would be unnatural to embrace with a gleeful spirit something that is by nature oppressive.

Responding in a humanly appropriate way does not give Christians an excuse, however, to be depressed, discouraged, and ornery. Along with the sorrow that was naturally brought by the temporary affliction of these believers, Peter also recognizes their great joy. They did not have great rejoicing because of the trial. Their joy came from a truth that was completely outside of their affliction. In verses three through five, Peter reveals the truth that brought them joy. They were thinking of God's mercy that provides the new birth; they were pondering eternal life in heaven and the power of God to keep them secure. In the midst of their trial, they rejoiced because of truths in God's Word that were worth rejoicing over.

Even on the worst of days or in the worst of circumstances, there is a wonderful hope that God's promises provide. Doesn't your heart rejoice when you really stop to consider that God loves you? Don't you want to sing when you ponder eternity in heaven? Isn't your spirit lifted when you think about God's magnificent salvation? You should be able to rejoice even in the midst of trials. The next time your illness burdens down your spirit, find a wonderful truth of Scripture and really think about it. Let God's truth lift your spirit.

"Father, in the midst of my illness with all its burdens, thank You for the truths of Your Word that are able to bring me joy."

Day 35

In this you greatly rejoice, even though now for a little while, if necessary,
you have been distressed by various trials.
I Peter 1:6

Have you ever half-wished that you would get a "normal" illness, just so you could experience recovery and healing? If you just had the flu or a broken leg or an infection, you would have a reasonable time table for healing. You could expect to be sick and feel lousy for a few days or weeks, but then you would get better. It isn't that way with your illness, is it? You refer to it in terms of "the third year" or "my second relapse" or "my latest flare-up."

Perhaps with enough time you will recover from your illness. Maybe you can beat it. Maybe you will be able to enjoy times of remission. On the other hand, you might deal with your illness for the rest of your life. Isn't the length of your illness one of the harder aspects to deal with? You don't want your trial to be forever; you want it to end.

Peter says that it will end. All trials are temporary in their nature. They are for a little while – just for a season and a short time. It is not God's intention to leave you in those trials forever, but only as long as they are necessary. They are necessary within God's plan, and He uses them for His purposes. When He has accomplished His purposes, however, the trial is no longer necessary, and God removes it. The God of compassion does not take joy in making you suffer. He desires to deliver you. Often God brings healing and deliverance after a time, and what a blessing that is.

What if your illness continues until God takes you home? Does that make His Word untrue? No, indeed. It's hard to think of thirty years as a little while, but in comparison to eternity, it is very short. At the very longest, your illness can only last until death. At that point all your trials will cease. Be patient. In a little while, all trials will be over.

"Thank You, Father, that this trial will end. I don't know when, but someday You will remove it. Help me to wait."

Day 36

So that the proof of your faith, being more precious than gold which is perishable, even though tested by fire, may be found to result in praise and glory and honor at the revelation of Jesus Christ.
I Peter 1:7

In the midst of your trial, have you felt as if your faith is really taking a beating? Do you struggle to believe and to have hope? Does it seem that your faith is being assaulted and subjected to very difficult challenges? Well, that is exactly what is happening. Your faith really is being worked over and put to the test.

God does sometimes put your faith through a time of harsh and intense testing, but the testing is not without purpose. As stated in verse six, the trials are necessary for your profit; that's why God sent them. They are never sent capriciously or by accident. They have the important task of interacting with your faith, and specifically of proving your faith. They test its trustworthiness, like the value of gold is tested by fire. The test shows you if your faith really has value, demonstrating whether or not it is the "real thing."

The expectation of the verse is that the answer is "yes." If you question whether there is anything real in Christianity, coming through a trial by fire shows you that there is indeed something very real. Your faith does have value. It is proven to be real, because it is your faith that makes the difference in how you survive the trial.

While it may be very hard to go through the trial even *with* faith in God, it would be impossible without faith in God. It is your faith, weak and shaken as it sometimes may be, that allows you to emerge victorious. Your faith passes the test, resulting in the encouraging certainty that you can truly depend on God.

"My faith is in the fire, Father. As brutal as the fire is, thank You that my faith in You is real and will survive. You will not let it down."

Day 37

So that the proof of your faith, being more precious than gold which is perishable, even though tested by fire, may be found to result in praise and glory and honor at the revelation of Jesus Christ.
I Peter 1:7

Our faith is very precious. That statement expresses God's evaluation. God is the one who declares our faith to be more precious than gold. It is very precious to Him even when it passes through a fiery test. The trial doesn't make our faith any less beautiful in His sight. Because it is so precious to Him, God does not want to destroy our faith, but rather desires to protect it through the trial.

The trial of our faith has an amazing result. There are, in fact, many benefits that come through the trial; the result stated clearly in this passage is that our victorious faith will bring praise and glory and honor to God. Isn't it something, that in our weak, human condition, even with all of our struggles, we are able to magnify God? We are able to exalt Him.

It is helpful for us to note when this will take place. This verse speaks of the praise and glory in our trials being expressed at the time of Christ's revelation. The deadline is the appearing of Christ. If we're struggling at the moment, there is still hope and still time for Him to work and bring His glorious result. It is never too late to give God glory in the trial. Perhaps God would receive more glory if we reacted correctly through the entire trial, but if we ultimately turn to Him, then at whatever point we do so, He receives glory. There is no need to despair when we seem to struggle and mess up, because we can always turn to Him *now* and He will be glorified.

"I haven't always had great responses, Father. Help me now to pass the test so that I can bring praise to You."

Fire (Sonnet 6)
Harsh trials by fire common seem to run.
No random things, they are designed above,
And when the temporary trial has done

Its needed work, 'twill be removed in love.
The fire seems much danger to employ,
But God protects His children through the flame.
The fire will not damage or destroy;
When we come out, we'll not be scarred or lame.
We leave so vastly changed by His design.
The fire burns the dross we have inside
Until for Him we now can purely shine –
A treasure in which He is glorified.
Oh, Master Craftsman, work so carefully
That I'll become what You want me to be.

Day 38

Surely goodness and lovingkindness will follow me all the days of my life,
And I will dwell in the house of the LORD forever.
Psalm 23:6

There are days and weeks in your illness that are not so bad. Mercifully there are some reprieves and good days. Then there is the other end of the spectrum. There are days that are just plain hard. You don't sleep well, your symptoms flare up, or just entirely too many things intersect at the same time. Those days are extra tough. On the days that you feel worst physically, your spirit also tends to sink. You easily become discouraged, and even your thinking about God suffers. You begin to wonder if He really is with you and if He really does care.

Thankfully God's goodness and lovingkindness are with you every day, whether you feel them or not. You may not always be aware of His goodness and love, or maybe only to a limited extent, but the verse is still true. Those blessings are not dependent on how you feel; they are dependent on a faithful God who never changes. His goodness and love are not with you only when you feel like it or only on good days, but *all* the days of your life. They are just as real on the hard days as they are on the easier days. His goodness and love are with you now, and they will be with you for all of eternity. When you die, your situation will only get better, because then you will dwell in heaven with Him forever.

"Help me, Father, to believe Your goodness and love every day,
whether I sense them or not."

Day 39

Be anxious for nothing, but in everything by prayer and supplication with thanksgiving let your requests be made known to God. And the peace of God, which surpasses all comprehension, will guard your hearts and your minds in Christ Jesus.
Philippians 4:6-7

There are plenty of things in our situations that we could be anxious about, aren't there? The particular list would vary from person to person, but among ill people the overall list would be pretty similar. We have concerns about how to accomplish the required tasks each day, questions about how successful our treatment will be, and doubts about how severe the side effects will be. We worry about whether we will recover and what will happen to our family if we don't.

God tells us not to be anxious about anything, and He gives us an alternative. It is to make all of our requests and burdens known to God. The word *but* tells us there is a contrast. Taking our requests to God in prayer is the opposite of being anxious. When we take our requests to God, we expect Him to figure out what to do. We expect Him to work out the answer and take care of the situation. On the contrary, when we are anxious, it is because we are trying to figure out on our own what to do. We are trying to come up with an answer and work it out. We can't possibly accomplish that expectation. No wonder the attempt makes us anxious.

The result on the other side is quite different. When we take our requests to God and allow Him to be in charge of all those things, He gives us His peace. If we choose to take our anxious thoughts to God, His peace takes up guard duty, protecting both our hearts and our minds. It allows our minds to be at ease, rather than filled with troubling and puzzled thoughts. His peace also allows our heart to be calm, without assaulting emotions that threaten to overwhelm us. It may seem amazing that anything can have such influence, but God's peace is so great that we can't even understand it. God can win the victory in our hearts and minds to an extent that doesn't even seem possible to us.

Yes, we will sometimes have troubling thoughts. That is a natural part of life and of the circumstances in which God has placed us. Instead of dwelling on those thoughts and making them the starting point for a downward journey, we need to acknowledge those thoughts and take them to God. We need to talk to God about them and then leave the burden there. God can make a change in our lives. Even in anxious situations, we can have peace as we commit those situations to God.

"Father, You know the thoughts and worries that assault me each day. Help me to leave them with You and let You figure them out. I would much rather have Your peace than my worries."

Day 40

For though the LORD is exalted,
Yet He regards the lowly,
But the haughty He knows from afar.
Psalm 138:6

God is exalted and great; there is no question about that. He created the entire universe. He maintains every system on the earth and every living creature. He controls the very largest and the very smallest events. He is the King of everything. No one can come close to matching Him.

It really doesn't make a lot of sense why this incredible God would pay attention to man, but He does. There are some people with whom He interacts distantly. The proud are not able to come very close to God. They don't think they need Him. They say things like, "I'm strong enough to handle this on my own." They claim, "I don't need anyone's help." They boast, "God must think I'm pretty tough since He dumped this on me." Those haughty comments come from a heart that cannot approach God.

On the other hand, there are people to whom God is very near. He pays close attention to the lowly. God listens when people say, "This is too much for me. I am not adequate." He hears when they admit, "I can't handle this on my own." God gives His attention when He hears people cry out, "I need Your help." With a humble attitude and a realistic recognition that I can make it through my situation only with God's help, I gain the interest of God. In such a needy state, I can be closer to God than the most elegant social figure, the most prestigious leader, or the most powerful ruler. Though I am nothing, the mighty God looks on me.

"Father, it would be absolute folly to think I could survive without Your help. Please look on me and give me the aid that I desperately need."

Day 41

You are the God who works wonders;
You have made known Your strength among the peoples.
Psalm 77:14

Our God is the God who works wonders. He performs miracles and does mighty acts that defy belief. No other person does wonders of this magnitude. We often take for granted the amazing things that God does because we have heard them so often and because they are what we expect God to do. It would be good for us to stop and really consider some of the amazing things that God has done.

When nothing existed, God created the heavens, the earth, and everything in them, using nothing but His voice. God caused a flood that covered every mountain on the entire earth. God caused an old woman to have a baby. God caused fire to fall from heaven and destroy two entire cities. God sent plagues so severe that they destroyed a powerful nation; in the midst of those plagues He protected another nation that lived in the same area. God made dry paths through a sea and a river. God enabled a shepherd boy to kill a giant warrior with only stones and a sling. God protected three men in the middle of a fire that killed the guards who threw them into it. God caused leprosy to disappear. Jesus turned a boy's small lunch into a meal for a multitude. Jesus made blind men to see and lame men to walk. Jesus brought a man back to life who had been dead for four days.

This list is just a small sampling of the wonders recorded in Scripture. Even after we list every miracle found in the Bible, there are many others that we don't even know about. Although we tend to associate miracles with Biblical events, God still works wonders today. In the history of the world, in the lives of people past and present, and even in our own lives, God does amazing things for which man has no explanation. The word *coincidence* is a pitifully laughable attempt to justify supernatural intervention. God truly does incredible works. No human would even think of them, let alone attempt them. These wonders are reserved for the God who watches over us.

"You are awesome, Father. You are incredible, unmatched, and phenomenal. You are wonderful, amazing, and extraordinary. Thank You for being my God."

Day 42

"Call unto Me in the day of trouble;
I shall rescue you, and you will honor Me."
Psalm 50:15

This verse presents a sequence of three steps. Those three steps occur within a specific context: a day of trouble. Those troubling days do come. God knows they will come, and He has given instructions for what to do when they occur. He is very aware that we will have days of trouble, often completely outside the realm of our control. Because God knows those days are coming, He tells us how to handle them. Meanwhile, He is standing by, ready to hear and help.

The first step in the sequence is for us to call to God. He is the one who can help us. We can't help ourselves, but there is help. We don't need to throw up our hands helplessly and give up. There is help available if we will call to Him.

The second step is that God will rescue. We don't know how He will rescue. We don't know when He will rescue. While those details remain unknown, we do know that God will rescue. He will deliver us in His way and in His time.

The third step is that we will honor God. In the midst of the trouble in which we are helpless, it is God who does the rescuing. We must acknowledge and praise Him as the rescuer. We must be careful not to take the credit for ourselves. We must guard against quickly forgetting the rescue or taking it for granted. Instead, we must clearly proclaim to others that God is the one who makes it all happen. It is His glorious work, and He deserves the praise and honor.

"Thank You, Father, that You know trouble is coming. Instead of condemning me for it, You help me in it. Help me to praise You as my Rescuer."

Day 43

Commit your way to the LORD,
Trust also in Him, and He will do it.
Psalm 37:5

Some people have lives that seem pretty simple, but your life does not fit into that category. You have so many decisions to make and so many things to consider that your mind can't even keep up with all of them. Your life presents one complication after another, a constant parade of new adjustments and variables to work through. It's hard to know what to do next. Even when you do come up with a plan, you are unable to make it work. Your best wishes and intentions fall miserably apart.

The reality is that humans are not really competent to handle life's problems. Someone bigger needs to take care of those difficult things. If you will commit your way to God and trust Him to make the arrangements, He will guide your path. He will lead you through each step and decision, each change and adjustment. You don't have to figure everything out or make a workable plan. That's God's job. God knows just what needs to happen next, and He knows precisely how to arrange your steps.

Part of that guidance and decision-making involves timing. While humans focus on how long something takes to happen, God focuses on making it happen at precisely the right time. Psalm 37:7 tells us to rest in God and wait patiently on Him. Just as we trust Him for what will happen, we can also trust Him for when it will happen. Perhaps you have seen numerous setbacks and delays. Why did your doctor's office fail to run all the tests they were supposed to run? Why did it take so long to reach a diagnosis? Why has the promised new drug not yet been released? Why has your recovery been so slow?

Each of these details rests within God's control. God's timing is perfect, and He is never late. When you follow His plan, everything happens precisely when it should and lasts for exactly the length of time that God deems best. Instead of yielding to your natural inclination to chafe at the delays, respond with patience and submission to God's perfect timing.

"Father, I don't know what to do or when to do it. I trust You to make the decisions about what should happen in my life. I trust the timing that You choose."

Waiting (Sonnet 32)
How hard to wait when guidance is not seen;
The holding back would seem to crush my soul.
The search for answers shows an empty screen;
I can't advance or move toward a goal.
Though I don't see, Your hand is not at rest.
Your plan's not lost; it's in Your memory.
Your thinking's not confused; You know what's best.
The timing You ordain is also key.
You know my heart and fully understand;
You watch me with compassion and with care.
Each day I wait You'll hold me by the hand;
Your faithfulness means You'll be always there.
Lord, when it's time, You'll show me what to do;
Till then, give grace. I place my trust in You.

Day 44

"If it be so, our God whom we serve is able to deliver us from the furnace of blazing fire;
and He will deliver us out of your hand, O king."
Daniel 3:17

God is able to deliver His people. The book of Daniel gives some powerful illustrations of this fact. Shadrach, Meshach, and Abed-nego faced the raging anger of a powerful king. They had dared to defy his order, and when he gave them a second opportunity, they remained firm in their resolve. The king threatened to throw them into the blazing fire of the furnace, confident that no god could deliver them. The three friends did not hesitate in their answer or waver in their confidence. They did not know if God *would* deliver them, but they had no doubt that He *could*. A blazing fire was no match for God. Even when the furnace was made seven times hotter than normal, hot enough to kill the men who threw them in, the flame did not exceed God's ability to deliver.

Daniel also faced a situation in which he needed deliverance. Evil men plotted against him, and he was sentenced to be thrown into a den of ravenous lions. Even the heathen king was aware of God's power to deliver. Though a little uncertain perhaps, he was hopeful and optimistic, ready to at least consider that God could deliver. The next morning the king approached the den and asked Daniel if his God had been able to deliver him from the lions. Of course, God had been able to and had done so. The king then commanded that Daniel's accusers be thrown into the pit; the same lions that had left Daniel in peace proceeded to tear those men apart before they hit the floor.

These stories provide just two examples of the many times in which God delivered His children. In addition to the many small ways and "easy" situations in which God has delivered, He has also delivered just as easily in impossible situations. No situation is too hard for God to give deliverance.

"Father, in the difficulty of my situation, help me not to doubt Your power."

Day 45

The eyes of the LORD are toward the righteous
And His ears are open to their cry.
Psalm 34:15

God is always watching over me. He always knows exactly what is going on in my life because He is always looking in my direction. No catastrophe can come without His being aware of it. No detail ever escapes His careful eye.

When I am hurting and needy, God sees. When I am alone, His eyes are on me. When I am confused, discouraged, or overwhelmed, God knows, because He is watching me. With so many people, so many events, and so many problems in the world, I am never out of the sight of my God. Nothing can distract His gaze. Nothing else is so interesting that He allows His gaze to stray from me. Nothing else is so important that He must stop watching me in order to attend to it.

Other people may look in on me from time to time, but God is looking constantly. No one else looks at me so frequently. No one else looks at me with a gaze so tender, so compassionate, or so loving.

God sees better than anyone else sees. That fact is not surprising. God is the one who created the eye with all of its complexity. The eye of man is amazing beyond description. How much greater must be the eye of God! His ability to see everything is incomprehensible. God could use His magnificent vision to view so many things, yet He chooses to look at me. His constant gaze is prompted by a profound love that is tremendously comforting.

"Thank You, Father, for seeing little old me. Thank You for looking on me every moment of every day."

Day 46

To this present hour we are both hungry and thirsty, and are poorly clothed, and are roughly treated, and are homeless; and we toil, working with our own hands; when we are reviled, we bless; when we are persecuted, we endure; when we are slandered, we try to conciliate; we have become as the scum of the world, the dregs of all things, even until now.
I Corinthians 4:11-13

Paul and his companions were certainly not in a position to be envied. Things were not going well for them at all. They were suffering greatly. They had physical needs, as they were hungry, thirsty, and inadequately clothed. They were homeless and had to perform hard physical labor to support themselves. They also had relational needs; they were being roughly treated by others. They were being reviled and slandered. Some of these attacks involved persecution because of their relationship with Christ. In summary, they were the off scouring of society, the scum of the earth.

Needs, abuses, attacks – problems come in life, especially as we serve God. Life will not always be a bed of roses. What should our response be when we find ourselves in challenging situations? Well, it is a different response than what the world would expect. The world would complain, fight back, steal, rebel, become bitter, become angry with society, and blame others for their problems. Those are natural responses.

A Christian responds differently. He has a supernatural, rather than a natural, response. In the midst of trials, a Christian's response stands out as different. Instead of giving up, he endures. Instead of retaliating against those who are injuring him, he responds kindly. Our particular trial may not match up with Paul's situation, but the spirit of our response should be the same. Our response should stand out as being godly, rather than the natural response of the world.

"Help me, Father, to be different in my responses to hard things. By my actions may I show others that I belong to You."

Day 47

But know the LORD has set apart the godly man for Himself;
The LORD hears when I call to Him.
Psalm 4:3

God has set me apart for Himself. What does that mean? At the most basic level, it means that He notices and pays attention to me. He cannot set me apart without first seeing me and knowing who and where I am.

It means that God chose me. He has picked me up and put me in a special place. He has placed me in a special group of people. I belong to Him. If He has chosen me for Himself, then He is claiming me as His own.

It means that God loves me and places value on me. He would not choose something that He did not want. He has not chosen me merely as a gift for others, but for Himself personally. He could have anything He wants, and He chose me.

It means that God has a special purpose and plan for me. He did not choose me just so that He could sit and look at me. There was a reason for His choosing. I am to be of some value or use to Him. I am to be used in His service.

It means that I can call on God. He wants me to have communion with Him. Because He chose me, He will hear my cries. He will care for me and protect me. God will guard, keep, and cherish what He has chosen.

Because God has set me apart for Himself, I know that He will continue to watch over me. I can be assured of His ongoing love. I can rest in His plan for my life. I can know that He will always hear me. I can have confidence that He will take care of me.

"I am nothing, Father, and yet You have chosen me. Thank You for the glorious privilege of being set apart for You."

Day 48

For You are great and do wondrous deeds;
You alone are God.
Psalm 86:10

There is only one God. God, the Creator and Savior of the world, is the only one. There aren't hundreds of others who could do what God does. There aren't even dozens of others who strongly resemble Him. He is the only God. God is unique, and His uniqueness is clearly illustrated in what He does.

What are the responsibilities and tasks that fall to God? He has designed and created a phenomenal world. The study of the stars, planets, and galaxies is vast beyond man's ability to comprehend, yet that realm works perfectly. God has designed a variety of living creatures that man could not dream up in his wildest imagination. Many animals and plants have distinct characteristics that make them wonders to man. God has created the human body with numerous well-designed systems and intricate parts, all of which work together to make up a person. Beyond creating these things, God sustains all of them and keeps them running. He also controls the events of the world. History is merely a record of what God has done. God's masterpiece was to establish a means of salvation that could reconcile sinful men to Himself while maintaining His holiness.

God surely has done great and wondrous deeds. No one else could have done them. Even if all the greatest minds of the world pooled their strengths, they could not come close to doing what God has done. As the only God, He doesn't need anyone or anything else in order to exist or do His great works. He needs no advisors, cabinet members, counselors, or task forces. All by Himself He is capable of doing the wondrous works that He claims as His responsibility. The job is so huge that we can't even comprehend it, but it is not hard for God. In relation to everything else God does, the problems in the daily lives of man are such trivial things. Since He can easily do those other incredible tasks, it is no challenge for Him to take care of His children.

"Father, sometimes I think I can handle my life, but I can't. Neither can anyone else. You are the only one who is capable. You are the only God."

Day 49

When He entered the house, the blind men came up to Him, and Jesus said to them, "Do you believe that I am able to do this?" They said to Him, "Yes, Lord."
Matthew 9:28

God has compassion on those who are hurting. His compassion makes Him kind and merciful so that He wants to help. Unlike humans, God's compassion has real power behind it. God is not limited to empty words of sympathy or half-hearted offers of help. He can actually meet the need. God has power to heal. No act of healing is too difficult for God. God's healing power was displayed over and over again throughout the Bible, in both the Old and New Testaments. Many of those instances of healing are very familiar to us, and we could fill many pages if we were to list out all of the examples. God healed even the most difficult cases – life-long lameness, blindness, leprosy – as well as the milder, common illnesses of life.

We do not live in a day when miracle-working prophets or even Christ Himself is walking in our midst. The healing that we see today is not usually miraculous in nature, but God does still heal, sometimes in amazing ways. We have all heard stories of healing that was beyond the doctors' ability to comprehend or explain. As Christians we don't lack the explanation. We know who heals. Any time someone is healed, whether the healing is dramatic or routine, it is God who gives the healing. Doctors may think it is their great skill and knowledge. They may attribute the healing to the medicines and procedures they prescribe. God does use those things, to be sure, but the bottom line is that God Himself is responsible for all healing. As part of the healing process, God controls both the speed and the extent of the healing, determining how much healing to give and how quickly to give it. We can depend on our compassionate Physician to do His work.

> *"Father, help me not to forget that whatever healing*
> *I experience comes from Your hand."*

Day 50

> *When my spirit was overwhelmed within me,*
> *You knew my path.*
> *In the way where I walk*
> *They have hidden a trap for me.*
> *Psalm 142:3*

I know I'm on a journey, but the path is daunting to me. Most of the time I don't know how I got here, and I certainly have no idea where I'm going. David said his enemies had hidden a trap on his path. As he walked on, he was in danger of being captured, yet what choice did he have except to walk on?

I can give different descriptions of my path that explain why my spirit is overwhelmed. As I look around me on my path, I see only barriers. I could describe them as tall buildings that block out the sun and threaten to fall on me. I could describe them as tall grasses and undergrowth, too thick to fight my way through. In short, my path looks impossible. I feel like I am trapped. It's no wonder that my spirit is overwhelmed.

When I am in such a condition, I can be confident that God knows my path. He knows it far better than I do. God knows every aspect of my path. Every path has a beginning; it started somewhere. God knows where my path started and where it has been. He knows the steps that I have taken already. He knows the past challenges. He knows the assaults that have come on that path. He knows the injuries and bruises that I still carry as a result.

Every path has a current location. God knows exactly where I am right now. He knows the condition of my heart. He knows how much it hurts. He knows what this tangled jungle path looks like to me. He knows how lost and scared I am.

Every path has a destination. God knows where I will end up. He knows the barriers and detours that will arise. He knows the bridges that He will build and the trees that He will chop down. He knows how and where I will walk out into a wide open field with warm sunlight surrounding me. Yes, God knows every aspect of my path. I can look to Him as a sympathetic friend and a faithful guide.

"This path is crazy, Father, and I don't know what to do. Thank You that You know all about it. Guide me and give me courage as I walk onward."

He Knows My Path (Sonnet 26)
God knows my path, and He can trace it back.
He knows where I have been and what's transpired.
He won't forget the turnings of my track;
He knows the source of bruises I've acquired.
God knows my path; He sees just where I stand.
He feels the burden of my aching heart
And in His comfort gently holds my hand.
He knows my current status – ev'ry part.
God knows my path, and where it now will go.
He has a plan to guide me on my way.
The weight that presses will not overflow,
For He'll walk with me ev'ry single day.
Though in my heart the sorrows overwhelm,
God knows my path complete; He's at the helm.

Day 51

The LORD is good,
A stronghold in the day of trouble,
And He knows those who take refuge in Him.
Nahum 1:7

We wouldn't say the words out loud: "God isn't good." That would be heresy. We would be alarmed if we even found that thought forming itself in our minds. If we're honest, though, haven't we believed it at times, whether we directly stated it or not? We try to make the statement less offensive by qualifying it. We might say, "I know God is good, but I don't really see how He is being good to me." Perhaps we limit His goodness by saying, "If He were *really* good, He would do *this* in my life." Doubting God's goodness is a common temptation in the midst of difficulty because our finite minds don't know what God knows, and therefore we can't figure things out. Our lack of understanding causes us to see only the pain, and our flawed interpretation is that God is not being good.

The truth is that God *is* good. His goodness is constantly expressed in His kindness and favor to us. Everything that God does is filtered through His goodness and permeated by it. God always does the things that are best for us, never what will harm us. He is pure, one hundred percent goodness. Goodness is at the heart of His very nature. It is His essence. Because God is good, it is impossible for Him to do anything that is not good. Regardless of our perception, everything that God does is good. If we had a correct view of God's goodness, we would say, "If God were *really* good, He would do *exactly* what He is doing in my life." In fact, God is good, and He is doing the best thing. In the next several entries, we will look at various aspects of God's goodness.

> *"Father, help me to believe in Your constant goodness*
> *regardless of how things seem to my eyes."*

Day 52

And Jesus said to him, "Why do you call Me good? No one is good except God alone."
Luke 18:19

God is good. Goodness is an expression of His character. In fact, God is the only one who is truly good. All others fall short, having only limited goodness. With people, even what seems to be goodness is often based on wrong motives. There is no other example of goodness that can compare to God's. No one else is good to the extent that God is; no one else is completely and purely good. God alone is the one we have to look to for an example and an accurate display of goodness.

God is often praised for no other reason than because He is good (Ezra 3:11). He expresses that goodness most notably through His lovingkindness, which lasts forever. He never ceases to love because He never ceases to be good. His character is one of unending and unlimited goodness.

When Moses asked God to show His glory (Exodus 33:19), God responded that He would make all of His goodness to pass by Moses. His goodness is the manifestation of His glory. His goodness is what reveals Him to us, and that goodness is immense. The revelation to Moses was just a small portion of God's glory, yet it was still more than Moses could look directly on. No one else has goodness that amounts to such amazing glory. When we see the magnitude of God's goodness, we easily see how He surpasses all others in His unique goodness.

> *"Father, I praise You that You are immensely good in a way*
> *that no one else can compare to."*

Day 53

Who satisfies your years with good things,
So that your youth is renewed like the eagle.
Psalm 103:5

God is good. His goodness is vast and undeniable. The Bible contains many reassurances regarding the reality and extent of God's goodness. He is *"truly"* good (II Chronicles 7:3), not like others who may just claim to be. He is *"surely"* good (Psalm 73:1); there is no doubt. He is *"indeed"* good (Psalm 85:12), and it cannot be denied. His goodness is described as being *"great"* (Isaiah 63:7) and *"abundant"* (Psalm 145:7).

God rejoices in doing good to His people (Jeremiah 32:41). He plans and promises to do good (Numbers 10:29). Because God is so good, He is not satisfied with doing just a little bit of good for His people; He does much good for them (Jeremiah 33:9). God's goodness is expressed in multiplied ways and in bountiful blessings (Numbers 10:32). God's goodness is not a random or one-time thing, but something that He shows consistently throughout our lives. Through the years we see it displayed over and over again (I Kings 8:66).

Beyond being merely genuine or even numerous, God's acts of goodness are satisfying (Jeremiah 31:14). They don't leave us longing for more. The gifts that He gives are either so good or so plentiful that they satisfy us. We don't need or want more than He gives (Psalm 103:5). Amazingly, the satisfying goodness that God has already shown to us is not the end. There are good things still to come that we have not yet seen through the law (Hebrews 10:1). God's goodness has not ended, and it will not end. What we have seen so far is just a shadow and a small portion of the plentiful goodness that He will continue to show.

"Thank You, Father, for the vast amount of goodness that You have shown to me. It is more than I can comprehend."

Day 54

God saw all that He had made, and behold, it was very good. And there was evening and there was morning, the sixth day.
Genesis 1:31

God is good. He is completely good. Because God is so entirely good, goodness permeates His every aspect and all that He touches. For this reason, we see many aspects of God that are good. God's name is good (Psalm 54:6) and deserves our thanks. God's house is good (Psalm 65:4), and being in it satisfies us. God's Word is good (Hebrews 6:5), and it does good for those who walk in it (Micah 2:7). God's commandments are good (Nehemiah 9:13) because they keep us on the right path. God's promises are good (Joshua 21:45) and will always be completed. His lovingkindness is good (Psalm 69:16), causing Him to act on our behalf. God's Spirit is good (Nehemiah 9:20), and He gives us that Spirit for our instruction. The way that God has established for His people to walk in is good (I Kings 8:36), and we can follow it in confidence and without fear. God's will is good (Romans 12:2), and He will always direct us into what is positive rather than detrimental. God's gifts and provisions are good (Deuteronomy 1:25). Everything that God made was very good (Genesis 1:31). How could it not be, when God is the one making it? In summary, everything relating to God is good, because God Himself is very good.

"Father, thank You that everything about You is completely good, with not one speck of evil or weakness, so that I can safely trust You."

Day 55

"If you then, being evil, know how to give good gifts to your children, how much more will your Father who is in heaven give what is good to those who ask Him!"
Matthew 7:11

God is good. His goodness is expressed in many ways, both by what He does and by what He gives. God's goodness causes Him to look kindly on those in need and desire to help them (Psalm 68:10). God shows His goodness through specific acts, such as delivering His people (Exodus 18:9). God's goodness is often displayed through physical blessings and in meeting practical, everyday needs (Psalm 85:12). His good provision is so great in both quality and quantity that it satisfies those who receive it (Psalm 104:28). In addition to meeting our basic needs by blessing our efforts, God goes on to give us extra blessings and gifts that we have not even worked for (Psalm 21:3). His good works are plenteous, as if His goodness overflows into action without restraint (John 10:32).

As a good shepherd, God cares for His sheep meticulously and provides for every need they have, even when He has to die to do so. (John 10:11). God's good hand prospers our way and moves forward the events of our lives in order to bring about His desired ends (Ezra 7:9). God's good desires will always be accomplished; He will never promise something good and then fail to do it (Jeremiah 32:42). Earthly parents give good gifts to their children, but God far surpasses earthly parents in His giving of very good gifts, including the Holy Spirit (Matthew 7:11). Because God is good, He is ready to forgive us when we call to Him (Psalm 86:5). Instead of remembering the sins of our past, He remembers us according to His goodness and stands ready and willing to instruct us even though we are sinners (Psalm 25:7-8).

"Father, You are good to me in more ways than I can even comprehend. Help me not to forget your goodness or take it for granted."

Day 56

The LORD is good to all,
And His mercies are over all His works.
Psalm 145:9

God is good. He is good to everyone. This is hard to believe to some extent. We want God to be good to the righteous, but we're not so sure about the wicked. Because God is good by nature, however, He can only do what is good, regardless of the recipient. That goodness may be expressed in different ways to different people because of the needs they have. For example, God would be good to send hardship in order to bring someone to Himself.

Even with a gentler definition of goodness, the reality is that God's goodness is so expansive that everyone profits from it. There are many blessings shown to the world at large. If God were not good, the earth would fail, and things would cease to exist. Even the creatures of the earth are cared for and satisfied because God opens His hand in provision for them (Psalm 104:28).

God is good to those who are not right with Him. He instructs them as sinners, even when they are not good (Psalm 25:8). When people have failed to meet His demands, but come to Him with humble hearts, He responds compassionately because of His goodness (II Chronicles 30:18).

God is good to those in need; He looks kindly on the poor and provides for them (Psalm 68:10). He does seem to care in a special way for those who belong to Him. He is good to Israel and to the pure in heart (Psalm 73:1). He doesn't withhold anything good from those who walk uprightly (Psalm 84:11) and His words do good for them (Micah 2:7). He is good to those who fear Him and who take refuge in Him (Psalm 31:19). God is good to those who wait for Him and seek Him (Lamentations 3:25), and they will not lack any good thing that they need (Psalm 34:10). God gives good gifts to those who ask Him (Matthew 7:11). Expressed in so many different ways, God is indeed good to everyone.

"I am undeserving, Father, and yet You are good to me. Help me to increasingly become someone who fears and seeks You so that I can see Your goodness increase."

Day 57

O give thanks to the LORD, for He is good;
For His lovingkindness is everlasting.
I Chronicles 16:34

God is good. He deserves praise for His goodness. We need to praise and thank Him because He is good. The refrain in the verse above was a common phrase in Israel's hymns, being repeated six additional times in Scripture. It is an important instruction and meant to be heeded. Apart from this specific phrase, there are eleven more references to praising, thanking, worshiping, and blessing God specifically for His goodness. This thanking is presented as a voluntary and willing expression (Psalm 54:6). It is done with exuberance and singing (Ezra 3:11). There should be rejoicing and gladness of heart as we stop to reflect on all of the good things God has done (I Kings 8:66).

The people in Nehemiah's day had a great celebration in which they recited a lengthy song of praise to God. It was a tremendous testimony service as they remembered specific acts that God had done for them through the years (Nehemiah 9:25 & 35). When we stop to remember all that God has done for us in His goodness, we should be ready to eagerly and enthusiastically share those blessings and memories with others (Psalm 145:7).

God has been so good! What a shame if we focus on only the negative aspects of our lives and fail to give Him the praise He deserves for His abundant and unfailing goodness! By failing to praise Him, we shortchange God of the honor due His name, we become negative and discouraged, and we fail to encourage others. Without God's goodness sustaining us day by day, we would be utterly lost. Let us not neglect to give Him the thanks and praise that is due Him for His unending goodness.

"Thank You, Father, for Your unfailing goodness. You have been so good to me every day.
May I not fail to give You the praise and thanks You deserve."

Day 58

Or do you think lightly of the riches of His kindness and tolerance and patience, not
knowing that the kindness of God leads you to repentance?
Romans 2:4

This is an appropriate verse with which to conclude our study on the goodness of God. The word *kindness* in this verse refers to moral goodness and is actually expressed with the word *goodness* in some translations. The question asked is whether we think lightly of God's goodness. As we have seen over the past days, God's goodness is not a light thing. It is not just a minor aspect that is kind of true about Him. No, God is good in His very nature. It is one of the things He emphasizes about Himself, and He shows His goodness over and over again in many, many ways. God's goodness is a big deal. In addition to its daily display in our lives, ultimately it led us to salvation.

What does it mean to take God's kindness lightly? Simply put, we just don't think it's that big of a deal. To take God's goodness lightly is to fail to remember it or be grateful for it. It is to doubt His goodness, saying things like "God isn't really that good to me" or "I'm not so sure I actually see God's goodness." It is to think, "God's goodness really isn't very meaningful in my life." How can that be? How can we utter such statements? His goodness is seen everywhere and expressed often, most notably in salvation. How much "gooder" can we expect Him to be?

We may not always see God's goodness expressed to the extent or in the ways we would like, but He is good nevertheless. If we truly open our eyes and look, we will easily see His goodness all around us. We should be aware of God's goodness and be exceedingly grateful for it. In the context of the verse above, knowing how good God is should also prompt us to turn from sin.

"Father, forgive me for taking Your incredible goodness lightly. Help me to focus on the good things that You do for me each day."

Day 59

He will be like a tree firmly planted by streams of water,
Which yields its fruit in its season
And its leaf does not wither;
And in whatever he does, he prospers.
Psalm 1:3

God gives a beautiful illustration of the man who walks in His ways and delights in Him. God compares this man to a sturdy and fruitful tree. God establishes His people, and when He does, He does so thoroughly. This is a firmly planted tree, one with deep and stable roots. It is not weak. It is not moving or even leaning, but is standing straight, strong, and tall.

This tree is planted by streams of water. It has the nourishment it needs to thrive and flourish. It's not barely surviving, weakened and hampered by drought. This tree's leaves do not wither, and it yields fruit at harvest-time. The tree is healthy and fulfills its purpose. It produces what it is supposed to produce. It prospers in everything.

A man like this is able to prosper in all he does because he is following God's plan. His mind is saturated with God's truth, and he delights in that truth; therefore, what he does is blessed by God. It is interesting to compare the righteous man to the wicked man described in the second half of the psalm.

While the godly man is firmly planted and can't be torn down or uprooted, the wicked man will not stand and is compared to chaff driven by the wind. There is a vast contrast between the two. The first is so firmly established that even the fiercest winds cannot shake or tumble it. The second is so weak that it cannot withstand even the gentlest winds, no matter how hard it tries.

The stability and fruitfulness of the righteous is not dependent on positive circumstances. God maintains the righteous even in the face of the harshest situations. The same brutal wind that easily drives the chaff is unable to tear down the tree. The fact that the righteous man does not fall in the wind is a testimony to himself and to others that he is planted and cared for by God's hand.

"Thank You, Father, that You can help me to be stable and fruitful. Thank You that I need not fear the wind, but that I can trust You to hold me firmly in place."

Brutal Winds (Sonnet 28)
The raging winds plunge down the mountainside,
And through the fissures, crags, and rocks they screech.
The winds burst fiercely through ash, elm, and beech,
And mighty oaks are from their bases pried.
The winds march harshly through the countryside;
Their mangling fingers through the gardens reach.
The driving winds rush o'er the plains and beach,
Propelling dust and whipping up the tide.
When winds like these assault my feeble soul
And blow so harshly, oh, how can I stand?
I'm shielded and protected by God's hand;
He's ever at my side and keeps me whole.
He makes my roots grow strong, holds firm my feet;
The weath'ring makes my character complete.

Day 60

My soul thirsts for God, for the living God;
When shall I come and appear before God?
Psalm 42:2

Throughout the ages of civilization, people have worshipped many, many gods. They have worshipped things they have made or gathered with their own hands: idols carved out of wood and stone, figures of creatures, sticks and rocks. Man has worshipped nature; he has feared and worshipped the rain, the sun, the rivers, or animals. Man has worshipped people; he has exalted another human to the level of a god and has whole-heartedly given his life and service to another man. Man has worshipped gods created in his own imagination. He has dreamed up what God must be like, and has even built entire religions based on these invented gods.

Each of these gods is false. Every one of them is dead. Even those who enjoy life, do so only for a limited time. They often die sooner than the man who worships them. These false gods have no ability to help man or to control what happens in his life. Being dead, they aren't even aware of the worship given to them, nor can they hear the prayers that are offered.

The true God is different. He is the Living God. He is alive, and He will be forever. God isn't just a mystic power out there somewhere; He is a real live person who interacts with man. Because He is alive, He can hear cries for help. He can watch the lives of His children. He can decide what to do. Because God is alive, He is able to help in the situations His children face. He can manage and control their lives. He can receive worship, and He can respond in very real ways to those who worship Him. God is not dead. He is not powerlessly trapped inside a hunk of wood. God lives!

"Thank You, Father, that You are alive. I don't have to helplessly depend on something that can never respond, but I can trust in a God who can do something."

Day 61

For this finds favor, if for the sake of conscience toward God a person bears up under sorrows when suffering unjustly. For you have been called for this purpose, since Christ also suffered for you, leaving you an example for you to follow in His steps.
I Peter 2:19 & 21

Endurance is required in difficult circumstances. We might even be asked to endure something that is not fair and never should have happened. Sometimes a physical ailment is due to a doctor's mistake or a surgery gone wrong. It may be the result of a freak accident or an injury due to the carelessness of others. The severity of an illness can often be traced to a belated diagnosis, a misdiagnosis, or a doctor who would not listen to the patient's concerns.

The Bible instructs us that we ought to bear up under sorrow, even when the situation is unjust. We are to do so because of conscience toward God – because we are doing it for His sake and because we believe it is what He wants us to do.

When we endure under these circumstances, we find favor with God. God is pleased with this response.

Don't we want God's pleasure and His approval? If we wonder how to respond in this way, God's Word shows us exactly what to do. The way to walk is not a mystery or something we have to make guesses about. The Bible gives us an example to follow. We can look at the life of Christ, a real man in real circumstances, and we can see how He walked.

Christ suffered for our sakes. This was unjust suffering due to no fault of His own. He suffered greatly on our behalf, yet He endured. He didn't sin in the process. He didn't fight back. He didn't speak wrong words against those who attacked Him. He didn't destroy them in anger or frustration. Instead, He kept entrusting Himself to God as the righteous judge. He allowed God to take care of the results. This is what God expects of us as we follow the example of Christ. When sorrows and sufferings come, even unjustly, we are to endure.

"Thank You, Father, for the example of Christ. Help me to please You as He pleased You by bearing up under sorrow."

Day 62

Behold, as the eyes of servants look to the hand of their master,
As the eyes of a maid to the hand of her mistress,
So our eyes look to the LORD our God,
Until He is gracious to us.
Psalm 123:2

A servant is dependent upon his master in two ways. First, the servant depends on his master for guidance. The master lets him know what the tasks are for each day. He tells the servant what to do first, second, and last. The master instructs the servant how to do the task and provides training if necessary. The master tells the servant where to go for supplies or for additional help. The master gives the servant a goal to aim at and a task to be accomplished.

Second, the servant depends on his master for provision. The master has to provide everything for his servant. He provides a context for living and a place to belong. He provides shelter, clothing, and food. He provides the materials needed to perform the tasks that are put before him. When education is required, it is the master who provides it. Without the master, the servant would have nothing and would not know what to do.

The Bible compares a Christian's relationship with God to that of a master and a servant. Like the servant, we depend on God for guidance. He lets us know what to do with our days and how to live our lives. He gives us our priorities. He teaches us how to do the things that we must do. He shows us where to get help. Just like the servant is nothing without his master, so we are nothing without God. Only He can show us how to live each day. We depend on Him for instruction.

We also depend on God for provision. We have nothing that God has not provided for us. Only He can provide meaning and purpose for our lives. God gives us the supplies we need for each day. He provides the tools we need for every job He gives. We must lift our eyes to Him, awaiting His provision. Only He can provide everything we need for life.

The picture of a servant may at first seem repulsive, but when the Master is kind and benevolent, the servant is carefully guided and completely cared for. The servant is in good hands because the Master is supremely gracious. When we look in dependence to God, we will not be neglected.

"Father, I look to You to tell me what to do. I wait for You to guide me. I depend on You for my every need. I am lost without You."

Day 63

Trust in the LORD with all your heart
And do not lean on your own understanding.
In all your ways acknowledge Him,
And He will make your paths straight.
Proverbs 3:5-6

There are many decisions before you. Which treatment plan should you pursue? Should you try to keep working or be involved in ministry? How long should you avoid making commitments? How far into the future should you make any plans at all? In the midst of these questions, have you found yourself wondering in frustration, "What is going on here? What should I do?"

Because you are human, you want to know what is going on and what the future holds. You want to understand the purposes for your situation so you know how to proceed. You want to be able to say, "Since God is doing *this*, I will do *this*." Unfortunately, your life seems like a huge, jumbled mess. You don't understand it at all.

If you don't understand what God is doing, you certainly can't rely on your own understanding. You need God's understanding instead, because His understanding is far better than yours. What doesn't make any sense to humans makes perfect sense to God. He is a big enough God to trust.

Instead of making decisions based on your own understanding, acknowledge God in each decision. Trust His guidance, asking, "God, what do You think?" Step aside and let God decide. Leave every decision to Him, resolved to follow whichever answer He chooses. He is a wise enough God to decide correctly.

With God's understanding as a basis and with His decisions as a guide, God can make your paths straight. He can lead faithfully no matter what the path looks like, and He will properly direct. He will produce a better outcome than you could have arranged. He is a sovereign enough God to arrange your life.

Because you trust God, you let Him make the decisions, and because you let Him decide, He does everything just right. You can lean on Him even if you don't understand a bit of His plan. When you are so far from understanding His plans, you are unlikely to do the right thing on your own. Slow down so that you are sure each of your plans is God's plan, because only then can you walk the right path.

"Father, I don't understand, so I must trust Your understanding. Make the decisions that You know are best, and I will trust You and follow Your guidance."

Trust His Understanding (Sonnet 27)
I cannot trust myself; I am too weak,
But I must trust in God with all my heart.
Completely helpless, He's the one I seek.
I lean on Him to show me ev'ry part.
My God knows things that I can't understand;
His thoughts are so much higher than my own.
I cannot lean on help from my own hand,
But humbly seek wise counsel at His throne.
In ev'ry path I must see my great need
And look to Him to be my trusty Guide.
Acknowledging His wisdom, not impede;
Remove myself and let my God decide.
Then He will wisely lead me through each gate,
And He'll direct each path and make it straight.

Day 64

He will cover you with His pinions,
And under His wings you may seek refuge:
His faithfulness is a shield and bulwark.
Psalm 91:4

Is there any human need deeper than the need for love? We long for someone to care about us and to express that caring in tangible ways. Illness brings along with it a greater sensitivity and vulnerability. More than ever we crave gentle nurturing and loving support.

God describes His meeting of that desire in a very beautiful way. One of the tenderest pictures of love is that of a mother bird who nestles her babies snugly at her side. With her wings she gently holds them close to her warm body. She surrounds them with her protective wings so they cannot be lost. She makes them secure in that sheltered position. So God holds us close to Himself. He nurtures us in tenderness. He shelters us from the cruel world that exists outside of the refuge He provides.

Can we doubt the love of one who holds us so gently? Can we feel unloved when He cherishes us so intimately? God knows the emotional needs of our human hearts, and He responds to those needs in a beautiful way. In case we fear that God is all kindness and fluff, merely a compassionate person filled with sweet-sounding but empty words, God reveals a second aspect of Himself in this verse.

Yes, He is as gentle and nurturing and as loving as can be, but He also has strength. He is also a shield and bulwark. Our doubts might tell us that the surrounding wings are not strong enough to fend off danger. Well, God also protects us with large, surrounding shields. These mighty shields are able to keep harm from coming to us. God surrounds us with both tenderness and might.

*"Father, how wonderfully You hold me close to You under Your tender wings.
How powerfully You protect me with Your surrounding
shields. Thank You that I can rest in Your care."*

Day 65

*"Behold, how happy is the man whom God reproves,
So do not despise the discipline of the Almighty."
Job 5:17*

Sometimes God sends an illness in response to specific sin. An illness can be judgment from the hand of God. A man who is disciplined in this way is actually blessed because of what God's judgment prevents. The Bible repeatedly teaches that God brings judgment on His people in order to keep them from more severe chastening in the future. God's common practice is to gradually escalate His judgment, increasing its intensity until it is effective. An illness can be an early step in the process. It can be an attention-grabbing tool that not only makes harsher judgment unnecessary, but also protects the person in question from the dreadful results of continued sin.

Job's friends believed that his illness was the result of his sin. In the New Testament, the disciples believed that a man's blindness was because of sin. Both of these assertions were incorrect. In neither case was the illness a consequence of specific sin. As sick people, we like to cling to these situations. We like to claim them as a general principle that illness is not the result of sin. We cannot, however, make such a blanket statement.

The truth is that illness is often the result of sin. The Bible reveals this through specific examples and through clear teaching. Most notably, First Corinthians 11:30 speaks of illness and even death as the result of sin. Job's friends were not crazy to present their argument, and the disciples were not foolish in asking their question. They happened to be wrong in those two specific cases, indicating that an illness is not an absolute indication of judgment.

On the other hand, the fact that God sometimes uses illness as a tool impels us to consider the possibility. We cannot blindly assume that we are the exception just because Job was. We must soberly allow God to search our hearts and reveal a sin-based reason for our illness if one exists. If our illness is not because of sin, we will have a clear conscience before God, but if it is the result of sin, we need to make things right so that God will not need to intensify His judgment.

"Father, help me to search my heart. Have I made a sinful choice that has resulted in my illness? Am I heading in a wrong direction? Do I need to confess and come back to You? Show me, Father."

Day 66

I sought the LORD, and He answered me,
And delivered me from all my fears.
Psalm 34:4

"What if?" Is this a frequent question upon your lips? Does your mind often find itself in turmoil, troubled by uncertainty and fear? An illness is an ideal breeding ground for doubts and questions. Everything about your life has suddenly become less certain.

Will you be able to finish school? Get married? Have children? Will you be able to resume your job or ministry? Will you ever be able to take that trip or tackle that project you've always dreamed about? Will the doctors know what to do? Is there any possibility of a successful treatment? Will the side effects be too harsh? Will you live long enough to see the fruits of your labor?

It is impossible for you to know the answers to these questions. It is easy for these doubts to give way to fears and worries. If you're not careful, you could become obsessed with these questions and your heart could become overwhelmed by fear.

What can you do in these times of threatening fears? Go to God. God is always there to listen to you. When you talk to Him, He will always hear. When you seek Him, He will always answer. Tell Him the fears that plague you. Express to Him your concern. Pour out on Him the uncertainties. He is gentle and kind to hear all of your troubles.

Seek God as the solid, unchangeable Rock. He can be the unwavering constant in your life. He can be your stability. When the uncertainties, doubts, and fears are carried to God and placed on Him, He can provide a solid foundation on which to depend. He can make you so secure that the fears no longer have power over you. Instead of fears, they become merely questions for which He has the perfect answers.

"Father, the fears are assaulting me. Help me to leave the questions with You. May confidence in Your knowledge give me peace."

Day 67

"He will cry to Me, 'You are my Father,
My God, and the rock of my salvation.'"
Psalm 89:26

What does a father do? First of all, our fathers give us life. Without them, we would never even exist. Second, our fathers give us our names. Our identity comes from them. Third, our fathers provide all that we need to survive. This provision is most notable during the most vulnerable times in our lives, when we are tiny and helpless. Fourth, our fathers protect us. They shield us from dangers and attacks. Fifth, our fathers teach us. They give us skills for life and decision-making. Sixth, our fathers love us. They care about our lives and desire good for us.

God calls Himself our Father, and He performs all of these same tasks. In fact, He performs them much better than any earthly father can. God gives us physical life, but, more importantly, He gives us spiritual life when we accept Him. He makes us truly alive. God gives us our identity. We are children of the King. God provides for us, meeting needs that our earthly fathers are powerless to do anything about. God also meets our needs in our weakest times. God protects us. He shields us from the attacks of Satan and does not allow any situation that we cannot handle with His strength. God teaches us. His Word provides wisdom for the challenges of life. God loves us. He pours out His love in countless ways. His love is inseparable and constant.

God is indeed a wonderful Father. There are people who don't have an earthly father, or who have a poor one, and that loss leaves a terrible lack in their lives. God declares Himself to be the Father to the fatherless. To those people who are most alone and most needy, God Himself wants to be the Father. He wonderfully fills the huge, gaping need that they have. He fills the role like no human father can. What an amazing substitute father He is! Who could be a better Father than God?

"Thank You, Father, for being my Father and for meeting all these needs in my life. Where would I be without You?"

Day 68

And not only this, but we also exult in our tribulations, knowing that tribulation brings about perseverance; and perseverance, proven character; and proven character, hope; and hope does not disappoint, because the love of God has been poured out within our hearts through the Holy Spirit who was given to us.
Romans 5:3-5

How can we have a positive response toward our illness? Is it possible? Isn't the illness an entirely negative thing? No, not when we look at it from God's perspective or when we consider the results it brings. We can exult in our tribulation. *Exulting* is a response that is directed toward God. It does not mean that we are jumping up and down with happiness; rather, it is the act of rejoicing and glorying in what God is doing.

We rejoice not in the trial itself, but in what the trial is accomplishing. God is indeed doing something profitable through the trial. Tribulations bring perseverance as a result, but that's not the end. Perseverance brings about a change in our character, making it proven and trustworthy. Our character becomes firm and reliable, having passed the test. Finally, proven character gives us hope and confidence. We have hope because we can see that God has worked a change in us and has helped us to endure. Based in the great love that God has poured out on us, this hope will not let us down.

If we work backwards, the fact that God pours out His love on us means that we can have a sure hope in Him. We can have that confidence because of the tried and tested character that God has worked in us. That tested character has come as a result of endurance through tribulation. Exulting in tribulation is possible because of what we know God is doing through it. We don't know all that He is doing, but we can rejoice in what we *do* know – that He is using it to bring godly character. Our character will mature, and we will have greater confidence in living for God. This confident stability is grounded not in ourselves, but in the fact that God loves us.

"Father, thank You that this trial is not without purpose. You are accomplishing something worthwhile that can give me hope."

Day 69

The steps of a man are established by the LORD,
And He delights in his way.
When he falls, he will not be hurled headlong,
Because the LORD is the One who holds his hand.
Psalm 37:23-24

God directs my steps. He directs the steps that I view as good, and He also establishes the steps that I perceive to be bad. Whatever the steps may look like, they're not actually my steps at all. Yes, they are the way that I will walk with my feet, but really the path is just the way that God is leading my steps. They are His steps appointed for me. Just like an invention belongs to the man who invents it, the steps that God designs belong to Him.

God takes great interest and delight in my path as He marks it out before me. He doesn't take the trailblazing lightly; He does it masterfully well. Can I not trust the path that God has designed for me? Who better to mark the path? I could not possibly do a better job on my own. God makes a good path on which I can walk safely and without slipping.

Or does He? In my experience, there have been times that I have not only slipped, but I have also fallen. These falls have been painful, yet I have not fallen to the bottom of the mountain and lain there broken at the foot of the trail. I have not been left disabled by the rocks or floundering in the mud without the strength to stand up again.

Oh, no. When I fall, the falling is not permanent. It is not destructive. It would be perhaps if I were walking by myself, but I'm not. I have someone walking the path with me, and that someone is holding my hand. When I fall, He lifts me back up, heals my injuries, and sets me back on the path. He will help me to continue the journey, and He will keep holding my hand as I continue to walk. Falling does not mean the end of the journey. In my weakness, I may stumble, but in His strength, I will never be defeated.

"Father, plan my steps as You choose. Guide me on the path so I don't slip. If I do fall, lift me back up. Help me not to give up but to continue with Your strength."

Day 70

But if any of you lacks wisdom, let him ask of God, who gives to all generously and without reproach, and it will be given to him.
James 1:5

A person who is ill needs a lot of things; one of the things he needs most is wisdom. He needs wisdom for choices to be made: to work or not to work, which treatment plan to use, when to call the doctor, when to ask for help, how to manage the diet and medications. He also needs wisdom for spiritual discernment: how much Bible study he is capable of, whether or not a struggle is spiritually based, why he becomes angry, what makes him fall into discouragement, what initiates his wrong thinking. In the midst of illness, there is so much that one does not know and so much that he is confused about.

If the person himself does not have the answers, it is quite unlikely that anyone else does. There is, however, one person who has all the answers. God has the best wisdom, so He's the best source to go to. He is completely willing to give the wisdom because He is *"full of compassion and is merciful"* (James 5:11). Instead of scolding, He is completely willing and ready to share that wisdom. One does not have to doubt that God will give it, because He promises that He will.

A greater blessing is that God doesn't allot only tiny fragments of wisdom. He gives wisdom generously and in abundance. He gives all that we need. God does have one requirement – that the man ask in faith, without hesitating or wavering. If a man doesn't think he has the faith to ask for wisdom, he can ask for faith, or he can simply decide to believe God and ask with the tiny bit of faith he has. The very act of asking would imply some level of faith; otherwise he wouldn't be asking at all. Then he must simply be ready to respond to what God shows him and to follow the counsel and guidance that God supplies.

"Give me wisdom, Father, not only for the practical decisions, but also to evaluate my limitations, to face challenges and temptations, and to pursue my relationship with You."

Praise to the God of Answers
No answer that God does not know –
No mystery is beyond His ken.
For He has planned each course just so,
Both what will come and what has been.
Oh, praise to God who knows it all.
In gratitude I humbly fall.

This knowing God can also show
His answers unto seeking men
So they can know the path to go.
He lets them know what, where, and when.
Oh, praise to God who shows to me.
My thanks to Him each day shall be."

$\longrightarrow$

His answers are worked out also.
Effective power He will send
To do what from His mind did flow.
His plans succeed once and again.
Oh, praise to God who works it out.
My feet can follow without doubt.

Day 71

Many are the afflictions of the righteous,
But the LORD delivers him out of them all.
Psalm 34:19

Psalm 34 presents God as a great and compassionate deliverer. This compassionate God pays attention to those who are needy and fearful, and He answers their cries for help (vs. 4-6). God sees His children in their need, and He fills them with good things (vs. 9-10). God shows His compassion by keeping His eyes directed toward His children and by keeping His ears available to hear their cries (v. 15). This compassionate God is near to those who are hurting; He helps those who are brokenhearted (v. 18).

God's compassion is very comforting, but it is really reassuring only because there is power to back up His comfort. God is not limited to having a heart that feels another's pain or to offering empty words. God has enough power to effectively respond to those for whom He has compassion. His power is shown by His ability to completely and thoroughly protect His own, as illustrated in the final four verses of the psalm.

Verse nineteen shows that the quantity of trouble doesn't matter to God. Regardless of how many trials there are, God's deliverance is able to match them. He can deliver from every single one. Verse twenty reveals the extent of God's protection. When God delivers, He can even protect every bone from being broken. His deliverance is not merely adequate, performing the major task of saving the life, but it is also detailed, down to protecting each little bone. Lest we think that deliverance from trials is something that just happens in life, verse twenty-one informs us that the wicked are not saved. The righteous are special, and God exercises His saving power on their behalf. Finally, verse twenty-two declares how many people God can save. It states that none of those who trust in Him will be lost. God has many children all around the world, and He is able to protect every one of them. God's deliverance is thorough. He has tremendous power that supports His profound compassion.

"Father, my troubles are many and deep. Thank You that You care about each one and that You are entirely able to meet them all."

Day 72

On the contrary, who are you, O man, who answers back to God? The thing molded will not say to the molder, "Why did you make me like this," will it?
Romans 9:20

God is God. He knows what He is doing, and He can do what He wants. The Bible presents many pictures of God that help to illustrate this concept. God is the master potter. He skillfully designs the kind of vessel He wants, and He works the clay for as long as He needs to. The clay cannot respond by asking, "Didn't you know what you were doing when you made me?" God is also the sovereign general of heavenly and earthly armies. He directs His subjects as He chooses, and no one can ask, "Why are You doing it that way?" God is the master pruner. He cuts off the branches that He chooses. The branches can't respond with "Why did You cut me off?" God is the refiner of metals. The gold can't say, "The fire is too hot" or "Why are You putting me in the fire again?"

Because God is the master in all of these areas, we cannot question His decisions or skill. Instead, we need to submit to what God is doing. We don't need to understand it, approve of it, or agree with it; those don't fall within our responsibility. We just need to submit and allow Him to do His work. That submission is not a one-time assent. The vessel can't agree to be molded, but then jump out of the potter's hands each time he makes a cut. The vessel must remain under the potter's hands for each step of the process, from the initial shaping to the final detailed work.

We may have accepted from the beginning the illness God chose, but we must also accept the day-to-day implications. We must continue to submit when we get worse instead of better in the course of treatment. We must continue to submit when we realize the end is further away than we had hoped. We must continue to submit when new symptoms develop and when we are left to suffer alone. It can be relatively easy to submit to the big picture because it tends to be a concept. It is often harder to submit to the daily details which affect us more regularly and practically. If the overall illness is God's plan, then all of the daily details resulting from that illness are His plan too. We must submit to all of His work until the job is finished.

"Father, You are the potter. You know what You are doing. Every step of the process is necessary. Please do what You need to do in order to make the product You desire."

Day 73

> *But You, O Lord, are a God merciful and gracious,*
> *Slow to anger and abundant in lovingkindness and truth.*
> *Psalm 86:15*

In this psalm David cries out to God in a time of affliction. He lifts up his soul to God and trusts in God as his source of help. He recognizes that there is no one else like God and no one else who can do the works that God does. The psalm is filled with these expressions of trust. Then in verse fifteen David shares five specific aspects of God's character. These five aspects make Him a God who is worthy of trust. They make Him a God to whom it makes sense to turn in time of trouble.

First, God is merciful. This refers to God's compassion and tender love. He cares about those who are hurting and in trouble. Second, God is gracious. He is a God who is above everything, yet He stoops in kindness to bestow His goodness on those who are below Him. Certainly those who are in times of affliction can profit from this kindness. Third, God is slow to anger. He is patient and does not easily give way to wrath at the actions of people. In the pressures of suffering, with all the accompanying temptations, man needs a God who is patient toward his failures. Fourth, God is abundant in lovingkindness. He has vast quantities of kindness and favor towards man. He repeatedly overflows with expressions of gentle love. Fifth, God is abundant in truth. He is certain and trustworthy. With all the doubts and fears that suffering people face, they need truth that will not change, that can be depended upon, and that will anchor them. Yes, David was right. God is the right place to turn in time of affliction. There is no one else like Him.

"Help me, Father, not to take You for granted or to take my relationship with You lightly. You are an amazing God who is perfectly ready to meet the needs of hurting people."

Day 74

> *Is anyone among you suffering? Then he must pray.*
> *Is anyone cheerful? He is to sing praises.*
> *James 5:13*

Going to God is always the correct response in life. If we are cheerful, we can go to Him in singing of praises. If we are suffering, we can pray. When we are suffering, we *need* to pray. This may seem like a very obvious statement. Of course, we're going to pray about our need. But haven't we often found ourselves in the midst of suffering, observing that we don't know what to do? When we are at a loss, here is the answer – pray.

Even though we know that prayer is helpful, we often neglect it or use it to a minimal extent. We are not to offer just an isolated prayer and consider that to be sufficient. We need to be serious about praying and persist in it on a regular and continual basis.

The verse says that we *must* pray. It does not say that we *can* pray, that we *might* pray, or even that we *should* pray. Prayer is presented not as an option, but as an imperative. We cannot survive without it. Suffering presents a very real threat to our spiritual life and to our faithfulness to God. We must pray for strength to endure and to be able to make it through the trial. Prayer is an admission that we need God's help. It is a sign of our dependence on Him. It is an acknowledgement that He is the right source to help us in our need.

Prayer is also a great privilege. God is the mighty King of the universe, and He is able to help us. He invites us to come to Him with our needs – needs that He is abundantly able to meet. What should we pray about? Help? Yes, and anything else that is on our hearts. It is important that we do not limit our prayers only to requests for physical healing, but that we also pray for the spiritual growth and progress that God wants to accomplish through our trial.

"I am suffering, Father, and I need Your help. Help me to endure. Help me to remain faithful. Help me to grow in the ways that You intend."

Day 75

"And being fully assured that what God had promised, He was able also to perform.
Romans 4:21

Abraham was waiting for a child when it seemed impossible that one would ever come. Was it impossible? Yes, it really was, but Abraham believed anyway. Because of God's promise, Abraham's faith did not become weak, but grew instead. He did not waver in unbelief. His response of faith gave glory to God. He was fully assured that God was able to do what He had promised. He hoped when there seemed to be no reason to hope.

Abraham's responses were based on a specific promise of God. Every expectation for God to keep His promises will be met with an affirmative answer. We can go to God with a promise and ask Him to fulfill it through Christ, and He will always do what He has promised. Are there promises in God's Word that you think will never be fulfilled and that you think He never will complete? God's promises might seem as unlikely or as impossible as can be, yet He is still able to keep every one of them.

This assurance is not a blank check to demand anything you want. It does not mean God will do everything you ask. You might not be healed. You might not be accepted for a clinical trial. Your insurance prices might continue to go up. God has not promised to do those things. He has promised that He will always be with you, that He will supply your needs, and that His grace will be sufficient. Those are things you can be sure of. Because they are God's promises, you can know He will do them. Like Abraham, your faith in those things can be certain, regardless of how impossible they may seem. Your faith to believe will give glory to God, and as you see Him faithfully keep His promises, your faith will grow.

"Father, help me never to doubt that You will keep Your promises, no matter how impossible the situation seems."

Faithful Promises (Sonnet 12)
At times God's promises can seem untrue;
We wait and wait, but don't see His reply.
They seem forgotten, weak, and distant, too.
And every circumstance would them deny.
But God's dependable and cannot lie;
His Word stands firm for all eternity.
His promises will never, ever die;
They're true for you and also true for me.
Not wavering, we must trust and believe.
The human mind can't always comprehend,
But in His time we surely will receive.
Without a doubt fulfillment He will send.
Our faith in God will always see reward,
For He's our faithful and trustworthy Lord.

Day 76

And we know that God causes all things to work together for good to those who love God, to those who are called according to His purpose.
Romans 8:28

This is a common verse and one that perhaps we tire of hearing. After all, we've heard it so many times. Besides that, what we see in front of us is so far from what seems good. Perhaps most annoying, this is the one verse that everyone wants to throw at us to make everything all better. So let's forget about it as a challenge coming from others. Let's take it instead as a precious verse from God Himself. He has a comforting message for us and a great reassurance.

We can know and understand that all things work together for good to those who love God. The individual things of life may be hard, but within God's plan they cooperate in a team effort. Together they produce a good result. God orchestrates each individual thing so that He can ultimately do for us what is best. It seems impossible for some things to be anything but bad; because God is so good, however, He can take all things, even those that are bad and hard, and turn them to His good purposes.

With His power, God is in absolute control of our lives. Everything that happens to us passes through His hands and is designed to bring about His good purposes. We will not always like the things that happen, but we must submit to God's plan and control. God's plan is not merely acceptable; it's not even restricted to simply being good. God's plan is best. From our limited perspective, we can't understand how something "bad" can be the best, but we must submit to God's greater knowledge and to His statement that it is so. In time God may allow us to see something of His good plan, but even then our insight will be partial. We can't completely comprehend all of the good that God is working out; we simply need to trust. He is accomplishing good things.

"Father, I don't see the good, but I trust You to make even the difficulties of my illness work as part of Your good plan."

Day 77

For those whom He foreknew, He also predestined to become conformed to the image of His Son, so that He would be the firstborn among many brethren.
Romans 8:29

This is an important follow-up to verse twenty-eight. As we think about the good that God works from all things, the end result specifically mentioned in the passage is that we become conformed to the image of His Son. God wants us to look like Christ. How many times have we prayed, asking God to make us more Christlike and asking Him to produce godly character in us? How often have we longed to be like our spiritual heroes? Haven't we desired to have a testimony of greater sanctification that would bring honor to God and would increase the usefulness of our service?

Wouldn't it be nice if that would happen simply through reading and studying His Word? That certainly is part of the process, but God knows that sometimes it takes a trial to advance our sanctification. We are to be made more Christ-like through all that comes our way, including difficulty. This truth all by itself would make the trial worthwhile. What could be better than becoming like Christ?

Now, as we are in the trial, isn't that what we want? Don't we want to come out of it closer to God and looking more like Him? Don't we want to please Him? Don't we want Him to be glorified through these trials in our lives? If we truly want to come closer to that goal, then we must embrace and appreciate the methods that God chooses to use to achieve that goal. As God changes us to become more and more like Christ, we lift up Christ as the one worthy to be imitated. Our pursuit of Christ-likeness exalts Him as the ultimate pattern that we all want to be like.

"Father, may I give glory to You by increasingly reflecting the image of Your Son."

Day 78

"Do not fear, for I am with you;
Do not anxiously look about you, for I am your God.
I will strengthen you, surely I will help you,
Surely I will uphold you with My righteous right hand."
Isaiah 41:10

As I look at this verse, I can ask myself a series of questions. First of all, what is my condition? I am fearful. I look anxiously around me. I do not know what will happen, and the uncertainty brings fear. I am weak and in need of help. I am in danger of falling. I can barely stand, and I desperately need support.

Second, what do I want when I'm in that condition? When I am fearful, I want someone to reassure and comfort me. When I am anxious, I want someone to fix things for me, to defend me, and to protect me from the dangers. When I am weak and ready to fall, I want someone to support me. I want someone to steady me and keep me moving forward on the path. When I need help, I want someone to carry the load.

Third, who is at my side? My God is with me. He is never far away. I never have to doubt His presence. He will never leave me. He is my God, and He is full of strength. He is close enough to help me and near enough to hold me with His hand.

Finally, what will God do for me? First, God will be with me. He will not desert me or leave me on my own. The presence of such an amazing God is enough to silence my fears. Second, God will be my God. He will look on me very personally as His dear child and willingly claim me. Belonging to such a God quiets my anxiety and stills my desperately searching eyes. Third, God will strengthen me. He will give me the strength and stamina that I need to face each new day. He will not let anything be too hard for me. Fourth, God will help me. He will assist me through the trying days and the daunting struggles. He will help me to meet each challenge so that I do not have to face it on my own. Fifth, God will uphold me with His hand. God's hand is kind, powerful, and righteous. With His hand He will do the right thing to uphold me and keep me going. His hand is always with me, supporting me and assuring me of His love and help. Every weakness that I have can be wonderfully overcome through my great God.

"I am fearful, Father, and weak. I need help. Thank You for Your presence and care. Thank You for Your hand that holds me and helps me."

Day 79

"As one whom his mother comforts, so I will comfort you;
And you will be comforted in Jerusalem."
Isaiah 66:13

Sometimes in the midst of illness, we are in need of comfort. Whether we've received bad news, whether we're suddenly overwhelmed with the prospects of the future, or whether our hearts are heavy with the burden of on-going illness, we are often hurting, and we just want someone to comfort us.

In the verse above, God promises that He will give comfort. This promise is given to those who love Jerusalem. While the ultimate fulfillment of this prophecy lies in the future, the verse does indicate two reassuring things about the comfort of God. First of all, He does comfort. He does realize the needs of those whom He loves, and He responds with comfort. He knows the frailty of our hearts, and He offers the appropriate response.

Second, we see a picture of what it looks like when God comforts. He compares the method and extent of His comfort to that of a mother with her child. What more tender picture of comfort could there be than that of a mother holding her child close, stroking his face and kissing him? To see a mother and child in this interaction is a beautiful thing. We know that the mother-heart responds deeply to the hurt of her child. Her actions are pure love. The repeated expressions of that love are designed to ease the hurt so completely that it is forgotten. Every touch and caress is intended to bring calmness and rest. The gentle, loving mother doesn't stop her caresses and tender words until she has accomplished her goal. This is the picture that God chooses to illustrate His own comfort. He truly does care, and He continues to express that caring until He brings the comfort that we need.

"Oh, Father, do You know how much I hurt? Please hold me. Hold me close. Let me feel Your gentle touch and let me hear Your tender words."

Day 80

For which I suffer hardship even to imprisonment as a criminal;
but the word of God is not imprisoned.
II Timothy 2:9

Paul tells Timothy to suffer hardship like a good soldier (II Timothy 2:3). Soldiers go into training or on a mission or onto the battlefield with the understanding that things will not be easy. They know they will face challenges, inconveniences, and discomfort. That's part of the reality of being a soldier. Similarly, suffering hardship is a part of serving Christ. Those hardships can reach some pretty high levels. For example, Paul was imprisoned as a common criminal. That is a pretty harsh trial, especially for a faithful preacher.

As we live our lives for God, they will not be entirely smooth and easy. There will be challenges and discomforts along the way. That should be an understood assumption for us as well. We are to recognize that what is happening is not out of the ordinary. It is to be expected as we live for God in this world. Like Paul, we don't get to choose the difficulty of the hardships we must bear. Our response to these hardships should be the same as what Paul instructed Timothy – to endure. We must simply continue on, like a soldier continues plodding through the muddy field or fighting his way through a dense thicket. We must continue faithfully toward our objective.

The suffering that we do is for the cause of Christ and so that His work can be furthered. We endure because we realize endurance is part of our service to God and part of His greater work. We may not see how our illness can possibly make an impact within God's greater plan, but God uses all things, both large and small, to accomplish His purposes. He has countless factors that are all interacting to work out His desire, and our illness is one of those small factors. Though we may not understand how, our suffering is part of God's method for achieving His objective.

"Father, help me to be a good and faithful soldier. Help me to endure."

Day 81

For from days of old they have not heard or perceived by ear,
Nor has the eye seen a God besides You,
Who acts in behalf of the one who waits for Him.
Isaiah 64:4

God is unmatched and unmatchable. If all the historians and storytellers of the world were to unite and begin reciting amazing events, they would not be able to top God's exploits. They could tell of everything they have personally heard and seen. They could recount stories that have been told to them and that they have collected from others. They could review the history books, ancient documents, and all the written materials that have been collected. They could scan all of the visual resources available. They could take the most amazing accounts from all available sources and compile them into a showcase presentation. With all of that, man would be unable to come up with anything as amazing as God. There is no one else like Him. There is no one else who can compare to God.

This unmatched God interacts with man. He acts on behalf of those who wait for Him. This God who is able to do incredible things does them for those who depend on Him. What a privilege it is to belong to this God who takes an interest in us and who involves Himself in our lives! From the beginning of time man has not been able to comprehend or appreciate the things that God has prepared for those who wait on Him. The wonders of what He can and will do for us as we depend on Him are beyond our human imagination and comprehension. God's presence and actions are awesome and overwhelming. As we wait on this incredible God, He acts on our behalf with great blessings.

"Father, I'm humbled as I think that a God as incredible and unmatched as You would be interested to work on my behalf."

Day 82

Therefore we do not lose heart, but though our outer man is decaying, yet our inner man is being renewed day by day.
II Corinthians 4:16

Was Paul in a difficult situation? Yes. Was it hard on him physically? Absolutely. His body was being worn down by the trials. His body was growing weaker and was moving constantly closer to death. In the midst of his physical frailty, Paul recognized something more important than what was happening on the outside. There was something that overshadowed the physical decay.

God was doing something on the inside of Paul. God was continually renewing his spirit. Every day He was renovating Paul's spirit and giving him increased strength. The benefit was worthwhile, as inwardly Paul kept being revitalized by God. He was made progressively better and better.

There is lasting value that comes from the things we suffer. The trial is doing something, and that something is significant. The weakness of our bodies doesn't prevent God from doing something in our spirits. Physical weakness in no way impedes spiritual growth and strength. Sometimes it is only through difficulty and struggle that we really turn to God or look to Him for help and answers. Sometimes God must bring us up short in ourselves so that we can really grow. Struggles are good in that they bring growth and dependence on God.

In the midst of our physical weakness, others may perceive us as having less value or yielding less profit, but for God that is not the case. Instead of being hindered in creating profit in us, His ability to work is often enhanced in our physical weakness. God can give us the more valuable aspect of a spirit that is healthy and thriving in Him. The outer man is going to decay anyway; everyone will die. It is the inner man that will last. That is where we most need to be strong. God builds up what is most important.

"My body is weak, Father. Don't let my spirit be weak. Do Your renewing work in me so that I can grow spiritually stronger day by day."

No Change? (Sonnet 33)
Through passing days and weeks I see no change;
My heart desires to progress and grow.
When things seem stagnant, Lord, I think it strange,
For I seek You; I long Your ways to know.
When I look to Your Word with unveiled face
And seek to learn, I see Your glory there.
You are transforming me by Your good grace;
Your Spirit modifies the shape I bear.
And when You send afflictions to my way,
Immense eternal value they produce.
You are renewing me day after day,
So for Your work I'll have a greater use.
No change? Oh, weakness of my human eyes;
Your Word and work will do what You devise.

Day 83

Teach me to do Your will,
For You are my God;
Let Your good Spirit lead me on level ground.
Psalm 143:10

There are so many questions for which I need guidance. Should I pursue treatment or just let the disease run its course? Which treatment option should I choose? How much should I tell my family? Which aspects of my life and ministry should I try to maintain through my illness? These are hard questions, and only God has the wisdom to answer them.

If I want to do God's will in these scenarios, then I must ask Him to teach and lead me. I need God to teach me His will because I don't already know it. My human knowledge is limited and ignorant. I need God to teach me, because my ability to do His will is incomplete. I still need to grow in doing His will. I need God to teach me to do His will because both the desire and the ability to do so come from Him. I need God to teach me because He is God. When I recognize Him as God, I want to follow Him and submit to Him in whatever He asks. As I look at Him as God, I also realize that He knows the answers because He is omniscient. To whom else could I look for answers? I need God to teach me because He sends His Spirit to guide my steps.

I need God's Spirit to lead me on level ground. The decisions to be made are hard to discern, and I need God to make the way very plain and smooth. I need Him to lead me clearly so that I have no doubt. God's Spirit is good, and, as such, He will only lead in good paths. God's good Spirit will give a good answer and lead me properly. I don't need to doubt His leading. There are so many reasons why I must look to God for guidance, and just as many reasons why I cannot depend on myself.

"Father, I don't know what to do, but You do. Teach me Your will. Lead me plainly on Your good path so that I have no doubt."

Day 84

"Peace I leave with you; My peace I give to you; not as the world gives do I give to you. Do not let your heart be troubled, nor let it be fearful."
John 14:27

Being ill is not exactly conducive to having peace. You are shuttled from one doctor to another. Your days are filled with managing medicines, scheduling appointments, and haggling with insurance companies. Your mind is exploding with questions about what will happen and doubts about what to do next. You are bombarded by the advice and ideas of family and friends, each of whom has his own idea of what is wrong with you and how to treat it. You must also absorb the widely varied reactions of those who either treat you like a half-dead invalid or those who expect you to completely maintain your life and responsibilities. After dealing with all these scenarios and more, it can sometimes take a while to get your thinking turned around and your mind back to a peaceful state.

God wants you to have peace. He desires to give it to you. Christ promised to leave peace with His disciples, and He told them that He was giving it to them. Christ is the source of that peace; it is His peace. Imagine experiencing the same peace that Christ did. This is a different kind of peace, not like the world's peace which is so ineffective. The world's peace may seem at times to work, but it is at best a fleeting and superficial peace that does not fully satisfy. Christ's peace, on the other hand, is complete and satisfactory. It allows your heart to be untroubled and unafraid. When your heart rests quietly, without turmoil or fear, then you are at peace. This peace is possible, because it is a peace that Christ determines to give.

"Father, with so many things assaulting me on a constant basis, I need peace. Please give me Your peace that is able to keep me from being troubled."

Day 85

He who dwells in the shelter of the Most High
Will abide in the shadow of the Almighty.
Psalm 91:1

God is called the Almighty. The Hebrew word refers to someone who is powerful, full of muscles, and cannot be conquered. God is so strong that He can never be defeated or destroyed. There are a lot of powerful people within the knowledge of man. We could discuss real people like Samson, who carried city gates on his shoulders. We could consider Olympic weightlifters, who can lift more than seems humanly possible. We have heard stories of people who had rushes of adrenaline in extreme circumstances; these people have been known to lift cars. If we move into the realm of legend, we find even more amazing stories. We hear of Beowulf who ripped the arm off a monster. We read of the mighty tasks accomplished by Hercules and of Atlas who held the world on his shoulders.

The truth is that whether we look at reality or in the imaginary realm, there is no one who has the strength that God has. As we consider the name *Almighty*, we can easily see the two components of the word: *all* and *mighty*. Only God has all might. No one can stand before Him or defeat Him. Not only can God never be defeated, but He has the power to defeat anyone and anything that rises against Him. He can do this because of His unimaginable and unmatched might. No one can even present a worthy challenge. This is a God who can do anything He desires, and there is no stopping Him. This Almighty God is on our side, and He offers us the shelter of His care. With such a powerful protector, we are completely safe. No threat can defeat us, and no danger can conquer us.

"Thank You, Father, for Your great might that You use on my behalf. Thank You that I can rest in Your strong and capable hands."

Day 86

Your word is a lamp to my feet
And a light to my path.
Psalm 119:105

God's Word is a light for our path. It gives us illumination for living life. We cannot walk properly if we can't see where to go. If God's Word is important for everyday life, it is even more crucial in the midst of a trial. In the murkiness and deepening darkness of illness, God's Word is the thing that gives hope, comfort, stability, answers, and guidance. It contains the promises to cling to and the petitions to pray. No other thing or person can be leaned on so effectively.

We must then be in God's Word. We must diligently seek the light that it has to offer. This can be an incredible challenge in the midst of illness. Because of sheer exhaustion or decreased mental ability, getting anything from the Bible or even reading it with any comprehension can be very difficult. The mind can be challenged to capture anything well, and there can also be a gap between comprehension and application. The heart can have difficulty assimilating what is understood by the mind.

In spite of the challenge in taking in new light, we can live for only so long on the built-up reserves. We must have fresh insight from God's Word. We may not be able to take in much, but we need to try. We can use some very simple methods: reading a single verse repeatedly, using a devotional book, copying portions of Scripture, keeping note cards of special verses, or discussing Scripture with a friend.

God can help us to learn, and He can make our hearts responsive. He says that His Word will not return void. If we will put forth the effort, He can make His Word effective beyond what we expect. Our capacity for meaningful intake may be very limited. We may not see any noticeable progress, but we are not in charge of that. We can only do our part by attempting to take in God's Word. God will be in charge of how much effect that will have.

"Father, You know how hard it is for me to read Your Word. Help me to be faithful in trying. Bless my limited effort and make Your Word profitable in my life."

Day 87

Submit therefore to God. Resist the devil and he will flee from you. Draw near to God and He will draw near to you. Cleanse your hands, you sinners; and purify your hearts, you double-minded.
James 4:7-8

A major illness often acts as a catalyst in a person's life. The effect of the illness is not neutral; it changes people one way or the other. The time of illness has great potential for leading to one of two responses, and those two responses are very different. People either draw very near to God, or they drift away from Him.

This verse presents two terms that are opposites: resisting and drawing near. Resisting someone creates an increasing distance between them. Drawing near decreases the distance. Particularly in the case of God, when I draw near to Him, He also actively decreases the distance from His end. These two responses on my part – resisting or drawing near – will determine the outcome achieved in my life through the illness.

The question for me is this: Am I resisting God or drawing near to Him? This is a question that I should ask myself frequently, because those broad terms show up in the many ways I act and respond throughout each day. In order to effectively answer the question, I need to understand what is involved in each term.

There are many ways in which I can resist God. My resistance can show up in a defeated spirit, doubting thoughts, fear, frustration, cynicism, anger, bitterness, resentment, discouragement, stubbornness, and many other responses. All of those things introduce a wedge that drives me further from God. There are also many ways in which I can draw near to God. I can do so by repenting, submitting, praying for help, talking to Him, focusing on truth, asking for discernment, resting in Him, admitting my need, and other similar activities.

At each point in the day, I am headed in one direction or the other. The question therefore needs to be asked often throughout the day: Am I resisting or drawing near *right now*? The end result will be the cumulative effect of all the individual choices I make. Every time I resist, I am impeding the process of drawing near. I need to consistently stop the resistance and choose to draw near instead.

"Father, I have resisted You in so many ways. Help me to draw near to You instead.
Make me sensitive to recognize the direction I am headed
through the little things I do each day."

Day 88

Your eyes have seen my unformed substance;
And in Your book were all written
The days that were ordained for me,
When as yet there was not one of them.
How precious also are Your thoughts to me, O God!
How vast is the sum of them!
Psalm 139:16-17

God made me. He formed me and gave me life. He put together every aspect of my tiny body. God's work at forming a baby is beyond human comprehension. Man has very limited understanding of the intricate systems that God designed in the human body and the marvelous way in which they all work together.

God very skillfully made my body. He did not make any mistakes. His fingers did not slip. If I was born with a birth defect or a genetic predisposition or a weak immune system, God is the one who made me that way. The work of His hands was very careful and deliberate. He made me exactly as He wanted to make me.

God is able to make those choices because He knows everything. God knows my future. Before I was even born, He saw me. He knew me, and He wrote down all the things that would happen in my life. Before I had lived a single day, God knew everything about every day that I would ever live. He knew what He had ordained and determined for me.

I have only known about my illness for weeks or months, but God knew about it before I was born. He knew every symptom, every struggle, and every treatment. He knew what every day would be like. He knew how He would help me through it and what the final outcome will be. Nothing about my illness is a surprise to God. He knows it all because it is all part of His plan.

Even now, His plan and my part in it are important to Him. He thinks of me constantly. His thoughts about me are more than I could ever count. With such careful planning before my birth and such precious thoughts about me constantly, I need not fear or despair. God has always taken care of me and He always will.

"Father, thank You for Your intricate preparation of my body. Thank You for Your careful designing of my days. Thank You for Your constant thoughts about me."

Day 89

For we do not have a high priest who cannot sympathize with our weaknesses. . . . Therefore let us draw near with confidence to the throne of grace, so that we may receive mercy and find grace to help in time of need.
Hebrews 4:15a & 16

In times of need and weakness, Christ is sympathetic. Because He has suffered, He can understand my suffering. He is the one who best understands what I am going through. Other people might think I'm exaggerating or dramatizing, but God knows the truth. He knows every aspect of the trial, even ones that I haven't identified or don't know how to articulate.

Christ was tempted in all points just as I am. He can relate to the agony of soul that threatens to crush me. In the Garden of Gethsemane, He was in intense agony.

Jesus understands anguish of spirit. He understands my intense struggle when the challenges seem to be too great, yet I want to do what is right. It is because of His ability to understand that He sympathizes. His compassion makes Him the best source to go to for help.

As my high priest, He helps me by bringing my situation before the Father. He also invites me to come personally for help. I am instructed to come to Him in my need. What do I need? I need help. I need grace. I need mercy. These are the things that I may freely come to receive. He gives His sufficient grace to help me through each day because He understands how frail I am. When I falter under the weight of the test, He gives His mercy rather than the judgment I deserve, because He understands my weak humanity. I don't need to be fearful about asking for His help; I can come boldly and with confidence. I don't need a big explanation – just that I am in need. I don't even need to ask; all I need to do is to draw near to Him, and I will find grace and mercy there in His presence.

"Father, You know how weak and needy I am. I need grace. Please pour it out on me."

A Helpful Sympathizer (Sonnet 30)
Our suff'ring leads us through days dim and black.
We find ourselves in need in days so bleak,
Assaulted by temptations which attack.
Susceptible to fall, we are so weak.
Like us, we know our Savior suffered too,
And with His pain, temptation came along --
Not once or twice, but tempted through and through.
Each time triumphant, He would do no wrong.
Our suff'ring Savior has much sympathy;
He understands the weakness of our frame.
He's strong to help with His ability;
His wisdom met each testing as it came.
His invitation's plain: "Be bold; draw near.
Find here the grace you need, My child so dear."

Day 90

Seeking to know what person or time the Spirit of Christ within them was indicating as He predicted the sufferings of Christ and the glories to follow.
I Peter 1:11

God has guidelines and systems that He has established. He has determined that certain things work in certain ways. His plan and order must be followed. They can't be violated or changed. God has ordained that sufferings come first, and then the glories. This is actually very logical. How can we appreciate the glories (or even recognize them) if we don't have the sufferings first?

This principle was true even in the life of Christ. Christ's sufferings were predicted. He had to live on the earth. He had to be poor and homeless, persecuted and hated. He had to be falsely charged, brutally abused, and savagely crucified. Then *after* all of that suffering, Christ received glory. He conquered death and He was restored again to the glories of heaven. He is there now as our Savior and as the beloved Son of God.

In First Peter 5:1, Peter tells that he had personally witnessed the suffering of Christ. The suffering had already happened, and Peter had already seen it. He was a companion with Christ in suffering. Peter was aware that the suffering would lead to the revelation of glory. Peter also expected to be a partaker with Christ of the glory that was to come. The glory had not yet been revealed to Peter; he was still waiting for it. He knew, however, that the time of glory would come.

Suffering does lead to glory, but the glory always comes later. We have to wait for it. We can also expect glories to follow our suffering. We can expect our suffering to yield growth in sanctification, compassion, and usefulness in service. We can expect our suffering to end in deliverance and ultimately heaven. What more? We don't know all that God will do through us or for us, but He will bring glories after the suffering.

"Help me, Father, to patiently wait and endure the sufferings, knowing that they are necessary before the glories that You have for me."

Day 91

Like a shepherd He will tend His flock,
In His arm He will gather the lambs
And carry them in His bosom;
He will gently lead the nursing ewes.
Isaiah 40:11

God illustrates His care for those who are most needy by speaking of Himself as a shepherd. Sheep are noted for their helplessness. In order to survive, they need a shepherd to look after them. Within the scenario of a shepherd with his sheep, God chooses the most vulnerable of the flock to illustrate His point. He speaks of the young lambs and of the recent mothers who are caring for their newborns.

God tells of His care for the delicate lambs and for the over-worked mothers with fragile bundles to care for. Far from leaving these vulnerable ones out, God makes a point to express His care for them. The picture created is a very tender one. God doesn't simply fulfill His obligation to these needy lambs and ewes. He takes the time and effort to do so appropriately. He takes special care to treat them tenderly. He tends all of His flock, leading them to pasture so they can find the food they need, but with the fragile ones, He is especially attentive.

God sees the tiny lambs who are tottering on their skinny legs and who don't have the energy to walk for long distances. He gathers those lambs into His arms and carries them close to His heart. He doesn't expect from them what they cannot do. Neither does He handle them roughly, slinging them over His shoulder. Instead, He cherishes them and carries them in the most tender and safest way possible. Similarly, He does not hurry the nursing ewes along or push them beyond their limits. He leads them gently because He knows their limitations. He loves them, and His kindness is expressed every time He leads them. Our Father, the Great Shepherd, knows how to deal gently with those He loves.

"It's just like You, Father, to recognize weakness and need. It's also just like You to respond gently and lovingly. Thank You for Your tender care for me."

Day 92

But realize this, that in the last days difficult times will come.
II Timothy 3:1
Alexander the coppersmith did me much harm;
the Lord will repay him according to his deeds.
II Timothy 4:14

The caution of verse one is followed in verses two through seven with the reason for those difficult days. It will be because of the type of men who live in them. The evil attitudes and actions of wicked men will be a huge contributing factor to the difficult times. Some hardships will come simply because men are wicked and reject God's truth.

Paul gives the example of Jannes and Jambres in verses eight and nine. In Second Timothy 4:14-15, he gives the example of Alexander the coppersmith. These men presented opposition and did much harm. They are good examples of the fact that some of our afflictions do come from other people.

Paul gives a few instructions about how we are to respond in those situations. We should make it our practice to avoid these evil men if possible (II Timothy 3:5). We can also be confident that they will not prosper (II Timothy 3:9). We should be wise and cautious in regard to these people, but ultimately we must allow God to take care of the consequences (II Timothy 4:14-15).

What in the world does this have to do with illness? Illness isn't one of those hardships brought on by evil men, is it? Not normally, no. There are situations, however, in which it could be. We might suffer from a disease that has its origins among wicked men but that we acquired innocently. We can suffer as a result of violence – injuries brought on by an assault or sustained in a car accident by someone who should not have been driving. Physical afflictions can be brought on or aggravated by a doctor's incompetence. What should our response be to these hardships brought on by wicked men? As Paul instructed, we must leave these men to God. We need to allow God to take care of them.

"Father, free my spirit from anger and spitefulness directed at those who have caused my condition or made it harder to deal with."

Day 93

For You have been my help,
And in the shadow of Your wings I sing for joy.
Psalm 63:7

God is our Help. Receiving help first requires the existence of a need. Humans are full of needs. Just in the realm of illness, our needs could include the following: the right medicine, a good doctor, successful surgery, an organ donor, effective treatment, physical strength, sleep, and relief from pain. If our thoughts move beyond the physical realm, we also need money, someone to cook and clean for us, a friend to talk to, a hug, patience, and encouragement.

When we consider these needs, we often "know" what the solution is. We have our ideas of how the need should be met. In reality, God is the help that we need. We may think that we need a thousand dollars, a phone call from the pastor's wife, or two aspirin. While those may offer solutions to some of our needs, what we really need is God.

In whatever situation we face, God is the one who takes care of our needs. He knows what our most pressing needs are, and He gives us His help to meet those needs. Not only does God know which needs really demand His attention, He also knows how to best meet those needs. He uses whatever method or means that He knows is effective. His help will always be equal to the need. God, our help, is ready to meet every need that we have. In a life that is so needy, it is wonderful to know we have someone who can help with every need.

"Father, You know my needs better than I do. What I really need is You. You are my help, and You can take care of anything that needs attention."

Day 94

*"Be strong and courageous, do not be afraid or tremble at them, for the LORD your God
is the one who goes with you. He will not fail you or forsake you."*
Deuteronomy 31:6

There are fearful things in the midst of illness. We fear what the tests will reveal. We fear what the doctors will say. We fear that no progress will be made. We fear the side effects of treatment. We fear a terminal prognosis. We fear the helplessness of physical decline that precedes death. We fear for the well-being of our families.

God does not want us to be fearful. In order to allay our fears, He reminds us of His presence. In fact, throughout Scripture, perhaps the most common application of the assurance of God's presence is that we need not fear. God's presence with us is faithful. He won't fail to be at our side. He will never forsake us. No matter what the circumstances are, and no matter how dark the path may be, God will be close by. He is always with us everywhere.

Think about what this ever-present God is like. He is the God who created the universe. He is the God who parted the Red Sea and gave manna from heaven. He is the God who single-handedly killed armies of His enemies. He is the God who brought water from rocks and sent fire from heaven. He is the God who healed the blind and raised the dead. That is the God that walks with us every day and that stays by our side every step along the way. If that God is with us, why should we fear? We can be strong in the face of danger and courageous in the face of bad news. We don't need to fear. We don't need to even tremble or quiver. The mighty God is with us.

*"Father, my heart wants to quiver in fear, but You, the mighty God, are at my side. May
Your presence give me courage as You face the trials with me."*

Day 95

*I will meditate on all Your work
And muse on Your deeds.*
Psalm 77:12

In this psalm Asaph is a man in agony. He is afflicted day and night, he can't sleep, and he doesn't even want to talk to other people. He finds himself in the depths of discouragement and doubt. He finds no comfort, even when he thinks about God, because it seems that God has forsaken him. As he ponders his past and present life, he comes to the erroneous conclusion that God is no longer who

He used to be. Asaph believes he has trusted in a God who has proven to be empty and unreliable.

Happily, Asaph turns his thinking around, and he does so by deliberately choosing to think about the works of God. It would seem natural for Asaph to do so by recalling situations in which God has worked in his own life. He does not do that. Instead, he thinks about God's mighty works in history.

He meditates on the flood, about God's great control over the waters and the skies, and about how God caused them to do something they had never done before. He thinks about the majesty of that storm and of the terror that it brought to man and to the earth itself. Then Asaph meditates on the exodus, when God amazingly delivered His people from Egypt. God brought them out of slavery, opened the sea on their behalf, and led them to a new land where He established them as a nation.

Asaph focuses on historical deeds because he realizes that God is not his personal servant. God's greatness is not limited to His working in Asaph's life. God is great because of who He is. He controls the most significant and unbelievable acts in the history of the world. God is still that same God today. He is still a mighty God whose acts of greatness extend far beyond the life of a single individual. Asaph came out of his despair not by thinking of himself at all, but by focusing on the wondrous works of his mighty God.

"When I am discouraged, Father, and doubting Your goodness, help me to get my focus off of myself. Help me instead to focus on You and on Your mighty works."

Day 96

O give us help against the adversary,
For deliverance by man is in vain.
Psalm 60:11

In Psalm 60, David and his people had suffered a great defeat, one that had left them shaken and in great difficulty (vs. 2-3). Oddly enough, God Himself had allowed His people to be defeated (v. 1). It is hard enough to face failure and trouble that shakes us to the bottom of our souls. How much harder it is when we see the situation defying reason by coming from the hand of God!

Instead of giving up or bitterly turning from God, David instead turned to God for help (v. 5). In such a situation, it may seem that God didn't really care about His people. It may seem that He had abandoned them to suffer in vain and without hope. God responded to this possible accusation by declaring that it was His intention to give the victory and to do His work (v. 6). God's people are very precious to Him and He can't forget them. God is very aware of who belongs to Him and of how special they are (v. 7). God knows whose side He is on, and He determines to defeat the enemy (v. 8).

God will indeed fight for His people and deliver them, yet sometimes His people must wait for that deliverance. David continued talking to God about the situation of rejection in which he remained (v. 10). Within the psalm, the answer was never shown, and David spoke of deliverance only in the future tense. He found himself remaining in that difficult situation.

In spite of the delayed relief, David did not give up or stagger under this situation that seemed wrong and difficult to understand. His confidence remained firmly fixed on God (v. 11). David expected not just a slight victory, but a valiant one (v. 12). This answer would come only from God, because no one else was capable of giving such a victory. David did not yet see the answer, but he knew from where the answer would come, and he knew that the answer would be dramatic. We can learn along with David that our deliverance is only through God, and that He is the only one who can give outstanding deliverance. We may not understand how He is working, but we can trust such a mighty God.

"Thank You, Father, for being on my side. I don't know how or when the victory will come, but I know that only You can do it. I trust in You."

Reflection on Psalm 60 (Providential Defeat)
O God, the battle's done, and we have lost.
No small defeat, we're broken and split wide.
The hardship is too much; we stagger on.

What's worse is that it comes from Your own hand.
We don't know why You'd break us or reject;
Your anger causes us this pain and loss.

And yet we know You honor those who fear,
And so we ask for healing. Please restore.
Dear God, please answer us and save us now.

You know, O Lord, each one that is Your own,
And they are precious – valued in Your sight.
You won't abandon them nor yet neglect.

Your enemies, by contrast, will be judged;
On them You'll bring dishonor and defeat.
Your work will bring the change we yearn to see.

But, still, dear God, in agony we wait;
We cannot see the answer that You'll give.
Still struggling, Lord, we long to see You work.

Great God, our trust is placed in You alone,
For man's unable to defend or save;
It's only by Your hand that we can win.

Why let us lose, then suffer on and on?
I guess to make us see it's You we need;
The valiant vict'ry only comes through You.

Day 97

Therefore, those also who suffer according to the will of God shall entrust their souls to a faithful Creator in doing what is right.
I Peter 4:19

This verse clearly states that there is suffering that happens according to the will of God. It is then within God's plan for people to suffer sometimes. God Himself ordains and arranges it. If the suffering is according to God's will, we have some comforting reassurances.

We realize that there is also a way within God's will for us to respond to the suffering. In verse sixteen, we see that our suffering is not something to be ashamed of. There is no cause for shame in suffering when it has come by God's design. Verse sixteen also tells us that suffering provides an opportunity to glorify God. As we endure suffering according to God's will, we are able to bring glory to Him because His will is accomplished.

We must also realize that the trial is too much for us. We cannot have confidence in ourselves to handle it. Instead, we must entrust our souls to God to keep us through the trial and to help us do what is right. On our own we would fall and be defeated. We need a stronger source than ourselves.

God can help us to stand firm. He can help us to respond correctly through the testing. Think of who it is that we can entrust ourselves to. He is the powerful Creator of the earth; nothing is too hard for Him. Additionally, He is always faithful. This Creator has faithfully kept the universe functioning for many centuries, and He will also faithfully stand by us. He is a worthy source for our trust. We can trust our souls to Him in the midst of trials and know that He will care for us.

"This trial is too much for me, Father. I need Your help. Please keep me."

Day 98

"The steadfast of mind You will keep in perfect peace,
Because he trusts in You.
Trust in the LORD forever,
For in GOD the LORD, we have an everlasting Rock."
Isaiah 26:3-4

Let's begin our consideration at the end of the selection; let's start with the Rock. The word refers to a cliff or boulder used as a place of refuge. That's what God is. He is a Rock that cannot be conquered and that can provide unfailing protection. He is a Rock that is everlasting. That strength and protection will never end.

Because we have an everlasting Rock, we are to trust in Him forever. Our trust will not be disappointed because God is a strong enough Rock to defend us. We can trust forever and never be let down, because that dependable and effective Rock is everlasting.

There is a certain kind of person who trusts God in this way; it is the steadfast of mind. This is the person whose mind is propped up on God and resting firmly on Him. This man trusts God so securely that he places his entire being on that single source of help. He is so confident in God's protection that he leans wholly on God. His knowledge of who God is sustains him.

The rest of the verse is completely logical. If a man is confident in God's ability to defend him forever, and if he leans his entire life and being on that confidence, he has no fear of falling. He is not holding himself up, and the one who is holding him up cannot fail. This is an extremely safe and secure place to be.

Because this man trusts so completely in God, God maintains him in a state of perfect peace. What other state could his mind and spirit possibly be in, when he rests so confidently in God? This trusting man depends entirely and constantly on someone who cannot fail; therefore, no threat or advancing trouble is able to shake his peace.

"Father, I long for such peace. Help me to keep my complete confidence
in You, the unfailing and everlasting Rock."

Day 99

Samuel said,
"Has the LORD as much delight in burnt offerings and sacrifices
As in obeying the voice of the LORD?
Behold, to obey is better than sacrifice,
And to heed than the fat of rams."
I Samuel 15:22

Man tends to put his focus and emphasis on what he does. Many Christians become caught up in doing the right things, saying the right things, going to the right places, wearing the right clothes, and giving the right amount. Those actions become the basis for evaluation of spirituality.

This practice is dangerous for anyone, but it takes on a new wrinkle in the midst of illness. A sick person is not able to do all of the things he once did. This can create a high level of frustration. The person views himself as spiritually weak because he is not able to do all of the things he used to do, or he is not able to perform them to the same degree that he used to.

The verse above teaches that God is not very interested in outward actions that are done merely for the sake of formality or routine. He is much more interested in the condition of the heart. When the heart is right, man will obey. He will do the right outward actions because his heart is directed toward God. God wants the heart's desire to be right.

No matter how badly he wants to, someone who is seriously ill may not be able to go out on visitation. In spite of his desires, he may be able to read the Bible and pray for only five minutes at a time. While his heart may long to go on a mission trip, his body is not able to. God is pleased with those heart desires. God does not require outward actions that are beyond one's ability. Instead, He requires a heart that delights to obey Him within the opportunities or limitations of the individual's life.

"It has bothered me, Father, that I can't do more. Help me to focus instead on my heart. May it be devoted to you so that I will obey in whatever You ask of me."

Day 100

The LORD opens the eyes of the blind;
The LORD raises up those who are bowed down;
The LORD loves the righteous.
Psalm 146:8

Psalm 146 presents two possible choices in which man could trust. First, man could trust in people (vs. 3-4). The passage informs us that, unfortunately, man is mortal. Other men face problems just like we do, and they will die just like we will. How can someone who is the same as us fix our problems? There is no salvation to be found in man, even in princes. They too will die and return to the dust. Their thoughts will not continue any longer than their lives. Help by man is vain.

Second, man could trust in God (vs. 5-6). God provides real hope because of who He is. God created the heaven and earth and everything in them. That is a pretty amazing God. He remains faithful forever. Here is someone worthy of our trust.

Peggy Holt

It would be a great disappointment to find out that such a wonderful source of help existed, but that we could not access Him. What if we are not important enough for Him to take note of? Verses seven through nine indicate for us the kinds of people that God notices and helps. God sees the oppressed who are being treated unfairly, and He works justice for them. God sees the hungry, and He gives them food. God sees the prisoners, and He frees them from their bonds. God notices those who are blind, and He causes them to see. God looks on those who are bowed down under heavy burdens, and He raises them up. God sees the righteous, and He showers His love on them. God sees the strangers in their disadvantage, and He protects them. God sets His eye on the orphans and on the widows who have no one to care for them, and He supports them. If God looks on all of these people and helps them, we don't need to have any worry that He won't notice and help us. He is a trustworthy God, able to give help. He is also a compassionate God, looking on those who are most needy.

"I am needy, Father. I look to You for help. Man will let me down,
but You are perfectly able to help."

Day 101

Grace and peace be multiplied to you in the knowledge of God and of Jesus our Lord.
II Peter 1:2

Here are two things that would be wonderful to have in the midst of a trial: grace and peace. Those are two wonderful things to have at any time, but they are particularly important in a time of suffering. When you are hurting, you need God's grace. You need His gracious favor and intervention in your life. You need Him to ease the rough patches and heal the hurts. When you are in a time of trouble, you need peace. Everything about your situation threatens your peace. From a human standpoint, the hardest situation in which to have peace is in the midst of affliction. God can give you both grace and peace.

Because those gifts are coming from God, they are far more effective than man's meager attempts to give the same things. God gives real grace and real peace. Not only does He give them, but He can give them in multiplied fashion. He can pile grace on top of grace and can layer peace on top of peace. He can give those gifts abundantly.

Notice the medium through which the grace and peace arrive. They come through the knowledge of God and of Jesus. Doesn't this make sense? God is amazing. The more you come to know God, the more amazing He is in your eyes. When you begin to get first a glimpse and then a growing picture of what God is like, you cannot help but to be awed by how great He is. Knowing that you have such a wonderful and loving God will fill you with grace and peace. The more you know Him, the greater your grace and peace will be. So how well do you know your God? Pick a topic about God – any topic. Meditate on it for a while and see if it doesn't minister grace to your soul and bring peace to your spirit.

"Father, help me to know You better. May that increasing knowledge of Your greatness multiply grace and peace to me in my need."

Day 102

You enlarge my steps under me,
And my feet have not slipped.
Psalm 18:36

Perhaps you have seen a mountain climber on a rock wall. You have seen his hands clasp knobs of rock. You have seen his toes cling to tiny bumps or support themselves on the narrowest of ledges. Sometimes it seemed there was nothing at all to support his hands or feet; he appeared to be magically glued to a sheer wall. You may have marveled at his skill, but thought to yourself, "If I were climbing, I would need the footholds to be as wide as possible." That certainly would make the climb easier and safer. When groups of mountain climbers scale a sheer rock wall or traverse a smooth icy expanse, they have to make the path as safe as they can. With their axes they carve out steps for themselves and for those who follow. A careful climber will make those carved-out steps as wide and as smooth as possible.

This is the picture that God gives in this verse. He makes the steps wide so that you can walk without falling. He enlarges your steps so they are safe and sure. The path you have to travel is not always completely smooth, but God intervenes to make it as sure and as safe as possible. He sees the steps that are too narrow and that would present a danger for you, and He enlarges them. He makes them wider and safer so that you can tread the dangerous terrain without slipping. God is very good at this preparation and does it well enough to give success. The psalmist claims that God's efforts were effective. The psalmist was able to walk without slipping. God can prepare your steps just as effectively.

"Father, this is an awfully difficult terrain that I have to climb, and I sense the danger. Please make large steps for my feet so that I can walk without falling."

Steps That Don't Slip (Sonnet 40)
God knows and counts each step I take, for He
Delighted to establish all my way.
The path is straight with steps enlarged for me, $\longrightarrow$

So I won't slip while walking there each day.
And if I slip, my loving God, I know,
Will hold me safe so I will not fall down.
If I should fall, He will not let me go,
But He'll sustain and raise me from the ground.
If God's with me, how can I fall at all?
It's sadly a result of my own sin,
For when I shift my gaze from Him I fall.
I need God's Word as light to vict'ry win.
A pattern sure is found within God's Book;
'Tis safe to follow steps that Jesus took.

Day 103

The LORD's lovingkindnesses indeed never cease,
For His compassions never fail.
Lamentations 3:22

God is a God of compassion. The Bible does not leave that fact open for debate or question. Instead, it clearly and simply states that compassion is a characteristic that God possesses and shows. In addition to the meaning that we associate with compassion, the word also includes the idea of loving and fondling, even to the extent of lovingly caring for a baby in the womb.

God is compassionate because He has decided to be. God chooses on whom to show His compassion, and when He chooses to show compassion, He follows His intention with action (Exodus 33:19). Compassion is one of the characteristics that God makes a point to identify as part of His character (Exodus 34:6). God wants to have compassion on His people, and He waits for opportunities to be able to do so (Isaiah 30:18).

Nothing can stop the compassion that God has for His people. He faithfully maintains it, even in the face of great terrors and calamities (Isaiah 54:10). The mountains can be removed, and the hills can be shaking, but God will maintain His compassion. Perhaps that is the most comforting aspect of God's concern. Kindness and care could be intense and deeply felt, but if they cannot be relied upon, what comfort do they impart? God's compassion is comforting because we know that it will always be there. God tells us that His compassion never fails. It never ceases. We can't exhaust it. We can't wear it out. We can't run away from it. His compassion does not fail.

"Father, thank You that Your compassion is so faithful. Thank You that I can count on it day after day, week after week, and year after year. Thank You that it will never end."

Day 104

My soul clings to You;
Your right hand upholds me.
Psalm 63:8

There are a lot of uncomfortable things about an illness. The most uncomfortable of them do not have to do with pain, confinement, or medical treatments. Instead, the greatest discomfort lies within the inner man – the heart, the emotions, and the mind. It is uncomfortable to have questions without answers. It is uncomfortable to have expectations without fulfillment. It is uncomfortable to have doubts and fears. It is uncomfortable to be lonely, neglected, or misunderstood. It is uncomfortable to have ugly and rebellious thoughts, especially when you can't understand where they came from or how to get rid of them. All of these and many more create an inner discomfort that you long to assuage.

You need something solid, something firm, something certain, something supportive to help you through these struggles. All of those answers can be found in God. You need Him desperately, and the good news is that He will never let you down. When your soul is sinking and on the edge of drowning, it must cling to God. When everything else is swirling and uncertain, and when nothing else gives you a firm place to put your feet, you can cling to God. In the midst of the raging storm, He is the only thing that stands stable and firm.

Cling to God as tightly as you possibly can. Don't let go or weaken your grasp for a second. Recognizing your human weakness in the midst of such a precarious position, it is encouraging to realize that you aren't the only one who is clinging. God is also holding on to you. His hand is holding you up, and His grip is far stronger than yours. When you no longer have any strength to cling, God's sure and mighty hand can hold on to you. He can hold you so that you do not sink or drown.

"Father, may I have an unquenchable thirst and a desperate dependence for You. When I'm too weak to cling to You, hold me with Your unfailing hand. Don't let me slip away."

Day 105

Therefore, we ourselves speak proudly of you among the churches of God for your perseverance
and faith in the midst of all your persecutions and afflictions which you endure.
II Thessalonians 1:4

Our response to affliction can be a great encouragement to other believers. This is particularly true when the afflictions are multiplied, as they were in the lives of these believers. A godly response can be a blessing to those who observe, and it can encourage them to continue faithfully in their own lives.

The verse above shares two particular aspects of an appropriate and godly response: perseverance and faith. We must persevere. We just can't quit. We must go on day after day and in the face of each new struggle. How can we possibly endure when life is so hard? How can we keep going when just the daily routine is enough to wear us out? How can we keep fighting when there is no end in sight? What gives us the strength to persevere? In seeking the answer to these questions, we need to consider our faith.

Our faith in an unchanging God allows us to continue on. As we rest in His Word and its promises, we are given the help to continue. We must believe that God is present and faithful. We must believe that He is fully in control and completely able to uphold us. Even when things seem darkest, there has to be at least the slenderest thread of faith that keeps the sufferer from wandering from God. That faith eventually brings him back to stability, trust, and hope. When the way seems blacker than midnight with no hope in sight, our soul must cry out, "O God, I see no hope right now, but I know that when it comes, it will come from You." This unshakeable confidence in God allows us to persevere through the darkest of days and through the weight of multiplied afflictions.

"The way is not easy, Father. Help my faith in You to be strong so that I can continue to walk the path before me."

Day 106

"For this reason I say to you, do not be worried about your life, as to what you will eat or what you will drink; nor for your body, as to what you will put on. Is not life more than food, and the body more than clothing?"
Matthew 6:25

There are a lot of things to worry about in the midst of an illness, and some of them may seem even more serious than the examples in the verse above. What to eat and what to wear may be the least of your worries. Food and clothing are, however, the most basic needs of life, and they represent survival. Jesus instructed His disciples not to worry about those basic needs, or any other needs, for that matter. He taught them that there was no reason to worry about life's needs, because God cares very deeply for His children, and He meets all of their needs.

Jesus gave two illustrations to demonstrate God's care. He spoke first about the birds. The birds are not farmers. They don't plant crops. They don't gather and store food for the winter. They go out each day and eat what they need for that day.

Even in times of harsh weather, the birds find food to meet their needs. How do they do it? God provides for them. Jesus specifically stated that His children are more valuable than the birds.

The second illustration was that of flowers. The flowers don't spin wool or make cloth. They don't sew clothing. They can't even move about, yet they are clothed very beautifully. How do they get such beautiful clothing? God provides it for them. Jesus then referred to the frailty of the plants, and indicated that He is even more attentive to His children than He is to the fragile and short-lived plants.

God has dedicated Himself to care for the needs of His children. He loves them much more than the vulnerable birds and the frail flowers. If God cares so carefully for birds and flowers, He will surely meet the needs of His children. God won't fail in any provision, because He knows every need that you have.

"Thank You, Father, for Your thorough care. Sometimes I forget, and I need the reminder that You care for every need of my life."

Day 107

With all humility and gentleness, with patience, showing tolerance for one another in love, being diligent to preserve the unity of the Spirit in the bond of peace.
Ephesians 4:2–3

Oh, boy! These verses must not have been written for sick people, were they? I mean, that's all well and good for normal Christians, but it's just different when we're sick. We're tired, we don't feel well, we're always a little off balance, and we're just challenged all the time. So it must be different! Different? No. Harder? Perhaps, but not impossible. As sick people, we don't get our own set of expectations. Since there is no abridged version of the Bible for us to follow, let's take a look at what is expected.

First, we are to be humble. We are not to think too much of ourselves, not to think we are special just because we're sick. Although it may be necessary for others to serve us, we should not have a sense of entitlement, thinking that we deserve their constant and exclusive attention.

Second, we are to be gentle. Instead of being harsh and demanding, we should make our requests humbly. We should appreciate the effort that others are making for us, rather than growling at them as they do it.

Third, we are to be patient. We should be willing to overlook things for a long time. People may forget what they've promised. Conflicts may arise unexpectedly. We can't be quick to snap at others every time something doesn't work out just as we would like.

Fourth, we are to show tolerance in love. We are to put up with frustrations and offenses out of our love for others. In ignorance people will make statements that are unkind. They will place expectations on us that we can't fulfill. They will set up situations that are inconvenient and uncomfortable for us. We just have to let things slide.

Fifth, we are to work hard at keeping unity and peace. We may want to shift this responsibility to others, but it rests a lot on us. In order to keep peace and avoid conflicts, we are going to have to do more than our share of giving in. We will have to bite our tongue, put up with inconvenience, forgive, overlook, and give the benefit of the doubt. When things hurt us, we have to forget and move on.

It is definitely a challenge for us to meet all of these expectations. How can we possibly do something so difficult? It will only be by the grace of God. He can help us to do what seems impossible.

"Father, I don't like this teaching. I want others to give me the benefit of the doubt and be patient with me. Help me to do my part by also responding correctly to others."

Day 108

As for God, His way is blameless;
The word of the LORD is tried;
He is a shield to all who take refuge in Him.
Psalm 18:30

I see two paths. The first is one that I imagine in my mind, the path that is built of all my hopes, dreams, and ambitions. It is the journey that I have laid out for myself since the time I was a teenager. It's not an extravagant path. I didn't plan to become a millionaire, the president of the country, or a universally recognized figure. It is a good but simple path. It includes a good education, marriage, children, a job I enjoy, a nice home, freedom from financial worries, a ministry I can devote myself to, and a peaceful retirement enjoying travel and grandchildren.

The second path is the one I am on, the one that God has placed me on. It is not such a nice path. It includes illness, pain, isolation from friends, limited time with family, an interrupted ministry, financial burdens, the inability to work, and the unlikelihood of ever reaching retirement age.

When I make the comparison, it sure seems that the path I designed is better. God's path just seems wrong – but that cannot be. The Bible states that God's way is blameless. It is perfect and entirely sound. There is no evil in it. It has no blemish. It is without a single spot or error. There can be no fault whatsoever in God's path.

This is true because the path that God has for me to walk is by His decree. It is based on His word; it is established on what He says and on what He commands to be done. God's words are tried. They have been thoroughly tested by fire. They have faced the most comprehensive and demanding tests imaginable, and they have been proven true and reliable. They do not contain a single speck of impurity or evil. If His words are so pure, then the way that He commands is also pure. There can be nothing wrong with it. It is right.

"Father, I would not have chosen this path, but You have chosen it for me. Help me to believe, even if I cannot see, that it is a good and perfect path designed by You."

The Path (Sonnet 36)
The path I'm on is rough and hard to walk;
I strain upon a road that's all uphill.
With frequency I tread on rut and rock;
I labor on and find it winding still.
But then I realize it's the path God chose;
He chose my way with purpose and with care.
Each obstacle and twisting turn He knows.
With spirit calm and peace I trust Him there.
He chose a path that leads me to His end;
Each step along the path is good and right.
I'm confident wherever He may send,
The destination's precious in His sight.
My God is there each moment on the trail;
Because He keeps me safe, I cannot fail.

Day 109

God will hear and answer them –
Even the one who sits enthroned from of old – Selah.
With whom there is no change,
And who do not fear God.
Psalm 55:19

God is *"the one who sits enthroned from of old."* He is established as the King and Judge. Some people filling those positions care nothing for justice. They may be there only to serve their own interests. Some of those rulers are novices, lacking the experience to make wise decisions. Recently coroneted or newly appointed, they have little idea of how to handle the affairs before them. Some people filling those positions are even completely incompetent. Human kings and judges are inconsistent and unreliable; they make mistakes and pass bad verdicts.

God has none of these problems or limitations. God is the eternally just and righteous Judge. He always makes the right decisions. One reason He is able to do this is because of His permanence. God has been established in His position from of old, from the beginning of time. God has been forever. As far back as anyone can remember or think or even imagine, God was there. That gives Him permanence and reliability. God can correctly answer all questions and make all decisions because He has been around to see it all. Nothing is new to God. There is no situation that He has not seen before. There is no dilemma that He has not already correctly solved. From the beginning of time, He has been making correct judgments, and He will continue to do so through the end of time.

"Since I lack wisdom, Father, I thank You that You know best how to respond to every situation. You have an awful lot of experience, and You haven't messed up yet."

Day 110

"Can a woman forget her nursing child
And have no compassion on the son of her womb?
Even these may forget, but I will not forget you.
Behold, I have inscribed you on the palms of My hands."
Isaiah 49:15–16a

It would be a strange thing indeed for a mother to forget about her infant. It would be appalling for her not to care at all when he cried. It would be shocking for her to ignore his needs. The small baby depends on her for life, and she has already put her life on the line for him. The bond between them is incredibly close. Is it possible that a mother could forget or ignore her baby? Though very unlikely, it is sadly possible.

God's love and attention exceed even that of a mother for her newborn. Mothers might occasionally fail, but God will never fail. He will never forget His children. God remembers His children every moment of the day and night. Because He never sleeps, He is able to remember them constantly. He remembers how tiny and fragile they are. Regardless of the infinite number of things He must attend to, God remembers each person who belongs to Him. God never callously ignores the needs of His children. He hears them every time they cry. He takes note of each whimper. His heart is moved by their hunger, their discomfort, and their need for security. He cares about the major needs and about the ones that are really too small to warrant attention.

God remembers and attends to each of His children individually. He loves and knows them so well that each one is unique and special to Him. God has written their names on His hands. Is this so that He won't forget? Oh, no. God doesn't need help like that to remember. He won't forget the name of a single child. Rather, writing those names is an indication of how special His children are to Him and of how permanent the relationship is. He claims His children gladly and without shame.

"Oh, Father, thank You that You have never forgotten me and You never will. Thank You for being attentive to me and for caring about my every need."

Day 111

Blessed is the man whom You chasten, O LORD,
And whom You teach out of Your law;
For the LORD will not abandon His people,
Nor will He forsake His inheritance.
Psalm 94:12 & 14

The intended purpose of chastening is to teach us to walk in the right direction. Though chastening often looks like punishment and correction, it can also take the form of guidance and instruction. A father might chasten his child by spanking him, or he might chasten him by talking to him. Either way, the desired result is that his child would be encouraged to do the right things.

Chastening by God is not capricious or without value. To the contrary, those who are chastened by God are blessed. If God can get us to walk on the right path, we will be far better off. We will be walking the path of blessing. God teaches us and guides us so that we know how we ought to walk. Experiencing the chastening of God is actually a very positive thing. It indicates to us that we belong to God and that He cares about us.

God will not abandon or forsake His people. Sadly, we sometimes stray far from where we ought to be. We sometimes act foolishly, seeming to have no discretion at all. These failures on our part do not cause God to ignore us. Instead of giving up on us when we are so slow to learn or so obstinate toward His guidance, God teaches. We are so far from perfection that we could not fault God if He gave up on us, but He doesn't do that. He continues to guide us, often teaching the same lesson over and over again.

Without His intervention, how could we ever end up at the right place? How could we ever make good decisions? God's discipline is necessary. We are blessed when He faithfully continues to work with us and when He cares enough to lead us further along His path.

"Father, I don't like the chastening, but I realize it is an expression of Your care for me. Help me to learn the lessons well so that I can walk the right way."

Day 112

> *Remember, O LORD, Your compassion and Your lovingkindnesses,*
> *For they have been from of old.*
> *Psalm 25:6*
> *Hear my prayer, O LORD,*
> *Give ear to my supplications!*
> *Answer me in Your faithfulness, in Your righteousness!*
> *Psalm 143:1*

When we come to God in prayer, we have some wonderful foundations on which to base our requests. We are not coming to a god who is weak, ignorant, cruel, capricious, or uncaring. We are coming to God as He is, in all of His splendor and with all of His attributes. Our God has amazing attributes that do not change, and He always acts according to those attributes. We can use His character qualities as a basis for making our requests, and we can be sure that God will answer in compliance with His character.

We have examples of such prayers in Psalms 25 and 143. David asks God to remember him first of all based on His compassion. God is a compassionate God. He cares about the needs and struggles of His children. His answer will always be based on His compassion.

Second, God is asked to remember David based on His lovingkindnesses. God is full of lovingkindness, and He has consistently shown it since the beginning of time. Because of that, He will answer in kindness and mercy and favor.

Third, God is asked to answer prayer according to His faithfulness. God is dependable and steady and trustworthy. He will answer prayer based on time-proven consistency and unfailing support.

Fourth, God is asked to answer based on His righteousness. God always does the right thing. He always makes the right judgment. When He answers prayer, He will do so correctly.

Fifth, God is asked to remember David based on His goodness' sake (Psalm 25:7). God is good; goodness is one of His most defining characteristics. He cannot answer in a way that is bad.

Finally, God is asked to respond based on His name's sake (Psalm 143:11). God will always do what will bring honor and glory to His name. His responses will always maintain the integrity of His reputation.

We can confidently ask God to respond to us based on His character. He will always answer according to His compassion, His lovingkindness, His faithfulness, His righteousness, His goodness' sake, and His name's sake, because those qualities define who He is. God cannot deny Himself or change His character.

"I may not know Your answer, Father, but I know it will be right, because You will answer as the amazing and dependable God that You are. I need not fear an answer filtered through these qualities."

Day 113

Just as it is written, "For Your sake we are being put to death all day long; we were considered as sheep to be slaughtered." But in all these things we overwhelmingly conquer through Him who loved us.
Romans 8:36-37

Our lives contain times of great difficulty. Sometimes everything seems to pile up at once. As we look at the mountains before us, everything seems hopeless. There is no way to surmount the difficulties. There is no way to conquer the challenges. We seem like helpless little sheep, destined to be slaughtered. We run around frantically, but to no avail. There is no escaping. The end is coming, and there is nothing we can do to prevent it.

Yes, these situations really do happen, and they happen to Christians. It would seem that defeat is inevitable, but we are never completely defeated. We are never left entirely without hope. Even in the worst of times, we are able to have the victory. Our situation is never too hard for God. He can conquer it. In each of our trials, no matter how difficult they are, we are able to conquer with God's help.

Victory does not mean that we just squeak through by a narrow margin; it means that we can overwhelmingly conquer. We can have a rousing defeat over the enemy. This victory is possible only through Him who loves us. It's not in us. We can't gain the victory on our own, and we can't make it happen. It is a faithfully loving God that allows us to triumph. In these times of distress, we can focus on the one who loves us. Remembering that His love is inseparable and unending, we can be sure that He will give a great victory. Our trials do not defeat us; they do not ultimately win.

"Father who loves me, in the midst of great affliction
I look to You as the One who is able to give the victory."

Day 114

This hope we have as an anchor of the soul, a hope both sure and steadfast and one which enters within the veil.
Hebrews 6:19

I believe the hope referred to in this verse is the hope of heaven. Whether it is that, or whether it is the truthfulness of God or the dependability of the Scripture (both are also mentioned in the context), the point is that we have hope. Our hope is centered on God and His promises.

The hope that we have is no small thing; it provides an anchor for our soul. We do not have an anchor in ourselves. On our own we would be tossed, battered, and broken by the wind and waves of the storm. We would be driven so far off course that there would be no hope of recovery – by ourselves. In such storms as we face, survival would be impossible if we did not have an anchor.

The hope of God changes all of that. God's hope provides an anchor, a single point of contact that keeps us tethered safely. To depend on a single line to hold us secure may seem risky, but there is nothing unreliable about this anchor. It is sure, and it is steadfast. God's promise will never change. It will never weaken. It will never fail. It is so certain, that with only that one thing to hold us, we are completely safe. That one thing is enough to give us hope and to keep us going.

When our soul threatens to lose its bearings and to be carried quickly away on the currents, our anchor keeps us properly located. Because the anchor is on a chain, it always keeps us within a chain's length of the proper position. With such an anchor, we can never be far off course and certainly cannot be lost. Our hope is just an anchor, but it is an anchor that will never fail.

"Father, I am being terribly tossed, and this old ship can't survive. Thank You for Your anchor that can hold me steady and that will always keep me sure."

The Steadfast Anchor (Sonnet 29)

At times my feelings tell me that I'm wrong,
And following their lead, my thoughts agree.
My circumstances sing a plaintive song –
All shouting out that things are bad for me.
In spite of all that looks as if it's true,
There is unchanging truth that helps me cope.
For come what may, no matter what's in view,
On this one thing I firmly fix my hope.
My God will always be my faithful Friend;
He'll never change through all that passes by.
His presence, love, control will never end.
An anchor sure – on Him I can rely.
When, of all reasons, only faith remains,
May that suffice to break doubt's binding chains.

Day 115

My lovingkindness and my fortress,
My stronghold and my deliverer,
My shield and He in whom I take refuge,
Who subdues my people under me.
Psalm 144:2

God is *"He in whom I take refuge."* He is the one I flee to for protection. This phrase describes an urgent situation, one in which I have no time to lose. This is the refuge I go to when I desperately need somewhere to hide. When danger threatens, when difficult circumstances present themselves, or even when emergencies arise, God is the place that I can run to. I can run headlong, knowing that God will be there and that His protection will be enough.

Whom else would I trust? Other people may care about me and may even have some wisdom and ability to help, but they are limited. God cares about me more than anyone else does. He is the only one with sufficient wisdom to know what to do. There are many situations that are far beyond the ability of any human to do anything about, but God is equal to every task. The help of others would be insufficient at best and sometimes completely powerless. God, on the other hand, is entirely worthy of my trust.

When I run to Him and hide in Him, He can shelter and protect me until the troubles have passed, no matter how long that takes. His protection is thorough; not only can He keep me from being destroyed, but He can also keep me from being injured or bruised in the process. God is indeed a sufficient and wonderful source of refuge. I can go to Him with confidence. When troubles arise, He should be the first source I turn to.

"Father, there is no other refuge like You. Thank You that I can run to You in time of trouble, and that I don't need to worry that You won't be there."

Day 116

Be of sober spirit, be on the alert. Your adversary, the devil, prowls around like a roaring lion, seeking someone to devour. But resist him, firm in your faith, knowing that the same experiences of suffering are being accomplished by your brethren who are in the world.
I Peter 5:8-9

The devil is our adversary and wants to devour us. No minor threat, he is prowling about like a lion seeking its prey. This description of the devil's activity is linked with the phrase *"experiences of suffering."* In other words, at least some of the suffering that we experience is part of the devil's tactics to destroy us. As Satan attempted with Job, he would love to send suffering our way that would cause us to turn from God and deny Him.

In this situation we are instructed to be sober and on alert. We need to be vigilant and seriously look around us in order to perceive the threats and coming attacks. Whether or not our illness is a planned attack by Satan, he would love to use it as a foothold for his work. He will seize any opportunity to turn us toward sin.

Once we have identified the attack of the devil, we are to resist him and to stand firm in our faith. We have to fight back against the enemy. The best way to do this is with Scripture. Because the trial is prolonged, we face the same battles and the same challenges over and over again. One day we might use God's truth and be victorious, but when the same challenge comes the next day, we often forget. In the midst of an extended trial with its repeated temptations, we need frequent reminders of God's truth. Those truths must be constantly recited and recalled so that we have the tools for each new day and so that those truths can become a firm foundation for us. When we resist Satan, he will fight back. The battle will not be easy. We must stand firm in our faith, believing that God's Word will faithfully defend us.

"Father, help me to be realistic about the severity of the battle, to be on guard against Satan's attacks, and to face him boldly with Your Word."

Day 117

For since He Himself was tempted in that which He has suffered, He is able to come to the aid of those who are tempted.
Hebrews 2:18

Suffering does bring with it temptation. That is part of the process of suffering. Temptation comes not so much when life is rosy and sweet as when things turn difficult. It is in the times of suffering that the temptations really hit hard. In the midst of hard times, we are more vulnerable to fall. In suffering and assaults, we are weaker, off guard, and less ready to respond defensively. This is probably most true of the temptations that deal with our thinking and emotions.

Christ understands that concept, and He is able to help us with it. Christ faced temptations in the midst of suffering. Probably two examples are most notable. After He had been alone and hungry in the desert for forty days, Satan came with specific assaults. Later as Christ suffered in the garden, knowing what was to come,

He faced temptation to turn from the cup of suffering. In both cases, He met the temptation victoriously and conquered it.

Because Christ was tempted, He understands our weakness and the challenge in responding. Because He was victorious, He knows how to combat the temptation and how to win the victory. He was thoroughly tested but always victorious; therefore, He knows what to do. Christ is not just sympathetic, though He is that, but He is also able to deliver.

Temptation is common. It will come to us in the midst of our suffering. There is also a way to escape. We are never inevitably doomed to fail or to give in to certain temptations, but we cannot be victorious on our own. We need God's help to keep us from falling. God is able to help in temptation. He knows how to win the battle, and He is ready to come to our aid when we are tempted.

"The temptations assaulting me are numerous and brutal, and I don't know how to defeat them. Help me, Father, to conquer as Your Son conquered.

Day 118

If I have to boast, I will boast of what pertains to my weakness.
II Corinthians 11:30

Sufferings are not something to boast about. Boasting about how much we've suffered may seem like a strange idea, but there is something in us that wants others to know how much we've gone through. We want to be seen as people who have withstood a lot and have come through strong. Somehow the idea creeps into our heads that we must be pretty good Christians for God to trust us with these trials.

It is not appropriate to boast about how much we've suffered, as if that makes us a better Christian or more pleasing to God. In verses twenty-three through twenty-eight, Paul gives a long list of things that he suffered for Christ, yet his intent is not to boast in these things or take any glory for himself. Neither the suffering nor the subsequent growth is our own doing. God decided what He wanted to accomplish in our lives, and He designed the method for bringing it about. Even knowing the value it has produced, we would never have chosen such a path for ourselves. It is God's plan, and He chose it. When there is growth and maturity in the trial, we can't claim credit. We would never even have been in the arena to learn those things if God hadn't designed the setting.

Additionally, without God's encouragement, without His urging us to continue, and without His careful tutoring, we never would have made it this far. We never could have handled the illness, lived victoriously in it, or grown through it. Our survival or success is not found in us. The growth is all of God too. The only thing to boast about is that God can take someone so weak and display His power.

"Help me, Father, not to think of myself as deserving special recognition. May I remember that You have done all the work."

Day 119

We are destroying speculations and every lofty thing raised up against the knowledge of God, and are taking every thought captive to the obedience of Christ.
II Corinthians 10:5

Do you know about crazy thinking? Do you know what it is like to have your thoughts bouncing all over the place? Are they out of control, topsy-turvy, scrambled, and changing rapidly? This scenario can commonly occur in the midst of an illness. It can also happen frequently in the midst of a spiritual battle, when you are struggling to comprehend what God is teaching and to submit to His direction. An illness is a great setting for that type of spiritual battle. For both reasons – the effect of the illness itself and the accompanying spiritual struggle – you are in a prime position to be at war with your thoughts. How should you handle that battle?

First, you need to be aware of the enemy. It is simply reality that you have thoughts that are confused, sad, painful, and so on. Those are natural responses. You can't really stop them from happening, and it is helpful to acknowledge they are there and perhaps to understand why they are there.

Second, realize how dangerous the enemy is. You are aware of how rapidly your thoughts can spiral downward. They are not something to be taken lightly. Because of their dangerous potential, you cannot focus on those negative thoughts or allow them to linger. Learn to recognize the thoughts that are especially dangerous – the ones that take you to the deepest depths or that return with the most frequency.

Now you are ready for the third step, taking those thoughts captive. It is not okay for your thoughts to be crazy. You must take control of those thoughts and bring them captive to the obedience of Christ. They must be made prisoners to what Christ would approve. Use God's strength to avoid traveling down those dangerous paths. Remember that the further you travel down the wrong path, the further you will have to come back once you do turn around. Learn to quickly substitute God's good thoughts for your faulty ones. Because of the very real challenges you face, the battle may be constant, but you cannot give in. Keep recognizing the enemy, keep reminding yourself of the danger, and keep taking prisoners.

"Father, give me Your help to stop my wrong thoughts, to bring them into captivity, and to think right thoughts instead."

Day 120

Jesus wept. So the Jews were saying, "See how He loved him!"
John 11:35-36

The story about the death of Lazarus provides a comforting realization about our Savior. Jesus was sensitive to the pain of others. The two sisters, Mary and Martha, had hoped Jesus would arrive in time to heal their brother. Instead, Lazarus had been buried four days before Jesus' arrival. The sisters were apparently dependent on Lazarus for their livelihood, but they also had great emotional pain at the death of their beloved brother. In their pain they expressed their dismay that Jesus had not come in time to heal their brother.

Jesus was completely in control of the situation. He knew what would happen. He had not been upset when He had informed His disciples about Lazarus' death. In fact, He had spoken positively of the greater purposes to be accomplished through the situation.

Jesus' emotional display came only after He observed the pain of His friends. The passage states twice that He was deeply moved in His spirit, and it also reveals that He was troubled. The reason for these responses is clearly stated as being a response to Mary's tears. It was when He saw Mary cry that Jesus wept. His heart responded to the grief and pain of His friends.

Christ's compassionate and sympathetic response was the result of love. The narration informs us of His love for the three friends, and the Jews present were also impressed with His great love. Jesus' love caused Him to cry as He observed the sorrow of His friends.

We have a Savior who cares when we hurt. He is moved when we cry in sorrow. Even though He is in control of every situation and knows how He will use it for His good purposes, He still responds tenderly to our pain. We are never alone in our sorrow. We are never unnoticed in our pain. Not a tear falls that Jesus does not see. When we are hurting, the heart of Jesus shares our pain, and He responds in compassion and love.

"Thank You, Father, that I never have to cry alone. Thank You that You always know about my sorrow and that You always care."

Day 121

He said to them, "Why are you afraid, you men of little faith?" Then He got up and
rebuked the winds and the sea, and it became perfectly calm.
Matthew 8:26

When storms come, it is wonderfully reassuring to know that we have God with us. The disciples were in a boat out on the sea when a gigantic storm arose. The waves were covering the ship. In fear the disciples woke Jesus and desperately begged for His help. They were afraid they were going to die.

The storm was too much for the disciples. Even though several of them were men of the sea, this storm frightened them badly. They couldn't do anything about the storm. They couldn't stop it or even make it less intense. They couldn't sail out of it. They didn't think they could wait it out. They couldn't protect themselves or find shelter. These men were in great trouble.

Though they were completely powerless in the teeth of the great storm, Jesus had absolute power. He had only to speak to the storm, and both the winds and the waves became still. The disciples had been hoping just to survive. Far beyond merely sparing their lives, Jesus stripped the storm of all its fury and caused it to cease. He left it completely powerless and entirely empty. When Jesus conquered the storm, it had no more power to instill fear.

Like the disciples, we often experience fear in the midst of our storms. Like them, our faith is weak and we easily forget how capable God is. While storms may be far beyond our power to control, and though they may threaten our very lives, Jesus still has all power. There is no storm that He cannot calm. No wave can lift up and crash upon us when Jesus has ordered it to be calm. No wind can thrash and buffet us when Jesus has commanded it to be still. No storm is a match for God; when we are under His care, we need not fear the storms.

"Father, in the overwhelming onslaught, I am perishing. Save me. Calm the storm and
bring it under Your control."

The Storm (Sonnet 3)
The storms of life may seem to me unjust.
I feel the wind too strong, the waves too high.
The tossing tempest never seems to die,
And drowning threatens with each wave and gust.
The search for answers leaves me in disgust,
For to my mind appears no reason why.
But as I wonder how to just get by,
My Father whispers, "Trust, my child, just trust.

One day it will be time to understand;
My promises will be enough till then.
I realize what you need and also when.
I'll lead you through and bring you safe to land.
I will not fail; I'm found when I am sought.
I am the Master of the storm; fear not."

Day 122

Be gracious to me, O LORD;
See my affliction from those who hate me,
You who lift me up from the gates of death.
Psalm 9:13

This verse is part of the personal testimony of David, a man who served the same God that we serve today. God's work in David's life is illustrative of the way He also works in our lives. David acknowledged that God was the one who lifted him up from the gates of death. Many times in David's life, he was at the very edge of death. Often his life could have been, and logically should have been, snuffed out.

At times he was only seconds or inches away from death, yet over and over God delivered him. God gave him strength over wild animals when they could have easily torn him to pieces. God caused a stone to fly powerfully from David's sling to its target, killing a warrior who could have crushed him. God caused a javelin thrown at close range to miss David and pierce the wall instead. God allowed the diversion of a fake body in a bed to be successful, causing the search for David to be delayed for precious minutes. God provided food, weapons, and men for David when he had nothing. God hid David from an army that pursued him relentlessly for many years. God caused foreign kings to fall for David's ruses. God protected David in many battles and civil wars.

David could have died dozens of times, but God preserved his life over and over again. Only God has such power. David's own efforts did not keep him alive; his life was preserved only by the direct intervention of God. God has the power to preserve life as long as He chooses and as many times as necessary. He kept David alive, and He can keep us alive until His time for us has come.

"Father, as I face the possibility of death, I acknowledge You as the preserver of my life. You can deliver me as many times as You choose, in spite of the strength of the enemy."

Day 123

How great is Your goodness,
Which You have stored up for those who fear You,
Which You have wrought for those who take refuge in You,
Before the sons of men!
Psalm 31:19

God's goodness is abundant and plentiful. There is always enough to go around. He never has to ration it out or make people take turns. God has sufficient goodness to extend it to all of His people. His supply of goodness reaches levels so high that man cannot even imagine them. God has displayed His goodness in the past, and He continues to display it in the present.

Not only does He have enough goodness for everything needed in the present, but He also has reserves stored up for the future. God saves up His goodness in great storehouses. He has such huge stockpiles of goodness that He will never run out. If all the goodness in the world were used up, with none to be found anywhere, God would still have an abundant supply. He holds His extra goodness in reserve so that He has it available to pour out on His children.

God saves His goodness for those who fear Him. He works it out on those who take refuge in Him. When a man seeks God in these ways, he will find a good God. No one who takes refuge in God will find Him to be cruel or heartless. No one will find God empty. God is full of goodness, and He is ready to pour out His stores of goodness on those who flee to Him.

"What a precious truth, Father. I need lots of goodness, and I can find enough in You. Thank You that You are always good and that You will always have enough goodness."

Day 124

That I may know Him and the power of His resurrection and the fellowship of His sufferings, being conformed to His death.
Philippians 3:10

Knowing God is an important desire for any Christian, but it is even more expedient for those who are suffering. The Bible reveals great value and numerous benefits in knowing God. Those benefits are especially precious and helpful to those who are in need.

Knowing God is the basis for our relationship with Him. It puts God on our side. Knowing God frees us from the power of sin. Not only does He forgive our sins, but He helps us to escape the staining of the world. Knowing God gives us a peaceful life. As we know Him, we have rest and confidence in Him. Knowing God leads to fearing Him, which is the foundation for knowledge and understanding. It gives us guidance for life. Knowing God helps us to hear His voice. Knowing God provides the basis for our commitment to Him and gives us strength and courage in time of trouble.

In short, knowing God is the basis for practical Christianity. It affects our spirits because we know He is worthy of our trust, and it affects our actions because we have the understanding and courage to live for Him. No wonder Paul yearned to know God. He counted everything else as worthless in comparison with knowing God, and he was willing to count all other things as loss for the higher goal of knowing Christ. Knowing God is the most important thing. Knowing God is worth the loss of other things, including our health.

While the Bible is the best source of the knowledge of God, He also reveals Himself through the events of our lives. A serious illness is actually a great venue for learning about God. We get to know Him through His mighty acts on our behalf and through the deliverance He gives. We learn to know God through His answers to prayer and through the blessings He provides. We learn to know Him through the correction that He sends into our lives. We learn about God as we seek Him, something that happens more readily in a time of trial. We need to look for God's hand at work in our illness. When we learn what He is like, we are much better prepared to face the difficulties of life.

"Father, I need to know You better so that I can face life more effectively and serve You more faithfully. Help me to recognize Your hand at work so that I can learn more of You."

Day 125

O LORD, You have heard the desire of the humble;
You will strengthen their heart, You will incline Your ear
To vindicate the orphan and the oppressed,
So that man who is of the earth will no longer cause terror.
Psalm 10:17–18

To whom does God give His attention? He hears the humble. He listens to the orphans and the oppressed. God pays attention to the needy and cares about those who are in trouble. God hears the desire of these people when they cry out to Him. He knows what they long for. He understands the yearnings of their hearts.

When God hears those who are oppressed, He also helps them. That help does not always come in exactly the way they desire, because the Almighty God knows things that man doesn't know. He understands things that are beyond the comprehension of those who are faltering in the midst of assaulting troubles. God knows the burdens and desires of their hearts, and He knows whether or not He will grant those desires as they have come to Him.

God is able to answer the cries of the needy by giving great victory and deliverance. He can conquer each enemy and beat down every foe. Even if God chooses not to answer in such a dramatic fashion, He still gives help. He does not fail those who depend on Him in time of need. If God chooses not to grant the desire of the needy, He will strengthen their hearts. He can give strength, both internal and external, to those who are weak. He gives them help so that they can walk the path before them. He will not leave them to stumble or suffer on their own.

"Father, You know the desire of my heart. If You answer it, I will praise You. If You don't answer, strengthen my heart to follow You and praise You."

Day 126

I will sing of the lovingkindness of the LORD forever;
To all generations I will make known Your faithfulness with my mouth.
Psalm 89:1

Psalm 89 talks about two wonderful aspects of God's character. It mentions His lovingkindness and His faithfulness seven times each. God has established those two characteristics forever. They will always exist, and we can always count on them. They are such an inseparable part of God that they surround Him and are with Him wherever He is.

God promised to show His lovingkindness and faithfulness to David and his descendants, and He shows them to all of His children. The amazing thing about God is that He will never break a promise. When God says He will do something, He will always do it. God's promises are not dependent on man's behavior. God vowed that if David's sons forsook Him, He would not go back on His word. He would still deal with them in lovingkindness and faithfulness.

These two characteristics that are forever an inseparable part of God's character provide encouragement for the troubles we face in life. Because of God's lovingkindness, He desires the best things for us. He desires to take care of us. He desires to provide for us and protect us. He cherishes us.

Because God is also faithful, He will never change. The desires that He has for us now are the same desires that He will continue to have for us. God doesn't show His lovingkindness for just a little while and then give it up or forget about it. He will faithfully show His lovingkindness day after day and year after year. He will never stop caring for us.

Verses five through ten reveal an additional aspect of God's character, one that works together with His lovingkindness and faithfulness. These verses discuss God's power. His wonders are seen in the heavens. No one, no matter how mighty, can match God. He is awesome and feared. He controls the oceans, and He crushes nations at will. God's power means that He is able to work out the lovingkindness that He faithfully intends for us. Nothing can stop God from performing what He desires to do for us.

"Father, thank You that You love me. Thank You that Your love will never change or cease. Thank You that You are powerful enough to display Your love faithfully."

Day 127

"He must increase, but I must decrease."
John 3:30

In his well-known book *Humility*, Andrew Murray states, "Humility is the only soil in which virtue takes root." When we are humble, we are in a position that allows God to effectively do His work in our hearts. An illness is a great venue in which humility can be learned because it teaches us how weak we are. We learn first of all about our physical weakness. Things that used to fall into the routine of daily life – things we used to do without even thinking about them – have now become challenges. It's pretty tough to boast about how great we are when we can barely walk across a room.

Even more humbling than our physical limitations are the tremendous spiritual struggles that we face. Whereas we used to mostly cruise through life, now we are assaulted daily by temptations that seem nearly impossible to resist. In general, we like to keep up a good image before others; we resist allowing our faults and struggles to be seen. After several months of illness, however, we realize that we have no good image, except as Christ's image is reflected in us. It's hard to be proud when we see how weak our inner man is.

Growth and maturity do come through trials, but even this growth leads us to humility. Because we have come to see how weak and vulnerable we are, we realize that the growth is all from God and entirely by His grace. We have nothing to boast about in regard to our performance through the trial. The profit that is worked in us through our trial comes only as we humble ourselves, admitting our weakness and our great need for God. Only then do we properly present ourselves to God so

He can do His work in us. Only when we become nothing can the light of Christ-likeness shine clearly through us.

"Father, I am learning that I am truly nothing. Help me to learn even more how much I need You. Help me to humble myself so that You can be seen more clearly in my life."

From Nothing to Nothing

The ugly vase was placed upon a high top shelf
Back in the darkest corner of the lonely room.
As dust collected, cobwebs formed, and paint peeled off,
The vase stayed hidden in the humble, quiet spot.
'Twas unimportant, and it met no want or need.

The scraggly plant was in the grown-up garden plot,
Hid deep amid the tangled and neglected mess.
As weeds entwined, and fallen leaves collected there,
The plant retained its lonely and forgotten state –
Unnoticed and ignored, a flower without blooms.

So this is what it means to learn humility;
It is a lesson that I need and want to learn.
Although it hurts and is not fun, I need to yield.
Retain me here while You do all Your work and plan;
I must see that I'm useless, nothing without You.

The decorator enters the neglected room
In search of something new to use in his display.
He finds the unremembered vase, removes the dust.
He shines and polishes till it begins to glow;
At last its beauty brings a sparkle to his eye.

The gentle gard'ner comes to the abandoned plot.
He cleans the mess and takes away the leaves and weeds;
He cultivates the flower, frail and delicate.
He helps it grow and beautifies it with his love;
Its beauty and its bloom are giv'n to him alone.

If vase or flower come into the public eye,
Allowing others to observe the work that's done,
Then once again, I must be taught humility.
I must remember all is by Your choice and skill;
It's not my beauty. I'm still nothing without You.

Day 128 _____

For You have been a refuge for me,
A tower of strength against the enemy.
Psalm 61:3

This verse contains two descriptions that reveal the power and strength of God. First, God is a Refuge. The refuge is a place of shelter and hope in a time of danger. It is a place that those who face harm can run to and confide in. More than merely a pleasant place to rest, a refuge is a place of protection. The concept can be illustrated by thinking of someone who is caught in a fierce storm. He is pummeled and perhaps threatened by the elements, but he knows where to go. He knows of a sturdy cabin in the woods or a protected cove along the coast. He knows that if he can just get to that place, he will be safe. He will be protected and will have hope of waiting out the storm. Because of the intense danger, there is a certain level of desperation in finding that place and getting to it quickly enough. The desperation is quickly forgotten, however, when he finds safety in the refuge. Because the refuge is so effective, it provides hope and peace to combat the fear.

The second picture presents God as a Tower of Strength. This particular word for *tower* focuses especially on the size and height of the structure. This tower is large and imposing. It is something that people notice. When people look at the tower, they think, "Wow, that's big!" In addition to being big, the tower is also strong. It has force and majesty. Because of its strength, it is effective as a place of defense and refuge. This tower is strong enough to protect, but it also inspires awe and admiration. The tower of strength is much like a large and beautiful castle that fascinates while at the same time providing protection.

"Father, thank You that I can hide in You. With such a sure refuge and such a strong tower, how can I fear? You are completely able to protect me."

Day 129 _____

Thanks be to God for His indescribable gift!
II Corinthians 9:15

If ever you begin to feel worthless, consider this. You were far from God and He brought you near. You were darkness and He made you light. Though you were hostile to Him, He reconciled you to peace. You were dead till He made you alive. You were nothing and He gave you existence. You were foolish, weak, and base, but He made you prudent, strong, and distinguished. You were a humble earthen vessel, but He made you a box fit for treasure. You were a slave and He made you free. You were an alien who didn't belong, but He made you a citizen of heaven. You were an orphan, and He made you His child. While you were once a beggar, He made you an heir of the King. Though you were a sinner, He made you a saint. You were an enemy of God, but He made you His friend.

These striking transformations are hard to believe. Surely they were not easily accomplished. Oh, no! They came at incredible cost. You were bought with a price you could never repay, a price greater than silver and gold. The gift was so precious it can't be described. To bring these great changes, Christ suffered and died. His body was broken. For you the only Son of God became a curse. He chose poverty so that you could be rich.

What possible motive could warrant such an investment? It was clearly not because of what you deserved. Neither was it done from a sense of obligation, in order to gain wages or reward, or out of a philanthropic heart. What motive is left to explain such a gift? Jesus gave up Himself and did all that for you based only on love. For no explainable or understandable reason, He decided that He wanted to. His mercy and grace poured out in abundance from a heart of incredible, incomprehensible, incomparable, unselfish, inseparable, and undying love.

"Father, it is amazing to think that You would love me so much that You would give so much for me and do so much for me. Thank You."

Day 130

Trust in Him at all times, O people;
Pour out your heart before Him;
God is a refuge for us.
Psalm 62:8

The weeks and months of your illness have included many long hours and days. One thing you have discovered in those extended quiet hours is how much you have to think about. In contrast with the curtailed activity of your body, your mind seems to be working overtime. In spite of the fact that your life is on hold, it seems you have more to think about and evaluate than ever before, and your mind cannot keep up. You think about living with your illness. You think about the changing symptoms, the tedium, the frustration, the progress, the decisions, and the plans. Beyond that, you think about all of the things God is teaching you. You ponder your areas of struggle and the lessons you think you're learning but can't quite figure out.

Your heart and mind are exploding with things you want to talk through, and you wish you had someone to listen to you. As you search for that listening ear, you may find that your family is busy with your care and tired from increased responsibilities. Your friends may be caught up in the activities of their own lives. Perhaps those around you lack the spiritual depth to offer you help. Maybe they are so far removed from understanding your situation that talking to them is more frustrating than profitable. Maybe your thoughts are too deep and private to share with anyone.

In such an absence of suitable listeners, God invites you to talk to Him. You can pour out every thought and struggle of your heart to Him. Tell Him the truth. Dump it all on Him. Just let it flow. You may not have the mental stamina for long, structured prayer times, and that's okay. Just talk to Him whenever you feel a need. As you practice doing this consistently, you will find your prayers becoming deeper and more frequent. You will find yourself turning more instinctively to prayer. When you talk to God, He will not let you down. You can trust Him to always be there. You can trust Him to listen to every word. You can trust Him to completely understand. You can trust Him not to betray your confidence. You can trust Him to be a refuge. God is ready to listen to you.

"Oh, Father, there is so much I want to share. Help me to remember to talk to You about what is in my heart."

Day 131

He gives strength to the weary,
And to him who lacks might He increases power.
Though youths grow weary and tired,
And vigorous young men stumble badly,
Yet those who wait for the LORD
Will gain new strength;
They will mount up with wings like eagles,
They will run and not get tired,
They will walk and not become weary.
Isaiah 40:29-31

Human strength is limited. That strength can disappear faster than what would seem possible. When a capable young person is struck with a debilitating illness, his youthful vigor can quickly turn into feebleness. A diseased person may wake up feeling strong and energetic, but that energy can disintegrate by lunchtime or even by the time he gets dressed. The Bible points out a more alarming scenario which falls outside the realm of illness. Even youths and vigorous young men grow weary in the course of normal life. The many demands of life take a toll, causing even the young to be tired and to stumble.

When having consistent strength is so hard even for healthy people, how can those who are sick survive? They certainly can't do it in their own strength, but with God's help they can. God sees those who are weary and who lack might. He gives them strength and power. God is the source of all strength, and He can give it to whomever He wants.

With God's power infused, the weak person gains new strength. Instead of lying helplessly on the ground, he can now soar into the air like a mighty eagle. Instead of staring helplessly at a fifty-yard dash, he can now run a marathon without getting tired. The pictures are, of course, comparisons to illustrate the point. The bottom line is that those who seem completely exhausted and without resources can, through God's help, do far more than they ever dreamed possible. When it seems impossible to take another step, God makes it possible to continue on and on. God gives this kind of strength to those who wait on Him. He gives it to those who look expectantly to Him for what they know they don't have apart from Him. Those who wait on God will have renewed strength for the journey; they will be able to proceed mightily without growing weary.

"Father, I'm weary physically when I wake up in the morning and weary emotionally in this impossible, unending illness. Give me the strength to walk and even to run day after day."

Day 132

Therefore, do not throw away your confidence, which has a great reward. For you have need of endurance, so that when you have done the will of God, you may receive what was promised.
Hebrews 10:35-36

The writer of this passage addresses the need for confidence in God that will endure through a trial. The primary reason for this enduring confidence is the knowledge that faith will be greatly rewarded. The readers are encouraged in this truth by being reminded of a situation in their past. They had experienced great sufferings because of their identification with Christ and their loving sympathy for others who were suffering (vs. 32-34). In spite of these great sufferings, which had included the seizure of their properties, they had responded with joy. They had been able to face the loss of property (and other afflictions) joyfully because they knew there was something better to come. They knew they would enjoy an eternal possession that would far surpass what they had lost in the present.

Just as these believers were encouraged by recalling the truth they had lived out in the past, so we need to remember that our sufferings are only temporary. There is something better to come. We can remain confident in God, and our confidence will be rewarded. We need to endure and continue doing His will through the trial, and we will then receive His promise. All of God's promises are faithful, and all of them will be kept. They will not all be fulfilled right away, so we must wait patiently until God does fulfill them. We must have endurance so that we can make it through the preliminary stages of obedience and arrive at the end result of seeing the blessing. Instead of giving up, we need to continue serving and following God, and He will fulfill His promise.

"Father, there are days when I just want to quit. Help my confidence in You to endure and keep me going forward until I see the reward that I know You will give."

Day 133

Now to Him who is able to do far more abundantly beyond all that we ask or think, according to the power that works within us.
Ephesians 3:20

Father, this is not an outrageous demand that I've invented; it is a claim that You make for Yourself. You are able to go beyond my boldest prayers, doing more than I can ask. You are able to go even beyond my most daring imaginations, doing more than I can think. While You could merely meet my prayers or expectations, You choose to go much further. Your claim includes numerous added superlatives: *"far more abundantly beyond."*

These amazing answers come through Your power, the same power that created the earth and that works miracles. Because Your ability is beyond what I can think, I can't even comprehend what this verse means. What *can* You do? Where *will* You stop in Your amazing work? When I see Your work, my faith grows and my imagination expands. Even then the verse does not change. You can still do far more than I can imagine.

My thoughts are limited to thinking mostly of physical healing. Are You able to do more than I can think because You work in areas that I don't even think about? Are You focusing on the spiritual battles more intently than I am? When I look at that side of myself, I become very discouraged. It doesn't seem possible to have consistent spiritual victory or significant spiritual growth. I don't even see how to retain what I've learned so far. I don't see how I can ever be useful again. If You bring hard things as preparation, however, then the preparation has to be *for something*. Are You really preparing me to serve You more effectively? That would require Your power, because in myself it will never happen.

While I may have doubts, there really is no need to fear that I can't grow or that I'll never have victory in challenging areas. What seems impossible to me is not impossible for You. You can give me the desire to change, the confidence in Your ability, the steady teaching and training, the gradual strengthening of conviction, and even the eventual outworking of that into practical action. Nothing is too hard for You. When the amazing things are done, whether they be physical healing or spiritual growth, You will be the one responsible.

"Father, You may not always do exactly what I ask, but You are always able. I leave the physical realm to You, and in the spiritual realm, I ask You to do more than I think possible."

Far More
He'll do far more abundantly than I can ask,
For His pow'r is not limited by any task.
When my life seems confused and in much disarray,
He gives answers beyond any prayer that I pray.
He'll do far more abundantly than I can think;
He can do such sensations – in wonder I blink.
When my soul is in need that His hand should revive,
He is plentifully able to make me alive.
Oh, I know He is able; His power can't fail,
And it's only His hand that could work such detail.
When my faith gains more strength and my thinking expands,
Even that's not too much for His capable hands.
Since my thoughts are so finite, His work I can't know,
So that I am left asking, "How far will He go?"

Day 134

Great is my confidence in you; great is my boasting on your behalf. I am filled with comfort; I am overflowing with joy in all our affliction.
II Corinthians 7:4

In the midst of many afflictions, Paul had joy. In fact, he was overflowing with joy. Where did such super-abounding delight come from in the midst of trials? Paul shows us that joy can be found in things outside the affliction. Paul's joy came as God gave him comfort through external and unrelated factors. Paul was filled with comfort as he thought about the growth and testimony of the church. He was excited about what God was doing in them. He had something else to focus his thoughts on and to rejoice about, rather than becoming fixated on his own problems.

He did have some rather intense problems which were causing some very strong reactions. In verses five and six, Paul mentions multi-pronged conflicts, internal fear, and even depression. He was without rest and found afflictions everywhere he turned. God knew the desperation of his situation, however, and responded by sending comfort. On this occasion it was in the form of a visit from Titus, who brought a report of how well the church was doing. In First Thessalonians 3:7, Timothy was the bearer of good news about the church and encouraged Paul in another time of affliction. Good news about others encouraged Paul in those very difficult times.

Can we not profit from Paul's example? Instead of dwelling on the very real challenges of our situation, let's look for some good news. What good work have we heard about recently? What has God done in a loved one's life? What victory has He given to a friend? What church or missionary work has He blessed? Let's take a break from our troubles and rejoice in God's goodness to others.

"Father, it is so easy for me to be self-centered and to forget about the good things You are doing all around me. Encourage me as I focus on Your blessings to others."

Day 135

O taste and see that the LORD is good;
How blessed is the man who takes refuge in Him!
The young lions do lack and suffer hunger;
But they who seek the LORD shall not be in want of any good thing.
Psalm 34:8 & 10

God is very good. He does good things and provides good things for His children. The psalmist is so absolutely sure about this aspect of God's nature that he issues a bit of a challenge. He invites the reader to taste God's goodness – that is, to test it or to run an experiment. There is no doubt as to how the experiment will turn out. The psalmist knows what the result will be: the experimenter will see that God is good. If someone tries God, he will find out that God is good.

God can't help but to be good, because goodness is an intrinsic part of His nature. Those who put God to the test in this way will not be disappointed. God's goodness is complete, and because His goodness is so deep, God does what is good for His children. He provides what is good for them. Those who seek the Lord will not lack any good thing that they need. If something is a true need, God will supply it.

There are two descriptions given of the people to whom God responds in this way. These people are referred to as those who take refuge in Him and those who seek Him. If we hide in God and look to Him, He will meet every need by supplying every good thing that we need. Young lions are bold, brave, proud, and self-reliant. These kings of the beasts go out to hunt with a great deal of energy, skill, and bravado. Sometimes they come back empty and hungry. Similarly, if we rely on our own strength and cunning, we will find ourselves lacking. When we seek God, rely on Him to supply, and trust Him to be our good God, He supplies all that we need.

"Father, I want to take refuge in You. I want to believe that You are entirely good. Please fulfill those desires by allowing me to taste Your wonderful goodness."

Day 136

But in everything commending ourselves as servants of God, in much endurance, in afflictions, in hardships, in distresses.
II Corinthians 6:4

Every day and in all things we are to commend ourselves as servants of God. That is, we are to exhibit by our responses that we belong to Him. Affliction is no exception. We are not exempted from demonstrating our relationship to Christ just because things get difficult. Being in difficulty does not give us an excuse for living any way we want to or for having ungodly reactions. If we are showing ourselves as servants of God in the midst of difficulties, there will be an obvious difference between the way we handle troubles and the way the world handles them. The difference exhibited in these hard times is one of the best proofs and most powerful testimonies that we indeed belong to God.

From Paul's own example, we see that those afflictions can include some pretty difficult things. In verses four and five, he mentions some rather extreme scenarios in which we are to display that we are of God. He goes on to give contrasting pairs in verses eight through ten, showing that both positive and negative scenarios exist in the life of a Christian. In either case, we are to show ourselves as servants of Christ. This allows us to be positive even in negative situations. In particular, verse ten notes that it is possible to be sorrowful, yet always rejoicing. Sorrow and joy can both exist at the same time. In the midst of trials that bring only sorrow to the world, our sorrow is tempered with an underlying joy because of the fact that we belong to God.

"Father, I have You as my God and my help. I should not respond in the same way as those without You. Help me to have godly responses that point toward You."

Day 137

Come, let us worship and bow down,
Let us kneel before the LORD our Maker.
Psalm 95:6

God is our Maker. He made everything. The world itself would not exist without God, and neither would anything or anyone on it. While it is remarkable to consider the intricacies of the plants, the uniqueness of the animals, or the complexity of the solar system, God chose man to be His masterpiece. It is man who has the capacity to glorify and honor God. When God made the human body, He made a remarkable thing. Our minds cannot comprehend how amazing the body's systems are. For example, man has taken great strides in understanding DNA, yet he is really just beginning to peer into the edge of that complex system. God understands it perfectly because He designed it and produced it. This is just one facet of the amazing way God made us.

Since God is our Maker, that makes Him incredible. He deserves our admiration, respect, and worship. Since God is our Maker, that makes Him our sustainer and caretaker as well. God is the one who created our bodies, and He is the one who keeps them going day after day. He knows exactly what they need and precisely how to fix any problems. Since God is our Maker, that makes Him right. He designed us exactly as He wanted us to be. Any deformities or birth defects were purposefully made by our Maker. When our bodies break down, they do so under His care and within His purposes. Since God is our Maker, He is also our master. Something created belongs to the one who made it. God deserves our submission and obedience. As His workmanship, we should serve Him well. He is a Maker who is worthy.

"Father, You are my Maker. I am humbled at Your involvement in my life. May I allow You to use me according to Your design."

Day 138

"Had it not been the LORD who was on our side
When men rose up against us,
Then the waters would have engulfed us,
The stream would have swept over our soul."
Psalm 124:2 & 4

Life is tough enough on a normal basis, but when a significant hardship is introduced, life gets even tougher. How can anyone survive such a thing without

God? The nation of Israel asked that question. They pondered this horrible possibility: what would have happened to them if God had not been on their side? Israel then responded with some pretty horrific, but entirely likely, answers to that question. If God had not been on their side, they would have been swallowed up alive. If God had not been on their side, they would have drowned in the raging waters. If God had not been on their side, the tumultuous waters would have swept over their souls. Their lives would have ended in tragedy without God.

Israel's reminiscing did not stop there, because, wonder of wonders, God *was* on their side. God stood by them and He helped them. God saved them from being torn apart by vicious teeth that wanted to rend them. God saved them out of the trap that had been set to entangle them. God helped them to escape. It is no surprise that God was able to deliver His people. He is the God who made the heaven and the earth. Having done that task so masterfully, what task is too hard for Him? God can deliver.

That same God is on our side today. If we were alone, we would be overwhelmed by the challenges of our illness. We would be plunged into despair. We would be helpless. But we are not alone! God is with us. He can deliver us from the fierce storms just as He delivered Israel. He can save us from drowning in our problems just as He saved Israel. He can protect us from being devoured just as He protected Israel. Without God on our side, life would be a disaster indeed, but with God there is always help and hope.

"Thank You, Father, for being on my side. Sometimes I forget, and the floods threaten to drown me. Help me to remember that I am not alone."

Day 139

"He will call upon Me, and I will answer him;
I will be with him in trouble;
I will rescue him and honor him."
Psalm 91:15

This verse shares several reassuring truths that bring comfort to our souls. First, God answers us when we call to Him. When we are in need, there is no better place to go for help. God is able to help us better than anyone else can. Because of His tremendous ability to help, it might seem that He would be very busy. We could imagine that He has a backlog of requests and that He must limit Himself to the most important or most urgent requests. This is not the case. God is never too busy to answer our call. He never has so many things to attend to that He can't take care of us. Our need is never too insignificant for Him to care about. When we call on God, He will answer.

The second truth is that God will be with us in trouble. We certainly don't want to be alone in a time of trouble. We want someone to be with us. Again, there is no better person to have at our side. The God who created the universe with His power stays by us, and His power is sufficient to meet our needs. This capable God will never leave us alone. Others might flee when trouble comes, but God remains faithfully with us.

Third, God delivers us. God is able to dramatically change our situation. He can take a seeming tragedy and turn it into something amazing. He can rescue us from fear, from defeat, and from destruction. He can turn our situation into one of honor as He upholds us and prospers our faith. These are indeed wonderful truths: God hears us when we call, He is with us in trouble, and He rescues us.

"Thank You, Father, that You answer when I call. Thank You for being with me in trouble. Thank You that You can rescue me."

Day 140

Immediately the boy's father cried out and said, "I do believe; help my unbelief."
Mark 9:24
The apostles said to the Lord, "Increase our faith!"
Luke 17:5

Faith can be a puzzling thing. It is based on things that we cannot see. It often defies logic or reason. It seems to defy reality. Faith asks us to believe without seeing proof and without having understanding. This response is hard for humans to do. It seems that the less proof we have or the more something seems to contrast with what we see, the harder it is to have faith regarding it.

We want to have faith. Often our spirit longs to believe God's truth. We have moments and even stages in life in which our faith takes leaps. At times our faith tenaciously clings to God's truth even when we see no support for it. Then at other times we refuse to believe even the most basic concepts.

I think we understand the dilemma of the boy's father in the verse above. We want to believe. We choose to believe. Our faith puts forth tentative fingers toward belief. We feel as if we are on the verge of confidently believing, and we want those fingers to take a firm hold. Faith and unbelief both exist, and we want the confidence of faith to overpower the doubts that unbelief is still trying to introduce. We want faith to take complete control.

The disciples also had faith, yet they recognized that their faith was weak. It had room to grow. While they could believe the easy things, they were still challenged in believing the more difficult things. In that struggle, they asked God to increase their faith. Like the disciples, we find that some of God's truths are harder to believe than others. In our trial it may be hard to believe God's love or to accept the truth of abundant life available in Him. What can we do when we want to believe and when we know we need to believe, but everything in us protests?

We certainly should confess our doubt. We can definitely ask God to increase our faith. We can also specifically target the area in question. When we come across a verse or concept that we doubt, we can turn it into a prayer. We can say, "You say that You love me, but I struggle to believe it. Help me to believe. Help me to see Your love." This topic, like everything else recorded in God's Word, is true. Why would God not want us to see and believe it? The growth may not be immediate, but if we continue to earnestly pray this way, God will increase our faith.

"Father, increase my faith. Help me to firmly believe what You say,
even when I don't see how it's true."

Faith's Conflict (Sonnet 46)
The God who guides my path is true and tried;
He answers every promise with a "Yes."
His faithful Word can never be denied.
He will not fail; He promises no less.
In spite of facts like these, my faith is weak;
My humanness demands the way be plain.
I long for resolution when I seek;
Believing the unseen is just insane.
That He is right, I know I must concede;
In Him alone support and hope I'll find.
Why does my soul resist just what I need?
It's not in me - the faith that God designed.
For faith that sees beyond, I humbly plead;
I must believe He'll do what He decreed.

Day 141

Casting all your anxiety on Him, because He cares for you.
I Peter 5:7

This verse mentions two things that are factors within any illness. First, a seriously ill person has a lot of anxieties. There are a lot of threats and uncertainties that can cause anxiety. There are many burdens to carry. Second, a person who is sick wants someone to care for him. He wants someone to sympathize, to sit by his side, and to be concerned. If there is someone who really cares, then the anxieties are not as bad, because there is someone to help carry them.

God gives us a wonderful invitation. He tells us that we can throw all of our anxieties on Him. He will carry them for us so that we don't have to carry them at all. Some of our concerns are so small that they aren't worth anyone else's attention, but God cares about them. When we have a small quantity of concerns, we may be reluctant to share them with others whose lives probably also have burdens. God cares even when our pack of burdens is small.

More often, though, our burdens are so many that neither we nor any of our friends are able to bear them. Some of our concerns are so large that no one else could possibly manage them. God has no problem with those heavy burdens, and no quantity of burdens is too great for God to handle. God can carry every burden, and He invites us to cast each one on Him.

This relief from the burden is coupled with the wonderful knowledge that someone truly cares about us. God loves us. He is on our side. His heart is touched with our grief, and He shares our pain. He cares more than we can even imagine. He cares more than the most attentive of our friends or family. He cares more than everyone else put together. When others tire of our distress and long for us to move on, God continues to extend His compassion because He is love and He deeply cares for us.

"Father, my anxieties are many, and I need someone to care. Thank You for caring for me so much. I can hardly believe such love, but I thank You for it."

Day 142

That in a great ordeal of affliction their abundance of joy and their deep poverty overflowed in the wealth of their liberality.
II Corinthians 8:2

The churches in Macedonia were going through a time of great affliction. Their personal need and challenges did not stop them, however, from having abundant joy or from reaching out to others. While we are not told the specific source of their joy, we see that they were able to find a source of joy in spite of their affliction. Stemming from this abundant joy, they reached out to others even though they were in the midst of their own time of need.

The realm in which they ministered was actually the same as the area of their own need, as they sought to alleviate for others the very thing that was causing their own suffering. The Macedonians were going through a time of great poverty. In spite of their financial challenges, they gave monetarily to meet the needs of others. Being in a particular situation gave them a compassionate desire to help others who were suffering in the same way. They felt and understood the need. They were willing to put themselves out, to sacrifice, and to give even though it hurt, because they were so sensitive to that particular need. They knew very well what it was like to suffer in that way, and they wanted to relieve the pain of others.

Being in need does not require you to withdraw from all service and ministry to others. In fact, your particular affliction makes you better able to understand and respond to the same need in others. You must be careful to exercise God's wisdom. Physical limitations may keep you from ministering to others as much as you would like. Your limitations may, in fact, allow you to minister only in very small ways. It does seem, however, that God honors your desire and attempt to do so.

"It seems, Father, that I can do nothing for others. Give me the desire and ability to minister in whatever small way You choose."

Day 143

> *Those who trust in the LORD*
> *Are as Mount Zion, which cannot be moved but abides forever.*
> *As the mountains surround Jerusalem,*
> *So the LORD surrounds His people*
> *From this time forth and forever.*
> *Psalm 125:1-2*

In these verses God encourages His people with two comparisons involving mountains. The first comparison likens God's people to Mount Zion. This is the mountain most closely associated with Jerusalem. It is very special to God, illustrated by the fact that there are several psalms written about it. God determined that Mount Zion would abide forever and that it would not be moved. This comparison speaks of stability. God says that those who trust in Him are like this mountain. They will be stable, unshaken, and unconquerable. No one will be able to destroy them.

The second comparison speaks of God's surrounding His people just like mountains surround Jerusalem. He is using a geographic reference that would have been very familiar to His people. When they went to Jerusalem to worship, they had to go up. This comparison speaks of protection and care. The mountains surrounding Jerusalem are like the surrounding arms of God around His people. He is on every side. He forms a barrier against those who desire to attack. As God surrounds His people, He holds them within the circle of His care. He shelters them in a place of safety.

Both comparisons use the word *forever*. God's care for His people will never end. He will never neglect them, nor will He ever stop watching over them. They are stable and protected under His care.

"Father, thank You that You will always care for me. Thank You that You will always hold me firmly and that You will always surround me with Your protection."

Day 144

"Just as the Father has loved Me, I have also loved you; abide in My love."
John 15:9

God's love for us is a wonderful comfort. While we are unable to fully comprehend God's love, the Bible does share some amazing insights about that love. In the verse cited above, we see that Christ loves us in the same way that the Father loves Him. We have no doubt that the Father loved Christ very deeply. That love is perfect and is displayed in a relationship that has been constantly peaceful and eternally unified. How could there be any greater love than that? Christ loves us with that kind of love.

John 17:23 tells us that God loves us the same way He loves Christ. We have the same foundation for comparison: the love of the Father for the Son. We have already seen that Jesus loves us that way; now we see that the Father also loves us that way. Both the Father and the Son love us with the very love expressed within the persons of the Godhead. If that seems impossible, we must remember that God's love is perfect. He loves perfectly no matter who the recipient is. There is no way for His love to become any better than it already is.

How great can love be? In John 15:13, Jesus reveals the greatest expression of love. He says there is no greater expression of love than someone willingly giving his life for the one he loves. That is exactly what Christ did for us. He laid down His life for us so that we could live. There is no greater expression of love in all the world. The quality of the love expressed by Jesus is exactly the quality of love expressed by the Father. They both love us that deeply – with the absolutely most spectacular type of love that exists.

"Father, I do not understand such deep love, but I thank You for it. Day after day I desperately long for love, and You offer it to me freely."

Day 145

The LORD is my light and my salvation;
Whom shall I fear?
The LORD is the defense of my life;
Whom shall I dread?
Psalm 27:1

God is our Light. He provides all of the illumination we need in order to see our surroundings. God provides light in a way similar to how the sun functions. When the sun rises in the morning, the darkness disappears. Things that were completely hidden or were only bulky shadows become bright and clear. It is easy to see what objects are and even the details that make them up. In the sunlight we are more cheerful, and we are able to function more effectively.

These descriptions of the sun powerfully illustrate how God is the light for our lives. Without Him we can't see clearly. Life before us seems like vague shadows and frightening gloom. In the darkness and confusion, we stumble and fall. We cannot make forward progress because we can't see either a destination or the path for reaching it. With no light to cheer our way, we are despondent and dull. It is an awful thing to live without light.

When God comes into our lives, everything is radically transformed. With God's light, we are finally able to understand things, including the purpose of life itself. Things start to become clear and make sense. We have guidance for our lives, and we can see the path to follow. We are no longer blindsided by unseen obstacles. Instead of a dreary and dull journey, we can walk joyfully in the radiant light that God provides. Living a life with God really is like the difference between night and day.

"Thank You, Father, for the many times You have kept me from stumbling. Thank You for lighting my path and brightening my days. There is no light more effective than You."

Day 146

The law of his God is in his heart;
His steps do not slip.
Psalm 37:31

There are paths that are difficult to walk. It is one thing to manage to make our way down a treacherous path, all the time stumbling and falling. We may make it to the end, but we are left bruised and spattered with mud. It is an entirely different experience to walk that path safely, without slipping and without being injured or soiled. To walk a dangerous path victoriously is a difficult thing, because our feet are constantly threatening to slip.

If we are to walk such a path without our steps slipping, we must have the law of God in our hearts. We must be seeking to learn and follow His truth. It is God's Word that will establish our steps and protect us from iniquity. When we are firmly grounded in God's Word, sin will not have power over us, and our feet will not slip. When we try to walk in our own way and in our own strength, we will fall. If, however, we walk in God's way and with His strength, only then will we be able to walk without slipping.

What a challenge is before us to examine ourselves as we set out on each new path and each new day's journey! We will not be able to walk successfully without God. We will stumble on the path if we allow sin to gain a foothold. We must earnestly seek to love and follow God's Word, because it is His Word that gives light and guidance to our path. We need the Bible to keep us from the sin that threatens to pull us down. Any path, no matter how treacherous, is possible when we have God's Word to keep us from slipping.

"My path is slick and slimy. My feet are constantly sliding. Help me, Father, to cling to Your Word so that my steps can be stabilized and my heart can be cleansed."

Day 147

But the vessel that he was making of clay was spoiled in the hand of the potter; so he remade it into another vessel, as it pleased the potter to make.
Jeremiah 18:4

As a human, I am hopelessly flawed. I have defects and impurities. As strong as my desire may be and as hard as I may try, I cannot come out perfect. The only hope for me is to be placed in the hands of a Master Craftsman who can form me properly.

If the truth be told, I don't even know exactly what He wants to make of me. Even if I could do something to mold myself, I would not end up being what He has planned for me. He knows what type of vessel will please Him. He knows precisely what He needs and envisions exactly how it should be shaped.

With His end product in mind, the Potter considers the spoiled lump of clay in His hand. He can take what is ruined and hopeless and make it into something worthwhile and pleasing. That transformation can only happen if He changes what I am. Right now I'm the wrong shape, and I must allow Him to break me down so He can make me into the right shape. Being broken is not easy or pleasant, but that does not mean that it is bad.

When the Master Craftsman remakes me, I will never be the same again. I might always feel humbled and subdued by the breaking He has done. I might always be aware of how different I am. I may feel the loss of something that had always seemed a part of who I was. All of these are necessary; they are God's way of making something He can use. I must continually recognize my need to keep yielding to Him. I must be workable and pliable clay, constantly allowing Him to do the work without resisting. I must not fight being broken, but rather trust that His breaking and remaking will produce something useful and valuable to Him.

> *"Father, would You break the spoiled me? Would You remake*
> *me into a new vessel that pleases You?"*

The Vessel (Sonnet 20)
The potter sits intently at his wheel,
His full attention given to the jar.
Then suddenly his probing fingers feel
A flaw or lump or pebble that would mar.
The jar is spoiled; it must now be remade.
His hands reduce the clay into a ball.
His skill is followed and His will obeyed;
The clay is pliant, yielding at His call.
The potter works to press and shape and squeeze;
The quality no longer will be poor.
The final product is designed to please –
Without a doubt, far better than before.
Effective when the clay remains the clay,
And lets the skillful potter have his way.

Day 148

For if these qualities are yours and are increasing, they render you neither useless nor
unfruitful in the true knowledge of our Lord Jesus Christ.
II Peter 1:8

Have you felt that you are useless and that you aren't accomplishing anything worthwhile? Have you wondered what possible value God sees in you? It would be a disaster for a Christian to be useless and have no impact for Christ, and you may feel that you fall into that category.

Being sick doesn't make you worthless. God says there is an assured way to avoid being useless or unfruitful. God declares that you are useful and you bear fruit when certain qualities are found in you, especially when those qualities are increasing. Second Peter 1:5-7 gives the list of seven qualities, and being sick does not prevent you from growing in any of them. In fact, your illness can be used by God to increase these qualities. Your illness can also be a powerful setting in which to display them.

The first quality is moral excellence. Are you growing in making right choices and in being above reproach? Second is knowledge. Are you learning more about your God? Third is self-control. Are you learning to more consistently hold your tongue, keep your temper under control, and stabilize your emotions? The fourth quality is perseverance. Are you growing in your ability to withstand discomfort and keep going day after day? Fifth is godliness. Are you being less influenced by the world and drawn closer to God? Sixth is brotherly kindness. Are you learning to speak kindly to those around you and to do little things to brighten their lives? The final quality is love. Are you growing in your love for others? Your trial is likely bringing growth in several of these areas. God says that if these qualities are increasing, you are useful to Him and you are bearing fruit for Him.

"Help me, Father, to be useful and fruitful by growing in moral excellence, knowledge, self-control, perseverance, godliness, brotherly kindness, and love."

Day 149

But we have this treasure in earthen vessels, so that the surpassing greatness of the power will be of God and not from ourselves.
II Corinthians 4:7

Humans live in weak, earthly vessels that are affected by trials. In Second Corinthians 4:8-11, Paul admits to several manifestations of that realization. He says that he was being afflicted in every way. He was perplexed, without seeing the way out. He was persecuted, struck down, and in constant danger of death. He faced the pressure of many afflictions, and he did not understand them or know what to do.

Paul's afflictions did not overwhelm him, however. In spite of the afflictions, he was not crushed or in despair. He wasn't forsaken or destroyed. His trials were definitely hard, but they were not completely overwhelming. They did not have victory over him.

How could Paul remain in such desperate situations without being conquered by them? God made all the difference. For example, Paul was at a loss for what to do, but not at an utter loss, because he knew that God knew what to do. In each of his challenges, an ever-present and all-knowing God was with him. That fact kept Paul under control in his trials. It wasn't his human strength that got him through.

Because our weak, earthly vessels can't handle trials, our trials serve the purpose of displaying God's power. In circumstances such as these, it becomes obvious that the incredibly great power seen in us has to be God's and not our own. Our very human weakness is an opportunity to display God's greatness as He handles situations that are far beyond our ability. Not only are we put in a position in which we can exalt God, but we also have the wonderful privilege of seeing God's power manifested in us.

"I'm too weak, Father. I can't do it. Show forth Your great power by doing in my life what I could never do in my own strength."

Day 150

For whatever was written in earlier times was written for our instruction, so that through perseverance and the encouragement of the Scriptures we might have hope.
Romans 15:4

This verse reveals two things about the Scripture. It was written for the purpose of instructing us, and it was also written for the purpose of giving us hope. At the time the book of Romans was written, the Scripture referred back to was the Old Testament. The instruction of the Old Testament comes as we read God's instructions to His people, as we see those people respond correctly or incorrectly to His instructions, and as we watch God respond to their choices. This instruction lays the groundwork for the hope that the Scripture provides. While we are instructed by the stories of those who responded both correctly and incorrectly to God, we are encouraged specifically by the stories of those who responded correctly to God.

Hebrews 11 is perhaps the most extensive New Testament commentary regarding the Old Testament characters. Whether we read about those characters in Hebrews or in the Old Testament itself, we find two encouraging themes that are repeated often. God always keeps His promises and God always rewards faith. Time after time we see God keeping His promises. Regardless of how doubtful or impossible the Old Testament promises seemed, God always completed what He said He would do. He was always faithful to His people.

Time after time we also see God rewarding faith. God asked His people to do some pretty crazy things: pick up a snake by the tail, walk between towering walls of water, use pitchers and trumpets to fight against a large army, wait for birds to deliver food, and many more. When those people obeyed in faith, God always rewarded that faith and showed His power.

As we read about God's faithful dealings in the Old Testament, we are encouraged. The Scripture provides hope as we realize that God is the same today as He was then. He is still just as faithful. He will continue to keep His promises, and He will continue to reward faith.

"For thousands of years, Father, You have taken care of Your people. You have proven Yourself over and over again. You are certainly worthy of my trust today."

Day 151

And what is the surpassing greatness of His power toward us who believe. These are in accordance with the working of the strength of His might.
Ephesians 1:19

An illness quickly shows us how weak and helpless we are. We are challenged in performing the simplest tasks. Our mildest attempts to re-enter life leave us exhausted. Even physically fit people lose their robust physique. In addition to physical weakness, our inner self also struggles. Our emotions are unstable, and our thoughts are undisciplined. We struggle to resist temptations. Weakness pervades every aspect of our person. The good news is that our strength does not have to come from ourselves. Instead we can rely on the power of God.

Paul described the power of God as being surpassing great. It is grand and magnificent beyond anything we have seen before and beyond anything that we can imagine. God has used His power to do some amazing things. Probably the two most cited examples in Scripture are the creation of the world and the raising of Christ from the dead. Doing those two tasks requires more power than we can imagine. In fact, we wouldn't consider either of them possible even with an assembled team of the world's mightiest forces.

God extends this incredible power toward us. It is His power that allows us to live with Him. It is His power that gives us protection. It is His power that enables us to continue on through our weakness. When we consider our inward struggles, it is also His power that strengthens us in the inner man. We could not do any of these things on our own, but we don't have to. We have the amazing resource of God's power, and He manifests that power in our lives.

"Thank You, Father, for Your great power. Thank You for strengthening me with it. We both know the task is too hard for me, so I thank You for Your help."

Day 152

Oh, the depth of the riches both of the wisdom and knowledge of God! How unsearchable are His judgments and unfathomable His ways!
Romans 11:33

There is no question that human understanding is limited. There are many, many things that we do not know and cannot understand. There are many situations in which we are puzzled about what to do. God is not so limited. He knows and understands everything. Things that are far beyond human understanding don't even scratch the surface of God's wisdom. His wisdom and knowledge are so incredibly rich that we cannot imagine the extent of them. His decisions are beyond our ability to figure out. They are based on such incredibly deep wisdom that our human minds are not able to make sense of them. The paths that God works out in our lives are not capable of being comprehended by man.

God not only understands all of these things, but He was wise enough to come up with the complex thoughts and plans in the first place. With His astronomical knowledge and infinite wisdom, God is in control of all things. God has never made a mistake or been caught by surprise. We can safely trust a God this wise. He has all the wisdom necessary to make the right decisions. Along with His immense wisdom, He also has tremendous love so that He wants to help us and unlimited power to be able to do so. There is no way that God is going to do the wrong thing. Whether we understand or not, we can trust Him to do what is right.

Don't we trust our doctors in this way? We allow them to do painful procedures, dangerous operations, and uncomfortable treatments. We face side effects worse than the actual disease. Why? We are looking forward to the end result, and we trust the doctors to use the proper, though painful, steps to bring that about. God is far wiser in knowing the best steps for reaching His desired result. Though the individual steps along the way may be difficult or distasteful, His wise plan will accomplish something beautiful in the end.

"Father, I've been trying to understand what is beyond my comprehension. Help me to trust Your great wisdom instead."

Day 153

But after we had already suffered and been mistreated in Philippi, as you know, we had the boldness in our God to speak to you the gospel of God amid much opposition.
I Thessalonians 2:2

Affliction can make us want to give up. When struggles drag on, we want to stop fighting, and we refuse to put forth any more effort. God doesn't want us to give up. He can help us to overcome affliction and to continue on in spite of it.

Paul and Silas had some very rough days in Philippi. They were harassed for many days, being followed everywhere they went by a demon-possessed girl. When they finally responded by delivering the girl from the spirit, they were seized by her owners. These men dragged Paul and Silas to the authorities, where a mob testified against them. Without even a fair trial, they were beaten, thrown into jail, and placed in stocks. Soon afterward they moved on to Thessalonica, where they continued to face opposition. A mob set the entire city in an uproar, blamed it on Paul and Silas, and chased them out of town. Then they followed Paul to his next stop and caused trouble there also.

After all of this trouble, wouldn't you think Paul and Silas might be tempted to give up? In spite of the cruel treatment they had received in Philippi, and in the face of ongoing opposition in Thessalonica, they continued to preach the gospel. They faithfully continued to serve God.

Affliction should not stop us from doing what God has asked us to do. Instead of faltering under continuing trials, we must remain faithful. God can give us the strength to persevere. He can equip us to persevere until the job is done.

"Father, You know how many times a day I want to give up. This situation is just so hard. Give me Your strength to continue faithfully in what You have for me."

School's Not Over
The student hurried off to school
With thoughts of all he'd do and learn.
To read would be a helpful tool,
And other triumphs he would earn.

He learned of A and B and C,
And one plus one must equal two.
A student bright and good was he
And learned what teacher told him to.

Now off to play. Oh, school was fun!
And what a scholar he did make.
"But hold on, lad; you are not done.
For that was only recess break."

He went to school all day, till three.
Two days, a week, then had a test.
He learned much more, this busy bee.
At Christmastime he took a rest.

Oh, what relief, for that was work,
And now at last he took a break.
"It's January – you can't shirk.
To think school done was your mistake."

So then he learned to read a book,
To add, subtract, and write down words.
And what an effort all that took;
He's thinking school is for the birds."

135

Comes summer and at last he's free.
What joy to make it through the year.
"But wait, my son, pay heed to me.
There are eleven more, I fear."

Year after year he filled his brain;
He learned each lesson, read each book.
His mind could hardly stand the strain,
But he gave effort - all it took.

Until at last with cap in hands
He's finished all that work and strife.
There's so much now he understands;
Today he starts to live his life.

Go off to college? No, not that!
He's had enough; he wants no more.
He has the answers all down pat;
His brain is filled with facts galore.

But off he goes for four more years.
The work is harder, more intense.
At times it nearly leads to tears -
The projects, papers are immense.

With focused study, knowledge grew.
The scope of things to learn was vast -
A new expanse of what he knew.
Four years are over – done at last!

So long in school – it finally ends.
With knowledge now he'll seek a job -
For years of study make amends.
With joy his heart begins to throb.

But then – it still is not enough?
He should pursue advanced degree?
To study more – oh, this is tough.
He fears more books his end will be.

So many years have passed him by -
Not easy years, but filled with toil.
"Please let me just be done," his cry,
"From one more lesson I recoil."

So sad he does not see the worth
Of hard-fought lessons brought his way.
His training gives success its birth;
The things he's learned will make the day.

> *Are we not too much like this lad?*
> *Content to learn a thing or two.*
> *When tiny bits of "school" we've had,*
> *We think there's nothing left to do.*

We've no idea of what's left,
Of how much further we must go.
Though knowledge sadly is bereft,
We have no yearning more to grow.

> *The simplest lessons come at first.*
> *Though needed, they are not so deep.*
> *The ones of value seem the worst;*
> *To learn them, faith must take a leap.*

By choice we would too soon drop out.
No, we must learn to stay in school.
When hard – press on! (we cannot pout)
Till work is done and learning's full.

> *Our Teacher knows how much we need;*
> *The lessons are by His design.*
> *The length of years He has decreed;*
> *His school is best – the bottom line.*

Day 154

> *Cast your burden upon the LORD and He will sustain you;*
> *He will never allow the righteous to be shaken.*
> *Psalm 55:22*

Throughout your life you have carried some heavy burdens. Perhaps in your current situation you acknowledge that you have never been required to carry a burden quite this heavy before. You have learned how weighty an ongoing physical problem can be, and you've also learned how much greater the burden is than just the physical aspect. This burden is more than just heavy and demanding. It is worse than simply strength-sapping and challenging. This burden is crushing. It is impossible. It threatens to completely destroy you.

What can you do with such an overpowering burden? Throw it on God. God invites you to cast that burden on Him and allow Him to carry it for you. Oh, what a relief it is to surrender that crushing burden to someone who is much stronger!

Perhaps even when the burden is lifted, you continue to feel vulnerable. Perhaps you recognize the danger in having carried something too heavy for too long. Even though the burden is now removed from your shoulders, you have been pushed beyond your limits and you are about to collapse. Here's more good news: not only can God carry your burden, but He can also hold you up.

No matter how fragile you are, and no matter how close to complete exhaustion, God can sustain you. He can carry both your burden and you. His arms are never too weak to do that. God can give you incredible stability and keep you from ever being shaken. How does He do that? Is it not possible that, in order to keep us from shaking or falling, God holds us in His strong arms? God can hold us close to Himself, firmly supported within His arms, so that even if we faint, we will not actually fall or even move. We are safe and secure in His arms.

"Father, I feel myself about to collapse under this crushing weight. I can't hold it anymore, and I can't even stand up any more. Father, take the burden on Yourself and hold me tight in Your loving arms."

Day 155

For as many as are the promises of God, in Him they are yes; therefore also through Him is our Amen to the glory of God through us.
II Corinthians 1:20

Have people let you down? Have they promised to call you or come for a visit only to leave you waiting and alone? Have the offers of cleaning, transportation, and meals fallen through? Do you doubt whether those promised prayers are really being offered? All of the above scenarios are possible, because people will fail. That is just a fact.

God, on the other hand, cannot and will not fail. God always keeps His promises. It matters not how many promises God makes, because He is able to keep them all. When you come to God with one of His promises and ask Him to keep it, it is a sure thing. A request like that will always be answered with a "yes" because God will always do what He has said He will do. In First Kings 8:56, Solomon blessed the Lord for His goodness and reminded the people that God had done *everything* that He had promised to Moses. He stated that not one single word of God's good promise had failed.

God keeps His promises completely and thoroughly. He doesn't keep them half-way. He doesn't keep them mostly or sort of. He keeps every word and every detail. There is nothing that He has promised that is impossible for Him or that He will fail to do.

So how many promises will God keep? According to our verse, He will keep as many as there are. How many is that? Why not start writing them down? Make a list as you find them in Scripture. You know that God can keep them all, and a list of them would give you hope to cling to and something to ask Him to do. Then all you have to do is wait for Him to answer with a "yes."

"Father, thank You that You are dependable, reliable, and faithful. Thank You that I can believe every word You say and every promise You make."

Day 156

The LORD is my light and my salvation;
Whom shall I fear?
The LORD is the defense of my life;
Whom shall I dread?
Psalm 27:1

David called God *"the defense of my life."* God is the fortification that defends our lives. He is the reason that our lives continue. We are not kept alive due to good genes, good nutrition, or exercise. We are not kept alive by doctors, medicines, surgeries, or any other available resource. From a human perspective, all of those things play a part, but in reality it is God Himself who allows our lives to continue.

Our human bodies are vulnerable and frail. There are so many things that could go wrong with them. We are susceptible to accident and disease. There are many ways in which we could very quickly or easily die. Without God's defending us, any one of those potential dangers could cause our death. Not one of us has the ability to extend his own life.

When God defends us, however, the story is completely different. If God chooses to prolong our lives, He can do so to the bafflement of those who look on. Because God is the defense of our lives, we can survive even when facing the greatest of odds. We can continue to live through circumstances that seem hopeless. When the doctors have given up, and when all of the medicines have been tried, God is still able to keep us. Our very lives are upheld by God's strength. We will live just as long as God chooses for us – not a day more and not a day less.

"Father, in the midst of all the resources You have provided, may I not forget that my life is in Your hands. With or without medicines, You are the defender of my life."

Day 157

No temptation has overtaken you but such as is common to man; and God is faithful, who will not allow you to be tempted beyond what you are able, but with the temptation will provide the way of escape also, so that you will be able to endure it.
I Corinthians 10:13

I find myself in the midst of a fierce battle. I look around me as it rages, and I see victory as impossible. It seems that I am too weak and that I cannot win. I am about to be finished off.

Indeed, that is how it seems, but that is not what God says. For God no battle is impossible. My particular temptation is not even unique to me. All temptations are common to the human race. I can't put myself in a unique category and claim to suffer as no one else has. Others have faced this same battle and have emerged victorious. How can that be?

God is faithful, and He won't let the temptation go too far. He won't send too much or allow more than I can handle. He does not say that it will be easy or pleasant. I do have to endure, but God will be my help. So I cannot give up or think the situation hopeless. It is never hopeless. God will provide the way to escape. I just need to keep enduring until I find the escape that God has provided. God always provides a way out.

No matter how strong the test that comes my way, it is possible to endure because God Himself provides the help. God wants victory, and He wants it even more than I do. Victory in the trial brings glory to Him. So the victory will come. I don't know how or when; that's the hard part. Perhaps I must continue fighting until my last ounce of strength is expended. Perhaps I will come close to being destroyed, but God will deliver. This is not impossible.

"I don't see the escape, Father, but You say it is there. Lead me to it and help me to be faithful until You bring the victory."

Day 158

Simon Peter answered Him, "Lord, to whom shall we go? You have words of eternal life."
John 6:68

This verse follows the account of the feeding of the five thousand. Many multitudes had been following Jesus, and He did a great miracle in their sight. In His teaching that followed the incident, Jesus taught some difficult things. The Jews struggled with Jesus' teachings, and many Jews stopped following Jesus because of those statements which they could not understand. Jesus asked the twelve disciples if they wanted to go away as well, and Peter gave this wonderful answer. Where else would they go? How could they turn from following God? Jesus was their source of life and hope. He was the only way, and they must follow Him.

We also face things that are difficult and that we don't understand. We could turn away and stop following God; many have. When we stop to consider, however, how can we turn from God? He is the only way. He is the source of life that we need. His words are the only ones that can help us. Where else could we find help and hope? Other people, other philosophies, and other tactics will all fall short. They will leave us empty. When other ways are so inadequate, why would we even want to try any other way? Turning from God would leave us completely without a source of real help. We may not understand what God is doing or what He is trying to tell us, but nowhere else will we be able to find answers that will help as much. How can we turn from God? We must follow Him.

"Father, in the midst of my lack of understanding,
please don't let me turn away from You, the source of life."

Where Else? (Sonnet 19)

O, struggling sinner, would you go away?
And does the gospel seem too hard to hear?
But Jesus' sacrifice provides the way,
And only He can save you from your fear.
O, faithless foll'wer, would you turn aside?
And does confusion leave you in despair?
Just hear God's Word, and it will faith provide,
For you can only find the answers there.
O, suff'ring servant, would you now give up?
And do you deem Him now not worth the pain?
In tender love He'll help you drink the cup,
And only He can turn your trial to gain.
Don't turn from God, for where else could you go?
Through Christ alone the words of life you'll know.

Day 159

For the LORD God is a sun and shield;
The LORD gives grace and glory;
No good thing does He withhold from those who walk uprightly.
Psalm 84:11

God gives characteristically to His children. Giving is part of His nature. As a sun, He gives warmth, illumination, cheer, and life itself. As a shield, He gives protection from danger and encouragement in the face of fear. He gives grace, the bestowal of His kindness and favor. He gives glory; He gives men honor and lifts them up beyond what they deserve. All of these are examples of how God, simply because of who He is, gives good things to His children.

God gives actively to those He loves. It would be possible for someone to take neither a positive nor a negative position towards others. Although that person may not cause harm, he wouldn't give anything helpful either. God is not like that. He is not neutral and disinterested; He doesn't stand idly by or casually allow gifts to fall from His hands based on whim or fate. God gives on purpose.

God gives willingly to those He cares about. A stingy or selfish person would want to keep as much as possible for himself. He would deliberately refrain from giving to others so that he could have more. God is not stingy or cruel. He never withholds good things from His children. He doesn't deny them the things that are best for them. God doesn't keep back blessings. If there is something good that His children need, God gives it.

God gives appropriately to His dear ones. He doesn't give thoughtless gifts or mediocre gifts. God's gifts aren't awkward or useless. No, the gifts that God gives are good gifts. God is an excellent judge of what is good, and He chooses His gifts very carefully.

God gives abundantly to His followers. God doesn't stop with just one gift or even two. God does not withhold *any* good thing that His followers need. If someone needs one hundred good gifts, God will give them all. Whatever God determines to be good, He will give, regardless of how big or costly the gift is. God will keep giving until His children have all that they need.

"Thank You, Father, for Your many, many gifts. Help me to let You choose the gifts that are best for me. May I accept them willingly from Your hand."

Day 160

When the Lord saw her, He felt compassion for her, and said to her, "Do not weep."
Luke 7:13

God is a God of compassion. At times we may find it hard to comprehend God's compassion because He is not a "real" person that we can see and touch. When Christ lived on earth, He was the flesh-and-blood representation of God. Christ demonstrated for us what God's compassion looks like. He put God's compassion into practical terms. What is most notable about Christ's compassion is that He always put His compassion into action. Christ met the needs of the people for whom He had compassion.

Jesus had compassion on large groups of people. When Jesus saw the crowds who were distressed and without a shepherd to guide them, He responded by teaching them many things (Mark 6:34). He saw another large crowd and had compassion on them. On this occasion He responded by healing those who were sick (Matthew 14:14). On a third occasion Christ had compassion on the crowds because they had no food to eat and needed nourishment. Jesus responded by providing food (Mark 8:2).

Jesus also had compassion on individuals. When two blind men called out to Jesus for help, He had compassion on them and restored their sight (Matthew 20:34). A leper approached Jesus and asked for help. Jesus expressed His compassion by cleansing the leprosy (Mark 1:41). Jesus had compassion on a demon-possessed man. He responded by casting out the demons and restoring the man to a normal life (Mark 5:19). Jesus met a woman whose only son had just died. In His compassion for her, He responded first by speaking comforting words and then by raising her son back to life (Luke 7:13). We know that God is compassionate. These examples reveal to us how God's heart of compassion is expressed in action.

"Even though You are not a person that I can see and feel, thank You that Your compassion is very real. Thank You for acting on my behalf because of Your compassion."

Day 161

But our God is in the heavens;
He does whatever He pleases.
Psalm 115:3

People trust in some pretty crazy and unreliable things. Psalm 115 describes people who trust in idols. The idols in which they trust are powerless; they cannot speak, see, hear, smell, feel, walk, or make noise. They can do nothing. The things people trust in today are just as powerless. There is only one true and trusted source of help, and that is God.

God is not lifeless, helpless, or powerless. God is different from all the other sources of trust. God can actually do what He intends to do. There is no stopping of God's plan. When He decides something, it will happen. When God puts something into motion, it cannot be stopped. The negative aspect is also true. If God does not want something to happen, there is no power on earth that can make it happen.

This concept has tremendous application. Whatever has happened in my life is what God has been pleased to do. He has accomplished what He intended. If my situation was not what God wanted, He would have stopped it. No person, no power, no fate or coincidence is strong enough to override God. If any danger or tragedy which is not in God's plan threatens me, God can stop it in its tracks. It will proceed no further than what God decides.

This concept is true of the past and present, and it is also true of the future. Whatever pleases God is what will happen. If God wants to give healing, He can do so against impossible odds. If God wants to take me to heaven, no doctor or treatment can force me to stay. God will always do exactly what He intends, and I can rest in His plan.

"I don't know the future, Father, but I know that You control it. Help me to rest in Your unstoppable ability to accomplish Your plan."

Day 162

By faith Noah, being warned by God about things not yet seen, in reverence prepared an ark for the salvation of his household, by which he condemned the world, and became an heir of the righteousness which is according to faith.
Hebrews 11:7

Hebrews 11 provides a long list of people who faced a variety of challenging life situations. In the midst of those challenges, God demanded faith and obedience. Noah had faith, believing a flood would come though it had never rained before. He obeyed by building an ark.

Abraham had faith to follow God from his homeland even though he didn't know his destination. He obeyed by leaving his home and wandering for years. Sarah had faith that God would be faithful to keep His promise of a child. She conceived and bore Isaac. Abraham also had faith that God could raise his son Isaac from the dead. He obeyed by preparing to offer his son as a sacrifice. Jacob had faith that God would bless his seed. Jacob demonstrated his faith by imparting his own blessing to his sons. Joseph had faith that his people would leave Egypt. He gave instructions that his bones should be carried with them when they left.

Moses' parents had faith that God could spare their son from the king's decree. They hid Moses to keep him alive. Moses had faith that God would reward His people. He rejected Egypt and chose God's people. Moses also had faith that God would lead Israel to the Promised Land. He demonstrated that faith with obedience, leaving Egypt and passing through the Red Sea. Israel had faith that God could conquer Jericho. They obeyed by marching around the city.

Many other men and women of faith suffered great things, some seeing victory and some seeing only apparent defeat. The results did not always seem positive, but God always accomplished His plan through the faithful obedience of His people. Whether or not the suffering people actually saw the results, all of them knew that God would keep His promise and accomplish His plans. They had God's approval because of their service and obedience in faith. What is the message for us today? We too must have faith and obey.

"I don't see what's going on, Father, or how this will work out. Help me to have faith in You and to simply obey what You ask me to do."

Day 163

Blessed be the Lord, who daily bears our burden,
The God who is our salvation.
Psalm 68:19

You do not have an ordinary, every-day illness. If you did, you would wake up one day feeling not so great. You would feel lousy for a couple of days and would lie on the couch, alternately napping and watching television. The third day you would start to feel better. That evening you would be ready for a decent meal and joking with the family. After a good night's sleep, you would wake up the next morning feeling fine and ready to go back to work.

That sounds like a nice scenario, doesn't it? Instead, you have symptoms that persist week after week and year after year. When you do have a better day, you know it's only a temporary lull before more of the same. Your illness never leaves. It affects you every day. Its limitations and frustrations are constant, and you bear that burden without reprieve. Don't you wish that just for one day you could be free from the physical, mental, and emotional burden of your illness?

This verse gives you great hope. God bears your burden, and He does it every day. Each new day when you wake up with a burden too heavy to carry, God is there to take it from your shoulders. When a new week begins and the burden persists, God still picks it up. Each month as the burden grows heavier, God continues to carry it. When those months melt into years, God is still there. It does not matter how many days you have that burden; God can always carry it. Your burden is ugly and it is heavy, but you don't have to carry it – ever. Although your illness affects you every single day, God can also carry the burden for you every single day.

"Oh, Father, this burden is too heavy for me, and I have carried it for too many days. Please take it from me and carry it on Your strong shoulders."

Day 164

"Ah Lord GOD! Behold, You have made the heavens and the earth by Your great power and by Your outstretched arm! Nothing is too difficult for You."
Jeremiah 32:17

Is it true that nothing is too hard for God? What if God promises something, but all of His actions seem to be in direct conflict with His promise? Jeremiah found himself in such a situation. For over forty years he had prophesied the destruction of Jerusalem. Now the destruction was imminent, and the besieging army had already placed ramps against the city walls. In this situation, God told Jeremiah that a cousin would come and ask him to buy a piece of land; Jeremiah was to proceed with the purchase.

The command seemed ludicrous, and Jeremiah's mind was filled with questions. He wondered how God could speak of the owning of property when He was actually in the process of removing the property from the hands of the people. God was bringing about the very opposite of what His instruction to Jeremiah seemed to indicate. Why should Jeremiah purchase a piece of land that was about to be snatched away by the enemy? God's answer was that the land would be restored and that God's people would own it again.

In this confusing and seemingly impossible situation, Jeremiah recognized truth. He remembered that God was the Creator of the heavens and earth. The creation which is so vast and incomprehensible to the human mind was created very easily by the hand of God. If God could do that – make incredible beauty and intricate complexity out of nothing – then He could also keep His word to Jeremiah.

Soon afterward God confirmed this truth to Jeremiah by giving him some reminders. God had kept His word in the past. He had told Jeremiah that his cousin would come with the offer of land, and he had in fact done so. God was keeping His word in the present. He had said that the city would be destroyed, and it was happening before Jeremiah's eyes. God would just as faithfully keep His word in the future, and He would restore the land to Israel. Jeremiah's God is still God today. No matter how impossible a situation looks, God's Word can be trusted. Nothing is too difficult for God. He is powerful enough to fulfill all that He is bold enough to declare.

"Father, forgive my doubt. Things look impossible to me, but You are not limited by anything. Help me not to doubt Your Word."

Day 165

"If you abide in Me, and My words abide in you,
ask whatever you wish, and it will be done for you."
John 15:7

Prayer is a wonderful privilege that is available to us. It is a resource we do not use as often or as effectively as we should. God invites us to come to Him and ask what we will. He tells us that whatever the request is, He will hear it. In some ways, it would be nice to have guaranteed answers to all of our requests. We would like to receive everything we ask for.

When we stop to consider, however, we realize that the "genie in a bottle" scenario wouldn't really work. How often have we desired something, only to find out later how harmful it would have been? God wisely places some requirements on the requests He will grant. We must be abiding in Christ and have His words abiding in us (John 15:7). We must ask with faith, not doubting (James 1:6). We must ask according to His will (I John 5:14). We are to ask in the name of Christ (John 16:23).

If these things are true, then God will honor our faith. If we are asking with Christ's words permeating our hearts, with knowledge of God's will, and for the things that Christ Himself would ask, God will surely hear and answer those prayers. If we don't know God's will, He still invites us to ask, but we should pray as Christ did, with the concession *"Not My will, but Yours be done."*

There is no limit to the prayers God can answer. In answer to prayer, God granted children to barren women like Hannah and Elizabeth. He delivered His people from overwhelming attacks. He rescued Peter from jail. He restored sight, healed leprosy, healed the lame, and brought the dead back to life. He made the sun go backwards in the sky. He brought years of drought and then abundance of rain. He did all of these because people dared to ask incredible and impossible things of God.

"Father, may I be filled with boldness to bring my requests to You, filled with Your will so I know what to ask, and filled with faith to see Your answers."

Day 166

For the LORD God is a sun and shield;
The LORD gives grace and glory;
No good thing does He withhold from those who walk uprightly.
Psalm 84:11

God is a Sun. This illustration speaks of both what He is and what He does. The meaning of the Hebrew word helps to reveal what God is like; the word singles out the brilliance of the sun. From an earthly perspective, nothing else shines as brightly. Whether we look at the sun directly, or whether it reflects off the water, the snow, or a window, we cannot maintain a prolonged gaze at the sun. It is so radiant that it makes us squint, close our eyes, or look away.

Similarly, no one has as much glory as God. He is also brilliant, to the extent that we cannot look at Him without being dazzled and amazed. If we tried to fully gaze on Him for an extended time, we would not be able to do so. God's brilliance would be too much for us to see and too overwhelming for us to fully consider. As much as we appreciate God, our human limitations do not allow us to do so fully.

The sun also illustrates what God does. The sun sustains life. Though the sun is only one thing, it is one thing that we cannot do without, either on a personal level or on a global level. Without it there would only be death and desolation. The sun provides light. It allows us to see and to carry out our life without stumbling or groping blindly. The sun provides warmth, both internally and externally. It keeps our bodies warm so that we don't freeze to death, and it also warms our souls and brings us joy.

Like the sun, God is absolutely vital to life. There would be no life without Him. God is so critical that comparing Him to the sun illustrates well the dependence that all people have on Him. Like the sun, God also provides blessings for life. He gives us light so we know how to live. He gives us the warmth of His love. He encourages our spirits and gives us joy. Without God, there would be no life.

> *"Father, You are so amazing that I cannot comprehend it. Help me not to forget*
> *Your brilliance, nor to forget how much I need You.*
> *Only You are the source of life and blessings."*

Day 167

> *For His anger is but for a moment,*
> *His favor is for a lifetime;*
> *Weeping may last for the night,*
> *But a shout of joy comes in the morning.*
> *Psalm 30:5*

We do sometimes find ourselves under God's anger. This involves punishment and correction for sin, but perhaps it could also refer to God's molding and discipline. Those growing times can be harshly unpleasant, and it does seem sometimes that we are under the frown of God. Weeping accompanies these times, as we struggle to respond correctly to God's prompting and to become what He wants us to become.

Sometimes this harsh discipline is necessary, but God does not discipline us for eternity or even for the rest of our lives. He does it only for as long as is needed. The pain of growth and molding is short-term. The anger, or discipline, lasts only for a moment, like the brief instant it takes to wink with the eye. The accompanying weeping is only for a night, like an overnight stay in a hotel compared to the course of an entire life.

The short-term pain is worthwhile because of the wondrous results it brings. The pain is the pathway for blessings and growth to come. It will lead to rejoicing.

What a wonderful thing it is to experience the favor of God and to feel His smile and delight upon us! The night of weeping will break into the glorious dawn of a new day in which joy will overflow.

Not only does the hardship have a wonderful result, but that wonderful result lasts for a long time. It completely overshadows the time of pain. The moment of pain becomes a lifetime of favor. The time of trial is swallowed up in blessing and joy so vast that the trial is no longer worth considering. The brief hardship is worthwhile in order to reach the extended favor and blessing on the other side.

"Father, as I walk through this night, remind me that it will soon be over. Give me hope in the glorious day of blessing that You will bring."

How Long? (Sonnet 11)
"How long, O Lord, how long?" my spirit cries.
"My outer man decays both day and night."
"Not long, my child, not long," my God replies.
"This test is momentary, brief, and light."
"How long, O Lord, how long?" my heart appeals.
"My constant weeping has left me forlorn."
"Not long, my child, not long," my Hope reveals.
"You'll see my joy come to you in the morn."
"How long, O Lord, how long?" my soul implores.
"My faith is tested in a fiery trial."
"Not long, my child, not long," my Rock assures.
"It will persist for just a little while.
Not long, my child. For I make no mistakes –
As long as to perfect my work it takes."

Day 168

I know, O LORD, that a man's way is not in himself,
Nor is it in a man who walks to direct his steps.
Correct me, O LORD, but with justice;
Not with Your anger, or You will bring me to nothing.
Jeremiah 10:23-24

Man has two common problems that seem to surface particularly in times of trouble. First, he doesn't know what to do. He doesn't know which steps to take. He doesn't know how to handle the major catastrophes or even the minor challenges that make up the larger ones. He doesn't know how to resist the temptations that assault him. The lack of wisdom may not be due to a lack of seriousness or effort;

it is simply because of who man is. He is merely a man who is limited to walking. He cannot compare to God who has no such limitations.

The second problem results from the first. Because man doesn't know what to do, he makes wrong choices. He takes wrong steps and performs wrong actions. Because he does not know how to protect himself from danger, he falls into temptations. This problem may not result from a lack of desire either. Again, it simply shows the weakness of man.

God, on the other hand, knows exactly what steps a man should take. God can direct man's steps on a straight and carefully laid-out path. God also knows how to get a man back onto the right path after he has strayed. God can correct man's steps and bring them back into line. The word *correct* in Jeremiah's prayer could refer to a harsh reconciliation brought about by blows or a gentle one guided by words. Jeremiah asks for the second. If God were to correct all of man's errors harshly, no man would survive. Thankfully, God also guides man gently by teaching His truth. God wants man to walk in the right ways. Man is totally dependent on God to show him the way to walk. God knows the roadmap of which man is ignorant.

"Father, the path is a mystery to me. Correct my steps and lead me so that I walk in the way You desire. I need You to show me the path."

Day 169

The LORD's lovingkindnesses indeed never cease,
For His compassions never fail.
They are new every morning;
Great is Your faithfulness.
Lamentations 3:22-23

All illnesses are different, even among people with the same diagnosis, but perhaps some of these scenarios sound familiar to you. You wake up every morning feeling fine, but by noon you're exhausted. You go symptom-free for weeks or months, and then your disease brutally reminds you that it's still there. You initially respond well to a treatment, only to have the benefit fizzle out after a brief time. You think you are on the road to recovery, only to suffer a relapse that makes you feel as bad as ever. As your illness starts to come under control, your doctors unexpectedly discover another major problem.

These scenarios and others like them rob hope. It's hard to face the loss of hope on such a regular basis. When hope disappears again and again, what you want is compassion and kindness. If you're counting on people to provide that compassion, you will face only more disappointment. People are busy and they forget. Your illness becomes routine to them. The initial announcement of your illness probably brought sympathy, offers of help, and assurances of prayers. Now that you've been living with your illness for months or years, people don't realize how hard it still is, especially if you don't look sick. People don't understand the on-going loss of hope or the recurring disappointment.

There is someone, though, who does understand. God has compassion that never fails. His compassion never diminishes or becomes desensitized. God always feels your hurt. Because God's compassion is constant, His expressions of lovingkindness never cease. He is just as faithful to care for you in the fourth year as He was in the first year. He cares for you as much today as He did on the day you were diagnosed. Every day that you wake up with your illness, God's compassion awakes with you. He is unfailingly faithful, and you will never face a day without His compassion and love.

"Thank You, Father, for understanding my frustration and pain in this continued illness. Thank You for giving me Your compassion every single day."

Day 170

The LORD is near to all who call upon Him,
To all who call upon Him in truth.
Psalm 145:18

In the midst of trouble, we long for someone to be near to us. We want someone reliable and dependable, someone that we can count on. We want someone who is close enough to be able to come to our side whenever we are in need. We can't always wait a few hours until someone shows up. We can't manage for a couple of weeks until someone can arrange a vacation. We need someone now.

God fits all of those requirements. He is near to us. He is so near that He can immediately appear at our side as soon as we call. He is so near that He hears every cry we make. He is so near that we will never lack a companion and helper. God is so near because He cares so deeply about us.

It is an incredible encouragement to have someone near. It is an even greater encouragement when that person can help us with more than just a comforting presence. God also fits that expectation. God is abundantly able to help us, and He is able to effectively meet our needs.

The verses surrounding the above verse describe some of the help that God provides for us in His nearness. God helps us and does good things for us because He is righteous and kind in everything He does. We know that our agony never goes unnoticed, because God hears the cry of those who fear Him. We can look forward to blessing, because God fulfills the desire of those who fear Him. We can expect deliverance, because God saves those whose cry He hears. We can be secure, because God keeps all those who love Him. We have a God who is near when we call. We have a God who does wonderful and loving things in answer to our call.

"Oh, Father, without You at my side, I don't know what I would do. Thank You for being so near. Thank You for always being available and for always helping."

Day 171

The LORD is my rock and my fortress and my deliverer,
My God, my rock, in whom I take refuge;
My shield and the horn of my salvation, my stronghold.
Psalm 18:2

This verse explodes and overflows with descriptions of God's help and protection for His people. How many ways can it be said? First, He is the LORD. He is Jehovah, the one who eternally exists all of Himself, without needing any help or anyone to give Him life or strength. Second, He is a rock. He is a lofty and craggy rock that can be used as a stronghold. Third, He is a fortress. He is a castle that is able to hold people securely. Fourth, He is a deliverer. He slips people out of their prisons and helps them to escape. Fifth, He is God. He is the Almighty One, full of strength. Sixth, He is a rock of refuge. He is a mighty boulder or inaccessible cliff to which His people can flee for protection. Seventh, He is a shield. He is a small and impenetrable protection for the most vulnerable parts of the body. Eighth, He is a horn of salvation. He is the protruding and aggressive weapon that pushes and fights to give deliverance. Ninth, He is a stronghold. He is a high refuge in which His people can hide and avoid the reach of the enemy.

With so many descriptions of the protecting God, can there be any doubt that He defends His people? A God like this cannot be defeated, nor can He allow defeat to come to His people. Perhaps the most amazing realization is that even this verse does not contain a complete list; it merely provides a sampling of the protective names of God.

"Father, You state Your mighty help and protection in so many ways, and yet I still find myself doubting. Help me to look not at the problems but at You, my mighty God."

Day 172

Let the words of my mouth and the meditation of my heart
Be acceptable in Your sight,
O LORD, my rock and my Redeemer.
Psalm 19:14

As a sick person, I almost wish this verse weren't in the Bible. My words and thoughts are so hard to control anyway, but the challenge is even greater when I'm sick. Because I'm sick and always limited, I live with a constant level of frustration. When that frustration hits hard, when I am extra tired, or when I am having a rough day, I can easily lose control of my words. I need God's help to restrain my tongue so I don't say things I shouldn't say. My mouth wants to spout words of cynicism, anger, discouragement, self-pity, and complaint. It's easy for me to say too much or to say things that I shouldn't say. It's easy to hurt those around me with my words.

Controlling what I think is even harder than controlling what I say. Sometimes I can control my words and keep myself from saying everything I want to say, but my mind still thinks those unacceptable words. I'm shocked and appalled at some of the things that come into my mind, the things that I want to say. I am aware of how easily and frequently my thoughts stray from God, of how far they stray, and sometimes of how quickly they stray.

I need God's help with my thoughts so that I can think His thoughts instead of the poisonous thoughts that come from my own heart. I can't dwell on thoughts that don't please Him; I must get rid of them as quickly as possible. Instead of helplessness, despair, discouragement, anger, and frustration (none of which please God), I need to think thoughts of hope, truth, faith, and trust. These thoughts are acceptable to God. I need to think thoughts from His Word, because these are always acceptable to Him. As the meditations of my heart become acceptable to God, they will come out of my mouth in words that are also acceptable to Him.

"Father, I really need Your help with this one. I pray that my spoken words and inner thoughts would be pleasing to You. Fill me with Your words and thoughts."

Day 173

And He took with Him Peter and James and John, and began to be very distressed and troubled. And He said to them, "My soul is deeply grieved to the point of death; remain here and keep watch."
Mark 14:33–34

I don't know about you, but I have described my battle (the one that goes beyond the physical realm) as "anguish of spirit." I feel as if my soul is being pressed, twisted, and torn. It frustrates me when other Christians give the impression that anguish of spirit is inappropriate. As they admonish me to cheer up and smile, they seem to imply that anguish of spirit should never happen. They seem to expect me to remain upbeat and happy, completely unaffected by the trials of life. Is that a reasonable or right expectation?

When I think about characters in the Bible, it seems that it is normal to chafe, to hurt, and even to despair under affliction. Job did. David did. Paul cried out to God about his thorn in the flesh. Those were three very godly men. Many other examples exist also, but perhaps the most poignant is the example of Christ Himself.

I think of three specific occasions in which Christ experienced intense anguish. The first was at the temptation. The Scriptures don't share a detailed description of His anguish of spirit, but they do reveal that physically He was weak. After the temptation, angels came and ministered to Him, indicating that He needed a soothing and refreshing of His spirit (Matthew 4:11).

The third instance was on the cross. Jesus, in anguish as He bore the sins of the world, cried out, *"My God, My God, why have You forsaken Me?"* (Matthew 27:46). His interpretation of the situation was correct; because of our sins, Jesus actually was separated from God. Though His cry was based on truth, it is interesting that He expressed His anguish so strongly.

The second situation is the most interesting to me. In the garden of Gethsemane, Jesus was in great agony of spirit as He faced the reality of the cross. He knew the battle ahead of Him, and His soul was very heavy and exceeding sorrowful to the point that He felt the squeeze of death. In His agony, His sweat became like great drops of blood (Luke 22:44).

While I can't truly relate to Christ's level of anguish, I do relate to the types of phrases used to describe it. They seem to describe my own battle also. I am not alone in facing this anguish of spirit and intense internal battle. I am in very good company. Like Christ, I also can turn to God in my anguish.

"Father, I'm sorry that Jesus had to suffer for me, but I'm also grateful to see the example of His suffering. It comforts me to see that I am not radical in my anguish."

Day 174

"But He knows the way I take;
When He has tried me, I shall come forth as gold."
Job 23:10

How many times have you said to yourself, "I have no idea what God is doing through all of this"? Your human brain is unable to wrap itself around what is going on. Why did you ever get sick in the first place? Why has the illness gone on this long? Why have you responded as you have (or failed to respond) to the treatments? You don't see any purpose in your illness or any reasonable explanation for your life to take this path.

The good news is that you don't have to understand. God is the one who has to understand, and He does. God knows the reason for all that has taken place. He knows why it has happened just this way. God is well aware of your path, because He designed it. God also knows how your path will progress from here. God has not forgotten you. He intends for your trial to end. You will exit and you will come out the other side.

God knows that you will come out of the fiery trial different from how you went into it. The trial has a purifying effect. God has placed this fire in your life to burn off the ugliness and the waste and the impurity. He is making you instead into something of great beauty. When you come out of the trial, you will shine brightly, reflecting His loveliness. The worthless aspects will have been burned away, and what remains will be of great value and worth having. Christ-likeness will compose a greater percentage of your character.

"Father, do Your purifying work in me. Make me into something
of beauty and value that reflects Your glory."

Make Me Beautiful
I desire and I long to be beautiful, Lord.
I want sweetness and grace to come out of my soul
So that others would see something lovely outpoured.
To encourage their faith I'd be used as a tool.

So I scrub and I primp and I preen every day
To create something lovely to shine out of me,
But I'm troubled to realize I can't find a way.
When I look, just an ugly black heart I can see.

Oh, how could I have thought there was beauty inside?
I am nothing but one whom Your grace has redeemed,
And my efforts to change things have all been denied.
What I thought was becoming was not what it seemed.

Only You, my dear Father, can make me look good;
It is possible when I reflect Your dear Son.
So please give me His beauty; I do wish You would,
So that my life would point to the Beautiful One.

Day 175

So I will sing praise to Your name forever,
That I may pay my vows day by day.
Psalm 61:8

Psalm 61 is wonderfully reassuring and comforting. In the psalm David cries out to God from the end of the earth. He takes refuge in God as a rock that is higher than he is. He sees God as a tower of strength. He dwells with God in His tent and hides under His sheltering wings. These are all beautiful pictures of God's protection.

David's dependence on God is not disappointed; in the second half of the psalm, David describes the answer of deliverance. David talks about victory and a prolonged life. He also acknowledges the reason for his added years. David reveals that he has been saved in order to serve and praise God.

The fact that David's life was spared meant that God had something for him to do. His life was not extended so that he could serve himself or bask in the pleasures of life. He was spared for a purpose, and David readily accepted that purpose. He declared his intention to fill his service to God and to sing His praises constantly.

What a wonderful thing it is to be able to tell others how good God is and to share with them the things He has done! Whether or not God spares our lives is not up to us. Whether He heals and gives the gift of more years, or whether He chooses a reduced lifespan, the truth is that as long as we live, it is by God's design. Each day of our lives exists because God has chosen to give us that day. Whether those days be few or whether they be many, each one is to be used to praise and serve God. As long as He chooses to spare us, we have a job to do for Him.

"Father, help me not to waste my days. As long as you give me life, may I honor You by giving You the praise that You deserve."

Day 176

My flesh and my heart may fail,
But God is the strength of my heart and my portion forever.
Psalm 73:26

God is the Strength of our heart. The word *strength* actually refers to a rock or boulder; it is something very solid and unyielding. *Heart* can mean the literal heart, but more frequently the term refers to the feelings, will, or intellect. Our heart represents all of our inner being. Our emotions, our minds, and our wills can be very weak and shaky. They can quickly yield to fear and uncertainty. At times they seem to tremble violently or even completely dissolve.

It is quite apparent why we need God to be the strength of our heart. He can take something that quivers like Jell-O® and can turn it into a rock. He makes it strong. It is amazing to think of the transformation God can make. It surprises us to see the incredible strength, determination, and resolve that we can have when our strength is from God. There is a remarkable difference when God replaces our unstable, trembling heart with one made of rock.

With God as the strength of his heart, Daniel rested in the lion's den; his three friends stood alone in a crowd though their lives hung in the balance. With God as the strength of his heart, timid Peter preached powerfully at Pentecost. With God as the strength of their heart, countless martyrs have remained faithful under persecution and torture.

With God as the strength of their heart, ordinary Christians can remain steadfast through trying situations. They can face illness and even death without falling to pieces. Without God's strength our hearts are faltering and, oh, so weak, but He is able to stabilize those trembling hearts and infuse them with His strength.

"Father, my mind can't focus. My thoughts are crazy. My emotions are all over the place. Please strengthen my heart so that I can be firm instead of faltering."

Day 177

> *For such is God,*
> *Our God forever and ever;*
> *He will guide us until death.*
> *Psalm 48:14*

What is God like? Have you found your view of God suffering? It's easy enough to picture certain aspects of God. You have no problem seeing Him as an intense refiner and as a sovereign general. But do you find it easier to perceive Him as an abusive father rather than a loving one? as a ruthless mugger rather than a mighty deliverer? as a self-serving politician rather than a benevolent philanthropist? Does it feel like God is beating you when He should love, attacking you when He should help, and taking advantage of you when He should be advocating for you?

These are not pleasant pictures of God; surely you want something better. At the very least, you want to feel Him as a rock of protection and a defense against the enemy. Beyond that, you want to feel God as a loving father, as a tender shepherd, and as a protecting hen. You want to experience the aspects of God that reveal His love. Why do those pictures seem to escape you?

In the midst of these conflicting and troubling pictures, you must step back and consider truth. God absolutely cannot be who He cannot be. God gives us pictures of Himself in the Bible. There is no picture of God as an abusive father, as a ruthless mugger, or as a self-serving politician. God cannot be those things, regardless of your perceptions or feelings.

The opposite statement is also true: God absolutely must be who He is. The Bible does give pictures of God as a loving father, a tender shepherd, and a protecting hen. God *is* these things. Your perceptions and feelings cannot change reality. By faith you must believe what your eyes cannot see at the moment. Maybe you don't always see God as a loving and cherishing Father, but it is still true. If He seems to be a ruthless mugger or selfish politician, that cannot be true. He is the God revealed in the Bible, and He will be that God forever – every day of your life, from now until death.

> *"Father, I admit that my view is sometimes skewed. Thank You that You don't change because of how I feel. Thank You that You will always be the God You declare Yourself to be."*

Day 178

> *Be not far from me, for trouble is near;*
> *For there is none to help.*
> *But You, O LORD, be not far off;*
> *O You my help, hasten to my assistance.*
> *Psalm 22:11 & 19*

Trouble sometimes seems to be nipping at my heels. It is so close that I can feel its hot breath on the back of my neck and its claws scratching at my back. This trouble is threatening and terrifying.

When trouble is near me, God, I need You to be nearer. I can't survive if You are far away. I need You to be closer than the trouble, closer even than my skin. I need Your faithful nearness to comfort and protect me. Oh, God, You promise that. You say that You will never leave my side. Thank You for being near to me when I am afflicted. You *are* close by my side, closer than any trouble.

When I am in trouble, I need someone to help. Most of the time when I look around, I see no one. Even if people wanted to help, no one else really can. You are on my side. You are my helper and never my enemy. A trial is not something that You do *to* me; rather it is something that You help me *through*. The results of sin have brought many difficulties, and trouble is common to man. You allow those troubles and use them for Your own purposes, but Your intent is never vindictive or cruel. You're not out to get me; You are there to help me.

You are a faithful helper. You don't get tired or annoyed when I find myself in need over and over again. You hear me every time I call; You never hide from my needs. You are a sufficient helper. You determine to help me through my trouble, and You are able to do so. No matter how great my weakness, Your strength is enough. Thank You, God, for helping when no one else is able to do anything. Help me quickly, Lord.

"Oh, Father, the trouble is near. I need You to be nearer. I have no one to help me. I need You to be my help."

Day 179

Therefore, confess your sins to one another, and pray for one another so that you may be healed. The effective prayer of a righteous man can accomplish much.
James 5:16

Our human nature contains a universal element called pride. We don't want to admit we need help. We don't want to let people see our weaknesses. If others do catch a glimpse of our weakness, we want it to be in little things, or at least in very small parts of bigger problems. Rather than being viewed as struggling Christians, we want to be respected and looked to as examples. It is hard enough to admit practical needs (like cleaning or transportation); it is even harder to admit spiritual needs. We don't want to let people know that we're struggling with bitterness, anger, lack of faith, or discouragement.

If we are struggling with those things, however, we need help. It would be foolish, especially in our weakened condition, to think we can win those battles on our own. To attempt it is to ask for trouble. Do we really think that we can live the Christian life and win ferocious battles without help? God has given us the fellowship of believers for a reason; we are to help and encourage one another. People can't help if they don't know there is a problem.

It requires humility to admit the deep struggles of our soul to someone else, but when the struggles are that deep, we need someone to encourage us and to pray with us. While it is true that not every friend is appropriate for sharing these weighty matters, it is also true that God has placed godly and compassionate friends around us. When these people are able and willing to help, we would be foolish and prideful to ignore that help.

God has given fellow Christians maturity and wisdom for a reason – that they might help others. While we may hate admitting our weakness and the extent of it, we need to have godly people praying for us and with us. We need their encouragement and wisdom as we face the daily battles. The number of people in whom we confide need not be large, but we must have some.

"Father, I have been very resistant to sharing my failures with others, but I realize now that I need their help. Please guide me to someone with whom I can share – to someone who will pray with me."

Day 180

Strengthened with all power, according to His glorious might, for the attaining of all steadfastness and patience; joyously.
Colossians 1:11

How many times have you said, "I just can't do this anymore"? How often have you protested, "I can't keep going"? Day after day, week after week, month after month, and year after year, your illness has persisted. Whether your condition remains the same, has ups and downs, or progressively gets worse, the duration takes its toll. This whole thing got old a long time ago.

You may hate to even consider the future or ponder how long you must continue to deal with the same challenges. Yes, it sometimes seems impossible to continue for even one more day. You have no steadfastness. Your patience has long since disappeared. Not only do you not have steadfastness and patience, you can't imagine ever having them again.

God says that you can attain these qualities. It is possible to endure patiently through something that seems as if it will never end. Where does this patience come from? This verse teaches that God can strengthen you to be able to attain patience.

In particular, God gives you strength out of His vast reserve of might, and that strength is used to give you patience. God is strong enough to do that. He was powerful and mighty enough to create the earth. He was powerful and mighty enough to do countless miracles. He was powerful and mighty enough to raise the dead. God still has that same power today. A God with such glorious might is surely able to strengthen you to have patience. Can you continue to endure your illness? Not on your own, you can't, but with the might of God strengthening you for the challenge, it is possible.

"Father, it seems I can't take this for another day. Please give me your power to help me endure. You are strong enough to do that. Strengthen me to be patient."

Day 181 _____

"But it is still my consolation,
And I rejoice in unsparing pain,
That I have not denied the words of the Holy One."
Job 6:10

A chronic illness is not an easy thing. It can, however, be a wonderful thing, because it can provide a powerful platform for faithfully following and exalting God. In spite of his severe trial, Job did not deny God. He still believed God's words to be true. In Job 27:3-5, he echoed this same concept. He firmly resolved that he would not speak unjustly regarding God, even if he was brought to the point of death. He refused to turn his back on God.

This unswerving testimony is poignant in the midst of pain, because a Christian acknowledges God's control over his situation. Typically, human faithfulness is short-lived. It follows a person or a program for as long as it works for him, but when the promised results falter, resolve quickly melts away. When life is falling apart, it doesn't make human sense to stubbornly follow a God who has promised to care for His children.

Continuing faithfully through dark days that seem to have no end isn't done by human strength. When faithfulness and enduring trust happen, therefore, they provide proof that something supernatural is going on. Such continued resolve and prolonged faithfulness are evidence of the work of God. They prove once again that God is real and that His way works. When someone is faithful in the face of prolonged suffering, others are challenged with the reality of God. They are encouraged that God really is true and that His grace really is sufficient.

Both the faithfulness of the sufferer and the acknowledgment by the observer bring glory to God. God is lifted up as His greatness is recognized. Being able to do such a thing brings both soberness and joy to the one who is suffering. The soberness is due to the realization of how ludicrous it is for a mere man to be able to exalt God. The joy is in realizing that it is happening. When others have fallen in the midst of trials, there is great joy in realizing God's upholding hand. Job had comfort and joy as God enabled him to be faithful.

"Father, I have a serious opportunity before me – the chance to demonstrate
Your faithfulness. Help me to remain faithful in spite of everything,
so that others will see how great You are."

$\longrightarrow$

The Value of Pain (Sonnet 2)
To suffer is to learn — such quantity.
I learn what's worthwhile in my life, what's dust,
Of human weakness, need, and sympathy,
The greatness of my God, that I can trust.
To suffer is to grow — so deep the span.
I grasp things now I've never grasped before.
My spirit sobers as I sense God's plan.
I reach new depths with Him. He shows me more.
To suffer is to change — no more the same.
I've lost a part of me that used to be;
Replaced it with the likeness of His frame,
So others see His face reflect in me.
Why learn? Why grow? Why change? No praise to me.
To bear more fruit for Him — O, may it be!

Day 182

Therefore, return to your God,
Observe kindness with justice,
And wait for your God continually.
Hosea 12:6

Hosea recounts the story of Jacob. Jacob was bad news from the beginning, grabbing his brother's heel even in the womb. Later he contended with God Himself. That wrestling match ended with Jacob's weeping and seeking the favor of God. Jacob's brokenness caused him to prevail, to find God, and to hear His voice. Jacob's pleading with God resulted in blessing.

Jacob's story serves as an example for us. Since God responded in that way to Jacob, we ought to do what he did. We ought to return to God, to be kind and just, and to wait continually for God. As we wait on God with a humble, obedient heart, we can also expect to receive God's blessing.

Jacob was a great conniver, inventing schemes and plans in order to get what he wanted. His own schemes had only limited success. He did not have true blessing until he gave up his plans and yielded to God. God longs to pour out blessing on His children, but sometimes He must wait for us to finally realize that He alone is the source of true blessing. Instead of depending so much on ourselves and trying to figure everything out, we ought to turn to God and plead with Him for His blessing. As we wait on God, we are to do so continually, implying that His help is essential every day and in every aspect of life. We can wait on God, looking to Him for blessing and for constant sustaining in life.

"Oh, Father, I need You so much every day. I can't help myself. I need Your blessing on me. Will You bless me by working in my life?"

Day 183

He caused the storm to be still,
So that the waves of the sea were hushed.
Then they were glad because they were quiet,
So He guided them to their desired haven.
Psalm 107:29-30

It is highly unlikely that you have not compared your situation to that of a storm on the ocean. You can easily relate to the Biblical description found in Psalm 107:23-27. The sailors, who made their living on the waters, were going about their business as usual when a fierce storm attacked out of nowhere. The winds were vicious and drove up mighty waves. The ship rose up high on the crests and then plunged brutally down into the depths. The sailors were in misery and their souls melted away. Staggering like drunken men, they could hardly walk. They were at their wits' end, having no idea what to do. (The description does fit, doesn't it?)

In this desperate and troubling situation, the sailors cried out to God. He heard them and delivered them. God calmed the wind and made it still. He hushed the waves and made them flat. Finally the fierce storm was over, but God didn't stop there. He took that poor, lost, and battered ship, and He led it to port. The sailors didn't end up safe on a deserted island. They did not land at the nearest port after being driven off course. No, God led them to the very port where they wanted to go.

What was the end result of the storm and subsequent deliverance? The sailors saw the wonders and the mighty works of God. They saw His might first in the storm itself. Who else could create such a thing? Who else can match God's power? They also saw His might in the deliverance. If no one else could even make such a storm, it is even less likely that anyone else could calm it. The amazing deliverance was a chance to see God's unmatched power at work and to praise Him for His goodness.

"Father, You know how rough this storm is and how often I feel like I am drowning. Please deliver me. Calm the storm. Lead me safe to port. Let me see Your wondrous power."

Day 184

Let the favor of the Lord our God be upon us;
And confirm for us the work of our hands;
Yes, confirm the work of our hands.
Psalm 90:17

Psalm 90 describes an eternal God, one who existed long before the earth was created. By comparison, man has a tiny window of life that passes quickly. Because of sin, even that brief life is full of sorrow and is precariously in danger of facing God's displeasure.

The psalmist, along with anyone else who loves God, responds in reverence, humbly desiring to please God during the brief opportunity he has. The most well-known verse in the psalm is probably verse twelve, in which the psalmist prays that God would teach him to number his days so that he can properly present himself before God.

Our hearts should echo that prayer. We should desire to use our days to their maximum potential for God's glory. We must make the most of them because we don't know how many days we have. Illness may significantly shorten our years. Even if it doesn't, the lifespan of man is brief. There is no time to waste. We must be diligent in completing the tasks God has given to us. What those tasks are varies from person to person; those with serious illnesses may have a shorter list comprised of simplified tasks. We must consider what God wants us to devote ourselves to: raising our family, knowing God better, encouraging those around us, praying for others, witnessing to doctors, or finishing that one project.

The psalm closes with a humble recognition that we cannot accomplish any of those tasks on our own. As strong as our desire may be, we are incapable of performing what we desire. We need God to confirm the work. We need His blessing. We need His favor so that our work can be effective. No matter what the task, and no matter how long we have to do it, only God's help will allow us to have success.

"Father, I want my few days to please You. Help me to be serious about not wasting them. Above all, place Your favor on me so that I can accomplish what You desire."

Day 185

God is our refuge and strength,
A very present help in trouble.
Psalm 46:1

God is my Strength. Of the Hebrew words translated *strength* in the Psalms, the most common one refers to a sharp rock or boulder. It is hard to imagine anything harder or stronger than a rock. In fact, rocks are among earth's hardest substances, so they are a good illustration of strength. A boulder would be a hard thing for anyone to effectively assault or break through.

The verse does not state that God *gives* me strength so that I become impregnable, but rather states that He actually *is* my strength. Because God is my rock, I am able to trust in His strength, which is far stronger than my own. I cannot face the assaults of life by myself. When things are difficult or worse, I need to lean hard on God. On my own I would fall. Others can give only tentative and temporary help. God is the only one strong enough, firm enough, and reliable enough to hold me up.

Leaning on God doesn't happen by accident; it is a very conscious thing. Leaning on Him also has to be constant. I can't lean on Him one day, but depend on myself the next. I have to lean on Him day after day, and day by day – one at a time. When even that is too overwhelming, I need to lean on Him one hour at a time or one minute at a time if necessary. The bottom line is that I need God desperately. He is my source of strength for every task and every challenge.

"I am so weak, Father. I can't do anything. I need Your strength. I need You for every task of every day. I need You to help me with each challenge I face."

Day 186

This is my comfort in my affliction,
That Your word has revived me.
Psalm 119:50

In the midst of affliction, when you are in agony and when you feel completely beaten down, you need comfort. Where can you turn? The radio or television? Ludicrous. An inspirational book? Disappointing. Food? Ineffective. Your pastor? Busy. Your friends? Frustrating. Your family? Inadequate. There is only one place to turn for effective help and comfort, and that is the Word of God. The Bible is unlike any of those other sources.

The Bible is personal, able to minister to your specific needs and concerns. It doesn't throw out a one-size-fits-all answer.

The Bible is certain, able to give you real hope. It doesn't glibly make wishful reassurances that "everything will be all right."

The Bible is understanding, able to address the struggles that your friends don't comprehend. There is no battle you face that is not mirrored by the Bible's characters.

The Bible is wise, containing all the answers. It can adequately address any question you have.

The Bible is available, never too busy. There isn't a day you can reach for your Bible that its pages won't open.

The Bible is eternal, having answers that last. The answers are there today, and they will be there for all the tomorrows too.

How many times have you gone to the Word of God with a spirit that was discouraged, a heart that was hurting, or a soul in distress? How many times has the Bible revived your spirit until you came away rejoicing at the wonderful things you'd seen? Sometimes the ability of the Bible to minister to your heart is absolutely overwhelming; it leaves you feeling like a new person. That change is not your own doing and can't be brought about by the influence of any other person. It is the Word of God that makes the changes, gives the growth, supplies the answers, and revives the spirit. That infusion of new life brings incredible comfort to the soul. On the outside, the battle may still be raging, but God's Word provides a safe and sure retreat. The life-giving supply of God's Word will never run out.

"I need comfort, Father. Peel back my despair so that I can receive the wonderful comfort of Your Word. Apply it like an effective salve to my hurting heart."

Day 187

I will rejoice and be glad in Your lovingkindness,
Because You have seen my affliction;
You have known the troubles of my soul.
Psalm 31:7

Being in affliction is difficult. Physical affliction can take many forms: pain, nausea, weakness, fatigue, limited mobility, mental shortfalls, and so much more. Those physical symptoms are hard to bear. They are also hard for someone else to relate to unless that other person has suffered something similar. Some of those physical symptoms cannot be observed, and it is especially hard for others to grasp the impact of those unseen symptoms.

More difficult than the symptoms that trouble the body are those that afflict the soul. It is very likely that the troubles of your soul far outnumber the troubles of the body. The afflictions and burdens of the soul can be very weighty and overwhelming. They are harsher and more difficult to deal with than the physical struggles. The physical symptoms pale in comparison.

Although the soul burdens are harder to bear, perhaps they are also harder for others to understand. These burdens can't be seen at all by others. As you think of your troubles, both physical and internal, you realize that others fail to understand. They might forget or overlook you. They might not realize the seriousness of your situation. They might care, but be unable to understand.

God never overlooks your troubles. He knows about every one of them. He sees your physical afflictions. He understands what they are like, and He cares. He also knows the troubles of your soul. He understands what no one else can. When God sees you in your need, He has a wonderful response. The result of His seeing and knowing is a response of lovingkindness. God understands your struggle, and He responds with gentle love.

"Yes, Father, my body is hurting, but my soul is hurting more. Look on me, see my trouble, and respond with Your love."

Day 188

And let endurance have its perfect result,
so that you may be perfect and complete, lacking in nothing.
James 1:4

James 1:3 tells us that trials do produce endurance. That's just a fact. Steadfastness and patience come as we continue through a trial. The next step in the process depends on our response. Endurance produces maturity *if* we let it. We have to allow the endurance to work and to bring about the end that God desires.

What does it mean to let endurance have its result? We must allow God to do His work. This requires submission on our part. We must respond when God indicates an area of change. We must yield ourselves daily to what He has chosen. We can't fight and connive to remove ourselves from the trial. We must wait through the process; it can't be hurried. Ultimately, we don't do anything; the work is all God's. We simply allow Him to do what He wants to do.

The end result is actually pretty amazing. Endurance has its perfect result; it does a complete work. That final product is to make us complete and perfectly sound in every part. It will cause us to be lacking in nothing. The endurance brought by the trial completely equips us spiritually, giving us all the tools and skills and knowledge that we need. Endurance has the wonderful result of making us complete and mature and of filling in the deficiencies in our character.

When we consider our natural condition, we realize that God is bringing about a pretty dramatic change. This verse, as well as other passages, implies that there might not be any other way for this dramatic change to take place. God has chosen to use trials as His means of accomplishing outstanding growth. God knows what the end product should look like, and He knows best how to bring it about.

"In order to accomplish the good work that You've designed, Father, I submit to You. May I be yielded daily so Your hand can work." $\longrightarrow$

Let It Work (Sonnet 38)

To let endurance have its perfect work,
I must remember first that it's God's tool.
It comes through trials from which I can't shirk;
I realize they will help to make me whole.
Beneath endurance I must daily stay;
It cannot work on me if I'm not there.
I can't escape or try to run away,
But rest and let my God His training share.
For it to do its work, I must submit
And yield to everything that God would choose.
It's He who works, and I can't do a bit;
I just surrender to what He would use.
I'll let it work so I can be complete;
He'll fill my lack, thus making me replete.

Day 189

Who will separate us from the love of Christ? Will tribulation, or distress, or persecution, or famine, or nakedness, or peril, or sword? For I am convinced that neither death, nor life, nor angels, nor principalities, nor things present, nor things to come, nor powers, nor height, nor depth, nor any other created thing, will be able to separate us from the love of God, which is in Christ Jesus our Lord.
Romans 8:35 & 38-39

In the midst of your extended illness, don't you sometimes just long for love? On some of those days when it seems that your condition has already stretched on forever, don't you just want someone to care? You want companionship, someone to sit with you, someone to hold your hand, someone to speak kind words.

Because of your illness, however, you are cut off from some of those very things and people that could bring you comfort. Because spending time with you would require a special effort and deliberate planning, you have less contact with others than you would have if you were healthy. You crave love more than ever, but see it less and less. Perhaps you never would have believed it possible to be separated from some of the loved ones whom you no longer see.

There is one truly dependable source of love, and that is Christ. Nothing can separate us from God's love. It will always be faithful and will always be true. There is absolutely no possible way for His love to be cut off. Lest we doubt and think that maybe trials could do so, the passage above specifically lists and focuses on those types of things. No, tribulation can't do it; neither can distress, persecution, famine, nakedness, peril, or sword.

Do those things happen? Yes, according to verse thirty-six, they do happen, but those things, as fierce as they may be, are powerless and incapable of separating us from God's love. In each of them, we have the love of God faithfully with us. We can trust in His constant love in hard times. His love is real. His love doesn't fail.

"Father, thank You for Your unfailing love that will always be with me.
Help me to rest in it."

Day 190

Who is like the LORD our God,
Who is enthroned on high,
Who humbles Himself to behold
The things that are in heaven and in the earth?
Psalm 113:5-6

What is man? Psalm 113 reveals several things about him. He is only a servant. He is only a human who dwells on the earth. Man is poor and needy. He is fallen in the dust and mourning in an ash heap. There is nothing important in man. There is nothing elegant or powerful. There is only frailty and sorrow and need. There is nothing that would impel God to pay any attention to man.

What is God? Psalm 113 also describes God. He is served by the earth. He is high above all things. He has glory that cannot be matched. He is the King who rules on high. He lives in heaven. God deserves praise from all the earth. He deserves praise for all eternity. He deserves praise all day long. God has no need of man because He is everything.

What does God do? God humbles Himself. He is above the heavens, yet He looks down. He is high above all nations and people, but He stoops to look at them. This lofty God examines what happens on lowly earth to lowly men. Amazingly, when such an exalted God sees such great need and such immense weakness, He does not turn away in disdain. Instead He takes the poor out of the dust and makes him sit with princes. He lifts the needy mourner out of the ashes and places him in a position of importance. He takes the sorrowful, childless woman and gives her joy with a family.

God, who is so high, has no reason to look on man. He chooses to condescend, to look down on frail and needy people. Best of all, when this great God observes incredible need, He intervenes. He troubles Himself to be interested in such weakness. He generously gives help, comfort, and joy.

"Father, I cannot comprehend how great You are, and I do not realize how weak I am. I
am amazed and forever grateful that You not only notice me, but You also help."

Day 191

All discipline for the moment seems not to be joyful, but sorrowful; yet to those who have been trained by it, afterwards it yields the peaceful fruit of righteousness.
Hebrews 12:11

In the midst of affliction, we need to remember the truth that God reveals in His Word. One of the truths we should consider is that at least some affliction is for the purpose of discipline (vs. 5-6). We are not to take God's discipline lightly or faint in the midst of it; rather we are to recognize that God, in love, disciplines His children.

We are to endure under the discipline, knowing it is an assurance that we are God's children (v. 7). If we did not belong to God, and if He did not care about us, He would not go to the trouble of disciplining us. His discipline is proof that He loves us.

As we respect the discipline given by our earthly fathers, we should much more respect and submit to the discipline of God (v. 9). Our earthly fathers at times discipline poorly, but God's discipline is with wisdom. He knows exactly how to do so, and His discipline is effective for the purpose of our growth in holiness (v. 10). It has the job of training us and preparing us and making us what we ought to be. God disciplines in order to purify us and bring us along in our maturity.

Discipline through affliction is not enjoyable, but in the long run it is worth it. Once the discipline has done its training work in our lives, it helps to make us righteous. It yields good and peaceful fruits. Although it is unpleasant at the moment, it will bring us future joy. We may have to wait to see the results, but God will bring them. The process itself cannot be the focus, but we must look forward to the result that God will bring about.

"Thank You, Father, for Your love that impels You to interact in my life. May I submit to Your training so that I can grow in holiness as You intend."

Day 192

By awesome deeds You answer us in righteousness, O God of our salvation,
You who are the trust of all the ends of the earth and of the farthest sea.
Psalm 65:5

It's pretty easy to trust God when you don't need anything. In that position, how could He possibly let you down? When life is not so bad, God pulls through pretty well. What about when your situation gets desperate? Can He still be as reliable? If you were alone at the remotest end of the entire earth, could He keep you there? What if you were on a raging sea, as far as possible from civilization? Could you rely on God then?

This verse says you can. Even in those situations, God is able to answer. He is a secure refuge and a dependable assurance for those who flee to Him. Anyone, whether he is at the darkest corner of the earth or in the wildest and remotest place in the oceans, can have this assurance. When troubling times come, you can flee to God and be confident in His protection.

This is not a weak God who barely manages to meet your needs. No, He answers with awesome deeds. How awesome are His deeds? This psalm shares some of them, just in case you wonder at His ability. God holds up the mountains. He stills the roaring of the sea's wild waves. He makes a dawn and a sunset so beautiful that they shout for joy. God causes the earth to produce vegetation. He provides water to maintain the earth. He gives bountiful harvests. He provides for the needs of man and beast. He fills the hillsides with flocks of animals. In summary, God created and maintains the entire earth. Such a God is worthy of trust, even by the most desperate among His children.

"You have so much power, Father, that You are able to meet my needs no matter how desperate they are. You can take care of me no matter where I am or what danger I face."

Day 193

> *You, O LORD, will not withhold Your compassion from me;*
> *Your lovingkindness and Your truth will continually preserve me.*
> *Psalm 40:11*

David introduces Psalm 40 by telling how wondrously God has delivered him in the past. He tells how blessed the man is who trusts in God. He describes his personal response of gratitude as he willingly offers himself to serve God. Through difficult times David has learned some wonderful truths about his God. He has given glory to God as he has gladly and freely shared these truths with others.

After those times of victory and rejoicing, David finds himself in another frightful situation. He is surrounded by evil situations that are too numerous to count. His sins have piled up so high that he is blinded by them. His heart is failing.

Does his new situation leave him in despair, forgetting all that God has previously done? No, in this horrid situation, David speaks with amazing confidence. He speaks with great certainty of God's compassion, lovingkindness, and truth. He knows that God will still give those things to him and that God will use those things to preserve him.

God has compassion. He cares for His children when they are in need, and He expresses that compassion to them. To do nothing, to hold back His compassion, would take no effort and would require no interest. God, however, does have interest, and therefore He puts forth effort. He acts by reaching out with His compassion.

God also offers His lovingkindness and truth. They go with His children to keep them. David realizes how constantly God shows these traits; he is never a moment without them. He expects them to go with him every step of his path. God loves and cares, and He actively and continually shows that love and care.

> *"Thank You, Father, that You will show Your compassion and lovingkindness to me just like You did to David. I can share his bold confidence that they will be with me at all times."*

Day 194

> *The LORD is my shepherd,*
> *I shall not want.*
> *Psalm 23:1*

God is my Shepherd. This picture is less familiar today than it was in Biblical times, but the fact that sheep desperately need a shepherd is still generally well known. Sheep are helpless. They need a shepherd to take them to water. They need a shepherd to direct them to new grass when they have exhausted their current patch. They need a shepherd to provide a place of shelter for them. He must take them to their home and show them where to sleep. Sheep need a shepherd to pick them up and set them on their feet when they fall over. They need a shepherd to protect them from attacks; on their own they would run panicked and without direction. They need a shepherd to keep them from wandering and getting lost. Sheep are not smart animals, and they have many needs.

God as my shepherd means that He is very involved in my life. Caring for me is a full-time job and a long-term commitment. God as my shepherd means that I need Him very much. I can't survive or meet even my most basic needs on my own. Because God is my shepherd, however, all of my needs will be met. I won't lack anything. He will not leave me hanging with some need that is unmet.

Trying to supply my own needs doesn't work. I only complicate things and leave myself with unmet needs. It can be uncomfortable to let someone else meet my needs, because I want to be self-sufficient and take care of things on my own. One of the best things I can learn is to stop trying so hard to meet my own needs and allow God to do the job. As my Shepherd, God fills the role of tending and ruling His flock. As He faithfully provides for me and makes decisions for me that I am not able to make for myself, I must respond by trusting His choices and by following Him without question.

"Father, everything about Your being my Shepherd is a good thing. There is no negative side. Thank You for caring, leading, guiding, and protecting. Thank You for meeting all my needs."

Day 195

And without faith it is impossible to please Him, for he who comes to God must believe that He is and that He is a rewarder of those who seek Him.
Hebrews 11:6

Faith is necessary. We cannot please God without it. God expects us to have faith that He is; the God described in the Bible does exist. He is who He says He is. God also expects us to have faith in His responses. He will do what He has said He will do. He will provide the reward to His promises. He will respond appropriately to those who seek Him.

God demands this faith, so what do we do when we don't have it? First of all, we need to recognize the danger. When our faith wavers and doubt starts to take over, a critical warning alarm should sound within us. When doubt controls us, we are walking in a danger zone. Not only is faith required in order to please God, but it is also very hard to maintain spiritual health without faith. As faith shrinks, remaining firm and stable becomes even more difficult. Without faith, we quickly start to spiral downward. In order to stop the doubt in its tracks, we need to be ready to take immediate action when we recognize the warning signs.

Second, we need to confess our doubt and ask for help. When we recognize the truth about lack of faith, we realize that it comes from Satan, the father of doubts. When we give in to doubt, we allow Satan to win. This is sin; we must confess our wavering and turn to God for help. We must ask Him for faith in both big and little things.

Third, we must remember that faith comes by hearing the Word of God. It is critical to have intake from the Word of God in order to combat the doubt. We must fight our doubts with God's truth. We should have appropriate verses ready and available so that our minds can quickly focus on them. We need to repeatedly read or quote those verses.

Fourth, we need to exercise the faith we have. God is pleased with even a small amount of faith. Jesus commended those who sought to exercise faith, even when that faith was small. We must go to God with the amount of faith we have. He can reward and even increase that level of faith. Faith grows as we use it. While lacking faith is a dangerous position, it is not hopeless.

"Help me to please You, Father, by exhibiting faith in You and in Your Word. Prompt me to take action quickly when I recognize doubt." →

Prayer for Genuine Faith (Sonnet 35)
In You alone I place my faith, oh, Lord,
For only You are worthy of such trust.
In every promise I can be assured;
To keep Your Word, You are completely just.
So give me faith that truly will believe
With confidence although I do not see.
What You have said, I surely will receive;
With peaceful heart, I'll wait with certainty.
And when I see the answers that You bring,
My faith must trust they really are Your plan.
In all You send in life – yes, everything -
Give faith to trust though I don't understand.
I'm longing, Father, for a faith that's real.
It's not in me; to You I must appeal.

Day 196

You turn things around!
Shall the potter be considered as equal with the clay,
That what is made would say to its maker,
"He did not make me";
Or what is formed say to him who formed it,
"He hath no understanding"?
Isaiah 29:16

When I protest God's work, I have things backwards. It makes no more sense for a mere mortal to question Almighty God than it does for a handcrafted item to claim independence or to assert ignorance on the part of the artist.

When I choose to fight with God over any issue, the issue itself is not the problem as much as my heart before God. As long as I continue to focus on the issue in question, I am drawing my focus away from God. When I make something into a point of conflict, I create a wall that hinders my spiritual growth. I create a battlefield. Hardening my will and refusing to submit put me in rebellion against God. If I refuse to yield over this issue, what will I refuse over next time? Obstinacy sets me up for continued rebellion against God.

Instead of fighting, I must submit and surrender to God. I can't resist based on uncertainty about what submission will mean in terms of follow-through. For now I only have to yield, soften my heart, and be willing to take the steps God shows me. I have to admit I was wrong – again. Some of those wrongs have been long-established patterns, and it's hard to face my failure, but God's forgiveness is complete. It is greater than my sin. It is sufficient to cover the worst and longest-standing offenses and to create a clean standing with God.

Yielding is not a loss; it is a victory. It is a means of blessing and grace. Conflict, guilt, and rebellion create a very heavy burden. I can't carry that burden and still function. It will wear me down. When I fight, I'm fighting against my own best interest. There is really no choice – no better option – than yielding. My relationship with God is too precious for me to damage it with rebellion. I can't allow that poison to build in my soul or to have a foothold. It is foolish for me to fight with God. I can't win. Fighting with God not only causes me to take the wrong path, but it also makes the journey itself very unpleasant.

"Oh, Father, my wretched flesh is so bent on doing exactly the opposite of what is best for me! Soften my heart and turn me toward You. Help me to lose the battle of my will."

Day 197

But You, O LORD, are a shield about me,
My glory, and the One who lifts up my head.
Psalm 3:3

David spoke these words in the face of increasing enemies who were rising up around him and declaring that he could not be saved. David knew that neither the abundance of enemies nor the threatening words they spoke could defeat him, because he was trusting in God. He had God as his protector. No enemy, however strong, could break through God's defense. No crowd of enemies, however numerous, could overrun God's protection.

David first referred to God as a Shield. This shield surrounded him with sufficient protection from any danger. Satan's attacks were fierce and frequent. They seemed overwhelming and indefensible, but God's shield was big enough and tough enough to meet the attacks. David did not have the defense in himself. He did not have the ability to defend himself from Satan's attacks. Instead, he had to trust in God and in His words. He had to keep telling himself the truth of Scripture.

Second, David identified God as his Glory. Anything good in him, anything positive in terms of progress and victory, anything to boast about or rejoice in was all of God. David was weak and had no glory of his own. It was only God's strength that produced anything worthy of note.

Third, David called God the Lifter of his head. God was the one who lifted David to his position as king. God was also the one who gave support to David's weak neck and kept his head above water. God was the one who held him up and kept him from drowning or being trampled. God was the one who helped him survive. All the protection, all the glory, and all the strength came from God.

"Father, help me to trust You to be strong enough to defend me from Satan's attacks. Help me to believe that no enemy is too strong for You."

Day 198

My flesh and my heart may fail,
But God is the strength of my heart and my portion forever.
Psalm 73:26

God is our Portion. He is our allotment or our inheritance. The idea comes from the word used for the smooth stones used in casting lots or dividing things up. God as our inheritance means that when everything is divided up, our share is God.

Of all the things that we could want or receive for an inheritance, God Himself is the best. All other things will be spent, used up, or lost. Any other inheritance will be temporary and meet only temporary needs. God, on the other hand, will never run out. He is permanent and will meet permanent needs.

Not only is God the only lasting inheritance, but He is also the most necessary. Some inheritances are not much more than a nuisance, while others are nice, pretty, or even valuable. God, however, is the most valuable inheritance. He will always be something we need, and He will always be useful. If we could choose between everything else in the world and God, God would be the better choice.

In reality, God is all the inheritance we will ever need. There is nothing else that can even compare. God will meet every need, including our very deepest needs, and He will do so for all eternity. People that we know will receive all kinds of things as inheritances, but our inheritance is God. How could we ask for any better portion than that?

"Of all the possible inheritances in the world, Father, I get You! Thank You for something that is truly valuable and eternal. With You, what could I lack?"

Day 199

That He might present to Himself the church in all her glory, having no spot or wrinkle or any such thing; but that she would be holy and blameless.
Ephesians 5:27

As we struggle from day to day with our fleshly nature that seems bent on doing wrong and doomed to failure, it is wonderful to know that someday all of that will change. We currently live in natural bodies, and those natural bodies are incapable of living supernaturally. They still reap the results of having lived in bondage to sin.

When Christ comes for us, He will give the ultimate deliverance from that bondage. He will deliver us from our mortal bodies of death that pursue sin. He will give us spiritual bodies to replace our natural bodies. The spiritual bodies will be completely different and far superior to what we know now. Those bodies will be so dramatically different that we won't recognize them, but they will be glorious and accepted in the sight of God.

As we stand before God in our new bodies, we will be blameless. We will be faultless and holy. We will be beyond reproof. We will not have a single spot or a single wrinkle to mar us. In fact, our transformation will be so amazing and so complete that we will be like Jesus Himself. When we are united with Him, we will be made perfect, just like He is perfect. We will stand gloriously before God, no longer having the capability of sinning. We will no longer have to do battle with the flesh and sin.

"Oh, Father, what a day is coming! Every time I turn around, I am falling into sin, but some day I will be changed to sin no more. There will be no more battle with sin."

Day 200

Search me, O God, and know my heart;
Try me and know my anxious thoughts;
And see if there be any hurtful way in me,
And lead me in the everlasting way.
Psalm 139:23-24

What is wrong with me? *Is* something wrong with me? How can I be so unspiritual? How can I struggle so much? How can I be the worst Christian I have ever met? My mind is filled with thoughts like these. I really don't understand. God has done so much for me. He has taught me so much. He has given me years of training and has been with me faithfully through my illness. How, then, can I struggle so deeply with so many things?

The most frustrating thing about my struggle is that I can't distinguish between what is a spiritual problem and what is a product of my illness. Am I unable to maintain control and stability, or am I just not doing it? Is my mind truly dulled by illness, or am I being undisciplined? This is maddeningly frustrating and disheartening.

God's wisdom tells me that I must be realistic. I must admit that my disease is real and has very real effects on me. I ought not to be unduly hard on myself for something that I cannot fix. On the other hand, I have no way of knowing what is merely a result of the disease and what is something more. I must also realistically face the possibility that something wrong in my heart could be affecting my relationship with God. I can't use the disease as an excuse for my failures.

Since these issues are too difficult for me to comprehend, I must take them to God. I must pray for God to search and understand my heart. I must ask Him to evaluate my thoughts. If there is something wrong in me, I need Him to show that to me and to lead me in the right way. I need Him to bring appropriate conviction when I need it. Because my struggles are constant, I must constantly ask and allow God to evaluate me. My evaluation will be jumbled and inconsistent, but God can accurately evaluate. He can show me the spiritual problems that exist, and He can lead me to the right solutions.

"Search me, Father. Show me any real problems that exist. Help me to be sensitive to respond to Your leading. Give me victory."

Day 201

You made men ride over our heads;
We went through fire and through water,
Yet You brought us out into a place of abundance.
Psalm 66:12

Psalm 66 contains many joyous words of exuberant praise to God. His works are awesome and His power is great. He turns the sea into dry land so His people can walk through it, and He carefully rules all the nations of the world. On a personal level, He keeps His children and doesn't allow their feet to slip. What a wonderful God!

Life doesn't always seem quite so exuberant or stable, does it? In the midst of his rejoicing, the psalmist also acknowledges the intense trials of life. He refers to being tried and refined. He talks about being captured in a net and having an oppressive burden placed on him. He recalls men riding over his head. He recounts his journeys through fire and water. He attributes all of those weighty trials to God's work. He repeatedly says that God made all of those things happen.

Isn't it easy to relate those various trials to your own life? As you read the psalmist's descriptions, you can easily say, "Yep, that's what is happening to me." The trying and refining, the net and oppressive burden, the riding over your head, and the fire and water are all very hard things; they seem beyond explanation or reason. Look though at that next precious word – *yet*. After all of those troubles, God brings His children out into a place of abundance.

You can't know what lies in the future or how God will work out your trying circumstances. You can know, however, that God will give the victory after He accomplishes His work through the trials. When the deliverance comes, it will not be just a marginal rescue, but it will be abundance and blessing. God protects you and loves you within the trials, and He leads through all of these very hard things. Then He brings you out into a place of abundance. The trials are not easy, but they are necessary. God works through them and wonderfully provides abundance after the trial.

"Father, do the refining work that You need to do. When it is finished, bring me out into a place of abundance. I wait and long for that day."

Transformation (Sonnet 24)
Our God can take what's dead; it comes alive.
He changes darkness into brilliant light.
The sinful soul in holiness can thrive,
And He can take what's wrong and make it right.
He issues good from what seems bad to me.
What once was ugly now is beautiful.
Great blessing comes from seeming tragedy –
From crushing sadness makes a joyful soul.
He takes what's very weak and makes it strong –
What's crushed and makes it vibrant with His love.
He turns my sorrow into praise and song.
To meet my pain, He sends grace from above.
He takes what's broken and makes it complete,
And gives a vict'ry out of sure defeat.

Day 202

So that we may lead a tranquil and quiet life in all godliness and dignity. This is good and acceptable in the sight of God our Savior.
I Timothy 2:2b-3

This question has probably come into your mind many times: How can I please God in my illness? In the midst of your affliction, you feel limited in how much you can do. You are keenly aware of the sense of expectation to handle your trial correctly. You are just as keenly aware of how short you fall and of how easy it is to fail. So the question is valid. In your current situation, with its restrictions, challenges, and temptations, how can you please God?

In His Word God specifically reveals several ways in which Christians can please Him. Some of these ways are completely unaffected by whether or not someone is ill, while others can be even more readily applied to those who are ill. For the next several days, we will look at some ways in which you can know you are pleasing God in the midst of your situation.

First, God is pleased when His children lead a godly lifestyle. He wants us to live in a way that reflects His character. He is pleased when we are able to lead a tranquil, quiet life in godliness and dignity. Instead of having a life of chaos and confusion, God wants us to be peaceful. We should not be the blaring source of noise in our community. We should have dignity, acting in appropriate rather than foolish ways.

Another demonstration of a godly lifestyle is when we exhibit patient endurance though suffering unjustly (I Peter 2:20). When people treat us unfairly or cause us pain, we should patiently bear with them. Don't we have opportunities to do that in the midst of illness? Because they do not understand, people treat us wrong, and we can respond with patience. We can please God by living in a godly way.

"Father, I long to please You. Help me to do that by reflecting Your character in my peacefulness and patience with others."

Day 203

He has told you, O man, what is good;
And what does the LORD require of you
But to do justice, to love kindness,
And to walk humbly with your God?
Micah 6:8

We can please God through our illness by having a heart that is turned toward Him. This general concept is expressed in various ways. God is pleased with those who love Him (Deuteronomy 10:12). We can please God by something as basic as loving Him. God is pleased with those who wait for His lovingkindness (Psalm 147:11). We please Him by expecting Him to act according to His character by demonstrating His love.

God is pleased with those who fear Him (Acts 10:35). We can please God by having the proper respect for Him and recognizing our proper place before Him. God is pleased by those who walk in His ways (Deuteronomy 10:12). We can please God by choosing to follow His path and plan. God is pleased with those who walk humbly with Him (Micah 6:8). We please Him when we forget our own importance and follow Him.

God is pleased with faith (Hebrews 11:6) and with the prayer of the upright (Proverbs 15:8). We can please God by believing His Word and by bringing our

Bible-based requests to Him. God is pleased when someone asks for wisdom rather than temporal blessings or power (I Kings 3:10). We please Him when we desire what pleases Him more than what pleases us.

God is pleased when people speak what is right about Him (Job 42:8). We please God by accurately describing Him to others. Finally, God is pleased when we accurately handle His Word (II Timothy 2:15). We can please Him by studying His truth so that we can know and communicate its true meaning. All of these actions and attitudes are expressions of a heart that is directed toward God, a heart that pleases Him.

"Father, I desire my heart to be tender toward You. In this time of physical weakness, draw my heart closer to You. Make me more sensitive to Your ways."

Day 204

And do not neglect doing good and sharing, for with such sacrifices God is pleased.
Hebrews 13:16

We can please God through our illness by showing kindness. This is an area that is perhaps a little more challenging for us, because when we don't feel well, we want other people to be kind to us. It is our human tendency to crave kindness and to want to be waited on and pampered. When we make the effort to be kind to others in the midst of our own need, God is pleased.

God is pleased with those who love kindness (Micah 6:8) and with those who cling to kindness (Proverbs 3:3-4). Being kind should be important to us and something that we continue to insist upon. God is pleased with those who do good and share (Hebrews 13:16). We may not be able to do the same things for others or as many things for others as we used to do, but we can still be kind. That kindness may take different forms for us now. It may be expressed by a smile, a card, or a phone call, rather than cookies, hand-made gifts, or physical labor. God is pleased with those who bear fruit in good works (Colossians 1:10). Again, our kind works may have to be much simpler and far fewer than they were before, but any that we do bring pleasure to God.

God is pleased with those who give gifts for the sake of the gospel, especially when it requires sacrifice (Philippians 4:18). When we are weak, it does require sacrifice to serve others. Finally, God is pleased with those who serve Him with consideration for the weakness and struggles of others (Romans 14:18). We should be sensitive to the things that others struggle with and serve them in a way that will encourage them. Although we may be limited to some degree, none of us are so limited that we cannot be kind.

"Help me, Father, to please You by being kind to others with my words and actions. May my spirit be friendly and sweet rather than cranky and disagreeable."

Day 205

"Now, Israel, what does the LORD your God require from you, but . . . to serve the LORD your God with all your heart and with all your soul."
Deuteronomy 10:12

You can please God in your illness by continuing to render faithful service to Him. God is pleased when you bring your sacrifices and your service to Him (Ezekiel 20:40). He is not pleased by the amount that you do, but rather by the fact that you do it. Depending on the severity of your illness, you may be quite limited. You may have had to give up a ministry that you had lovingly performed for years. You may have had to reluctantly step aside from leadership and areas of responsibility. God is not cruel to expect you to do more than you are capable of. He knows your limitations because He gave them to you. Your service now is more of a sacrifice than ever, and God is pleased by what you are able to do for Him and bring to Him.

God is pleased by those who serve Him whole-heartedly (Deuteronomy 10:12). Again, the emphasis is not on how much you do. Instead, the emphasis is on the attitude and the spirit with which you do it. If you are serving out of a heart that loves God, He is pleased. If you are serving from a fervent desire to do something for God, He is pleased.

God is pleased when you present your body to Him as a sacrifice of worship (Romans 12:1). Your body is not the same as it was before. It cannot do as much. Once again, God is not concerned with the quantity or ability. All He wants is one hundred percent of what you have. If you were willing to give your strong, healthy, energetic body to God, are you not willing to give Him your tired, weak, and broken body? The key is that whatever you do and whatever you are capable of, it is all for Him.

"Father, You know that I can't do all that I once did. Help me to joyfully give you my service within the new limitations that You have placed on me."

Day 206

I will praise the name of God with song
And magnify Him with thanksgiving.
And it will please the LORD better than an ox
Or a young bull with horns and hoofs.
Psalm 69:30–31

The final means that we will examine for pleasing God through our illness is that of praise. God is pleased when we praise His name with song. He is pleased when there is still a song in our hearts and on our lips that will lift up His name. He is still the same great God that He always has been. He is worthy of our song.

God is pleased when we magnify Him with thanksgiving. When we thank God, we are declaring that He is big enough to meet our needs and to do something good for us. Perhaps it is easier for us to think of things for which we are not thankful, but it is better for us to think of things for which we are thankful. There are always blessings given to us by God for which we can give thanks.

These actions of praise and gratitude please God more than some monetary sacrifice, no matter how impressive that offering might be. Praise and gratitude are genuine gifts from a heart that loves God. God is pleased when we show gratitude for the wonderful and eternal gifts He has given us (Hebrews 12:28). There are blessings of God that can never be taken away. We have received benefits from God that can never be undone or lost, no matter what our condition and circumstances may be. It is appropriate to give God our gratitude with a spirit of reverence and awe. We should always be a little bit amazed at what the mighty God has done for us. Praise and thanksgiving may not be the easiest things for us to do in the midst of our illness, but they are guaranteed ways to please our God.

"Father, when my heart is heavy and rebels against the idea, help me to praise and thank You for the goodness that You continue to show to me."

Gateways to Praise (Sonnet 25)
That trials and tests are hard I can't deny;
At times they seem to cruelly break my heart
And pierce right through me like a wounding dart.
With grief and heaviness they make me sigh.
I share what Christ faced when He came to die;
Like Him, in learning suff'ring has a part.
In tests, Christ-like compassion gets its start.
"You'll be more like my Son," is God's reply.
When testing ends, what blessings there will be
Because of how God ably brings me through.
I'll stand amazed at all my God can do
And see what otherwise I'd never see.
The glorious vict'ry yields abundant song;
His awesome answers bring praise sweet and strong.

Day 207

For the word of the LORD is upright,
And all His work is done in faithfulness.
Psalm 33:4

If I did not know my God, I would have serious questions about what He is doing. If it were another person doing all of this to me, I would be justified in thinking him cruel and unfeeling. Cruelty, in fact, would seem to be the only logical explanation for what is happening in my life – if it were being done by a person.

That isn't the case. It isn't a faulty human who is controlling things; it is an all-wise, all-powerful, sovereign God. He cannot act outside His character. He cannot be cruel or unfeeling toward His children. It is impossible. His Word, whatever He declares regarding me, is right. What He commands to happen to me and what He declares is best for me is always correct and appropriate. There is no mistake, nor can there be. God cannot make mistakes.

God's work to me is done in faithfulness. He is a God who always remembers me. He is reliable and dependable. He will never forsake me, ignore me, or turn His back on me. He will stand by me forever and do what is right.

A god that I invent in my own mind could make mistakes. That kind of a god could mess up. He could lose track of what is going on and could easily overlook something. A god of my own invention could make a wrong decision or ignore the personal aspect in his focus on the grand scheme. But the true God, the God revealed in the Bible, will never have those kinds of failures. He will always do what is right, and He will always be faithful to me. I can trust Him. I can hope in Him. I can wait for Him to do His work. I can rejoice in His control.

"Thank You, Father, that You are the amazing God that You are. You can't make mistakes, and You can't forget me. Help me to trust Your plan."

Day 208

By You I have been sustained from my birth;
You are He who took me from my mother's womb;
My praise is continually of You.
Psalm 71:6

God is *"He who took me from my mother's womb."* The verb used seems to refer to the actual moment of birth, indicating that, in essence, God is the one who actually delivers the baby. This insight highlights the reality of the role of doctors and medicine. They are merely instruments that God uses, but God is the one who is in control and who is actually doing the work.

In other words, God is the one who gives life. None of us would be here if it were not for Him. Some babies die at birth and many others never reach that point, but God chose to give life to us. His giving of life indicates that He has a purpose for our lives. He birthed us for a reason.

The fact that God was so involved in our births also means that God is and has been very involved in our entire lives. He has been interacting with us from the very point of our birth. We have not lived even a second of life without God's being in control. God has been there for every step and every detail.

Being involved since birth, He has carefully arranged every event of our lives. With His watchful care since our very earliest moment, He has monitored and directed our lives. God was there at the beginning, and He has sustained us in every step, every breath, and every heartbeat since then. The one who was instrumental in giving us life is worthy to be trusted for maintaining that life.

"Father, You have been with me from the beginning. Nothing has escaped Your watchful eye. Help me to trust Your continued care for me."

Day 209

If I take the wings of the dawn,
If I dwell in the remotest part of the sea,
Even there Your hand will lead me,
And Your right hand will lay hold of me.
Psalm 139:9-10

It is a wonderfully comforting thought that I cannot escape God's presence. It does not matter where I am or what I am doing; God knows all about it because He is there with me. Others may forget that I exist; they may have no idea what is going on in my life. In their consideration I may have fallen into the category of people that aren't really part of life anymore. By contrast, I will never be insignificant, forgotten, or unknown to God. I will never fall off His radar. God knows every detail of my very unexciting life. He knows when I stand up or sit down. He knows all my thoughts and everything about me. He knows my words before I speak them.

In addition to knowing me very intimately when others have forgotten, He is also with me constantly though other friends may be scarce. Even if I die, I will be with God. If I could escape life, as I often long to do, and go to some remote, peaceful place, God would be with me there. His hand would still be with me and would still guide me.

Sometimes I feel like my life is a big dark cloud that somehow obscures me from everything normal. That dark cloud makes no difference to God. There is no darkness to Him; everything is bright. There is no setting, no circumstance, and no situation in which I can be separated from God. No matter how desperate, no matter how lonely, no matter how far removed, and no matter how dark my situation may be, God is right there with me. He knows all about it, and His hand is resting on my shoulder.

"Father, this truth is so amazing. In spite of everything, I have You. Always. Everywhere. Thank You that I can't escape You, no matter what happens."

Day 210

Do not hide Your face from me,
Do not turn Your servant away in anger;
You have been my help;
Do not abandon me nor forsake me,
O God of my salvation!
Psalm 27:9

We need God's help. No one else can really help us. Without God, we fail miserably. With Him, we prevail victoriously.

In this psalm David has claimed God as his defense. Many enemies have risen up against him, but David has no fear because God is with him, and God is able to make his enemies fall. David seeks God and longs to live in His presence. He yearns for this nearness to God because when God is with him, He hides him in times of trouble. David cries out to God and seeks Him diligently when all others, even his own family, have forsaken him. He pleads for God's nearness because he can't afford to have God forsake Him. God can be his source of help when all other sources have disappeared. David's only hope is to wait on God; He needs God to be at his side.

God can do for David what no one else can do in the midst of his trouble. When God is near, He can teach David through the circumstances. When God is at his side, He can lead David in the right steps. When God stands by David, He can deliver him and give him strength. David knows how fierce the attack is. He knows how unreliable the help of others is. He also knows how effective God's help is. Because of all these reasons, David calls on God desperately. He asks God not to hide or turn away, not to abandon or forsake him. These are prayers that God will answer, because God does not turn His back on His people. He will faithfully stand by amid the harshest of threats and when all others have turned aside.

"Oh, Father, I need You so much. Oh, God, my Help, let me find You always at my side."

Day 211

Let us hold fast the confession of our hope without wavering,
for He who promised is faithful.
Hebrews 10:23

God is faithful. He always keeps His promises, and He always keeps His word. This fact can give us confidence that we can firmly cling to. We don't need to waver or fear in the least. We know that God will do everything He has said. Titus 1:2 tells us that God cannot lie. It's not just that He *won't* lie, but that He *can't*. It is impossible for Him.

The same verse refers to the promise of eternal life, which God made *"long ages ago."* God's promises are ancient, remaining firmly established down through the many centuries. He has faithfully kept His promises for all those years, and He will continue to do so. His lengthy performance record is spotless. God always does what He says.

Hebrews 6:17-18 reminds us again that it is impossible for God to lie, but then those verses go on. As if God's inability to lie were not enough to convince us to believe His promises, God reinforced His reliability with an oath. Oaths are not something that God takes lightly. For Him to make an oath is to bind Himself inextricably to what He has promised.

God's purposes are sure. He intends to fulfill them. The concept of unfailing faithfulness is foreign enough to us humans that God gives us these reassuring proofs and guarantees. He is faithful. He cannot lie. He makes a promise and then binds Himself with an oath to keep that promise. Any one of those factors is sufficient to prove His reliability, but God gives these redundant reassurances in order to encourage our weak faith and our humanly-influenced evaluations.

"Thank You, Father, for the confidence I can have in You, knowing that You will do everything that You have promised."

Day 212

May it never be! Rather, let God be found true, though every man be found a liar, as it is written, 'That You may be justified in Your words, and prevail when You are judged."
Romans 3:4

Sometimes I find it difficult to believe what God says because His statements don't seem true to me. At times I simply don't understand them, but sometimes I downright disagree with them. As if my unbelief is not enough, I even look for proof that I am right. When something disappointing happens, I jump on it, saying, "See,

I was right. God really doesn't care." I base my conclusions on my feelings and on my own interpretation of "evidence."

The Bible says that when my conclusions differ from God's statements, I am wrong, and He is right. When I deny His truth, I am exhibiting pride. I am in the dangerous position of trying to make myself more correct than God. In such a conflict, I need to humble myself and remember that God decides what is true and right. I cannot be greater or more correct than God.

No matter how hard something is to believe, God is always true. When something from God's Word does not seem true to me, the fact of its reliability does not change. In this conflict, the problem is always with my belief, never with God's Word. I don't have to understand how His truth works; I must simply choose to believe by faith. In an illness, I doubt things like God's goodness, His love, His control, or His presence. I don't understand how they can be true when my life is like it is.

I need to remind myself that there are lots of other topics in God's Word that I don't understand either. I don't understand how God answers prayer though He has already planned what He will do. I don't understand how Satan can do His work, yet God is always in control. I don't understand the balance between the sovereignty of God and the free will of man. I don't understand the concepts of eternity or of the trinity. Yet I believe all those things. In the same way, I need to believe God's goodness and love even when I don't understand them. If God says it about Himself, it is true.

According to this verse, all of my friends could look at my situation and agree with me. They could add their opinions, proclaiming that God really isn't fair or good. Even if everyone I know agrees with me, we are all wrong, and God is right. God's words will always be proven true. He will never lose against man's accusations.

"Help me, Father, not to promote my thoughts over Your truth. Keep me sobered about the danger of such a position. Everything You say is always right."

Feelings and Faith (Sonnet 23)

My feelings and emotions come and go
Like ocean waves, with no stability.
Distracting, blinding, leading to and fro,
Their end is doubt, despair, despondency.
But faith and truth will constantly abide,
Unchangeable and steady like a rock.
When made my focus, they're a trusty guide,
Stability and hope on which to dock.

Emotion tells me truth's not true at all,
But truth persists in spite of how I feel.
Repeatedly my feelings make me fall,
But truth–based faith provides an even keel.
Though feelings linger which my heart disdains,
My faith rests firm in truth that e'er remains.

Day 213

To Him who alone does great wonders,
For His lovingkindness is everlasting.
Psalm 136:4

God is *"[He] who alone does great wonders."* There is something unique about God. He is the only one who can do certain things, and He does them alone, without needing any helpers. Without the help of anything or anyone else, God is able to do these works by His great power.

God is able to accomplish and execute great things. The wonders that He does are things so wonderful and amazing that they are differentiated and separated from any other works. There is nothing else to compare with the things God does. God, without help and without needing to rely on outside resources, is able to accomplish what He has planned to do.

God's acts are worthy of being praised and magnified. By their very nature they place God on a level above everyone else. His acts are so wonderful that they distinguish Him as doing something that no one else can do. They effectively demonstrate that there is no one else like Him. God has no equal. In other words, only God can do miracles, and He doesn't need any help.

"Father, thank You that You are capable of doing what no one else can even dream of. You are unique in Your power. Thank You that I can call You my God."

Day 214

"In the wilderness He fed you manna which your fathers did not know, that He might humble you and that He might test you, to do good for you in the end."
Deuteronomy 8:16

There are lots of things in life that we don't understand. The Israelites found themselves in such a situation. When they needed food, God supplied manna for them. The manna was something new and unknown to them. They did not understand it. It was unfamiliar and uncomfortable to them. It demanded faith as they trusted God to supply it on a day-by-day basis. It demanded totally illogical obedience; five days of the week they couldn't gather more than a day's supply, but on the sixth day they had to gather enough for two days. It demanded the labor to gather it from the ground each day.

God Himself declares that He used the manna to humble them and to test them. There certainly were a lot of uncomfortable and misunderstood things about the manna. God states, though, that His ultimate purpose for the manna was to do them good in the end. The process of living by faith and obedience in relation to the manna was good for the people. They didn't realize that the good end was coming, but it was.

Likewise, our lives are full of things that are unfamiliar, uncomfortable, and incomprehensible. These things require faith and obedience. They require us to humble ourselves before God and simply follow His plan whether we understand it or not. Just like He did for Israel, God will bring us to a good end through the strange things He has chosen. As humans we don't always understand the good, but it is good nevertheless. The good things may not always seem good at first. We may not like them or want to accept them, but they are ultimately good for us. God will bring His good result in the end.

"Father, help me to trust You to take what makes no sense to me and to use it for good. Help me to humbly follow You through it all."

Day 215

He heals the brokenhearted
And binds up their wounds.
Psalm 147:3

Sometimes life just hurts. Our human hearts and emotions are frail; they are not made to withstand trauma. The burdens and challenges of our situation can be too much for us to handle. We might wake up in the night with a heart that is hurting, unable to stand the pain. The wounds are so deep we don't think they will ever heal. We may think of our distress as a constant ache or a soul in agony. These are wounds that no doctor can do anything for and that no medicine or treatment will help. What other way is there to describe our condition except that we are brokenhearted?

Does God understand the pain of our heart? Oh, yes. He records in His Word the cries of others who have gone before us. Some of them express their pain very strongly. The psalmists refer to things like constant sorrow and troubles of the soul. They speak of being crushed, benumbed, faint, and wounded in their spirits. They talk of groaning and weeping. Our similar cries of pain are no surprise or shock to God.

How does God respond to us in these times of intense hurt? God knows. He sees. His eyes are always on us. He does not miss a single trouble or hurt that comes into our lives. He is never unaware of our pain. He knows how hard it is, and He responds with loving compassion. God supports the afflicted. He heals the hearts that are broken, and He binds up the wounds that are deep in our souls.

God may heal partially through the love of others, but He can also give healing from Himself without needing to use any external sources. God is the only one who can give this kind of healing, and He can do it without help. God can heal the wounds completely, and any scars that remain are merely reminders of the healing He has given. When God heals, it doesn't hurt anymore.

"Father, I'm hurting beyond belief. Will You heal my broken heart? Will You bind up those wounds so that I can be whole again?"

Day 216

The LORD is near to the brokenhearted
And saves those who are crushed in spirit.
Psalm 34:18

We all face times in which we are brokenhearted and in which our spirits are crushed. These are very difficult times to face. Regardless of how others respond to us, whether they support us with comfort or ignore us in neglect, the question that we most want to have answered is "What is God's response toward me?" We want to know if God will be different. Will He pay more attention than other people? Will He understand our struggle? Will He care more than others do? We can bear the inadequate responses of others if only we know that God is constantly with us in our hour of deepest need. If we have His attention and concern, we can go on.

The Bible is very clear that we do indeed have God's attention when we are hurting. He notices, and His noticing has a direct effect on the way He thinks and feels toward us. When our heart is breaking, God is near to us. He stands nearby, showing His support. He is ready to steady us if we stumble and ready to comfort us when we cry. He never goes far away, so that at a moment's notice, He can reassure us with the words, "I'm right here." Isn't that what we want when we're hurting – to have someone at our side?

God has compassion on us, and His compassion is active. When Jesus felt compassion, He always acted upon it by meeting the need. God doesn't just make a mental note of our pain and move on. He cares about it and takes upon Himself the responsibility of ministering to us in our need. He sees Himself as our helper, our sustainer, and our strength. When our heart is breaking, what a comfort it is to know that He is near to us!

"Father, thank You that You are near. Thank You that You never leave me in my time of pain, but that I can always find You at my side."

Day 217

> *Cast your burden upon the LORD and He will sustain you;*
> *He will never allow the righteous to be shaken.*
> *Psalm 55:22*

When we are brokenhearted, God's constant and compassionate nearness is a great comfort. It is not, however, the full extent of His response to us. Human companions are often very limited. In many situations there is nothing they can actually do to help us other than to express their concern. God is not so limited. Beyond the comfort-giving aspect, He is actually able to act on our behalf.

Some of God's actions are visible outwardly. God hears our prayers and answers us. He sometimes does that by rescuing us from the difficult situation we are in. Being delivered from the intense circumstance can bring immediate healing to our hurting hearts.

Even if God does not rescue us outwardly, He is faithful to rescue us inwardly. It is our inner man – our heart and our soul – that is wounded and so shaken. That is where we need the most help. God sustains us. He gives us inner strength, holding us steady so that we don't waver. Instead of asking us to carry the weight of our burden, He carries it for us day after day. He lifts the weight that threatens to tear more deeply into our hurting hearts. God is with us in our trouble, and He restores our soul that is so wounded. Instead of the hurt, He is able to put boldness and strength into our soul.

Ultimately, God heals our broken hearts. He doesn't leave the hurt to continue indefinitely. He doesn't expect us to continue with that pain. He takes the pain in our hearts, and He alleviates it. He makes it better. God heals our hearts.

"Father, the physical struggles are hard enough, but the inner hurts are far worse. I need Your healing for my hurting heart and Your strength for my soul."

Day 218

> *He restores my soul;*
> *He guides me in the paths of righteousness*
> *For His name's sake.*
> *Psalm 23:3*

When we understand God's response to broken hearts, how should that affect us practically? It should, of course, encourage us as we comprehend that God knows and cares, that He wants to help, and that He can help. We don't have to be ashamed to come to Him with our hurt, no matter how bad it is. We don't have to be embarrassed that we are still hurting or that we are hurting so badly. God knows we are human and that we can be overwhelmed by the pain of things that come our way.

In His compassion, God will hold us, comfort us, and surround us with His love. His compassion, however, is not limited to mere sympathy or empty words. God is able to do something about our hurts. He can heal the hurt and take it away. No one and nothing else can alleviate this kind of pain. We may determine just to give it time, to lean on the support of others, or to push through by sheer willpower. These things may have some effect, but they cannot give real and complete healing. That only comes from God.

We can pray for this healing. If we realize God's ability to alleviate this pain of the heart and His great compassion in wanting to be the healer of our hurts, then we can come confidently to Him and ask. Instead of trying on our own to conquer the pain, and instead of seeking comfort from other sources, let's turn to the one who can truly do something about it. Let's go to God, the Physician who can heal what no one else can even see. Let's ask Him for healing. Why suffer hopelessly, thinking there is no answer? It's such a simple thing, but proven by God time and time again to be effective – take it to Him in prayer.

"Oh Father, my heart is hurting so much that I can barely function. I can't do anything about this. I need You. Will You take away the pain?"

Day 219

*Therefore humble yourselves under the mighty hand of God,
that He may exalt you at the proper time.
I Peter 5:6*

There is a vast difference between us and God. No matter how good a Christian we may think we are, when we look at God, we are nothing. God had to teach this lesson to Job. He reminded Job of how completely the earth is under His control. He reminded Job of His power and of what He had done. In the process He also reminded Job of how puny he was; Job was incapable of doing any of the works God had done. Job responded by saying that he had spoken things he did not understand. He responded in humility, as he stepped back in the realization that God is God.

If we had any concept of who God is, what He knows, His power and wisdom, and if we truly understood how mighty His hand is, we would quickly recognize our own lowly state. God is the author, the potter, the craftsman, the creator, and the gardener. We are merely the material with which He works. We are to humble ourselves and lay ourselves low before God. We are to submissively allow ourselves to be worked on by His mighty hand.

We must submit to what God says and does no matter how much it hurts. God's hand is not poised to destroy us; rather it is creating something in us. We must be completely yielded to God, because that is how we learn and are changed. We can only know what He shows and teaches us. It is only as we respond to what He shows and teaches that we can grow and be pleasing to Him. Our progress can never go further than our submission to the teaching He gives. It is therefore important for us to always submit and agree with God so that we can grow as He intends.

"Keep my heart tender, Father, so that I will be as yielded
as I possibly can be to Your hand and work."

Humble Under His Hand
The mighty Creator has charge of my life;
His wisdom determines each blessing and strife.
His love overarches and always surrounds.
His presence is with me; His mercy abounds.

Humble under His mighty hand.
Humble in this – the way He's planned.
In everything I know His way is best.
I must obey; I will submit and rest.

The good and the bad both proceed from His hand.
He knows what He does when I don't understand.
In all of the big things He works out His will;
In each of the details my heart can be still.

Humble under His mighty hand.
Humble in this – the way He's planned.
In everything I know His way is best.
I must obey; I will submit and rest.

Day 220

"With weeping they will come,
And by supplication I will lead them;
I will make them walk by streams of waters,
On a straight path in which they will not stumble;
For I am a father to Israel,
And Ephraim is My firstborn."
Jeremiah 31:9

It is hard to walk day after day. It is hard to remain on the path. When your eyes overflow with tears, it is hard even to see the path. When you have difficulty following or seeing the path before you, you have a faithful Guide.

God is loving and gentle and compassionate and caring. He sees the tears that impair your vision, and He feels the burdened heart that produces the tears. He responds by leading you gently. He repeatedly gives words of guidance and instruction to lead you step by step. God provides your needs along the way. He leads you by gentle streams that comfort you and supply water for you.

God provides a path on which you can walk. He makes it straight so it is easy to follow. He makes it smooth to keep you from stumbling in your weakness. It is not God's intention for you to stumble and fall along the way. At each stage of your life, even in difficulty, God makes that particular path as straight and smooth as He possibly can. He adjusts and improves each path within the confines of where He needs to take you and the terrain that the path must of necessity cover.

When the path is difficult, when your eyes strain to see it, and when your feet struggle to follow it, listen for the voice of your gentle Guide. Trust your feet to the path that He has designed and modified for you. He will guide you all the way.

"Father, You know the weakness of my eyes and feet. I need Your help and guidance on the path. Help me to take the right steps and not to fall."

Day 221

For momentary, light affliction is producing for us
an eternal weight of glory far beyond all comparison.
II Corinthians 4:17

Paul did not lose heart in his affliction (v. 16) because he realized there were greater issues at stake than his personal suffering. There were eternally valuable things happening in the midst of his trial, and he kept the proper perspective between the temporary and the eternal. Yes, there was affliction, but he knew that it was momentary and only of this lifetime. It was also light in comparison to the eternal benefits. The trial was producing something; it was actively working in a positive way to fashion something valuable and lasting.

The positive work of a trial is not in doubt; it is not to be debated or wondered about. The clear statement of the verb is that the affliction *is producing* something. The product itself is amazing. The eternal weight of glory is so abundant and of such value that it is far beyond all comparison with the affliction. There is no question about the value of what is produced. The value of the eternal reward surpasses the temporal suffering in such a dramatic way that the difference is both obvious and overwhelming.

What were the eternal benefits that Paul was seeing? There is the inner renewing mentioned in verse sixteen, but it seems that Paul is specifically remembering the spiritual fruit that he had referred to in verse fifteen. God's gracious gospel was spreading to more and more people. Christ was being exalted, and God was receiving glory. How can affliction compare to things like that? Again, the comparison is not even close. Understandably, Paul was encouraged when he looked at the eternal benefit being produced in the midst of his earthly groaning (II Corinthians 5:2 & 4).

"Father, this affliction is hard to bear. Thank You that in heaven I will completely forget it as I see the eternal work that You have done through it."

Day 222

The LORD sustains all who fall
And raises up all who are bowed down.
Psalm 145:14

The burden on your back is heavy. It pushes your body toward the ground and sometimes forces you to your knees. The path upon which you walk is treacherous. In addition to the difficulty of the terrain which demands every bit of strength you have, there are many obstacles that cause you to stumble. With such challenges, is it any wonder that you sometimes find yourself on the ground?

God is compassionate, and He responds compassionately to those who fall. When God sees needy people bowed down beneath a heavy burden, He raises them up. When He observes His children fallen on a difficult path, He sustains them. God looks gently on the fallen and the needy.

Do you think this truth is not for you? Would you accuse God of letting you fall? Do you think He has left you alone, fallen in agony and unable to move on?

This cannot be the case. The word *all* is given twice; God sustains *all* who fall and He raises up *all* who are bowed down.

The timing varies from person to person and from situation to situation. God might know you need time to catch your breath. Perhaps you have sustained an injury that requires time to heal before moving on, but God is not going to leave you. He is not going to neglect you in your fallen condition. He will keep you and lift you back up.

The word *sustain* speaks of support. God gives the level of support needed. At the very least He props the fallen one up, helping that needy person to lean on His capable shoulders. If necessary, God even picks the fallen one up, holding him in His arms. God is compassionate. You may stumble and fall along the way, but God is always there to carry your load and to give you the support you need. He can set you back on your feet and keep you moving on the path.

> *"Father, my load is crushing me. I need Your strong arms*
> *to lift me up and carry my burden."*

Day 223

> *To Him who made the heavens with skill,*
> *For His lovingkindness is everlasting.*
> *Psalm 136:5*

God is *"[He] who made the heavens with skill."* God created the heavens, including all the planets, stars, and galaxies that stretch further than man is able to comprehend. The more man studies space and the more powerful telescopes he builds, the more he realizes how vast and intricate space is. God's creating of that vast realm speaks of His tremendous power and skill.

The emphasis in this verse, however, is on God's wisdom. Creating the heavens took an incredible amount of intelligence and understanding. God designed the solar system so that everything works. He placed things at the proper distances from each other. The moon influences the tides without causing chaos. The sun is close enough to sustain life but not so close that the earth is burned up. God created the sun, moon, and earth so that they work together.

God established the orbits so that they accomplish their purposes; they provide predictable seasons of seedtime and harvest. God established the orbits skillfully, so that after many millennia the planets' courses are still predictable. None of the planets have crashed into each other. The smallest error, compounded over time, could cause disaster. There has been no disaster, however, because God did not make the slightest error.

Astronomers have been studying the heavens for centuries and millennia, yet they still have not learned everything. They are constantly making new discoveries, and so much more remains that they haven't begun to learn about yet. The heavens are far beyond man's ability to understand, yet God had the intelligence to make something so complex.

"Father, Your wisdom is amazing. You completely understand things that I have no idea about it. Help me to trust Your wisdom and to remember that You know exactly how to do everything."

Day 224

Many, O LORD my God, are the wonders which You have done,
And Your thoughts toward us;
There is none to compare with You.
If I would declare and speak of them,
They would be too numerous to count.
Psalm 40:5

Sick people have a reputation for complaining. I don't want to accuse you of complaining, because not everyone does. Sometimes, however, you are asked a question, and you have to give an answer. You've thought about your condition enough and have described it so frequently that you know what to say. You rattle off your speech of explanations and symptoms, and you can't help but notice that it is quite a list. It's not a very exciting list; in fact, it can be downright discouraging.

Did you ever think that perhaps you're counting the wrong things? This verse refers to some pretty wonderful things to count. You can count God's wonders. Perhaps I should say that you can attempt to count God's wonders, because they are too many to count. How could you ever compile a list consisting just of the wonders He has done in your own life? When you add the wonders He has done for people you know and for people throughout history, the list is astronomical. There is no one else like God; there is no one who can compare with Him. He does so much for you, and all His deeds are wondrous.

You can also count (or try to count) God's thoughts toward you. God thinks about you all the time. Even if you knew all of God's thoughts, you would never be able to list them all. God thinks of you so much, and all of His thoughts are good. These are two wonderful lists to ponder: the list of God's amazing wonders and the list of God's loving thoughts. The list of your symptoms, needs, and troubles may be lengthy, but it has a limit. The lists of God's wonders and thoughts are endless. These lists never end, and the items on them cannot be counted.

"There is so much good in You, Father, that it overwhelming outweighs all the bad that I have seen. Help me to focus my thoughts on the right list."

Day 225

The LORD appeared to him from afar, saying,
"I have loved you with an everlasting love;
Therefore I have drawn you with lovingkindness."
Jeremiah 31:3

Sometimes my heart cries out in anguish that God doesn't love me. On occasion, the words even slip out when I speak to others. I can easily doubt His love when I look at my circumstances and interpret them with my human eyesight. Things are dark, painful, bewildering, and oppressive. I don't see how God's actions toward me can be good or kind. They seem only cruel and unfair, and someone who loves me would not treat me cruelly. All of these thoughts are based on my perception, my uncertainty, and my lack of understanding. Now let me examine the facts.

It is a fact that God loves me. God says so, and God cannot lie. The Bible is filled with statements and examples of God's love.

It is a fact that God tells me of His love. He doesn't hold Himself aloof, leaving me to wonder whether or not He loves me. He states it repeatedly, assuring me of His love. He backs up those statements with His actions toward me.

It is a fact that God's love is everlasting. He loved me even before I knew of His love. He will continue to love me forever, every moment of every day of my life – and then beyond. God's love for me will never change.

It is a fact that God's love has caused Him to draw me to Himself. I was unlovely, but God did not ignore me. He didn't wait for me to become lovable. When I was still a sinner, He made a tremendous sacrifice in order to show His love for me and draw me to Himself.

When I consider the facts, I must admit the truth. It is foolish to deny God's love. It is silly to complain of it to others. It is ludicrous to even think of telling God those words to His face. God does love me, and He loves me deeply and eternally.

"Thank You, Father, for Your patient, kind, and everlasting love. Thank You that Your love is dependent on Your character rather than on my perceptions."

Day 226

"For He inflicts pain, and gives relief;
He wounds, and His hands also heal."
Job 5:18

This verse contains some negative phrases. We see that God wounds and inflicts pain. While we may not understand all of the reasons for which God brings pain, we are certainly aware that it happens. Within His plan, God must at times bring some hard things into our lives. The discipline and molding do come from God's hands, and they are painful and wounding.

We don't like those hard times, but the good news is that God doesn't stop there. The process is not over when God has corrected or torn out or cut out. He does not leave us hurting. After God has done the "surgery," He also brings the recovery. There are positive phrases in the verse to balance the negative words. God also gives relief and healing. That needed healing comes from His own hands.

Can you imagine any doctor more skilled than God Himself? When God's hands give the healing, we can be sure it is effective. The pain is forgotten as God soothes it. The wounds are healed as God mends the injured places. God finishes the process. The painful wounds are necessary, but they are not the end. Healing and recovery are also part of the process. They are such an important part of the process that God will not forget them. When we are wounded and in pain, we just need to wait. The same God who of necessity brought the pain will also bring relief. His hands will heal our wounds.

"Father, help me to remember that I'm still in the middle of the process. May I not despair, but wait hopefully for the healing You will bring."

Healing to Come (Sonnet 41)
At times our God afflicts - not willingly.
He disciplines so teaching can be done,
For training yields a righteous fruit, you see,
And shows He won't abandon His true son.
The process is not done when our pain grows,
For then He heals and sweet relief He'll send.
With great compassion, His love overflows.
Let's turn to Him so He our wounds can tend.
As He perfects, He'll mend us and restore
And then confirm our faith in His true Word,
Establishing a base that is secure
And giving strength to trust in all we've heard.
And so the pain will last a little while.
Just wait, then for a lifetime feel His smile.

Day 227

For the LORD takes pleasure in His people;
He will beautify the afflicted ones with salvation.
Psalm 149:4

God's people are sometimes afflicted. The same verse refers to God's children as *"His people"* and as *"the afflicted ones."* Being a child of God does not exempt us from affliction. It does, however, put us into a special group, because it affects the way God looks at us and interacts with us in our affliction.

God takes pleasure in His people. He is pleased with them. He has affection for them. He delights in them and enjoys them. He has favor for them. All of these descriptions can be summed up in a very "human" way: these are people that God really likes.

God therefore pays close attention to what is happening in their lives, and He wants things to turn out well for them. We have all had similar responses in our desires for others. We have seen a friend suffering, and our hearts have been moved. We have earnestly desired for their situation to change and for them to prosper again. This is how God thinks of us. He cares for us so much that He knows what is happening, and He wants things to go well. As humans, we are limited to having hope for others without any means of actually bringing about relief or prosperity for them. God is not so limited. When God desires a blessed situation for us, He can make it happen.

God goes beyond just seeing what happens to the afflicted. He intervenes in their lives. He beautifies them. He makes their situation more attractive and worthy of note. What is the adornment that He gives to accomplish that purpose? He dresses the afflicted with salvation. He delivers them, giving great victory. He prospers them, giving aid and welfare. God intervenes for those He cares about, and He helps them in their situation.

"Oh, Father, you do care. You do want the best for me. You do act to help me. May I not doubt your interest and intervention for me."

Day 228

The LORD of hosts has sworn saying, "Surely, just as I have intended so it has happened, and just as I have planned so it will stand."
Isaiah 14:24

Remember when you thought your life was crazy? You had just been promoted at work and had inherited lots of new responsibilities. You were in the middle of a cross-country move. You had just paid to get your oldest child started with braces. You had just committed to a new ministry that took up hours of your time.

Those situations were challenging enough in themselves, and then the next round hit. Your pastor suddenly resigned, initiating a major transition at church. You realized that your parents needed extra care. One of your children started having problems that required extra time and wisdom. Your husband lost his job (with its health insurance) and had trouble finding a new one. By now, you were thinking that it couldn't possibly get any worse. Then your health fell apart.

When that happened in the midst of a year that was already challenging, God was not surprised in the least. Not only did He know about each of your challenges, He knew they would all happen at the same time. God didn't sit in heaven and say, "Oops! I scheduled things wrong. I should have saved one of those for next year." To you, the multiplied problems seem like overload on top of overload, but God purposefully orchestrated all of it to happen at once.

Everything always happens exactly as God plans it. What He plans stands, with not an ounce of variation. This was true in the past. Everything that has happened so far has happened exactly as God intended it. The same will be true of the future. Everything that He has determined for the future will stand exactly as He has planned it. God is still completely in control of what He planned and subsequently brought about. When He planned your situation, He also planned the resolution of it. God has a plan for how things will turn out, and that plan will also be accomplished precisely according to His plan.

"Father, I would never have planned it this way, but You did. I understand that what happened was no accident, but carefully prepared by You.
Help me to wait to also see Your planned answer."

Day 229

"Come, let us return to the LORD.
For He has torn us, but He will heal us;
He has wounded us, but He will bandage us."
Hosea 6:1

Sometimes God has to send hard things into our lives. God knows the reason for those hard things. Perhaps it is to mature us and teach us. Perhaps it is to discipline us. Whatever the reason, it doesn't feel good. These hard times call for descriptions like torn, wounded, broken, aching, and hurting. Although we don't like them, those things are necessary as part of God's work.

The pain, however, is only part of the process. Those hard things are not the end result; they are only the preparation so that God can work out what He really wants to accomplish. God doesn't leave us in our hurting and broken condition. He finishes the process by giving recovery.

After the pain God heals and bandages. He knows every cut and scrape, and He carefully tends to each one. He knows what ointment and comfort is necessary, and He gently bandages the wounds. God's healing erases the wounds and eliminates the pain. We are left better than ever. When God finishes the process by healing the hurts, He has then accomplished His purposes in us.

The verse calls us to come and return to this tender Physician. We have to allow Him to touch us and care for us. We have to trust Him to treat us properly. When God has disciplined, we must return to Him in submission and compliance. If, in the process of our trial, we have allowed impurities to get into our wounds, we must be willing to have those cleansed. When we go to God, we must go to Him with corrected hearts so He can heal the wounds with no infection remaining trapped inside. God does heal and bandage the wounds. Why then would we not turn to Him?

"I am hurting, Father, and I ask You to finish the process by giving Your healing. Help me to remove any impurities so that You can complete Your work in me."

Day 230

For of His fullness we have all received, and grace upon grace.
John 1:16

As you have gone through your illness, you have received grace from God. You are aware of that. You recognize that His grace has helped you through many difficult days. It has sustained you through bad news and trying symptoms. What a blessing to receive that grace!

As you consider your unworthiness and the unending need for God's help, have you ever wondered when God would get tired of you? Have you wondered how long He would keep giving you grace before He decides that you've had enough? What happens when His grace runs out?

The good news is that God's grace never runs out. He just keeps piling on more and more grace. The word *upon* in John 1:16 means *instead of.* We may think that we've received our share of grace and that God will now substitute something else instead. We find that what He gives instead is simply more grace.

God's grace is sufficient for every test. God does not meagerly portion out His grace. He makes His grace abound. There are no limits or rations; God pours it out in tremendous quantities. His grace abounds to the point that there is more available than we are even able to take in. His grace extends over our heads and beyond what our arms can hold.

Why does God pour out so much grace? He gives it so that we are completely sufficient and equipped for whatever He asks of us. We have more than we need so that we can continue in all of the good things that He wants us to do. There is no situation that is beyond our ability to withstand, because God gives abundant grace to enable and uphold us.

"Father, thank You for Your never-ending supply of grace.
I ask You for more of it for my needs today."

Day 231

"He who offers a sacrifice of thanksgiving honors Me;
And to him who orders his way aright
I shall show the salvation of God."
Psalm 50:23

When life stinks, it's hard to be thankful. Man's natural inclination is to complain instead. In a testimony service, perhaps you look around at others and expect them to participate; after all, their lives are pretty good. Why should you share anything? You used to, back when life was normal, and you will again if you ever recover, but for now, the task of giving thanks belongs to others.

Really? The truth is that God is always good. There is always something to praise Him for. He always deserves praise because of who He is. Giving thanks is a way of honoring God. Doesn't God deserve honor?

With the limitations of your life, don't you wish there were something you could do to exalt and serve God? In addition to your limitations for service, it may also seem that your daily responses and attitudes too often fall far short of giving God the glory He deserves. Giving thanks is a wonderful way to do something about that. It is something active and deliberate that you can do to give glory to God. By choosing to praise Him, you can be confident that God is receiving glory from your life.

This verse does refer to a sacrifice of praise. It isn't always easy to thank God. Sometimes it requires great effort and an overlooking of many negative things. God, however, is honored by that sacrifice. Thank Him for the blessings. Even what seems bad is actually good within God's plan, and you can praise Him for that good even when you don't understand what it is. It can be a battle to be thankful, but it is also a fail-proof way to honor God. You may not be able to do much else, so let thanks be your offering to God. What can you thank Him for today?

"Father, help me to be thankful even when it hurts. I do want to honor You. Help me not to shrink back from this method of doing so."

Day 232

For I am confident of this very thing, that He who began a good work in you will perfect it until the day of Christ Jesus.
Philippians 1:6

I am a work in progress. I'll be the first to admit that the job is not finished yet. There is far more work left to do than what has already been done. Sometimes (or, if the truth be told, most of the time) I think that the project is beyond hope. I'll never make it. I'll never be all that God wants me to be.

When I think this way, however, I am focused more on the project than I am on the Architect. The project may not seem to have much potential, but the one doing the job is beyond compare. God is doing a good work in me. What other kind of work would God do? He always does a good work.

God planned the work. He made the blueprint, and He designed something wonderful. Because He knows what His creation is supposed to look like when it is finished, He knows how to go about the process. He will use the proper tools and materials to achieve His desired result.

Additionally, I can have confidence that God will complete the work. God planned the work and started the work, and God does not quit. He will not give up on me. It is a life-long process; the work won't be completed overnight. God is patient to stick with it and to gradually lead me in sanctification and growth.

I can't do the work on my own, but I don't have to. God has taken that task for Himself. He has determined to do the work, and He will complete what He has started. I don't have to fret or despair. Instead of demanding instant results or creating self-made, unreasonable expectations, I can be as patient with myself as God is patient. He knows it is a long process, and He is committed to carrying it out day by day and year by year. I can let God work in His way and in His time. He will finish what He has started.

"Help me, Father, to stop being discouraged and unreasonable. Help me to place myself in Your capable hands and to allow You to do the work that You know how to do."

Day 233

"Abide in Me, and I in you. As the branch cannot bear fruit of itself unless it abides in the vine, so neither can you unless you abide in Me."
John 15:4

While some people may prefer to let others do things for them, most of us prefer to handle things on our own. We want to be strong and independent, able to take care of ourselves, and capable of handling what life throws at us. Instead of admitting weakness and need, we work fervently to present ourselves as being fine on our own.

This quest for independence influences our interactions with others. In our attempt to maintain an admirable, unwavering testimony through the trial, we hide all evidences of weakness – no public tears, no admissions of struggles, no requests for specific prayer.

It is one thing to keep ourselves independent from others, but it is another thing entirely when we try to keep ourselves independent from God. In our arrogance, we refuse to admit our weakness to God, attempting to prove to Him that we are good Christians who are able to rise above any trial. We want to rely on ourselves spiritually rather than being desperate for His help.

With this independent determination, we limit ourselves. We defeat our own purpose by making ourselves incapable of bearing fruit. It is impossible for us to produce fruit without God's help. We would be much better off acknowledging how completely we need Him and admitting that living through this trial is way too big for us. With our best and most dedicated efforts, we still struggle with being consistent or seeing complete victories. We need God so much. We will never be able to make it through on our own. Only through Christ can we have victory and bear fruit.

"Father, I need You desperately, and I don't want to ever forget it. Not only do I need You now in this trial, but I always will, even when my illness is only a memory."

It's God's Work (Sonnet 8)
Though former works for God form a long line,
I know I can do nothing on my own.
The power's always His and never mine.
Abide in Him so profit can be shown.
Because it's God alone who does the task
In every job, both large and very small,
How can I any private credit ask?
No glory's mine, for God deserves it all.
The choice is His, it certainly would seem,
Of whom I'll serve and how and when and where.
He might choose ways that I could never dream;
He knows what's best His glory to declare.
So here am I, Lord. Use me all my days.
Display Your pow'r alone; take all the praise.

Day 234

Therefore my spirit is overwhelmed within me;
My heart is appalled within me.
Psalm 143:4

Are you overwhelmed today? Or is *today* too narrow? Are you overwhelmed frequently or even constantly? It's easy to become overwhelmed when every day is full of challenges and nothing seems to be improving. Several of the psalms discuss people who are overwhelmed. The word, sometimes translated *faint*, occurs in five different psalms. The word picture is powerful; it conveys the idea of languishing and being shrouded in darkness. To be overwhelmed or faint is like being wrapped up in dark clothing or surroundings, except that it refers to the heart rather than the body.

In Psalm 61:2, the psalmist is in this condition. His heart is faint, and he feels like he is at the end of the earth. In Psalm 77:3, the psalmist's spirit grows faint, becoming more and more so, even when he thinks on God. Nothing seems to help. The title of Psalm 102 identifies it as a psalm of an afflicted man who is faint and crying out to God. The man is in the midst of a severe illness in which he is very lonely and is misunderstood by his friends. Psalm 142:3 tells of a man whose spirit is overwhelmed due to danger and a trap hidden in his path. In Psalm 143:4, the psalmist is overwhelmed due to external pressures that he faces.

Perhaps the worst thing about being overwhelmed is feeling like there's nothing you can do about it. You seem to be in a deep, dark hole where there is no help and from which there is no exit. The good news is that there is help. There is something you can do. Many of God's children in the past, including the psalmists described above, overcame their overwhelming situations. The next several entries will consider what these five psalms teach about definite steps to take when your spirit is overwhelmed.

"Father, I am overwhelmed, and it seems that there is no way out. Show me what I can do to encourage and stabilize my faint heart."

Day 235

From the end of the earth I call to You when my heart is faint;
Lead me to the rock that is higher than I.
Psalm 61:2

The first thing we can do when our heart is faint is to call out to God. In each of our five psalms, the psalmists begin this way (61:1-2; 77:1; 102:1; 142:1 & 6; 143:1). These men simply cry out to God and ask God to hear them.

When we are overwhelmed, we want someone to talk to. There will be times when no one else is paying any attention to us (142:4). That is never the case with God. His ears are always open to hear our cries. His heart is always receptive to care about our struggles. No matter how many times we have gone to Him before, we can still go again. Even if we are telling Him the very same things, God is still available to hear us, but He can't hear us if we don't call out to Him.

We must recognize God as the source we must go to, but just going is not enough. We also need God to hear us. The psalmists want to know that they have God's attention, and they ask God to hear them. They ask God not to hide from them, but to pay attention and notice them (102:2). It does no good to ask for help or to tell our heart burden to someone who is not listening. As we call out to God, we can be confident that He hears every word. He is not distracted, but is carefully paying attention to us.

As the psalmists call out to God, they pour out their complaints and tell God all the challenging and overwhelming details (142:2). These cries are not casual and half-hearted. They are desperate cries in desperate times. They represent souls in distress. When we are overwhelmed and distressed, we can confidently cry out to God, asking and expecting Him to hear us.

"Father, my heart is faint and I want to fall. Please hear my cry. Listen to my lament. Pay attention to me. I need to talk to You."

Day 236

When my spirit was overwhelmed within me,
You knew my path.
In the way where I walk
They have hidden a trap for me.
Psalm 142:3

The second thing that we can do when our spirit is overwhelmed is to know God's character. We need to remember truths about our God, recall His attributes, and remind ourselves of what He is like. We need to focus on these aspects of God's character. The psalmists make several good observations about what God is like.

First, God has all knowledge, including knowledge of our situation. The psalmist recognizes that God knows his path (142:3). It is comforting to remember that God knows about our troubles and our path. He is not blindly unaware, but knows exactly where we are and our condition. God knows all about us, all the reasons why we're hurting, and all the symptoms and details of our situation.

Second, God is sovereign. His sovereign hand is at work in every situation (102:23). The psalmist attributes his condition to the work of God and realizes that God does exactly what He has planned to do.

Third, God is a caring God. He cares about our struggle when no one else does (142:3-4). When we have no support from anyone else, God cares.

Fourth, God has faithfully and historically shown compassion to hurting people (102:12-13, 17, 19-20). That's who God is. He simply cares about people who are hurting.

Fifth, God is faithful and righteous (143:1). He makes right judgments on a consistent and continual basis.

Sixth, God is eternal. He never ceases to exist, and He is always the same – day after day and century after century (102:24-27).

These truths about God encourage our hearts and give us confident hope in Him, and this list is not exhaustive. We can add our own contributions to the list and ponder these great truths about who God is.

"Thank You, Father, that You know all about me and that You care about me. Thank You for Your character that makes You worthy of my trust."

Day 237

I stretch out my hands to You;
My soul longs for You, as a parched land.
Psalm 143:6

The third thing we can do when we are fainting inside is to lean on God. As frail humans, we really are as weak as we feel. We don't have the strength to stand on our own. We are indeed ready to topple over and be crushed.

God is not that way. God is strong. As we remember the characteristics of God, we realize that He is strong enough to support us and to hold us up. He provides the strength and protection that we need. Unfortunately, we don't always go to Him like we should. Sometimes we need God to lead us to Him so that He can be our source of strength (61:2). Once we are there, He will be sufficient to hold us.

We need to realize how very much we need God. Instead of trying to rely on ourselves, we need to reach out our hands to God and long thirstily and desperately for Him (143:6). We need to lift up our soul to Him and allow Him to hold it (143:8). We must lean hard on God and allow Him to be the one who holds us up.

The psalmists give a few pictures to help illustrate the strength that God can give us as we rely on Him. God is pictured as a rock (61:2). Not just any rock, He is a rock that is higher than we are. Because He is higher than we are, He is able to provide the protection that we can't give ourselves. God is also pictured as a refuge (61:3-4; 142:5). God is a place of safety in which we can hide. As we lean on God, we allow Him to be a rock and refuge for us.

Like the psalmists, we should want to remain under God's protection forever (61:4). We can rely on God because He is a place of safety, security, and shelter. What better place could there be, than with one who knows all and cares about us?

"Father, my own strength is only weakness. Help me to lean wholly on You for my strength. Help me to hide in You, my Rock and my Refuge."

Day 238

I shall remember the deeds of the LORD;
Surely I will remember Your wonders of old.
Psalm 77:11

The fourth thing we can do when we are overwhelmed is to think about God's mighty works. The attributes of God that we have reminded ourselves of are not empty theory. God backs up His character with action. Through the things that He does, God has consistently and historically proven Himself to be who He says He is. We have confidence to pray for God's help now because of what He has done in the past (61:3).

In Psalm 77, the psalmist makes a firm resolve to think about God's mighty works from the past (77:11-12). He then goes into an extended segment in which he remembers various things that God had done. Interestingly, he does not mention anything from his own life and experience. Instead, he looks back into history. He remembers God's impressive deliverance of His people from Egypt. He remembers how God protected and defended them. He remembers how God controlled nature on their behalf, even opening up a path through the sea. He remembers how God faithfully led them through the wilderness. This passage indicates that we are not necessarily to remember things just from our own lives, but to look back in history and see the mighty things that God has done for others.

We might wonder, "What does that have to do with me?" It demonstrates to us who God is, what He is like, and what He is capable of. He is the same God with the same power today as He was in history. As we think about the amazing things God did in the Bible, we can be reassured that we have a powerful God who can be trusted. It is certainly appropriate to also remember God's works from the past in our own lives and to meditate on what He has done for us personally. One of our psalmists does that as well (143:5). God has previously cared for us, and He will continue to do so. Whether we look only at our own lives or at more distant history, we find that God's record is good and reliable.

"Father, You have done so many things for me in the past. You have delivered and provided and guided so many times. I have no reason to doubt You now."

Day 239

"Give heed to my cry,
For I am brought very low;
Deliver me from my persecutors,
For they are too strong for me."
Psalm 142:6

The fifth thing we can do when our heart is overwhelmed is to ask God for help. The psalmists, supported by many other parts of Scripture, clearly indicate that we can ask God to act on our behalf. God is full of lovingkindness, and we can ask for His response on that basis (143:8 & 12). We can remind God of His lovingkindness and ask Him to filter His response through that quality.

We can ask God to answer our prayer by changing our situation (143:1, 7, 9, 11-12). We can go beyond just telling God about our troubles. We can experience more than just having someone to listen and care. We can ask God to respond. The psalmist trusts God to be able to do something about his dilemma. He knows that God can change and direct his path (142:6-7). God can change the challenging situation and make it better. God can take his path in a totally different direction. We do not know what God's will is or what He has planned. Perhaps the situation that He has us in is precisely the situation that He requires in order to accomplish His purposes. He may not change it, but certainly we are able to ask Him to do so.

One thing we can confidently request, knowing that it is God's will, is wisdom from God. In addition to His work in the circumstances, God can also work in us personally by teaching us how to proceed and by leading us in the right way (143:8 & 10). It can be hard to know how to respond when we are overwhelmed by something hard, but God can teach us. He can show us what steps to take. In our overwhelming situation, God is able to intervene, and we can ask Him to do so.

"Father, would You be pleased to change my situation? Would You look on me with compassion and lovingkindness and turn the direction of my path?"

Day 240 _____

> *So I will sing praise to Your name forever,*
> *That I may pay my vows day by day.*
> Psalm 61:8

The final instruction for when our spirit is faint is to determine to thank God. Many of the psalms express an intention to praise God even before the situation is resolved, and the psalms in our study are no exception. An intention like this is based primarily on two things.

It is first based on the expectation that God will deliver. The psalmists assume that God will deliver, because that is what God does. The second premise is a realization that God deserves praise (102:18 & 21). It would be wrong to withhold that praise by failing to give God the glory that He deserves. The deliverance can only come from God. No one else can achieve it. God has created each challenging situation so that He can showcase His power by solving it. When God wins a victory, that victory is designed to show how great He is.

When we don't give God the credit and when we don't tell others what He has done, we are robbing Him of honor that belongs to Him. It is important that the praise be not just within our own hearts, but that it also be shared with others. The psalmist determined to thank and praise God in the presence of those who surrounded him in his time of victory (142:7). Others can join with us and can extend our praise well into the future (102:18).

Our own expression of praise can continue through time. We can praise God day after day and sing His praises forever (61:8). How could we ever praise Him enough? If God gives healing, we must be forever grateful for the blessing of health. If He does not heal, we must praise Him for His love and care. We must praise Him for the work that He is doing in and through our lives.

"Father, may I not fail to praise You for Your work. I praise You now for what You have done so far in my life, and I determine to praise You later for what You will do."

Day 241 _____

> *Though the fig tree should not blossom*
> *And there be no fruit on the vines,*
> *Though the yield of the olive should fail*
> *And the fields produce no food,*
> *Though the flock should be cut off from the fold*
> *And there be no cattle in the stalls,*
> *Yet I will exult in the LORD,*

I will rejoice in the God of my salvation.
Habakkuk 3:17–18

In this passage Habakkuk makes one of Scripture's great affirmations of faith in the midst of trouble. He pledges to follow God even if everything around him fails. This is a hard thing to say – that if everything were falling apart, he would trust God anyway. A statement like this requires God's grace. Simply making the statement is hard enough; living it out when the time comes is even further beyond the ability of man. If life really does come to this disastrous condition, remaining firm and true to that conviction is possible only with God's help. While Habakkuk's statement may seem a little foolish, there are some strong and valid foundations for making such a claim.

First, God has shown how faithful He has been in the past. He has shown how completely in control He is. God has led this far down the path. What reason is there for turning from His guidance now?

Second, everything that has happened is part of God's great plan. Instead of rejecting that plan, it is wiser to wait and see that plan worked out. God is preparing for a great answer, so it is best to trust Him to see the plan through to its end. The finale will be worth waiting for.

Third, in the midst of the troubles, no one cares like God does. He will give help through all of the challenges. To stop trusting Him only leaves one on his own to deal with the trials.

In conclusion, life may look black right now. You may see no answer or even the expectation of one in the near future. In spite of the circumstances, you can still choose to trust God. An observer might express this thought to you: "Look at the circumstances you are in, with all of the accompanying challenges and difficulties. You even admit God is in control. This is all His fault." Your response can be, "I don't care about the circumstances. I'm going to trust Him anyway." God is worthy of that trust – no matter what.

"Father, I hope my life never reaches complete disaster, but even if it does, I will still trust You. You will still be with me. Where else could I turn?"

Faith in the Dark (Sonnet 31)
The darkness makes my heart shrink back in fear;
I firmly grasp my Friend whose hand is there.
I love Him more because He stays so near
And never falters in His tender care.
While in the dark, with naught to see or do,
My Friend in calmness gently speaks to me.

→

> *He tells me all He's ever said is true,*
> *And that He knows all things that e'er shall be.*
> *It's in the darkness that I learn to trust;*
> *He keeps me safe because each step He knows.*
> *Since I can't see, then lean on Him I must,*
> *And with His proven guidance, my faith grows.*
> *If in the dark I learn He does what's right,*
> *Prepared I'll be to live and serve in light.*

Day 242

> *The sons of Ephraim were archers equipped with bows,*
> *Yet they turned back in the day of battle.*
> *Psalm 78:9*

Why would soldiers turn back in the day of battle? They were trained to fight and they had the weapons they needed. They had a powerful God to support them. Why turn back? These soldiers retreated in battle because they had lost sight of how powerful God was. They had forgotten what He had done for them in the past.

Though they imagined Him as such, God was not weak. This chapter recounts the plagues of Egypt, the parting of the Red Sea, the mass destruction of the Egyptians, God's supernatural guidance, His miraculous provision in the wilderness, and the divinely-achieved conquest of the Promised Land. God had the power to take care of these soldiers, but they didn't have confidence in God's power because they had forgotten what He had done. They had forgotten His mighty deeds. The result of such forgetting was disastrous.

Turning back in battle was just one of the results. The rest of the chapter reveals many other consequences of Israel's forgetfulness. They didn't keep God's covenant. They refused to walk in His ways. They sinned and rebelled against Him. They spoke against God and tested Him. They stopped believing in Him and stopped trusting Him. They turned away from Him and provoked Him to anger.

Forgetting God's greatness has these same effects on us. When we forget who God is and what He has done, we no longer have a basis for faith or trust. When we stop trusting God, we no longer have any reason to walk in His ways or to obey Him. Our human nature emerges with rebellion and rejection of God.

We are in the day of battle, just like the sons of Ephraim were. What is going to stop us from turning back like they did? We can stand firm in battle only if we remember God. He is with us in the battle, and He is a great God. God can defeat any foe. He has done so in the past. When we remember what God has done, we can have courage to faithfully follow Him. We can have confidence because of our great God.

"When things get tough, Father, I'm tempted to give up. Help me to remember often how great You are so that I will continue to follow You."

Day 243

You who fear the LORD, trust in the LORD;
He is their help and their shield.
Psalm 115:11

God is a Shield. There are two words used in the Psalms to indicate different types of shields. One of those is a large shield. The meaning of the word has to do with placing a hedge around something to protect it. This is what God does for those who trust in Him. He offers protection by making Himself a large and encompassing shield. He completely surrounds His children and thoroughly protects them. Nothing can squeeze past God or get around Him.

The other word for *shield* is used more frequently, and it refers to a small shield or buckler. This word is associated with the scaly hide of a crocodile. Like a crocodile's hide, this shield would be rugged. It would offer good protection and would be hard to penetrate. Because it is a small shield, it would have to be held close to the body. Similarly, God is close to His children in their time of trouble. He is not on the fringes as an observer; rather He is with His people right in the midst of their dangerous situation. Instead of forsaking them, He is as near as He can possibly be. Because this shield is small, its job is not to protect the whole body, but to protect targeted spots. It would be moved quickly to respond to incoming threats. This shield would be used to protect the most vital parts of the body. Likewise, God's protection is focused on the most vulnerable areas.

Both types of shields are used as descriptions of God; therefore, He provides both types of protection. He surrounds His children with full-body protection, and He also responds quickly to shield their vital areas.

"Father, I need You to shield me. Attacks are coming on every side, and some of them come dangerously close. Give me Your protection."

Day 244

"Come to Me, all who are weary and heavy-laden, and I will give you rest. Take My yoke upon you and learn from Me, for I am gentle and humble in heart, and you will find rest for your souls."
Matthew 11:28-29

Are you weary? More than just the physical fatigue, are you weary in your soul? Are you weighted down under a heavy burden? Do you feel yourself staggering beneath the load? Jesus offers you a wonderful invitation. If you will come to Him, He will give you rest. He is the source and supply of all things, and He has reserves of rest that He can give to those who need them.

How can coming to Jesus provide you with rest? First, Jesus simply gives it. He is full of compassion and He knows the strain and weight that you are under. He can give you rest.

Second, Jesus asks you to learn from Him. When you learn from Him and learn to be like Him, your soul will find rest. Rest in the soul comes from being like Jesus. Jesus is gentle and humble. This makes Him a good teacher, especially for those who are weary and overwrought. He teaches gently. His gentleness and humility also provide the perfect role model to learn from.

Learning gentleness and humility softens the soul and lifts a weight. When you stop fighting and when you submit completely to God's plan, the burden lessens and begins to float away. When you learn to be like Jesus, your soul is able to rest.

Come to Jesus. Let Him give you rest. Learn from Jesus. Find rest in Christ-likeness. The invitation is given to all who are weary, and God's supply of rest is sufficient to relieve all who will come.

"Oh, Father, I am so weary and my soul needs rest. Please give me rest, and please teach me so my rest can increase."

Day 245

But you know that it was because of a bodily illness
that I preached the gospel to you the first time.
Galatians 4:13

We often have no idea of God's purposes for our illnesses. We may come to recognize some of what God is doing, especially as time passes, but the truth is that God is often doing far greater things than we can even comprehend. God is wonderfully able to use trials to accomplish His purposes.

Paul had his first opportunity to preach to the Galatians because of an illness. At the time Paul had no idea why he was sick, and being sick was not pleasant for him. He was removed from his intended plan and was left in an unintended city. While there, he continued serving God as was his habit, and he preached to those around him. The result was not merely someone coming to Christ. Far beyond that, many people were saved and a church was established. Paul could look back later and realize that the Galatian church had started as a direct result of his illness. There could have been no question that God had planned and approved Paul's illness for His purposes.

Although First Thessalonians 1:6 does not refer specifically to a physical trial, it reveals that tribulation can be the catalyst through which some people receive the gospel. In this case it was not the preacher who was suffering, but the audience. The people in question became sensitive and prepared to receive the gospel because of the difficult situation they were in. As you are in and out of hospitals and doctors' offices, you come into contact with a world that needs God. Perhaps God has sent your illness in order to put you in a place to share the gospel. Perhaps He has sent illness to others so that they will be receptive to the words you share.

"Father, help me to be sensitive to the needs of souls around me.
Give me opportunities to share You with others."

Day 246

My sorrow is beyond healing,
My heart is faint within me!
Jeremiah 8:18
"I, even I, am He who comforts you."
Isaiah 51:12a

Sorrow can be indescribably deep. It can be so overwhelming that it renders us incapable of doing much beyond merely breathing. When our sorrow becomes so great, what can we do about it?

We can't heal ourselves. We might try to lose ourselves in distracting activities, ignore the pain, or keep a stiff upper lip. We might go on a shopping trip, request a favorite meal, or splurge in some other way in an attempt to ease the pain. Try as we might, our attempts to do so fail miserably. Our own comfort doesn't work; it falls short.

Others can't heal our sorrow. Most of our friends and family are incapable of understanding the depth of our sorrow. Their words are empty, and their hugs are temporary. They can't say or do anything to make everything better. They can't stop the pain.

The only effective source of comfort is God Himself. He might use other sources or scenarios in order to demonstrate that comfort, but true comfort always comes from God. God knows our pain. He knows how long and how deeply we have suffered. He cares about our pain, and He responds with comfort.

We may have wounds so deep we think they will never heal. Then one day we realize it doesn't hurt as much as it used to. Perhaps one day we even unexpectedly recall a painful situation, and we realize that we haven't thought about it for weeks or months. God can give effective healing when we think it is impossible. When we can do nothing to comfort ourselves, God steps in and gives comfort so effective it surprises us.

"Father, You know I've tried. I've done everything I can think of to ease the pain. Will You do for me what I cannot do for myself? Will You comfort me and heal my sorrow?"

Day 247

I will say to the LORD, "My refuge and my fortress,
My God, in whom I trust!"
Psalm 91:2

God is my Fortress. Whether it be in the form of a fort, a castle, or some other type of stronghold, a fortress is designed for the day of battle. It is depended on when the surrounding cities and towns have fallen and when the outer defenses have been breached. The fortress is the strongest, most secure, and most formidable structure built within a kingdom, nation, or city.

During the peaceful days of normal life, the fortress may not seem very important. When the attack comes, however, the fortress becomes extremely important. It has been built for just such a day. The fortress has been designed and constructed to withstand mighty attacks. It is designed to last for so long and to be so hard to conquer that the enemy will eventually give up.

Because the fortress is designed as a secure place, its population swells during an attack. People in danger flee to the fortress and close themselves safely inside in order to be protected from whatever threat is coming against them. The fortress must provide more than mere protection for this multitude of people; it must also be capable of supplying food, water, and lodging for the duration of the attack. While humanly-built fortresses are not invincible, they are the most secure place available.

As my fortress, God is a place of great security in the face of battle. God's fortress is a place so rugged and so secure that no one can break in. No one can reach me, regardless of his level of effort, determination, or persistence. As long as I remain within God's place of defense, I am safe. God can protect me and meet my needs for as long as I need to stay there, while simultaneously doing the same for all others who have taken refuge in Him. When attacks come that are too big for me to face and perhaps threaten to destroy me, I can hide in God and allow Him to protect me from destruction. He is the final line of defense, and He stands firm when all others have fallen.

"I should come to You more often, but now in the day of battle, I need You desperately. Thank You that I can hide in You and that You can protect me in all attacks."

Day 248

Lead me in Your truth and teach me,
For You are the God of my salvation;
For You I wait all the day.
Psalm 25:5

When David needed instruction in his time of trouble, he waited on God. Psalm 25 expresses his dependence on God for guidance. David knew that looking to God would provide the guidance he needed, but that failing to look to Him would be disastrous. David's looking dependently to God in this way required humility. David had to admit that he needed help, not only in doing what he should, but also in knowing what to do.

David expressed his humility and displayed his waiting on God through various means. He lifted up his soul to God (v. 1) and trusted in Him (v. 2). He repeatedly asked God to teach him and lead him (vs. 4-5). David demonstrated submission by obeying God (v. 10). He also acknowledged his great sin and confessed it to God (v. 11). He recognized that God's guidance comes to those who fear Him (vs. 12 & 14).

David showed his dependence by constantly directing his eyes toward God (v.15). In his admission of great need, he cried out for God to look on him and help him (vs. 16 & 18). David believed that he would not be ashamed because he took refuge in God (v. 20). All of these actions were from a man who was obviously dependent on God.

As David humbly waited on God, he had expectations for what God would do. First, waiting on God made David expect that he would not be brought to ruin as a result of his trouble (v. 3). Instead of believing that his trial would finish him, he expected to continue on. Second, waiting on God made David expect guidance and teaching in his time of trouble (v. 5). When troubles assaulted, he believed God would give him wisdom regarding how to respond and how to proceed. Third, waiting on God made David expect to be preserved (v. 21). He knew that he would be kept because of his dedication to humbly walk in God's ways. David was right in his dependence on God; a time of trouble is a time to wait humbly on God.

"Father, I don't know what to do, and even if I did know, I wouldn't be able to do it. I need You for the answers. I need You for the strength. I need You for the deliverance."

$\longrightarrow$

Teach Me (Sonnet 7)
I do not know the answer or the way;
I'd be ashamed if left to my accord.
And so I wait to hear what You will say;
I lift my soul to You and trust, O Lord.
Your goodness and compassion make You kind
And willing now to guide me through my days.
I need divine instruction for my mind.
Please lead me in Your path and teach Your ways.
It is the humble soul that You will teach –
The one who fears and always looks to You.
So cleanse my many sins, I now beseech,
And give me help so Your commands I'll do.
Though troubles come, my confidence can grow
When I am walking in the path You show.

Day 249

For the weapons of our warfare are not of the flesh,
but divinely powerful for the destruction of fortresses.
II Corinthians 10:4

Do you ever feel like you are at a distinct disadvantage? Do you feel like you are in the midst of a heated battle, surrounded by fierce enemies and separated from any allies? To make matters worse, do you feel like you don't have any armor to protect you or any weapons with which to fight back? Even if you did have weapons, do you think they would make little difference, because you don't know how to use them anyway?

You may find yourself unable to think rationally – maybe from the disease, maybe due to fatigue, and maybe from discouragement. Because your judgment is impaired, your attempts at fighting the battle are weak. God's Word acknowledges that you are in a battle and that the battle is fierce. The Bible acknowledges the fearsome enemies: doubt, fear, anxiety, discouragement, bitterness, anger. The battle is tough because it is spiritual rather than physical.

There is good news, however. God's Word also reveals that you have weapons appropriate for the type of battle you face. The battle is not physical, and neither are the weapons. The weapons are spiritual. They are from God, and they are divinely powerful. These God-given and God-powered weapons are capable of conquering and destroying mighty fortresses. The battles you face do indeed seem like mighty fortresses, but God's weapons are more than adequate for the task. They can win the victory.

"Father, on my own I would be helpless in this fierce battle. Thank You that I have Your weapons, powered by You and capable of destroying the strongest fortress."

Day 250

Bearing with one another, and forgiving each other, whoever has a complaint against anyone; just as the Lord forgave you, so also should you.
Colossians 3:13

People will hurt and disappoint you. That fact might never be more evident to you than it is in the course of your illness. People will expect you to do far more than you are capable of doing, or they will think you incapable of doing anything of value. They will overlook your needs and forget to include you. They will give you well-intentioned advice that doesn't come close to fitting your scenario. They will look down their noses at you (and maybe even offer verbal rebukes) because you aren't studying the Bible as deeply, aren't praying as much, aren't attending church as faithfully, or aren't continuing all of the same ministries you used to do.

Those responses are disappointing, because you are in a situation where you crave more understanding rather than less. The reactions are hurtful, because you long for help and encouragement, but receive the opposite. The bottom line is that people who are not sick simply do not understand. They can't. People don't understand the reality of physical limitations. They don't understand the effects of a long-term illness. They don't understand the strong mental and emotional impact that a disease can have. As much as you may try to explain, people cannot understand how a disease is able to so effectively impact all of these areas. If you're honest, you will realize that before you were sick, you never would have believed it either.

The problem, therefore, isn't that people don't care or don't want to help; they simply don't understand. Do you have valid complaints against others? Of course you do. Are the hurts and misunderstandings real? Absolutely. The verse above does not question those realities. It merely tells us what to do when they happen. We are to bear with one another. We are to overlook things, let them go, and put up with them. Beyond that, we are to forgive just as Christ forgave us. Instead of keeping a mental record of offenses or allowing anger and resentment to build up, we must let those offenses go. We are to forgive, even when our complaints are legitimate.

"You know how much it hurts, Father, when people misunderstand and say the stupidest things. Help me to be gracious and forgiving, so that I can overlook those complaints."

Day 251

So faith comes from hearing, and hearing by the word of Christ.
Romans 10:17

Because it involves believing what you do not see, faith is a challenge. Faith is a struggle for the most ordinary Christians in the most ordinary circumstances. Is it any surprise then, that faith is a struggle for those who are in situations that are not ordinary? In the course of an extended illness, there are many challenges to your faith. You are challenged and stretched far beyond the boundaries of ordinary life.

It's easy to have faith in God's financial provision when you have steady work and everyday bills. It's harder to have faith when you are disabled and the medical bills are mounting. It's easy to have faith in God's strength when your body is healthy and you can work for hours on end. It's harder when your body is frail and the simplest tasks wear you out. It's easy to have faith in God's love when you are surrounded by family and friends. It's harder when you are isolated and forgotten for days or weeks at a time.

What do you do when you suddenly need way more faith than you've ever needed before? You can't make faith up. You can't manufacture it. It doesn't magically appear. It isn't mysteriously poured out simply because you are in need.

The Bible reveals the source of faith. Faith comes from exposing yourself to the Word of God. Faith comes when you read the promises and assurances of God's Word. Faith grows when you read about what God did for people in the Bible. Faith expands when you see the greatness of God revealed in the pages of Scripture. As you keep reading the Bible and keep reminding yourself of these things, your faith will be constantly encouraged, reaffirmed, and built up.

You must then be in the Word of God. You need the Bible. It is your means of survival. If you can't read the Bible well, you must find some other way to expose yourself to it. Have a friend read to you. Listen to recordings. Choose a verse or a small passage that is manageable for you and read it repeatedly. Whatever you have to do, make it happen. Your faith must be built by the Word of God.

"Oh, Father, the battle for faith is fierce. I need Your Word to bolster my faith. Help me to be as faithful as I can be to stay in Your Word. Build my faith as I see Your truth."

Day 252

Wondrously show Your lovingkindness,
O Savior of those who take refuge at Your right hand
From those who rise up against them.
Psalm 17:7

God is the Savior of those who take refuge at His right hand. The verse is based on the realization that there are people in trouble. The troubled people face a situation in which enemies are rising up against them. They are being attacked and are in danger.

What do these people do in their situation of distress? They take refuge in God. They flee to Him for protection. In the midst of grave danger, they run to God with confidence that He can deliver them. There is a specific place to which the people flee. They hide at God's right hand. There is no better place to take refuge. God's hand is stronger than the hand of anyone else. God's hand has proven itself over and over again. His hand is strong enough to give deliverance in any situation. This God to whom they flee is the Savior. He is the one who keeps people safe, frees them from danger, and helps them.

This verse does not record the testimony of a single individual. Rather it makes a blanket statement; it gives a habitual characteristic of God. This is what God does – He saves people. God doesn't save just one time, but He does so frequently. Instead of offering salvation only to specific people, the assurance is open-ended. God is the Savior of those who take refuge in Him. That is the requirement, and it holds out hope to anyone who will come.

The verse seems to indicate that the taking refuge comes first, and the result is that God saves. God waits for people to turn to Him so that He can display His power and ability to save. When the Savior responds to those who take refuge in Him, He does so by showing His lovingkindness. He pours out His tender love and kindness on them, and He does so wondrously. God doesn't love in a small way; He demonstrates His kindness abundantly.

"Father, where else could I turn but to Your right hand? You have saved me in the past, and I can be confident that You will do so again. Show me Your lovingkindness."

Day 253

But sanctify Christ as Lord in your hearts, always being ready to make a defense to everyone who asks you to give an account for the hope that is in you, yet with gentleness and reverence.
I Peter 3:15

Christians can have hope even in times of suffering. From a human standpoint and from the world's viewpoint, hope in the midst of painful circumstances does not make sense. It is so odd, in fact, that others take notice of it and ask questions about it. Observers want to know what it is that makes a Christian tick. They want to know what is so different about a Christian that allows him to have hope under trying circumstances. A proper response to trials provides opportunities to share Christ. What does this response look like?

First Peter 3:14 reveals several aspects of a question-prompting response. First, a Christian does not need to fear in times of suffering. There is nothing to be afraid of, because God is master over all. Second, a Christian does not need to be troubled. He can be at peace as he trusts in God's plan. Third, even in the midst of trouble, a Christian recognizes that he is blessed. He is a child of God and eternally secure in Him. A Christian can have these hopeful responses because he has set Christ as Lord. Everything is under submission to God and resting in God's plan.

The suffering Christian seeks to exalt Christ. He explains that Christ is the source of his response. Even the Christian's manner of explanation stands out as different. Instead of striking out in frustration or impatience, and instead of judgmentally expecting the world to have positive responses, the Christian responds graciously. His answers are given with gentleness and reverence. He is respectful, compassionate, and kind. Instead of condemning others for not responding with hope, a Christian gently explains that the only reason he can do so is through Christ.

"Father, it is only through You that I can have hope in trouble. May I truly rest in You so that I can present something different to the world."

Day 254

But we all, with unveiled face, beholding as in a mirror the glory of the Lord, are being transformed into the same image from glory to glory, just as from the Lord, the Spirit.
II Corinthians 3:18

How well do you know the roller coaster? I don't mean the physical roller coaster – good days and bad days, symptoms that lessen and worsen. I mean the emotional roller coaster – the one that has such an impact on you that you can't distinguish it from the spiritual roller coaster. You have sparks of light, days of hope, and moments of stability and peace. Then in a very brief space of time, you plunge back to the depths of despair. You have little mental or emotional control, and the flip-flopping causes tremendous frustration. You go from resting in God and finding comfort in His work to doubting whether He is doing anything at all. While you occasionally catch glimpses of lessons He is trying to teach, often your continued struggles seem to deny that you're growing at all. The constant bouncing back and forth makes you wonder if any real progress is being made.

This verse assures you that God is doing His work in you, particularly when you desire it to be done. Your desire for God to work is demonstrated when you earnestly and openly seek God. When you look into His Word without barriers or resistance, God uses His Word to transform you. It is your open heart and willing attitude that God requires; He understands any mental or physical limitations that may hold you back from seeking as actively as you would like.

When you doubt progress, rest in the assuring and certain words of the verse: *"are being transformed."* It is happening. God says so. When you look into God's Word openly as the verse describes, you see Christ revealed and you become more like Him. The change may be subtle and gradual; in fact, you may not see it at all. If God says He is doing it, however, then it *is* happening. He is transforming you to look like His Son. If He is transforming you, then you will be different. You will not be the same when God is finished with you, because He is doing His work.

"Father, most days I don't see anything happening, but I believe that You are transforming me. Help me to seek You earnestly so Your work can be most effective."

Reflecting Christ (Sonnet 14)
That I would be like Christ is God's chief goal.
Oh, such a thought – His beauty to reflect,
When I am nothing but a ransomed soul.
How can I glory unto Him deflect?
This work is nothing I can do at all,
But only done by God's amazing grace.
Each day I must see my deep need and fall
And humbly put Him in His rightful place.
It's not a work that can be quickly done,
But through my whole life long a constant climb.
No part of life is wasted – no, not one.
Let patience do its work in God's good time.
Though ups and downs may cause me times of doubt,
At last I'll see Him bring His work about.

Day 255

They all wait for You
To give them their food in due season.
You give to them, they gather it up;
You open Your hand, they are satisfied with good.
Psalm 104:27-28

Psalm 104 describes God's interaction with the natural world. God created the earth and established it so firmly that it cannot fall out of position. He covered the earth with water, and then He caused the waters to move aside so that the mountains could rise up and the dry land could appear. God made boundaries for the oceans and the seas. He established springs and streams of water to run through the mountains and valleys.

The psalm reveals that God provided water for the wild animals to drink. He made trees to flourish near the waters so that birds would have places to make their nests. He made the earth to be fruitful. God caused grass to grow for the animals to eat, and He made food to grow under the tending hand of man. God provided enough edible foods so that man would be provided for. God made a water table so that the trees can draw moisture through their roots.

God established appropriate habitats for every type of creature. He established the routine of daytime and nighttime and started the seasons on their constant rotation. He made animals to hunt by night and animals to hunt by day. He provided the animals with the skills to hunt for food. God made the great oceans and filled them with so many creatures that they cannot be counted. He made tiny creatures that can hardly be seen and massive creatures that strike fear in those they meet.

God filled the earth, the sky, and the sea with many, many creatures – and He provides for every single one of them. There is no animal that does not have a food source. There is no creature for which God does not provide. He meets the needs of each animal, both large and small. If God so wonderfully created the earth, if He so intelligently designed it, and if He so capably provides for every creature, can we not trust Him to care for us too?

"Truly, Father, You have done amazing work. You care for more creatures than I can count or imagine. I have no doubt that You can provide for me."

Day 256

On the day I called, You answered me;
You made me bold with strength in my soul.
Psalm 138:3

It is disheartening to call out for help and be ignored; it is discouraging to long for help and be neglected. We can easily think of times like that – when there was too much snow for us to shovel, when all the clothes were dirty but we had no strength to wash them, when the fatigue was so great that we couldn't fix even the simplest meal, or when we needed help just to get dressed. In these situations, we wanted someone to call on the phone or come to the door; perhaps we even cried out loud, "Someone, please come help me." Sadly, people will not always meet our expectations. They cannot always be there.

There is someone, however, who always answers when we call. God answers our cries for help, and He does so in a timely fashion. He doesn't wait until it's too late. He doesn't wait until we despair of asking. God answers us on the day that we call on Him. It doesn't matter if it's a weekday, a weekend, or even a holiday. It can be mid-morning, mid-afternoon, or midnight. God answers when we call. He won't leave us alone with needs that are unmet.

Perhaps most encouraging is that God meets the needs that no one else can meet. When our soul is weak and on the verge of collapse, God can meet that need too. He can give us strength in our soul. The strength in our soul is what equips us to go on and meet the other challenges. It gives us courage to face life for one more day.

"May I look to You, Father, to meet my needs. You will hear when no one else does, and You will meet the needs that no one else can."

Day 257

Let us also lay aside every encumbrance and the sin which so easily entangles us, and let us run with endurance the race that is set before us, fixing our eyes on Jesus, the author and perfecter of faith, who for the joy set before Him endured the cross, despising the shame, and has sat down at the right hand of the throne of God.
Hebrews 12:1b-2

We are running a race, and that race is a marathon. The race, with all of its challenges, stretches on and on. In such a long race, we are to endure. One thing that will help us endure is to lay aside sin and weights that would hold us back. God never intended for us to carry things that weigh us down. We cannot afford to carry anger, resentment, bitterness, anxiety, doubt, self-pity, discouragement, or self-reliance. Even other burdens that may not actually be sinful have the capacity to hold us back in the race. These heavy burdens would break our backs even if we weren't trying to run a race. They are much more limiting and harmful in the course of our marathon.

Another thing that will help us endure is to consider the stories of heroes from the past. The eleventh chapter of Hebrews contains many examples of people who ran difficult races. Because of their faith in God, these men and women were able to emerge victorious.

Most important in helping us endure is focusing on Jesus. He is our ultimate example. In the face of death on the cross, He endured, not considering the shame. He did so because of the joy He knew would come as a result. The suffering is always worth the reward that follows. It is important for us to think about the severity of our suffering compared with that of Christ. He faced incredible hostility and still endured. We have not faced that same level of hostility. Things haven't gotten that bad for us yet. Realizing Christ's response under much more trying conditions should encourage us not to be weary or lose heart. We must look to Him for encouragement and strength.

"Father, help me not to lose my focus in this marathon. Instead of focusing on myself, help me to keep my eyes fixed on You."

Day 258

But as for me, my feet came close to stumbling,
My steps had almost slipped.
Psalm 73:2

There are precious verses in the Bible assuring us that we can be prevented from slipping and falling, even in the midst of trouble. On the other hand, there are verses telling us that God will pick us up after we fall. This psalm puts us squarely in the middle; Asaph almost fell. Is there a contradiction in these verses? Can we fall, or will God always uphold us?

The answer is not pleasant, because it confronts us with the idea of sin. In this psalm, Asaph very nearly slipped and stumbled, not because the path was too hard, and not because God had left him, but because he got his eyes on the wrong things. Asaph was looking with envy at the wicked (v. 3). With his wrong focus, he reached the point of bitterness in which he didn't even think it was worth it to live for God anymore (vs. 13 & 21). He behaved badly toward God (v. 22), not accepting God's path for him or God's help on that path. With such an attitude, and with his eyes looking at other things instead of where he was walking, is it any wonder that he almost slipped? In fact, with such a sinful response, we should be surprised that Asaph did not actually stumble and fall.

Sin and failure to focus on God are very dangerous. Do we think ourselves above falling? If we are the least bit honest with ourselves, we realize how incredibly easy it is to fall. We dare not think ourselves exempt from such a fate. So many others, including respected and faithful Christians, have fallen in times of trouble, and we must soberly recognize our vulnerability and the weakness of our flesh.

In the midst of such sober realities, we can have hope. We can be reassured when we realize the reason that Asaph did not actually fall. In spite of his failures, God was always with him. God held him by the hand and continued to guide him (vs. 23-24). What compassion and love! God knows our weakness and works in spite of our responses. He stays with us even when we lose sight of the path.

"Father, I know I am weak. I could easily fall. Dozens of times a day my heart and mind face that battle. Take my hand and guide me. Protect me from myself and hold me up."

Day 259

*When my heart was embittered
And I was pierced within,
Then I was senseless and ignorant;
I was like a beast before You.
Psalm 73:21-22*

Oh, the horrid power and influence of our emotions! Our feelings are so easily influenced and so rapidly changed, and they have great danger of controlling every other aspect of our lives. Asaph's emotions affected both his thoughts and his actions. His heart was bitter, like he had just eaten something that tasted very bad. He had inner pain, like a sharp weapon had just pierced right through him. These are incredibly apt illustrations of what our emotions are often like.

These very natural human emotions had a negative influence on Asaph's thinking. He was so poisoned by his feelings that he became senseless and without knowledge. Once his thinking was affected, his actions followed the same path. He behaved like a beast and responded brutishly toward God. These downward steps can happen so quickly that we hardly know what is happening and we barely have time to respond.

Because of the great danger, we must be on the alert. We must corral our emotions and thoughts, and we must bring them into submission to God's truth. When our feelings clash with God's truth, our feelings are wrong. We must choose to believe God's truth in spite of what we feel or perceive. When we sense a wrong attitude, we need to stop and pray and think correctly. We must ask God to help us think His thoughts – Biblical thoughts.

It is so easy for our limited human minds to be confused and deceived. We can't always see what is really going on. Therefore we must choose to believe what God says even when we don't see it or understand it. Because our feelings can so easily misguide our thoughts and actions, we must focus on Scripture. We must focus on what is right, rather than on what we feel. Otherwise, we come very close to acting incorrectly toward God.

"I pray, Father, that my fickle human emotions would not cause me to respond foolishly toward You. Help me to believe Your truth rather than what I feel."

Day 260

But as for me, the nearness of God is my good;
I have made the Lord GOD my refuge,
That I may tell of all Your works.
Psalm 73:28

This verse concludes the psalm in which Asaph has described his near fall from God's path. He has told of his wrong focus, his pained emotions, his troubled thoughts, and his horrid response to God. Asaph shares his testimony in this psalm; he discloses unflattering things about himself that perhaps he would have preferred that others not know.

Asaph shares his personal struggle in order to tell the wonderful truth that he has learned. He tells his story so that he can relate the wonderful sweetness of a renewed relationship with God. Instead of being on the verge of falling, Asaph is now enjoying increased knowledge of God. He has an incredible new confidence in God's strength.

Perhaps the most precious truth he has learned is the one he mentions to introduce the psalm – that God is good. In spite of Asaph's failures and boorish behavior, God remains good. This God is very near to Asaph, never having left him. God remained faithful through Asaph's time of struggle. Asaph describes this nearness of God as the good thing that he has to cling to.

In these difficult days of illness, days filled with so much pain and frustration, what good thing do I have to cling to? What is the good thing that I can carry with me today? Answer: God is near. That is a good thing that will never change. If, like Asaph, I have stumbled and nearly fallen from God, I can have hope. I can learn, as Asaph did, of the faithfulness and nearness of my good God. I too can enjoy a glorious return and a refreshing restoration. I can experience the incredible sweetness of a renewed relationship with my God. I can joyfully declare the goodness, faithfulness, and nearness of this unmatched God.

"Though I fall, Father, thank You that You never fall. You are faithful to be near me with Your unending goodness. May I know the joy of being close by Your side."

Reflection on Psalm 73 (Trust in a Faithful God)
My eyes had wandered from my God
When other things distracted me –
The trials of life, with storms so strong,
And others' lives smooth seemed to be.
Oh, God is good to those who fear –
A refuge sure. I know He's near.

It seemed so pointless and so vain
To run the race, to fight the fight.
Is there a diff'rence anyway?
Is darkness just as good as light?
Oh, God is good to those who fear –
A refuge sure. I know He's near.

To see sin prosper troubles me.
How can it win, while I'm in pain?
But now at last I understand;
The final day makes all things plain.
Oh, God is good to those who fear –
A refuge sure. I know He's near.

My cast-down heart deceived my thoughts.
I was a fool to doubt my Friend.
Though I was weak, He stood by me
And will direct me till the end.
Oh, God is good to those who fear –
A refuge sure. I know He's near.

On whom but Him can I depend?
None better on whom to rely.
Though rough my way, He is my strength.
He'll go with me until I die.
Oh, God is good to those who fear –
A refuge sure. I know He's near.

Day 261

"I know that You can do all things,
And that no purpose of Yours can be thwarted."
Job 42:2

Job recognizes two important things in this verse, and they are actually complimentary sides of the same truth. First, God can do anything that He chooses. Second, no one and nothing can stop Him from doing it. God has the power to do anything, and no one else has the power to stop Him. If God chooses to deliver us, He can do it. There is no virus, no bacteria, no tumor, no condition whatsoever that is greater than God's power. He can defeat them all.

While the first part of the verse concentrates on God's omnipotent power, the second part focuses on His unstoppable plans. God's plans can't be changed; they will happen just as He has determined. Within that statement, Job recognizes the fact that God does have a purpose. When God does something, it is not a random incident based on a whim, but rather a very deliberate and focused act.

God's deliberate purpose cannot be squelched. If God wants to heal, He can, and nothing can stop His intent. If we are not healed, therefore, that can only mean healing is not God's purpose (at least for now). Likewise, if God's purpose had been for us to remain healthy in the first place, nothing could have stopped that from happening either. The very fact that we are sick and that we continue to be sick is an indication that God does have a purpose for our illness; if He intended otherwise, His plan could not be overruled. God is working out His purpose in a way that cannot be stopped. We may not know what God's purpose is, but we can rest assured that He does have one. What is happening is designed by God's deliberate plan and carried out by His unstoppable hand.

"Father, though I do not understand what Your purpose is, I know that You have one.
Thank You that nothing can stop You from doing what
You have determined to do in my life."

Day 262

You are my hiding place; You preserve me from trouble;
You surround me with songs of deliverance.
Psalm 32:7

God is my Hiding Place. The purpose of a hiding place is to avoid being seen, but there are different ways to accomplish that. I could hide behind something. I could hide under something or inside something. I could even hide high on top of something. I could depend on dark shadows to hide me. These different hiding places each have advantages and disadvantages. Some of these positions are hard to find or hard to get into. Ultimately though, these hiding places hide me from being seen only from a certain angle or under specific conditions.

It seems that the best hiding place would be one that simply prevents me from being seen at all, regardless of my location. The phrase used in the verse describes that type of hiding place. It refers to a covering or a disguise. I can think of it as camouflage. Because it blends in with its surroundings, camouflage can hide me in a variety of situations. I don't have to find a box to hide under or a tree to climb. When God has disguised me in this way, my enemies can look right over me and never see me. When trouble advances directly toward me with every intention of overtaking me, God conceals me in a disguise and keeps my presence a secret. Although the trouble may be practically right on top of me and there may be a sense of urgency and imminent ruin, God is able to keep the adversary from seeing me.

With God to hide me so effectively, I can trust quietly in Him even on the very brink of danger.

"Help, Father. Danger is all around, and I have no place to hide. Disguise me so that
the danger cannot find me. Though danger is so close I can smell it,
help me to rest peacefully in You."

Day 263

For He has satisfied the thirsty soul,
And the hungry soul He has filled with what is good.
Psalm 107:9

It doesn't take a sick person long to realize that his greatest needs are not physical ones. While the physical needs may be intense, other needs quickly present themselves to overshadow the physical ones. Mental and emotional needs can be quite challenging, but the deepest of all are the spiritual needs. When great needs of the soul exist, it becomes practically impossible to deal with some of those other needs. If the spiritual needs are met, however, it becomes much easier to face the other areas of need.

Happily, the spiritual needs can be met. When the soul is hungry and thirsty, there is a solution. While God is able to meet all types of needs, sufferers don't always see the answers they hope for in some areas of need. There may be no successful answer for the physical needs. The mental needs may defy reversal. The emotional needs might always remain. Unlike these needs, (which God can change if He wants to), the needs of the soul can always be satisfied. The spiritual answers can be realized.

Hunger and thirst can be agonizing. When, in the midst of illness, a person realizes how deep the needs of his soul are, a tremendous hunger and thirst awaken within him. He knows that He desperately needs God to fill those empty holes. The good news is that God does just that. He doesn't fill the holes with any random thing; instead, He fills them with what is good. The hungry soul would be willing to take just about anything, but there is no junk food from God. God doesn't give empty calories or delicious-looking food with little substance. God gives good stuff.

The hungry and thirsty soul would also be grateful for even the smallest amount of food or water, longing for something to take off the edge of hunger and thirst. God doesn't give a small amount, doling out just enough to keep the person alive. God gives enough to satisfy and enough to fill. God wonderfully meets the needs of the soul.

"Oh, Father, my soul is parched and starved. I need water and food from Your hand.
Quench my intense longings. Fill me with what is good."

Day 264

This verse describes Christ as He prayed in agony on the Mount of Olives, and we would certainly do well to look to Christ as an example. He was in a time of intense suffering – sweating great drops of blood, grieving in His spirit, and facing death. Christ's response was to pray fervently to God. These were passionate and heart-rending prayers. They were accompanied by loud crying and tears. His prayers were directed to God because God was the one who was able to save Him.

Can we not follow the example of Christ? We also can bring our anguish to God, the one who is able to help. Certainly we cannot help ourselves in such overwhelming times. It does little good to share our anguish with other humans. God is the source to which we must flee. We can pour out our heart to Him in desperate cries. We do not have to hide the anguish of our souls from God. Instead of turning away from our tears, He will listen to our loudest and most painful cries.

Christ's prayers were heard because of His righteousness. Lest we think His righteousness was only because He was God, verses eight and nine give further explanation. They tell us that Christ learned obedience through His suffering, something that was part of the perfecting process. We struggle to comprehend the simultaneous deity and humanity of Christ. We don't understand how He could have to learn anything or how He could be perfect as God but still be perfected (or proven perfect) as a man. If Christ needed to experience sufferings in order to learn obedience, however, is suffering not also a valuable contributor to our Christian growth?

"As You teach me through suffering, Father, I come to You for help. Thank You for understanding the intensity of my pain and for allowing me to cry out to You."

Day 265

The human ear is one of the amazing aspects of God's creation. He has intricately designed the ear to take in sounds so that information can be gathered and communication can take place. It is completely illogical that a God who has so carefully crafted the human ear cannot Himself hear. God deemed hearing and communication important, and His hearing is better than that of any human. It is extremely comforting to know that God's ears always work. He always hears you when you call to Him.

The psalms present several categories of people to whom God particularly listens. First, God hears the righteous. The man who is attempting to live in a godly fashion has God's ear. Second, God hears the humble. If a man will fear God and call out to His strength in the midst of human weakness, God will hear his cry. Third, God hears those in need. He pays special attention to the orphans, the poor, and the oppressed. He listens to those who are afflicted, distressed, and in trouble.

Are you striving to live for God? Are you humbling yourself before Him in admission of your need? Are you needy and afflicted? If so, God will hear your voice. He will hear the supplication that you make to Him. He will hear the desire that your heart pours out. God will hear your cry and your weeping; He listens carefully even to your quiet sobs when there are no words. God will hear your cry for help in the midst of your distress. No matter what you have to say to God, He will be attentive to hear it.

"Thank You, Father, for always hearing me when I cry to You.
No one else listens as well as You do."

Day 266

In my distress I called upon the LORD,
And cried to my God for help;
He heard my voice out of His temple,
And my cry for help before Him came into His ears.
Psalm 18:6

There is no doubt that God hears my cries. When I cry out to Him, He always hears me. The psalms have many ways of expressing the fact that my cries directed toward God never fall on deaf ears. These many descriptions should give me an unshakeable confidence that God always hears me.

I am told that my cry for help comes into God's ears. It does not just come near Him. The sound waves don't swirl nebulously in the vicinity; the sound is not lost. It comes into His ears.

I am also told that God inclines His ear toward me. He leans closer toward me so that He can clearly hear what I have to say. He makes sure He doesn't misunderstand or miss a single word.

I am told that God's ears are open to me. He doesn't wear ear plugs or stuff His ears with cotton. He has no hearing deficiency, and He doesn't live in a soundproof room.

I am told that God doesn't hide Himself, but that He hears me. God doesn't go on vacation. He doesn't make up excuses for why He can't listen. He doesn't run and hide when He sees me coming. God cares about me, and He certainly hears and gives heed to my cries.

It does not matter when I come to Him. God hears my cries in the morning, in the evening, and at noon. In case I should be tempted to think those are the scheduled times of day when I must come, the Bible also tells me that He hears me when I am in trouble. He hears me whenever I call and whenever my voice rises to Him. There is no occasion on which God does not hear me.

"Oh, Father, thank You for Your constantly open ear.
Forgive me for not coming and talking to You more."

Day 267

The righteous cry, and the LORD hears
And delivers them out of all their troubles.
Psalm 34:17

What a glorious position to be in! I have a God who always hears me, but He doesn't stop there. When God hears my cries, He feels my pain and He cares. My words mean something to Him – but He doesn't stop there either. When God hears my cry, and when He cares about my need, He responds by doing something.

God's response is deliberate and active. My situation is not put on the back burner. It is not ignored. It is not shelved to be looked at another day. No, God responds by acting on my behalf. I may not see the results of His work immediately, but I can be sure that God is working. He puts His response plan into effect.

The ultimate result is that God will deliver me. That is what my God does. He looks on those who are in distress, and He answers their cries by saving them from their desperate situations. God has a masterful plan for how to bring about that deliverance, and His plans never fail. It does not matter how severe my trouble is, and it does not matter how many troubles I have. God is able to save me out of every single one.

Does that deliverance always fit the idea that I have for it? Does it always mean healing? No, not always. God knows what kind of deliverance is best within His plan. That might be healing, but it might be grace. It might be help to resist temptation. It might be freedom from oppressive thoughts. It might be taking me to be with Him in heaven, a place where I will never again suffer. Whatever form God's deliverance takes, I can be sure that He will do it and that it will be good.

"Father, thank You for the work that You are already doing on my behalf, even though I don't see it yet. Thank You that You will deliver."

A God Who Hears
Creator God produced the ear of man;
What sense then that Himself He does not hear?
He hears far better than a mortal can;
His hearing's always sensitive and clear.

He hears the righteous, godly man who fears –
Also the humble, orphaned, and oppressed.
Afflicted, poor, and needy reach His ears;
He hears the troubled and the ones distressed.

But what precisely does this God take in?
My cry, my voice, my supplications deep,
He hears my heart's desire and vows to Him,
When I'm distressed, need help, and when I weep.

He gives His heed; most certainly He hears.
His hearing ear inclines toward my side,
Each cry I make comes to His open ears;
This Listener always hears and doesn't hide.

Each morning God can hear my prayer and cries –
In evening, morning, noon – He hears them all.
He hears whene'er my voice to Him does rise,
In trouble or at any time I call.

But more than hear, He answers when I call.
He looks on me when I am sore distressed,
He saves, delivers me from troubles all.
I love the One whose hearing is the best.

Day 268

For we are not bold to class or compare ourselves with some of those who commend themselves; but when they measure themselves by themselves and compare themselves with themselves, they are without understanding.
II Corinthians 10:12

Whether we like to be involved in the lives of others or whether we are inspired by their testimonies, it is true that we notice other people. We have watched others go through trials with seemingly impeccable testimonies. We have been amazed at their responses to their situations. We have heard them extolled by friends, fellow Christians, and even the pastor. We've been told that they never complain, always give glory to God, and never question Him. Perhaps someone has even been so insensitive as to throw those examples in our faces. In kindness or in judgment, they have urged us to be like those respected heroes.

In the midst of our own illnesses, we realize how far short we fall. We know that we don't compare to such stellar godly examples. We know how very much we struggle, and from all reports and appearances, others don't struggle at all. We soon come to see ourselves as dismal failures in our spirituality. We evaluate ourselves as terrible Christians, because we struggle so much while those around us have victory. We've never heard these godly examples voice the conflicts that we experience, and we assume we are the only ones who struggle so deeply. Our comparison to those role models and our attempt to be like them leave us discouraged and defeated.

God warns about the foolishness of making such comparisons. That type of comparison is faulty in two ways. First of all, what we see is not the truth. The amazing claims about those heroes' unfailing responses are at best generalizations. Everyone struggles. Like us, most people don't openly reveal their struggles. They share them only with a select few people, and many of the people exalting them don't know them well enough to support the claims they are making. What we see as near perfection is the "best foot forward" that is maintained in public. If we knew the hearts of those people, we would see that their battle for godliness is much like ours.

Secondly, the comparison is faulty because it uses the wrong standard. We are not to aim to be like others, but to be like Christ. He sets the real standard. While others may inspire or encourage us, our observation of them should not serve to create expectations for us. Our attempt to imitate them is legitimate only as they clearly reflect the spirit of Christ. We have a much greater and more consistent example to look to.

"Father, I have condemned myself over and over because I don't respond as well as someone else. Help me to forget them and to focus on You instead."

Day 269

For no one ever hated his own flesh, but nourishes and cherishes it, just as Christ also does the church.
Ephesians 5:29

While this verse is found in a passage regarding marriage, it reveals something important about Christ's relationship with His children. Christ nourishes and cherishes the church. In fact, those actions demonstrated by Christ are held up as the ultimate example of how husbands are to care for their wives. Christ does it better than the most tender and romantic of husbands. Neither a newlywed nor a doting husband of fifty years can match the devotion of Christ. His tender care is demonstrated in two ways.

First, Christ nourishes the church. He provides it with everything it needs in order to survive and flourish. If nourishing were done with children, it would involve taking care of everything so that they could grow up strong and healthy. It would mean providing for them to reach maturity. It would include protecting them so that nothing could destroy the work that had been done. Nourishment is demonstrated through constant and thorough provision of everything that promotes well-being and growth.

Second, Christ cherishes the church. This addresses the more tender side of the relationship. Christ loves them and thinks of them as very special. He holds them close to Himself, demonstrating His estimation of them. In a human scenario, it might involve holding someone close to share body heat and keep him warm. It would include gentle words and tender caresses. Cherishing is an expression of the love that is in the heart. Christ deeply loves His people, and He demonstrates that love through the nourishing and cherishing of His children.

"Oh, Father, thank You for such a tender picture of Your love for me. Thank You for caring for me so much and for providing what I need."

Day 270

"For My thoughts are not your thoughts,
Nor are your ways My ways," declares the LORD.
"For as the heavens are higher than the earth,
So are My ways higher than your ways
And My thoughts than your thoughts."
Isaiah 55:8-9

How often do you feel like your life makes no sense? How frequently do you protest that what is happening is wrong? How many times has it seemed like God is not answering your prayers correctly? Haven't you agonized over the fact that nothing in your life is turning out like it ought to?

The truth is that our understanding is awfully small. Because we don't think the same way God thinks, we wouldn't choose the same actions He chooses. Our understanding falls far short of God's understanding. His thoughts are so much higher than ours that there is really no comparison. God is doing things of which we have no idea.

The fact that God's thoughts and ways are higher than ours doesn't just mean we can't understand them. It also means that they are right. We would do something mediocre, but God does something wonderful. The fact that we can't see it as wonderful only serves to prove the point that our understanding is limited. Our lives may make no sense to us, but they make perfect sense within the wonderful and meticulous plan of God.

We may think everything that is happening is wrong, but God doesn't do anything wrong. He knows how "just right" His plan is. We may protest that God is ignoring our prayers or answering them in the wrong way, but God hears every prayer, and in His infinite wisdom, He sends exactly the right response. We may despair over the terrible way our lives are turning out, but God is working every detail into His masterfully designed plan that is nothing short of perfect.

Someday, whether here on this earth or later in heaven, when we come to understand something of what God has done, we will say, "Oh, I had no idea," and we will be entirely correct in saying so. God is planning and doing things that are far beyond our comprehension, but they are also wonderful beyond our imagination. God knows best, and He does best.

"I admit, Father, that I don't get it. I also acknowledge that You are infinitely wiser than I am. Please work Your good plan based on Your great understanding."

Day 271

I have become a marvel to many,
For You are my strong refuge.
Psalm 71:7

God is my Refuge. There are three different Hebrew words that are translated as refuge. The first refers to a high cliff that the enemy cannot reach or access. The second refers to a place of shelter in which a person can have hope. The third refers to a retreat to which people can escape. Of these three words, only the first one presents the expected military picture. The other two, which are used more often than the first, seem to indicate more of an emotional retreat than an actual physical one.

The need for refuge is not so much because I require a place of safety and protection against a dangerous attack. Instead, that need exists because I am being hemmed in by pressures; I feel like I just need to get away to a place where I can rest and relax. I need a place where I can escape the pressures of life and catch up to myself. In a human attempt to find such a refuge, I might curl up in a favorite blanket. I might sink into a hammock beside the water garden or go to a quiet cabin in the woods. I might find that one person who I know will hold me gently without asking questions.

These ideas of refuges provide beautiful pictures of what God does for me. Sometimes I am overwhelmed, stressed, and pressured, just wanting to explode. Then a quiet talk with God, resting in His comforting arms and loving care, quiets and calms me. God is a refuge. Yes, He is a cliff that protects me from the enemy, but He is also a hope-giving shelter and a retreat in which to escape. He can protect me as much from the overwhelming pressures of life as He can from the physical dangers.

"Father, I crave this kind of refuge. I need to be held in Your arms. I need to feel their surrounding comfort while the pressures of life slip away."

Day 272

Remove the false way from me,
And graciously grant me Your law.
Psalm 119:29

Don't we always have false ways that need to be removed from us? Nothing shows us the false ways any better than going through a challenging time. Our weakened physical condition has an effect on us, causing extra strain on every other aspect of our person. Suddenly every fault we've ever struggled with seems to come to the surface, along with other shortcomings that we didn't even know we had. Temptations that used to assault us occasionally now seem to be constant. Things we thought we had conquered years ago rear their ugly heads once more. So much ugliness oozes out of us that we start to wonder what is wrong with us and how we can possibly be so unspiritual.

The bottom line is that we are human. That makes us both weak and sinful. In our sinfulness, we desire the wrong things, and in our weakness, we struggle to resist the temptations. We are left keenly aware of the need to change and grow. Because we are weak and human, we cannot create that change on our own. We desire for the false ways to be taken from us, but without help we can't make them disappear. We need God's help. We need Him to do the work.

God desires to take those false ways from us, and He longingly waits for us to be ready for Him to do the work. Thankfully, God is loving and understanding. Instead of forcefully beating the falseness out of us, leaving us battered and destroyed, God is able to do His work gently. He teaches us His law so that we can conform to it.

When He teaches us, He does so graciously. He is gentle and patient as He carefully guides us away from error and into truth.

> *"Father, I see so much ugliness in my soul. Please remove it*
> *from me and gently teach me the right ways."*

Day 273

> *Surely I have composed and quieted my soul;*
> *Like a weaned child rests against his mother,*
> *My soul is like a weaned child within me.*
> *Psalm 131:2*

There are few sights that are sweeter than a young child resting in his mother's lap. The child is contented and quiet. He is not struggling, and he is not alarmed. The child is able to quietly and sweetly rest because he has no concerns or worries. There may be many concerns and worries facing him and his family, but the child doesn't bear that burden. The child has learned that his mother and father meet all of the needs that he has. They completely take care of him so that he has everything he needs. The quiet resting that allows a small child to fall asleep in his mother's arms is an indication that he completely trusts her. He is entirely comfortable because he knows she will protect him and care for him.

David records in this psalm that he had forced himself to become like this little child. He had adjusted himself and silenced himself so that he had no worries or protests. He had made his soul trust completely and confidently in God. Verse one reveals that this adjustment had to do primarily with his thoughts. There were things going on in his life that were too difficult for him to understand. They were great matters that extended beyond his comprehension. In such a situation, it is natural to try to figure things out anyway. Man wants to know why things are happening and wants to understand how things that are unpleasant could possibly be part of God's plan.

David realized that his brain was not big enough to decipher such things. If he thought, pondered, considered, and reasoned for his entire life, he would never understand the things that were intended only for the mind of God. Instead of fighting to understand, he humbled himself and recognized his position compared to God's. He made up his mind that it was okay for him not to understand. That decision being made, he rested quietly in the arms of God just like a young child rests in complete trust in his mother's arms.

"Father, I have tried and tried, but I can't understand what You are doing. Now I
realize that only You can understand things so profound. Help me
to rest and trust like a little child."

Reflection on Psalm 131 (Beyond my Understanding)
All of Himself, God lives forever up on high.
Compared to Him, my understanding is so small,
My intellect not lofty, high up in the sky.
I can't promote myself as if I know it all.
I can't walk paths too high for me; they are too grand.
Such things rise up so far above the commonplace
At levels I would not presume to understand.
No master of those paths, I fall flat on my face.
There are so many answers that I cannot know.
I am aware the understanding's not for me.
Not trying to work all things out, I must be low –
By choice positioning myself where I should be.
In quiet wonderment, my words have been suppressed.
My mouth is mute; I find I have no words to say.
Not filled with frantic moves or empty speech, I rest
Like trusting child in mother's lap at end of day.
Without alarm or fear, I can remain content,
Not needing comprehension of complexities.
Such heights of understanding are not for me meant;
In patience, I must wait and hope in God who sees.
No problem hard beyond His wisdom can extend;
He masters all things with intelligence sublime.
They're known to God who has no limit and no end,
And I can safely trust Him till the end of time.

Day 274

God is our refuge and strength,
A very present help in trouble.
Psalm 46:1

Life is full of troubles and attacks which we are unable to meet on our own. It is a
great consolation to know that our God can meet those attacks. He is a refuge in which
we can hide. He is our strength when we have none of our own. Perhaps the greatest
comfort comes from the final phrase of the verse: God is a very present help.

There is tremendous comfort simply in knowing that God is with us. Isn't that
what we want from our family and friends – for them to be with us? We know that

often there is nothing they can actually do, but we want to know that they are there. Unlike man, God is able to do something, but there is also great comfort in His presence alone. He is very near when we need Him most.

God's presence is displayed through the help He gives. God helps us throughout life, but His help is especially meaningful as it occurs in times of trouble. When we find ourselves in distressing situations that trap us, God is there. He is present and ready to help. There is no doubt of God's presence, because He is not just merely there, but He is *very* present. He is wholly and exceedingly there. When we are in one of life's troubling tight spots, which come frequently and in many forms, God helps us.

God is so obviously present that He is the focal point and key player in each situation. What kind of help does He give? The psalm states that God helps even if the earth changes. He gives faithful assistance even if the mountains shake and fall into the sea. God helps even if every nation rises in uproar; He can defeat them all. If God can help when the earth is falling apart and when the entire world gathers against Him in battle, then He can help us in each of our problems. He is a refuge that is very near.

"Thank You, Father, for Your help. Thank You that You are so near that I don't have to move one inch or search one second in order to find You."

Day 275

"Blessed is the man who trusts in the LORD
And whose trust is in the LORD.
For he will be like a tree planted by the water,
That extends its roots by a stream
And will not fear when the heat comes;
But its leaves will be green,
And it will not be anxious in a year of drought
Nor cease to yield fruit."
Jeremiah 17:7-8

A tree prospers by living in the right conditions. Ideally, a tree would be planted in healthy soil; it would have adequate sunlight, protection from harsh elements, and a good water supply. Additionally, the tree should be well cared for, fertilized, and pruned.

In this passage God compares man to a tree. God reveals that the primary basis for prospering or failing to do so is not the environment, but the source of a man's trust. If a man trusts in himself or in other men, he will be like a dry bush in a desert (vs. 5-6). This man will not prosper even in the best of conditions. Even in times of prosperity, he will be like a scrubby bush in a stony, barren wilderness. He will be dried and shriveled up, with nothing to sustain him.

If, on the other hand, a man trusts in God, the entire situation changes. With his trust firmly in God, a man does not require ideal conditions in order to survive. He can, in fact, prosper and bring forth fruit even in the worst of conditions. In the midst of the harshest drought and the most blistering heat, that man will still flourish. In those conditions, when all around is wilting and dying, God sustains the one who trusts in Him. His roots are deep in God and drawing from His refreshing strength. That man remains fruitful and vibrant. When the storm clouds gather on the horizon, or when the dust starts to blow unmercifully across the parched land, there is no reason to fear. God can make it seem as if nothing has changed. The man who trusts in God will endure, with healthy leaves and luscious fruit. The source of strength makes all the difference.

"Father, You know I want to bear fruit for You in this time of difficulty. I can't do that if I don't depend on You. Keep my trust where it needs to be so I can bloom for You."

Day 276

But God, who comforts the depressed, comforted us by the coming of Titus.
II Corinthians 7:6

People have interesting ways of handling the depression of others. The most sympathetic people might offer some comfort. For the most part, though, depression is viewed as taboo, and this leads to a variety of possible responses. The depression might be ignored altogether, as people simply pretend it doesn't exist. They act oblivious while they wait for you to snap out of it.

Most people seem focused on fixing the problem. They can do this by exhorting you to cheer up and smile. After all, life can't be that bad, and you should think of all the people who have it worse than you do. The exhortation might even be more forceful, as others bluntly inform you that you shouldn't be that way. They simply expect you to change.

It is interesting to see God's response to depression. God comforts the depressed. Instead of ignoring or condemning, He helps. God knows all of your needs, and He is not unaware of your internal struggles. He meets those needs just like He meets every other need. God finds a way to give comfort to those who are cast down. His particular method may vary from case to case, but He knows just what to send in each situation.

In the verse above, God sent Titus on a special visit to hurting people. Sometimes God uses other people; that may be through a visit, a phone call, or a card. God knows when you need someone to share a verse with you or pray with you, and sometimes He arranges that. He knows when to send a special blessing, maybe something you've waited for expectantly for a long time or maybe something completely unanticipated. Whatever the specific method, God knows your pain, and He knows just how to relieve it.

"Father, You know how much I am struggling. I don't know what You have in mind, but I sure could use something special. Can You please send Your encouragement?"

Day 277

But thanks be to God, who gives us the victory through our Lord Jesus Christ.
I Corinthians 15:57

Isn't it wonderful that in the midst of all the problems and challenges, there are also victories? Those victories may be small, and they might not come often, but there are victories. In a prolonged trial, the war is made up of many battles, but it is not over until the final outcome. We win some of the battles and lose others, but when we lose a battle, we must remember that the war is not over yet. More skirmishes will follow, and we must keep fighting. The war itself will end in victory, and we will also be victorious in many of the battles along the way. God is the one who makes those victories possible, and He does so through Jesus.

When we stop to think about it, God gives victories especially in the areas that are most important. He gives us victory over the world, by making us escape its corruption (II Peter 1:4). He helps us to have victory over sin. God will give victory over Satan by crushing Him (Romans 16:20). First Corinthians 15 tells us of His victory over death. God's victories are not puny. He gives us a triumphant victory through Christ (II Corinthians 2:14). He helps us to overwhelmingly conquer (Romans 8:37).

God does give victories, and He will bring about ultimate victory. If we truly align ourselves on God's side, the length of the battle may be uncertain, but the outcome is not. Though it may seem a long time in coming, God will give victory in the end. He does, in fact, also give victories as we struggle through life. We must thank God for His wonderful victories.

"Help me, Father, to remember to thank You for the victories. Help me not to get so discouraged by the defeats that I fail to notice Your deliverance."

Day 278

"Thus says the LORD of hosts, 'If it is too difficult in the sight of the remnant of this people in those days, will it also be too difficult in My sight?' declares the LORD of hosts."
Zechariah 8:6

There are many things that are too hard for people. Even the greatest doctors can't heal diseases. Even the most stoic people can't ignore continued pain. Under great affliction, the most strong-willed people reach their limits until they cannot face another day. The most emotionally stable people eventually reach a breaking point. In short, there are situations that simply become impossible for man because man has limitations.

It is one thing for man to acknowledge his own limitations, which are very real. It is something else altogether to transfer those same limitations to God. God does not share man's limitations. There is nothing too hard for God. The fact that man can't do something doesn't mean that God can't do it. In fact, when man thinks that God can't do it either, man's doubt does not stop God's power. Man's wrong thinking does not and never will change the facts about God.

God is who He is. He is the Almighty God – wiser, stronger, more patient, and more faithful than man. God can heal the most resistant disease if He chooses. God can give grace and endurance in trying days. God can give stability and hope in the bleakest of circumstances. Is the situation too hard for man? Absolutely. Does that mean it is also too hard for God? Never.

"Father, I don't see the way out. Everything in my life seems impossible. Thank You that it is not too hard for You. You can do what I can't even imagine."

Day 279

The righteous man will flourish like the palm tree,
He will grow like a cedar in Lebanon.
They will still yield fruit in old age;
They shall be full of sap and very green.
Psalm 92:12 & 14

Nature is often used to display God's truth and to mimic how God works in other areas. These verses make comparisons between men and trees. The verses describe two types of trees. Palm trees are fruit-bearing trees. They are trees that survive and even flourish in very dry conditions. Based only on their habitat, they might seem to have little profit, yet they are so bountiful that people depend on them for food and shelter.

The cedar tree often grows in great forests far from civilization, but it is a rather majestic tree. The cedars rise up straight and tall, stately and powerful. Not only are they strong, but they are also valuable and useful as a building material.

God compares the righteous man to these two types of trees. Perhaps in both cases the habitat would seem to limit their fruitfulness or usefulness, but that is not the case. Likewise, God can take men in unlikely circumstances and can make them prosper and be useful.

Verse fourteen continues the comparison to trees, and now God's work is even more amazing. This verse describes old trees. It is natural to consider old trees to be valueless. They have faced storms and disease. They have been battered and broken. They no longer bear fruit, and as the wood weakens, it is no longer suitable for building.

God doesn't view His older saints in that way. God can defy the expected course of nature. He can do what seems impossible and completely illogical. God can take those older saints, and He can cause them to bear more fruit than ever. He can make them continue to be full of life. He can make their leaves very green, the evidence of the flourishing that comes from within. God is not limited by the conditions and circumstances that would seem to limit man. God can take people who seem to have lost their fruitfulness and make them very fruitful indeed.

"Oh, Father, I feel so old and broken down, like I can no longer do anything for You.
Make me like these trees – strong, fruitful, vibrant, and full of life.
May I still bear fruit for You."

Day 280

It is good for me that I was afflicted,
That I may learn Your statutes.
Psalm 119:71

No one likes to go through hard times, but it is not difficult to see that great benefit often comes out of affliction. Especially as Christians, we have often observed in the lives of others that affliction made them more mature and brought them closer to God. In spite of this, it is a hard thing to ask for or even to appreciate affliction.

Unknowingly, sometimes we do ask for affliction. As we have struggled with areas of Christian growth or with some aspect of our relationship with God, have we not asked God to do a work in us? Have we not asked Him to change us and mold us? Some of those things can only be accomplished through times of affliction.

Sometimes God sends the affliction we need even when we don't ask for it; He longs for us to grow even when we don't actively desire it for ourselves.

The psalmist came to the conclusion that his affliction was good because it caused him to learn God's ways. None of us would ever choose the afflictions that God sends our way, but the experience is really priceless. We cannot put a value on the good work that God does through them. God's afflictions are good because they teach His statutes. They don't always seem good at the time, but in the end the afflictions *are* good because of the result that they give.

When we see the resulting growth, how can we doubt the benefit of affliction? God deepens our relationship with Him. He allows us to see Him in a greater way. He teaches us to know Him better. He smoothes the rough edges of our character. He even gives victory in areas where we've struggled for years. Yes, afflictions are good because they teach God's ways. The end result makes the pain worthwhile.

"Father, what You've done is good. Please don't stop teaching me. Make me forever different so that I will never go back to being who I was before. Do what it takes."

Dare to Pray

I've prayed, "O God, make me like Christ,"
And "Will You do Your work in me?"
"Restore and cause Your face to shine,"
And "Teach me, Lord, to do Your will."

Such prayers as these are Your delight.
Your interest in these things is great
Because You long to see me grow,
And Christ is praised when I'm like Him.

And when I pray You'd make me grow,
There's just one way to bring results.
The process is through trials and tests;
Great vict'ries come through pushing hard.

So when You work, Your favor's shown.
I can't resist or even fret,
But see tests as Your means to teach
And take the methods that You send.

I cannot quibble with Your plan –
Must let You answer in Your way.
Each day I must see everything
As opportunity to grow.

$\longrightarrow$

If I'd known what my prayers would mean
And how You'd bring results about!
But even now, knowing the way,
"Do what it takes," I dare to pray.

Day 281

My lovingkindness and my fortress,
My stronghold and my deliverer,
My shield and He in whom I take refuge,
Who subdues my people under me.
Psalm 144:2

God is my Stronghold. This word involves the idea of safety, and it refers to a place so high and inaccessible than no one can reach it. A pretty sure way to have guaranteed safety is to be in a place that no one else can reach or penetrate.

God is able to put me in just such a place. He can remove me so far from a problem that it can no longer touch me. He can place me beyond its reach. On a very small scale, the concept is illustrated by an older brother who climbs a tree in order to escape the reach of a younger sibling. It might also be illustrated by a cat perched on a high bookshelf beyond the reach of a pestering child. The child reaches and strains and stretches over and over again, trying to reach and thinking that maybe he will be able to, but he never can.

God can give me that type of protection. Satan may strain after me. The trial may be repeated over and over. The danger may reach its fingers higher and higher. In the midst of this imminent and threatening capture, God can be my stronghold. As He holds me above the danger, I may still be close enough to see the trial. It might, in fact, be nipping at my heels. It may seem very near and intimidating, but God can prevent it from reaching me. God can hold me safely out of its reach, either just barely or so far above the problem that I forget all about it.

"Father, the danger is on my heels. I can't escape. Will You lift me up? Will You put me in a high place so that the danger can no longer reach me?"

Day 282

Rejoice in the Lord always; again I will say, rejoice!
Philippians 4:4

Don't you hate it when people tell you to smile or look on the bright side? They expect you to rejoice in tribulation and to be encouraged in God. They apparently expect you to always appear cheerful. They don't realize that what looks like sadness may actually be exhaustion, pain, or the physical drain on your body. Being sick or tired or medicated are real factors with legitimate effects.

Those physical effects are real, and God understands that. He knows the limitations of your body. A study of Scripture indicates that God also knows the limitations of your spirit. Sadness is natural, and God portrays tears as a normal part of life. God understands crying and pain and difficulty. He does not place the unreasonable expectation that you must always rise above those things with your countenance.

What about this command to rejoice in the Lord always? Are sick people supposed to do that even when they feel awful and about to fall over? When someone tries to cheer you up in that situation, are you failing to rejoice because you're not smiling and don't even want to? What is rejoicing anyway?

Contrary to a common misconception, rejoicing is not the same as happiness, and it is not evidenced only by smiling. Rejoicing in the Lord is a confident assurance based on truth about God. It is a positive inward response to the knowledge that everything comes from God as part of His plan. It is confidence and expectancy that He is doing good. I have a friend whose common greeting is "What do you know for sure?" The answer to that question is the key to rejoicing even in trouble. You can rejoice in what you know for sure.

You know that God is in control, that He loves you, and that He has a wonderful purpose in all He does. You can have a confident assurance in those facts and rejoice in them. In the midst of your illness, there are many unknowns. Rejoicing allows you to say, "There are a lot of things I don't know in this situation, but I'm very glad there's one thing I know for sure: God is in control." Focusing on that may not always put a smile on your face in the midst of the trial, but sometimes it will. More importantly, it will put a smile in your heart. Seriousness is appropriate and sorrow does have its place, but rejoicing can happen even in trials.

"Father, in the midst of sorrow and confusion, I rejoice in what I know about You. I rejoice that You have planned it all and that You are in complete control."

Day 283

"Then you will call upon Me and come and pray to Me, and I will listen to you. You will seek Me and find Me when you search for Me with all your heart."
Jeremiah 29:12-13

Does it seem sometimes as if God is nowhere to be found? Do you search and long for Him, only to feel disappointed and abandoned? The trial is hard enough in itself, but to have to endure it without God's help is unbearable.

Sometimes the situation can be so dark that it does seem like God is hidden, but the truth is that He will always hear you when you call. God is never far away. When you make an effort to come near to Him and talk to Him, He will respond. This verse says that He will listen to your prayer. God is always pleased when people seek Him and is always available when His children look for Him.

Sometimes the problem is that His children don't call on Him; they try to live their lives without help and without prayer. Sometimes the problem is that they seek Him only when it is convenient and when they think He can do something for them. Sometimes the seeking is very casual and half-hearted. It may take a major catastrophe before someone becomes desperate enough to really seek God.

The afflicted one must come to the end of his own resources and realize that he is hopelessly inadequate. Only then does he understand that he really needs God. Now he is ready to search with all of his heart. Now he is willing to seek God earnestly, determined to do things God's way. Now he is inclined to let God be in control and to follow God no matter what.

Whichever your background – whether you are seeking God earnestly for the first time in a long time, or whether your habitual seeking seems frustratingly ignored – God will listen and He will be found. Just keep seeking earnestly. Don't give up. God will reward your desires by coming to your side.

"Oh, Father, where are You? I need You at my side. I come to You with an earnest heart, ready to follow and obey You. Please show Yourself to me."

Day 284

"God is not a man, that He should lie,
Nor a son of man, that He should repent;
Has He said, and will He not do it?
Or has He spoken, and will He not make it good?"
Numbers 23:19

Have you ever read a verse from God's Word or listened to a sermon and had your spirit rebel? Has your head shook in denial or has your heart involuntarily cried out, "That's not so!" With our limited human understanding, it can seem to us that some aspects of God's Word are faulty and don't apply to us. We fail to see how God's promises are being fulfilled in our lives. In such a dilemma, the short-coming is never with God. The failure is always with us. We are unable to comprehend the scope of what God is doing. We fail to see the intricacies of His hand at work.

God's promises are faithful. He will always keep them. God is not like us. We make promises and fail to keep them. Perhaps we simply change our minds. Perhaps we forget what we said. Maybe it no longer seems important. Sometimes we have every intention and desire to keep our promise, but the situation slips beyond our control.

God never does any of those things. He doesn't change His mind. He never forgets. He says only things that are worth carrying through. There are never extenuating circumstances that limit God's ability to fulfill His Word. Every promise of God is true. If He has said it, then He will do it. God is faithful, reliable, and dependable. He will always keep His Word. He will make good on all that He has promised.

"Forgive me, Father, for doubting. If You have said it, You will do it. I don't see how, but help me to have faith in what I cannot see."

Day 285

For after all it is only just for God . . . to give relief to you who are afflicted and to us as well when the Lord Jesus will be revealed from heaven with His mighty angels in flaming fire.
II Thessalonians 1:6-7

God is paying attention to what happens in the world. He sees the lives of individuals. He knows those who are causing affliction, and He also knows those who are suffering affliction. There is no suffering that escapes His gaze.

God not only sees the suffering, but He also responds accordingly. God will do what is just and right. It is just for God to give relief to those who are afflicted. God is in the business of taking wrongs and making them right. When He sees suffering, His loving heart wants to relieve it.

We who are limited by time don't always understand how that happens because we don't always see the results in the time frame we expect. Some of the relief God provides will not come until the time that Christ is revealed. The fact that God does send relief, however, and the intent of God to do justice in regards to affliction reveal the heart of God.

We have a God who cares. He is a God who is well aware of our afflictions. He knows they are hard, and He desires to help us and deliver us from them. When it fits His plan to do so on this earth, He does. If not, we can be assured of relief and healing in heaven. The ultimate relief that God will give will never be broken. When

He delivers us from earthly afflictions and gives us the blessed relief of heaven, we will enjoy a healing that we cannot imagine. It will be a healing that is complete and that will never end. God will give relief.

"Father, thank You that You care about my affliction and want to give relief. Help me to wait patiently until the time You choose to do so."

Day 286

You will make known to me the path of life;
In Your presence is fullness of joy;
In Your right hand there are pleasures forever.
Psalm 16:11

To live with God is to live a life of great blessing. When we are wearied, exhausted, and drained by our illness and when we are oppressed and discouraged by the long process, it can be hard to focus on those blessings. It would do us good to take our eyes off the negatives and look at the many positives that God has given us. Because God is always the same, these blessings are true whether we are healthy or sick.

Psalm 16 provides a detailed list of some of God's blessings. God is a refuge that preserves us (v. 1). God Himself is so good that all other good things pale in comparison (v. 2). God's people are described as majestic (v. 3). God's people do not have the multiplied sorrows that come from following false gods (v. 4). God is the inheritance of the righteous, supplying all of their needs (v. 5). The inheritance that God supplies is a pleasant and beautiful one (v. 6). God gives counsel and instruction to His people (v. 7). God is continually with His people, and He keeps them from being shaken (v. 8). God's presence provides safety and cause for rejoicing (v. 9). God will not allow death to be the end for His people (v. 10).

Verse eleven is a fitting ending for such a wonderful list of blessings. God does indeed guide his people in a path of life. He does fill them with joy as they remain in His presence. A life with God is filled with abundant blessings, and those blessings will last forever. When this life is ended, God's people will continue to enjoy abundant pleasures and blessings with Him for all eternity.

"Father, You understand my weakness and how easy it is to focus on the hardships. Help me to remember and rejoice in the numberless blessings You give to me."

Day 287

Even though I walk through the valley of the shadow of death,
I fear no evil, for You are with me;
Your rod and Your staff, they comfort me.
Psalm 23:4

God is always with me. He walks with me in pleasant times, but He also stays at my side during the darkest days. When I am surrounded by darkness, staring death in the face, even there He is with me. He will never leave – not for one day, one hour, or even one minute. No matter how dark and difficult the path is that I must walk, I do not need to fear. No evil, however threatening it may be, can hurt me, because God is with me to protect me. God, my loving Shepherd, walks every path with me. What a blessing and a wonderful reassurance to know that He is faithfully at my side! I do not need to walk any path alone.

Along with His protecting presence, God also supplies me with comfort in the dark valley. When facing death, or the threat thereof, God is able to give sufficient comfort. I am comforted by His constant presence and by the knowledge that He is not going anywhere. I am also comforted by His rod and staff, the objects that He uses to give guidance and protection. Knowing that He is guiding my steps perfectly and watching over them carefully gives me comfort. In these most difficult days, God presence is constant, and His comfort is sufficient. Certainly if God is with me and comforts me even on the darkest path, then He is also with me in every less threatening place.

"Help me, Father, to remember Your constant presence with me in all circumstances. Comfort me with that unfailing presence."

In the Darkness (Sonnet 43)
The inky blackness constantly surrounds
With darkness so intense it can be felt.
This black of night is filled with frightful sounds;
The murky gloom attempts my heart to melt.
Trapped in this darkness, I can't see a thing.
No change I see; no answers are in sight.
My blinded eyes see nothing happening;
I long for vision and for morning's light.
E'en in such times, God's work can't be denied;
All through the night His labor will progress.
When comes the morn, He'll draw the veil aside, →

And what He's done will powerfully impress.
So I must trust although I cannot see,
For God will not forsake His work in me.

Day 288

Therefore I urge you, brethren, by the mercies of God, to present your bodies a living and holy sacrifice, acceptable to God, which is your spiritual service of worship.
Romans 12:1

Our bodies are pretty important to us. When we are willing to give them to God, that act is very important to Him. It is relatively easy to give something simple to God, even to give money to God. It is harder to give Him what is more special to us, but because the gift is so hard to give, it is also more pleasing to God. God doesn't want us to give Him just things; He wants ourselves. He wants what is hardest for us to give, our body that we care so much about – our living, breathing body that can be used for His service and His glory. He longs for us to give it all up to Him, giving Him what He really wants.

God doesn't specify what that body has to be like. He doesn't ask for a perfect body; He merely asks for a willing one. If that body is broken, God can use it. If it is hurting, His grace can heal it. If it is weak, His strength can work through it. If it is brief, He can squeeze out the maximum potential. God wants us as He has made us, simply yielded to Him.

What does it mean when we give ourselves to God? Every time we yield ourselves to God, we are actually worshiping Him. Giving ourselves to God is a means of giving Him the spiritual service that He deserves.

The reason for that worship is interesting. The verse urges us to give ourselves to God because of His mercies. Our yielding is not based on duty or reputation or self-denial; it is based on a heart overflowing with gratitude for His mercies. He has truly done so much for us. In addition to providing salvation, He has given us so much more. He has guided us and cared for us throughout our entire lives; His care has not lessened at all in our time of illness. Through every day and every struggle, God has been at our side, carefully leading and tenderly caring for us. How can we not respond in sacrifice by giving Him what He wants? He is worthy of everything we have.

"Father, You have given me so much. I worship You by giving myself wholly to You, such as I am. Use me and do with me what You see fit."

Day 289

From the end of the earth I call to You when my heart is faint;
Lead me to the rock that is higher than I.
Psalm 61:2

How many times is my heart faint? How often am I completely overwhelmed? How frequently are my emotions fragile? My heart easily grows very faint. Though I do often feel like I am at the end of the earth with nowhere to turn, in reality I always have somewhere to turn. I can turn to God, my rock. God cares about my frail emotions. No matter how desperate my situation, He is the help I need.

God is able to help me because of the great contrast between us. God is a solid, unchanging rock of stability, contrasted with my changing emotions which cause me to shake and tremble. Not merely a rock, He is a rock that is higher than I am. The emphasis of this verse is that I am not very high; God is much higher. If I tried to be my own defense, I would crumble very easily; I would quickly be scaled and conquered. I'm so puny, but God is immense. Because of my low position, problems may seem impossible to me, but God is higher and stronger. None of my problems are impossible for Him.

Only a high rock would be truly effective as a defense in which to hide. A short rock would be quite simple to overtake; it would offer little protection. As a high and tall rock, God is far more effective than any other refuge. I could never protect myself as well as God can protect me. In every situation, taking refuge in Him surpasses being my own refuge.

When my heart is faint, God can do something about my emotional need. That's why I can have the confidence to call out to Him, asking to be led to Him. If I must ask God to lead me to that rock, it is clear that I am not already there. I need God to gently lead me. I may not know how to get to that rock on my own and may not even want to go, so I need God to direct me to that place of stability and protection.

"Oh, Father, my heart is faint. I need You to lead me to a place of refuge in You. Help me to trust in Your power that far exceeds my own."

Day 290

Let me dwell in Your tent forever;
Let me take refuge in the shelter of Your wings.
Psalm 61:4

Psalm 61:2 presents God as a strong refuge, a high rock in which we can hide. While this is a wonderful picture of strength, protection, and stability, it could also seem somewhat impersonal. It presents strength without the tender and gentle care that we also long for in hurting times. The reality is that God provides both; verse four of the same psalm provides the balance. God's care is too complex to be fully represented by a single picture. This verse provides two new pictures that reveal a different emphasis within the idea of God's protection.

First, when we are overwhelmed, we can dwell in God's tent. We can go to the dwelling place of God, His home. We can live in the same place where God is. We are not limited to a brief visit that lasts merely for an afternoon or even for a day or two. Instead, we can stay in that loving, supportive environment forever. We can remain constantly in the presence of our loving God.

The second picture is that of a mother bird who holds her chicks under her wings. We can experience the tender, mothering, effective protection that God provides. We can experience His gentle comfort and reassurance as He takes us in and holds us close to His side.

Both of these pictures, God's dwelling place and His covering wings, are very tender in nature. They speak to us of home, of care, of love, and of nurturing. Those words perfectly describe the setting that we want to be in when we are hurting. We long for an intimate place of complete acceptance. We desire to be important and cared for. There is comfort in knowing we are so close to God that an attack on us is of necessity also an attack on Him. God is willing to give us that level of caring protection.

"Help me, Father, to believe that You care about my emotions. Because You care, You won't allow me to flounder. You will invite me to be with You, and You will hold me close to Your side."

Day 291

We count those blessed who endured. You have heard of the endurance of Job and have seen the outcome of the Lord's dealings, that the Lord is full of compassion and is merciful.
James 5:11

Even the world admires someone who endures great difficulty without being defeated by it. Especially as Christians we consider those who endure to be blessed. Watching them is an encouragement to us and we respect those people. God identifies the Old Testament prophets (v. 10) and Job (v. 11) as examples of those who endured in suffering. We can look admirably on these people and see them as examples.

We consider them blessed, I think, because God considers them blessed. He, in fact, blesses them. If we look at the end of Job's story, we see God's great compassion and mercy to him, as God restored and increased his wealth. That was

God's response to Job's situation, but Job had to wait till the end of the trial to see it. The outcome takes time. We must be patient to wait for the final result. We must allow God time to bring the trial to its conclusion and to show His compassionate and merciful outcome.

Even as humans, we are often able to see the outcome of blessing that God sends to those in trials. We see the benefit and the growth that come as a result. We may not desire trials for ourselves, but to some extent we do think, "I wish I could be that mature. I wish I could know God that well. I wish I could see God's hand at work or experience His blessing like that." There is something worthy to be desired in the outcome that God gives. We never reach the point where we would not benefit from the profitable outcome that follows a test.

"I pray, Father, that I would be patient to wait for the end result of Your work, trusting that You will give an outcome of blessing."

Day 292

We count those blessed who endured. You have heard of the endurance of Job and have seen the outcome of the Lord's dealings, that the Lord is full of compassion and is merciful.
James 5:11

The fact that Job is the specifically named example of endurance is worthy of examination. The Bible assumes that people had heard of Job; he was legendary in the arena of endurance. In one day Job faced the loss of all his wealth and all his children with this response: *"The Lord gave and the Lord has taken away. Blessed be the name of the Lord."* Job was sad and he did mourn, but in the midst of it all, he worshipped. He did not sin or blame God. Truly Job was a righteous man. How could any of us hope to respond in that same way? Job displayed a response of humble acceptance and worship.

Job then faced an extended physical trial. He suffered great physical affliction for weeks and perhaps months. He was challenged to respond appropriately in this new area of endurance. There is no question that Job struggled; he struggled greatly. This means that struggle is normal even for an extremely strong Christian. We should never assume or suggest that it is easy to live through affliction. Easy or not, however, we can't give up. We must endure.

I think what is most instructive for us in the story of Job is his response in the end. Job learned more about God. He learned more about himself in response to God. Job's primary response was that of humility as He learned to let God be God, without arguing with Him or putting restrictions on Him. He learned that God can do what He wants, and that he must simply trust it to be best. Job endured the trial.

Through the ups and downs, and as intense pain was added to multiplied calamities, Job endured. He emerged from the trial still trusting in God and still following God. He did not allow the trial to turn Him aside.

"No matter what comes, Father, help me to cling tenaciously to You and to endure the trial without turning aside."

Day 293

Gird Your sword on Your thigh, O Mighty One,
In Your splendor and Your majesty!
Psalm 45:3

God is the Mighty One. The phrase comes from the picture of a strong man or a valiant warrior who prevails against his foes. God is powerful, but He is not powerful in the same sense that man is. God is not even in the same category as man; He is the most powerful. There is no man who has more power than God does. No warrior can face God and win. God can defeat the most well-educated, intelligent soldier. He can conquer the strongest, most physically fit soldier. He can prevail over the most intimidating and decorated soldier. Not one of them is a match for God.

The Mighty One can even take on entire armies and win. The Bible records several occasions on which God defeated entire armies all by Himself. God caused their fortified cities to fall down. He sent hailstorms to wipe armies out. He sent wind in the trees to confuse them. He caused them to turn upon themselves. He caused them to hear noises and flee in terror. No army has ever lined up against God and been victorious. Even if the armies of many nations banded together, they would not be able to defeat the Mighty One. Those confederations merely form larger armies, and there is no army so large that God cannot conquer it. In fact, at Armageddon multiple armies will join together in an attempt to defeat God, but He will be equal to the challenge. Those armies will not win.

The Mighty One is completely powerful and totally in control. Since God has all power and all control, He oversees everything that comes into our lives. God has the power to stop anything that threatens us. If an enemy does come into our lives, it is not because God is powerless to defeat it. Rather, it is because God allowed it within His plan. God has the might to control that foe and to make it serve His purposes. Not only should we be in awe of God's unstoppable might, but we should also trust Him to use His might according to His vast wisdom.

"Father, the enemies I face seem daunting to me. Thank You that they are no match for You. There is no problem I face that You are not able to conquer."

Day 294

But Moses said to the people, "Do not fear! Stand by and see the salvation of the LORD which He will accomplish for you today; for the Egyptians whom you have seen today, you will never see them again forever."
Exodus 14:13

Two times in the Old Testament, God gives His people this instruction: *"Stand by and see the salvation of the LORD."* The first instance was when His people were fleeing Egypt. These newly released slaves had no military training. They were burdened down with families, flocks, and all their worldly possessions. In that disadvantageous position, they became trapped between an impassable sea and an approaching army that was both angry and powerful. In the second situation, recorded in Second Chronicles 20, a great allied army came against God's people. The land of Judah was invaded, and Judah's army was outnumbered.

In both instances, the people were trapped in impossible situations. In both cases God told the people not to fear. He did not ask them to fight or even to do anything. He took the responsibility upon Himself, promising them salvation, while they were only to stand and watch it happen. God made good on His promises. For fleeing Israel, He opened up the Red Sea, gave them dry land on which to escape, and then utterly destroyed the pursuing army. For beleaguered Judah, He caused the factions within the allied army to fight among themselves. They killed each other until only corpses remained. God gave amazing victories.

The truth is that those victories were possible only through God. As hard as the Israelites might have tried, they could not have been successful in either situation. Don't we face similar situations? Sometimes we aren't physically or mentally able to do anything about the situations that confront us. When we can't do anything, we are exactly where God wants us, for then the answer is all of God. When the solution comes, it is very clear that God was behind it. When we can do nothing else, we must simply rest quietly, knowing that God is able to deliver. In our powerless state, we can watch while God does the work.

"Father, I am trapped in an impossible situation. I can't do anything. Instead of wasting my energy and losing my peace by trying to fight, I will be still and watch You give the answer."

Be Still (Sonnet 4)
Be still and let Me do My work in you.
You want the image of My Son to wear,
Preparing you for work I'd have you do;

$\longrightarrow$

Then I must make adjustments here and there.
Be still a while and wait for Me to lead.
The world surrounds you constantly with noise.
To ascertain the way that I've decreed,
Be quiet so that you can hear My voice.
Be still and see the work that I will do,
For your reaction would be far too small.
Do not distract, but let My might shine through;
My actions show that I control it all.
If you desire Me to work, I will,
But sometimes that demands that you be still.

Day 295

"Now I will arise," says the LORD,
"Now I will be exalted, now I will be lifted up."
Isaiah 33:10

An illness provides a lot of potential for disappointment and defeat. The accumulated effect of the enduring illness is bad enough. Along the way you might also face relapses, unsuccessful treatments, disappointing delays, unexpected complications, discouraging news, and life-altering phone calls. When these types of things happen, you feel as if your spirit has been crushed. You are deflated, and it's easy to think that your life has suffered a great defeat.

In those dark days, it is important to remember that God is in control of your life. He has laid out a plan for you, and He is working out that plan day by day and step by step. A defeat in your life, within the plan of God, would also be a defeat for God. God can't lose. His plans can't be defeated. God is never conquered, and He never loses a battle. When God decides to do something, it is accomplished as He has designed it. When God chooses to lift Himself up, nothing and no one can put Him down. Nothing has power over God. Nothing can stop what He determines to do.

As you walk down the path that God has put before you, you can be sure that you cannot be defeated either. Apart from God, there can be numerous and disastrous defeats, but as long as you are following His plan, there can be no defeat. While you may not know exactly what the victory will look like or when it will come, you can be sure that God will be victorious. Keep following your Leader. Keep waiting, and He will win the victory.

"Father, I feel as if I am defeated day after day. Thank You that You are never defeated and that You never lose. Help me to trust and follow You."

Day 296

But He gives a greater grace. Therefore it says, "God is opposed to the proud,
but gives grace to the humble."
James 4:6

I am in great need of grace. I need it so that I can live through today and so that I can face the future. I need grace for facing my disease, for interacting with others, and for responding to the struggles that arise within me. Even normal life for normal people requires grace. How much more do I need grace in my far-from-normal life?

God gives grace. He gives greater grace than what He has given before, meaning that as trials increase, He just keeps giving more and more grace. God doesn't, however, give that multiplied grace to everyone. He gives it to the humble.

I don't like to be humble. I don't like to submit myself to God, because frankly I don't like a lot of the things God has brought into my life. My life is a constant challenge, and there isn't much that is pleasant. I want to protest against that.

I realize, though, that when I protest against God, I am being proud rather than humble. The grace that I need – well, God doesn't give it to the proud or to those who rise up against Him in protest. Those people meet with His opposition instead. I don't want God opposed to me. There is a huge contrast between those two situations: God's opposition and His grace.

Now I face a dilemma; I need God's grace, but I don't want to humble myself. There is a lot of vulnerability in humbling myself. I am so crushed already that to yield to anything else would just destroy me. Yet submitting is the only answer. When I submit, God pours out His grace. Until I submit, I am carrying a very heavy burden, but when I humble myself, God's grace replaces that burden.

I must submit to God, let His Word be right, and allow Him to do His work. My will cannot be aggressive or demanding or important. It must be completely given to Him. Although my heart does not naturally want to be humble or pliant, I must learn to consistently say "Yes" to God. When I humble myself, God does not crush me or allow the humbling to crush me; instead, He pours out more and more grace to sustain me – *because* I have humbled myself. That's when He gives the grace. He gives it just to the humble.

"Father, when I am hurting and broken, help me to be willing to humble myself instead of
fighting with You. Help me to find strength and comfort in Your grace."

Day 297

Those who love Your law have great peace,
And nothing causes them to stumble.
Psalm 119:165

It's so easy to stumble. There are bumps on the outside that want to overwhelm me. The outward bumps are the circumstances – the pain and fatigue, the hassle of doctors' visits, the bills, the medicines to manage, and the responsibilities that I can't keep up with. They all add up to frustration. They make me feel inadequate and helpless. They make me impatient and angry.

There are bumps on the inside, threatening my spirit. The inward bumps are my thoughts and emotions. I struggle with fear, uncertainty, bitterness, doubt, and discouragement. These unending struggles make me feel like I'm losing my mind. I feel like a pitiful Christian because I can't control my thoughts and emotions. I don't know what to do about it, and it's driving me crazy.

On a road containing so many bumps that threaten to trip me up, I need something to give stability to my steps. I need something to protect my faltering feet. The thing I need is the Word of God. One of the most amazing things about the Bible is that it is unchangeable. It is incredibly steady. It has not changed for thousands of years. In the face of all of my life's upheavals, the Bible gives stability. The same promises that have helped many others are still there for me. They still say the same thing. The same instruction that has guided vast multitudes of Christians remains unchanged in God's Word. It can still guide me. The eternal truth of the Bible provides everything I need to steady my steps. It hedges me in, it illumines my path, and it holds me upright. When I am walking the path with those safeguards in place, I no longer have reason to fear. The stabilizing ability of God's timeless and proven Word brings peace to my mind and calmness to my soul.

"Father, You know my unsteady steps. Use Your Word to hold me firmly on the path and to bring peace to my troubled mind."

Day 298

Examine me, O LORD, and try me;
Test my mind and my heart.
Psalm 26:2

An illness provides us with plenty of time to ponder. Our minds fill with an abundance of thoughts, some of which are true and many of which are not. In the midst of this onslaught, our discernment is challenged. We find ourselves unable to correctly diagnose our heart and thoughts. We imagine a variety of spiritual problems and easily believe ourselves guilty of them. Those self-initiated accusations may seem to be confirmed by the advice and input of other people. With a body exhausted by illness and a mind hampered by its effects, we suffer in our ability to think clearly. It can be impossible for us to distinguish what is a real spiritual problem that needs our attention from what is merely a physical limitation or an imagined problem.

In the midst of such confusion, we need God to do the diagnosis for us. We need Him to examine and try us. Only He can test our mind and heart and decipher the jumble inside. He can identify the impurities and separate them out. When we suspect a spiritual problem or when someone else brings a potential problem to our attention, we must not be hasty to claim that problem and force ourselves to work through it. We must first bring the area in question to God. We must allow Him to decide whether or not we are indeed in the wrong. We must give God time to reveal the truth about the issue.

There may, in fact, be a problem. How often are we completely without sin? If there is something wrong, we need to know that. We need to confess it and humbly allow God to purify us. If the issue in question is not a problem in our lives, we need to know that also. We need to be able to rest without false guilt or self-imposed pressure. In these difficult evaluations, we must trust in God's right judgment rather than in the easily flawed judgment of humans.

"Father, I need You to try my heart. If there is sin, reveal that to me so that I can be purified. If there is not sin, reveal that so I can rest at peace."

Day 299

For He Himself has said, "I will never desert you, nor will I ever forsake you."
Hebrews 13:5b

As someone going through an extended illness, you realize how easy it is to feel alone. In fact, you might even use words like *neglected*, *forsaken*, and *forgotten*. You may be house-bound or limited in going out in public. Perhaps you feel the isolation most keenly in regard to church. You miss the fellowship and the loving, supportive atmosphere. You may be blessed to have family and friends who keep up with you, but it is very likely that you have less interaction than you used to. It is possible that people you used to see regularly are now only rare visitors. Other friends, or even family, may seem to have completely disappeared.

When you are feeling overwhelmed by loneliness, this verse offers a wonderfully comforting thought: God is always with you. At no point has He ever left your side

– not for one day or one minute of your ordeal. It may be hard for you to sense His presence tangibly, but that doesn't make it any less true. He is there. Not only has He always been there in the past, but He will also be there every day of the future. God is not going anywhere. He will never desert you, and He will never forsake you.

No matter how dark things get, God will be by your side. When you spend a day without seeing anyone else, God will be there. When you get the next report from your doctor, God will be with you. When your pain increases until it makes you cry out, God will be at your side. When all treatment options have been exhausted, God will still be there. Even if you come to the very last moments of your life, God will never forsake you. He will be with you through every difficult day, and He will be with you for all of eternity.

"When I feel alone, dear Father, thank You that You are my faithful friend. Thank You that You have never left my side and never will."

Day 300

If we confess our sins, He is faithful and righteous to forgive us our sins and to cleanse us from all unrighteousness.
I John 1:9

How many times have we blown it already today? Man has been compared to a tea bag, with the trial being the hot water that brings out what is inside. I'm sure I don't have to tell you that it isn't always a pretty picture. In "normal" life, without overwhelming pressures, we tend to think that we are not so bad, but since becoming sick, we realize more and more the ugliness that is inside us. Along with all of the common sins that everyone struggles with, there are certain temptations that seem custom-made for illness. We struggle with worry, fear, doubt, and anxious thoughts. We lack faith and patience. Our hearts want to be filled with anger, bitterness, envy, and resentment. We treat others unkindly. We become selfish. We fail to glorify God as we should.

The list could go on, but clearly there are many strong temptations for us. Because we are human, we sometimes fall to those temptations. Some of those failures are small and some are huge. The size really doesn't matter. Our response, however, is very important. Instead of continuing in our sin or pretending it didn't happen, we must simply confess it. With a humble and contrite spirit, we need to admit our sin to God.

The wonderful thing is that there is no question as to whether or not God will forgive. He always does. He forgives because of His character. In order to be righteous, God must forgive those sins that have been covered by Christ's blood.

God is faithful. He will not let us down by failing to forgive. Not only does He forgive, but He also cleanses. He washes those horrible and ugly sins away and makes us clean again. He gives us a fresh start, and He does so consistently. If we fall again tomorrow and again confess our sin, God will forgive again tomorrow.

"Father, make me sensitive to honestly and readily confess my sin. Help me trust You to completely forgive, as You say You will."

Day 301

You are good and do good;
Teach me Your statutes.
Psalm 119:68

We have a tendency to want to talk about the goodness of God when life is going well. Perhaps after a special blessing or an answer to prayer, we find ourselves joyfully stating, "God is good." While this is true, and while it is right for us to make such a statement, God's goodness is not limited to times of blessing.

Goodness is a fundamental part of God's character. Therefore, the psalmist can make his statement of God's goodness regardless of the circumstances. This verse is an unqualified statement from God's Word. It puts no restrictions on the conditions under which it is true, because there are no such restrictions. There are not certain situations or certain times in which God is good. God is always good. He is good every day and every night. He is good to young people and to old people. He is good to those who are sick and to those who are healthy. God is always good.

The verse tells us that in addition to being good, God also does good. His character expresses itself in His actions. Again, there are no restrictions placed on the goodness of those actions. Everything God does is good. We don't always understand how certain actions of God can be good, but His deeds are good whether or not we understand them at the time. Our failure to understand does not change the character of God.

We can grow in our understanding, and that is what the psalmist asks for. He wants God to teach him. As we learn more about God's Word and works, we will be able to comprehend more and more of His goodness. Whether we have full understanding or not, however, we can confidently say, "God is good." We can make that statement at all times, and when we do, we will never be wrong.

"Father, I admit that I don't always comprehend how You are good, but I believe it anyway. I freely acknowledge to You that You are good."

$\longrightarrow$

He's Right (Sonnet 37)
No circumstance escapes my God's control;
Each detail is directed by His might.
If joy arrives or sorrow fills my soul,
God's good, He does what's good, and He is right.
My God determines how to answer prayer,
If "Yes" or "No" or "Stay within your plight."
In what I want or grief that's hard to bear,
God's good, He does what's good, and He is right.
When God in wisdom does a challenge send,
My hurting heart does not escape His sight.
He gives His grace and helps my heart to mend;
God's good, He does what's good, and He is right.
From birth to death, each day, both morn and night,
God's good, He does what's good, and He is right.

Day 302

O LORD, You have searched me and known me.
You understand my thought from afar.
Psalm 139:1 & 2b

How often in the midst of your illness have you longed for a friend? You have been largely isolated from social situations and you are lonely. Beyond being lonely just for someone to talk to or be with you, you are lonely in your soul. There is something in you that just yearns for someone to go through your illness with you, someone with whom you can truly and deeply share your experience. Your heart is hungry for someone to pay more than just an occasional visit and show more than just a passing interest. Oddly, you may feel as if a particular doctor or nurse is the one who best fills that role for you. The bottom line is that you want a real friend.

For the next several days, we will look at some of the aspects that you long for in friendship, and we will see how God satisfies each desire. Have you often said, **"I want a friend who understands me"**? You want someone who understands your symptoms and knows what you mean when you talk about the level of pain or fatigue. You want someone who understands the mental and emotional challenges. You want someone who knows the difficulty of an on-going illness.

Consider these verses about God. *"And are intimately acquainted with all my ways"* (Psalm 139:3b). *"For He Himself knows our frame; He is mindful that we are but dust"* (Psalm 103:14). *"For we do not have a high priest who cannot sympathize with our weaknesses, but One who has been tempted in all things as* we are" (Hebrews 4:15). *"For your Father knows what you need before you ask Him"* (Matthew 6:8b). God is a friend who understands. He intimately knows every thought and feeling. He knows what life is like. He sympathizes and wants to help. He knows you and your needs better than you do yourself. God is a true Friend.

"Thank You, Father, that You understand me, that You know how very much I struggle, and that You are sympathetic to help me in my need."

Day 303

Trust in Him at all times, O people;
Pour out your heart before Him;
God is a refuge for us.
Psalm 62:8

Your heart cries out in its isolation, **"I want a friend who will listen to me and that I can talk to about what's on my heart."** There is so much that you want to say and want to share. Perhaps you don't always have the energy or the mental discipline to be able to say everything, but as you go through day after day, many thoughts flood your head. You want to share them with someone.

You want to talk about how you really feel. You want to talk about the long hours. You want to talk about the discouragement. You want to talk about the battle in your mind, the battle in your emotions, and the battle in your spirit. You want someone to evaluate whether your thoughts are crazy. You want to share the things God is gently teaching you. You want to share your heart, and you want someone who will really, truly listen. You want someone who will just let you say it all, who will accept what you say without looking down on you, and who will let you share all that is accumulating inside during this intense time of your life.

God always hears. *"The eyes of the LORD are toward the righteous, and His ears are open to their cry"* (Psalm 34:15). *"But certainly God has heard; He has given heed to the voice of my prayer"* (Psalm 66:19). *"Casting all your anxiety on Him, because He cares for you"* (1 Peter 5:7). God cares enough to listen every time you call to Him. He cares enough to listen to every struggle and every triumph. He cares enough to keep listening until you finish talking, no matter how long that takes. He cares enough to think that every word is important. God will listen to it all.

"Father, what a relief that I have You to come to. Thank You that I can pour out my heart to You and that You will always listen and care."

Day 304

> *The LORD is near to the brokenhearted*
> *And saves those who are crushed in spirit.*
> Psalm 34:18

Especially on days that are hard and hold disappointments, you have said, "**I want a friend who cares when I hurt.**" Do you want sympathy for the physical pain? Sure, that would be nice. There is, however, pain that goes far deeper than the physical. The inner wounds, the ones that no one can see, are the ones that hurt the most.

You want someone to care when a disappointment threatens to crush you. You want compassion when the treatment hasn't worked or will take longer than expected. You are frustrated when your insurance denies coverage. It can even hurt to receive good news about an upcoming wedding, birthday party, or awards banquet, because being unable to attend those events highlights the frustrating limitations of your illness. You are disappointed when an out-of-town visitor neglects to stop by, a friend forgets to call, and there is nothing in the mail again. The treatment process, as it drains you in so many ways, has become so long that you can't bear to face another day. Day after day you are kept from the job or ministry that you love. Some days it hurts simply to remember that others are healthy, while God has chosen illness for you. You cry out, "My heart is hurting," and there seems to be no one to respond.

There is someone who cares, however, and He cares very deeply. *"Just as a father has compassion on his children, so the LORD has compassion on those who fear Him"* (Psalm 103:13). *"I will rejoice and be glad in Your lovingkindness, because You have seen my affliction; You have known the troubles of my soul"* (Psalm 31:7). *"The LORD's lovingkindnesses indeed never cease, for His compassions never fail"* (Lamentations 3:22). God is unceasingly kind and caring. He knows all about every hurt, even the ones you can't share with others. God cares about the hurts that you don't even know how to express. His heart always feels your pain.

> *"Thank You, Father, for feeling my pain. Thank You for caring*
> *about the hurt that no one else sees."*

Day 305

> *Even though I walk through the valley of the shadow of death,*
> *I fear no evil, for You are with me.*
> Psalm 23:4a

When something difficult happens, friends tend to rally around. They give their support, they bring a meal, and they say a prayer. That's what Christians are supposed to do for each other. There are times, however, when helping becomes awkward. Some situations are so hard that people just don't know what to do, and they end up doing nothing. Some situations become inconvenient as the trial stretches on, and the helpers begin to drop by the wayside.

Doesn't it sometimes seem that in the trials that are the hardest and the longest, the companions are the fewest? Have you said in your frustration, "**I want a friend who will stick with me through the toughest times**"? You want someone who won't give up on you, but who will stay by your side no matter how difficult the situation becomes and no matter how long the trial lasts.

Thankfully, you do have a friend who stays with you in just those situations. *"When you pass through the waters, I will be with you; and through the rivers, they will not overflow you"* (Isaiah 43:2a). *"For He Himself has said, 'I will never desert you, nor will I ever forsake you'"* (Hebrews 13:5b). *"He will call upon Me, and I will answer him; I will be with him in trouble; I will rescue him and honor him"* (Psalm 91:15). When troubles are at their worst and when things seem as hopeless as can be, God is still there. He is always able to help because He is always near. Regardless of what human friends may do, God will never leave.

"Father, this is a very tough time in my life, and I thank You that You are with me in it. Thank You that You will never leave me."

Day 306

"Then you will call, and the LORD will answer;
you will cry, and He will say, 'Here I am.'"
Isaiah 58:9

You have limitations. You can't always get up and go when and where you want. Perhaps there are certain times of the day or certain days of the week in which you are better than others. There are times when you feel well enough to want to spend some time with a friend. At the other end of the spectrum, there are also times when you feel particularly bad, and you long for a friend to be there for you in those times too.

In either case, has it not happened that you've expectantly and hopefully made phone calls only to find that your friends were not available? You've thought to yourself, "**I want a friend who is available anytime and who will never be too busy.**" You want someone you can talk to in the solitude of the sleepless nights. You want someone to be available when you experience a sudden desperation to talk to someone. You want someone to talk to on lonely weekends when everyone else is involved in a flurry of activity. As it turns out, however, your friends have lives. They have to fix dinner, put the kids to bed, drive to the airport, go to work, attend meetings, and do all of the other common tasks of life.

People cannot always be there when you want them to be, but God can. He is never too busy to hear you. He never has too many things going on. He is never involved in something so important that He can't spend time with you. *"Evening and morning and at noon, I will complain and murmur, and He will hear my voice"* (Psalm 55:17). *"But know that the LORD has set apart the godly man for Himself; the LORD hears when I call to Him"* (Psalm 4:3). *"That they would seek God, if perhaps they might grope for Him and find Him, though He is not far from each one of us"* (Acts 17:27). Anytime, day or night, God is very near.

"Thank You, Father, that You are always available. Thank You that I never get a busy signal from You, but that You are there every time I call out in my need."

Day 307

"Simon, Simon, behold, Satan has demanded permission to sift you like wheat; but I have prayed for you, that your faith may not fail; and you, when once you have turned again, strengthen your brothers."
Luke 22:31-32

When you become ill, it is pretty much an automatic response to pray and to request prayer. As you become more and more aware of your weakness and of the limitations of the human body, it doesn't take long to become even more convinced of just how important prayer is. The strength for each new day and for the ups and downs of life is entirely dependent on prayer.

Perhaps you have all the time in the world to devote to prayer, or perhaps your brain is so limited that you can barely rub two thoughts together. In either case, whether you can pray for yourself or not, you have probably thought, "**I want a friend who will pray with me and for me.**" What a blessing it is to know others are praying for you! It is an even greater blessing and encouragement to have someone sit with you and pray, allowing you to hear their words as they lift you up to God.

Whether or not humans fill those roles for you, you are privileged to have both the Holy Spirit and Christ to pray on your behalf. *"In the same way the Spirit also helps our weakness; for we do not know how to pray as we should, but the Spirit Himself intercedes for us with groaning too deep for words; and He who searches the hearts knows what the mind of the Spirit is, because He intercedes for the saints according to the will of God. Christ Jesus is He who died, yes, rather who was* raised, who is at the right hand of God, who also intercedes for us" (Romans 8:26-27 & 34). "For there is one God, and one mediator also between God and men, the man Christ Jesus" (I Timothy 2:5). "*I ask on their behalf; I do not ask on behalf of the world, but of those whom You have given Me, for they are Yours. I do not ask on behalf of these alone, but for those also who believe in Me through their word*" (John 17:9 & 20). How amazing and wonderful it is to have these divine prayers offered on your behalf!

"Father, thank You for the Spirit who prays for me when I don't know what to say, and for the Son who also prays for me."

Day 308

"I am the LORD, I have called You in righteousness,
I will also hold You by the hand and watch over You."
Isaiah 42:6a

Maybe we're half embarrassed to admit it, but at times haven't our hearts cried out, "**I want a friend who will hold my hand and hug me**"? There's nothing wrong with that thought, though we are sometimes too proud and independent to express such longings. Wanting a physical touch is a common desire in the day to day life of ordinary people. The longing seems to increase substantially in the midst of illness. There is something quite natural, almost innate in us, that causes us to reach out and stroke the forehead of someone who is ill. Lots of hands get held in hospitals. These are normal and desirable responses. At those times when we are weak and hurting, we crave such gentle, caring, and loving touches.

If there is no one to stay by our side or to hold us, what then? Are we left alone? Oh, no. God is constantly at our side. He treats us very tenderly. He holds our hand and cradles us in His arms. We can rest in His kind embrace. *"Nevertheless I am continually with You; You have taken hold of my right hand"* (Psalm 73:23). *"Like a shepherd He will tend His flock, in His arm He will gather the lambs and carry them in His bosom; He will gently lead the nursing ewes"* (Isaiah 40:11). *"He will cover you with His pinions, and under His wings you may seek refuge"* (Psalm 91:4a). How reassuring it is to be held by the one who loves us more than anyone else. How wonderful it is to have our hand enclosed warmly and securely within His loving hand. How comforting it is to be gently wrapped in His caring arms.

"Thank You, Father, for Your touch that assures me of Your love and constant presence."

Day 309

I will instruct you and teach you in the way which you should go;
I will counsel you with My eye upon you.
Psalm 32:8

Life has so many questions right now. Should you look for another doctor? Should you get a second (or third) opinion? Should you change medications? Should you try the experimental drug? Will your diet make any difference? Is surgery the best option? Should you try to keep working? Should you go to activities or just stay home? Should you tell your family how serious things are? How long should you keep fighting?

The sheer number of things to consider is overwhelming, and most days your brain isn't alert enough to consider any of them. You think, "**I want a friend who is wise enough to give me good advice.**" Even the best of your friends, however, has limited knowledge. No human friend understands all the ins and outs of your illness, nor does he comprehend all the ramifications of the choices to be made. He or she simply doesn't know the answers. While human friends fall short, you do have an all-wise friend who knows the answer to every dilemma.

God knows the best thing to do in each scenario. No problem is too confusing or difficult for Him. *"Oh, the depth of the riches both of the wisdom and knowledge of God! How unsearchable are His judgments and unfathomable His ways!"* (Romans 11:33). *"For as the heavens are higher than the earth, so are My ways higher than your ways and My thoughts than your thoughts"* (Isaiah 55:9). *"But if any of you lacks wisdom, let him ask of God, who gives to all generously and without reproach, and it will be given to him"* (James 1:5). Your heavenly friend can guide you with the best advice in the world.

"Give me Your wisdom, Father. Show me the answers. Guide me in what I ought to do according to Your immense knowledge."

Day 310

"Ah Lord God! Behold, You have made the heavens and the earth by Your great power and by Your outstretched arm! Nothing is too difficult for You."
Jeremiah 32:17

You are grateful for your friends. Some of them have been very kind and compassionate. They have been helpful in practical ways and have taken care of things that you were unable to do. Some of them, limited by the demands of their own lives, have strongly desired to help. They would help you if they could. In fact, you have dozens and perhaps hundreds of friends who would happily take your illness completely away – if they could. They can't. No matter how much they care, no matter how sincere their intentions, and no matter how much they want to help, there are some things that are just beyond your friends' abilities.

You know that humans can only do so much, but still you find yourself thinking, **"I want a friend who is able to do something to help me when I need it."** Wouldn't it be wonderful if there were someone who could actually do something about your situation? Wouldn't it be great if someone could actually meet the needs that you have?

Again, God fits the bill. *"Now to Him who is able to do far more abundantly beyond all that we ask or think, according to the power that works within us"* (Ephesians 3:20). *"Call to Me and I will answer you, and I will tell you great and mighty things, which you do not know"* (Jeremiah 33:3). *"Oh give us help against the adversary, for deliverance by man is in vain. Through God we will do valiantly, and it is He who shall tread down our adversaries"* (Psalm 108:12-13). God's power is not limited. God is able to completely control your situation. He can do all that must be done.

"You have the ability, Father, to meet every need that I have. Help me to trust in Your power and to rest in that knowledge."

Day 311

Behold, God is my helper;
The Lord is the sustainer of my soul.
Psalm 54:4

Sometimes there appears to be no end in sight. The sunshine has darkened, and you see no hope. Your thoughts quickly spiral out of control, deeper and deeper into the abyss of discouragement. You don't want to be there. You don't want to stay there, yet you seem powerless to come up with a positive thought or to reverse your thinking on your own.

"I want a friend who can encourage me," you sigh. If only there were someone who could say the right words and bring you a little ray of hope. You want someone to help you turn your thoughts around and to direct you to something positive instead of the gloominess that pervades your spirit.

God is able to encourage. God has words of hope. God can lift up your troubled soul. He can take your heavy burden and replace it with His strength. God knows when you are discouraged. He knows it happens, and He is able to help. *"Cast your burden upon the LORD and He will sustain you; He will never allow the* righteous to be shaken" (Psalm 55:22). *"He heals the brokenhearted and binds up their wounds"* (Psalm 147:3). *"On the day I called, You answered me; You made me bold with strength in my soul"* (Psalm 138:3). Are you too feeble to stand on your own? God can hold you. He can keep your thoughts and emotions above the dark depths where they want to sink. God can give hope to your hopeless heart. He can encourage your soul.

"Oh, Father, I need Your encouragement. Please minister hope and strength to my soul."

Day 312

Not that I speak from want, for I have learned
to be content in whatever circumstances I am.
Philippians 4:11

Contentment in circumstances is something that must be learned. While it may seem easy to be content in good circumstances, contentment acknowledges the potential for change. Circumstances, by their very nature, are changeable. A content person gladly takes the good circumstances with the understanding that they are only for as long as God determines. On the negative side, those pleasant circumstances do not usually lend themselves as well to rapid growth or increased trust in God. When God leaves someone in pleasant circumstances, he must be content, even while realizing his growth may be more gradual and his spiritual adventure less exciting than that of others.

Contentment in difficult circumstances must also be learned. A sufferer must learn to be content until God changes his circumstances for the better. It is easier for someone to be content (or think he is) when he knows his situation will change, especially if he expects the change to be soon. What if God doesn't change the circumstances for the better? If the illness is life-long, rather than one that can eventually be cured, contentment is still possible and necessary. The man who is content only because he thinks his situation is temporary is not really content.

Another aspect of learning contentment is its completeness. Contentment is an internal attitude rather than an external action. Contentment, therefore, can't be compartmentalized. If someone claims to be content with his marital status, financial status, and family, but not his health, he isn't really a content person. He must be content in the daily symptoms as well as in the overall diagnosis. Contentment is not so much a test to apply to each situation of life, but rather a heart response that permeates all of life. It allows someone to have satisfaction in remaining within God's overall plan regardless of the circumstances that change daily. Contentment must be learned in good, in bad, and in everything.

"Father, help my heart to be content in every area of life. Help me to be content in the bad as well as in the good for as long as You continue each situation."

Humbling Places (Sonnet 10)
His servants can be transferred by the King
To humble places that are hard to bear.
It's not my choice nor does it pleasure bring,
For I am needy and dependent there.
By God's design brought lower than I choose,
I see how weak I am and my great needs.
I must be humble so that God can use;
A servant proud the work of God impedes.
So I must stay within that humble spot
As long as God's wise sovereignty decides,
And let Him work and mold me as He sought,
And listen as His voice instructs and guides.
It's hard indeed to stay in such a place,
But on the humble God pours out His grace.

Day 313

Forever, O LORD,
Your word is settled in heaven.
Psalm 119:89

I dread to admit it to anyone, including myself, but sometimes I doubt God's Word. I read verses and think that they cannot possibly be true. God says that He hears my prayers, but I don't see any answer in sight. God says that He delivers His people, but I don't see any deliverance coming. He says that He gives comfort, but my pain is unbearable. He says His grace is sufficient, but it doesn't seem so to me. He says He is good, but it's awfully hard for me to perceive His goodness. The list of my perceived contradictions about God's Word could go on.

It's not always this way. Sometimes I believe, and God's Word gives me hope. Then I wake up the next morning, struggling to believe the truth I believed yesterday and perhaps even the hope I shared with others.

So what do I do? I must choose to believe God's Word. Regardless of how much it hurts to admit that God is right, and no matter how much submission it requires, I must believe what God says. What I perceive as true in my circumstances (and colored by my emotions) is only apparent truth. What God says, on the other hand, is actual truth. Actual truth always supersedes apparent truth.

When it becomes harder and harder to believe God's truth, I must submit more fully, acknowledging that God's truth really is true. God's Word is everlasting. I must bow myself before it and let Him be true. I must trust what He says, no matter what. If it takes me all day to adjust my thinking, I must seek His Word until my thinking is corrected. If my doubts return again tomorrow, I must seek His truth and submit to it again. I cannot give up believing.

I must believe all of God's truth; I can't pick and choose what I think is true. If I start to throw out a few verses or concepts, I have undermined the entire foundation of God's truth. All of His Word is true. His Word is right. It does have the answers, and it will not change. His Word always has been true, and it always will be. It is forever settled.

"Father, some days my doubts are strong, but Your Word is unchanged. Help me to fully believe Your truth and to submit daily to what You say."

Day 314

The LORD is my strength and my shield;
My heart trusts in Him, and I am helped;
Therefore my heart exults,
And with my song I shall thank Him.
Psalm 28:7

I am weak. My body is so weak that I can barely stand. My mind is so weak that I can't hold on to right thoughts. My emotions are so weak that they want to crack. The battles before me are too intense. The challenges ahead are too numerous. The giants I face are far too tall. The journey that stretches in front of me is way too long. I do not have the strength.

There is no way for me to win in my own power – but I don't have to fight in my own power. I am weak, but God is my Strength. He is there to fight for me. He is there to carry me forward. He is there to help me to persevere.

I am defenseless. My immune system is broken down. I have no reserves with which to fight. My body can no longer fight back. My mind and emotions have faced more assaults than even seems possible; they can't fight off another attack. I can't face another day of battle. One more thing will knock me down and destroy me.

There is no way for me to fend off any more attacks – but I don't have to face them on my own. I am defenseless, but God is my Shield. He is there to defend me. He is there to protect me. He is there to absorb the shock of the assaults and to drive them back. His protection is sure; it is strong and secure.

I can trust in God to be my Strength and Shield. My trust in Him is well-placed and will be rewarded. He will help me. I realize how impossible my situation is and how certain defeat is on my own, and then I consider the amazing strength and protection of my God. The consideration floods me with wonder. My heart fills with amazement at His work, and my lips burst with a song of thankful praise.

"Thank You, Father, for being a strength and shield that is strong enough to repel any attack that I face."

Day 315

"For I satisfy the weary ones and refresh everyone who languishes."
Jeremiah 31:25

This verse gives two very apt descriptions of those suffering from illness. First, they are weary. They feel as if they can't go on. They are too weak and faint to continue another day. They are too needy and exhausted to continue the battle. Second, they are languishing. They mourn over the pain, the symptoms, and the struggles. They sorrow over the loss of their hopes and plans. Their hearts are heavy over the losses in their lives.

How does God respond to such people? He does not ignore them. He doesn't tell them to toughen up or to hang on. He doesn't look down on them for their weakness. He doesn't stand impatiently by, waiting for them to get over it. He doesn't offer empty words or false hope. No, far beyond all of these, God does something positive about their suffering.

God helps these sufferers and gives them hope. When God sees those who are weary from their burdens and struggles, He satisfies them. He offers them refreshment and replenishes them, like a man would give water to a thirsty animal until it wants no more. God gives new life and energy to continue on.

When God looks on those who languish, He refreshes them. He fills them with hope and makes them whole again. He renews their strength and their spirit so that they no longer feel completely drained. He restores them so they are ready to carry on. God recognizes the depth of their need, and His resources are vast enough to meet the need completely. God can give new life to the weary and renewed hope to the hopeless.

"This verse describes me, Father. Will You renew and refresh me? Will You give me the strength to face another impossible day?"

Day 316

Blessed be the God and Father of our Lord Jesus Christ, the Father of mercies and God of all comfort, who comforts us in all our affliction.
II Corinthians 1:3-4a

Life is not easy. You face new symptoms, recurring symptoms, and symptoms that just won't go away. You face the constant onslaught on your mind and emotions. You look forward and see only another week, another month, or another year of the same. As much as you may have surrendered all of those things to God, they are still not easy. It hurts to be constantly impaired. It hurts to miss out on life. It hurts to see no hope of change.

When life is hard and when life hurts, don't you long for comfort? Don't you want someone to care and to love you? You know that no one can change the situation, but you just want a friend to sit with you through it and sympathize. You want someone to care about you and to share in your pain. Isn't that comfort most meaningful when it comes from someone who understands at least a little bit?

God understands. He is a God of comfort, and He comforts you in all of your afflictions. There is not a single trial in which He does not give comfort. His comfort is a given. God's comfort goes hand in hand with affliction. This passage (II Corinthians 1:3-7) that mentions affliction and suffering seven times mentions comfort ten times.

God is your Father of mercies, and He cares for you tenderly as a father cares for his child. He is able to comfort because He is the source of all comfort. You can always find comfort in Him. God's comfort is not just a condition; it is an action. God does something about your pain. Beyond merely the knowledge that God loves you, His comfort is expressed through deliberate action on the part of God. This caring God comforts you during your time of affliction because He knows how hard life is and how much you need comfort.

"Help me to rest, Father, in the comfort that You offer. Thank You that it is present in every one of my afflictions."

Day 317

Who comforts us in all our affliction so that we will be able to comfort those who are in any affliction with the comfort with which we ourselves are comforted by God.
II Corinthians 1:4

God has a purpose in giving you comfort in affliction. When God has comforted you, you are then able to take the comfort given to you by God and pass it on to others who are also in affliction. You are not alone in suffering; others have the same type of suffering that you have, and you become able to share comfort with others who are hurting. You don't pass on your own comfort, which would be ineffective, but the comfort that God has given you. Through the trial God equips you to give appropriate comfort to others. This sharing with one another in suffering and comfort is a natural response of the church. It is a reality that the church should go through things together and empathize and share with one another (v. 7).

Not only does the comfort you receive from God serve to comfort others, but the trial itself also comforts others. They receive comfort as they watch you patiently endure (v. 6) as well as from the words you share. Since verse four says that *"we will be able"* (future tense), it seems that you are best equipped to share God's comfort after you have passed through your affliction and after you have fully experienced God's comfort.

Can you not clearly see the greater understanding you now have regarding those in trials? Don't you see the need for encouragement? Don't you see the importance of practical help, prayer, and expressed interest? Don't you know the craving for someone to patiently listen without giving advice? That is part of God's equipping you to meet the needs of others. He chose your trial with the training it would bring. Isn't it right that you reach forth to others with His help, His hope, His answers, and His comfort? Isn't it appropriate that He use you in the lives of others?

"Father, don't let these testings be in vain or wasted. Let them be not just for my benefit, but also for the benefit of others."

Day 318

For just as the sufferings of Christ are ours in abundance,
so also our comfort is abundant through Christ.
II Corinthians 1:5

Sometimes things do mount up one on top of the other. Perhaps you have thought to yourself, "If it were only my health I had to deal with, I could survive." But right on the heels of your illness came financial difficulties, problems with the kids in school, needed repairs on the house, a car accident, a job loss, a death in the family, or a split in the church. Troubles have multiplied.

Even within your own health, things have not remained simple. In the process of treatment, new problems have been discovered, or perhaps new problems have been created as a result of the treatment. The snowball keeps getting bigger, while you cry out, "How much can one person take?!"

The verse doesn't deny that sufferings can come in abundance. That does sometimes happen. The hope the verse gives is that along with the abundance of suffering, you also receive abundant comfort. As the level of suffering increases, God's comfort also increases to meet it. God gives the amount of comfort that you need. He does not give a wheelbarrow-full when you only need a bucketful. Neither does He expect you to muddle through on just a wheelbarrow-full when you are in need of a dump truck.

God's supply of comfort never runs out; He will always have enough to give you. The fact that He does increase the amount of comfort illustrates that He is very aware of how much trouble you are in. He is carefully watching as the troubles mount higher, and He will give the appropriate amount of comfort.

> *"Father, as troubles have increased, thank You*
> *that Your comfort and help have also increased."*

My God of All Comfort

When troubles greet me as the sparks that fly,
My caring Father always hears my cry.
He'll never leave nor forsake me, I see.
As father loves child, so He pities me;
A mother holds children close to her heart,
So does my Father His comfort impart.

Once Titus showed care to God's men distressed;
Through friends in Christ has God so often blessed.
His guiding presence sustains ev'ry breath,
E'en caught in the valley of shadow of death.
When I need new life in trials so sore,
God's precious Bible gives comfort and more.

God has compassion on my broken heart.
Both God and Savior comfort do impart;
The blessed Comforter lives within me.
So clearly merciful kindness I see,
And hope-giving grace descends from above,
Providing comfort through undying love.

God's hand in trials is so sure and plain.
His love won't send affliction once in vain.
My heart fills praising my great loving God,
So sure deliv'rance will come full and broad.
Such hope when my brothers see manifest
The strength from God evident through the test.

My God of all comfort, my Father of mercies,
He gives His hand; soon all turmoil flees.
In all tribulation, at my side He'll be found.
Trials increase; I see consolation abound.

Day 319

My soul waits in silence for God only;
From Him is my salvation.
He only is my rock and my salvation,
My stronghold; I shall not be greatly shaken.
Psalm 62:1-2

In the midst of great trouble, David waited on God. His soul rested silently as he relied confidently on God and expected Him to bring salvation. He did not look to his own strength or to other people. He looked only to God, because only God was great enough to deliver him. What made God such a dependable source of strength? What made God worth waiting on when everyone else had failed? Psalm 62 reveals the answers to these questions.

First, God was the source of David's salvation (vs. 1, 2, 6, & 7). It had always been God who had helped him, and God had often provided salvation in the past.

Second, God was David's rock (vs. 2, 6, & 7). He was strong and firm and steady.

Third, God was David's stronghold (vs. 2 & 6). He was a safe place in which David could enclose himself and be protected.

Fourth, God was the source of David's hope (v. 5). God was the only place that David could look in order to receive the encouragement that there could be an answer to his problem.

Fifth, God was David's refuge (vs. 7 & 8). David could retreat to God and be protected from the attacks of the enemy. He could be sheltered from the assaults.

Sixth, God was David's source of power (v. 11). Evil men thought they had power (v. 10). They depended on their riches and on their wicked tactics to give them victory. They failed. Only God had the power to repel attacks and to gain victories.

Seventh, in addition to those mighty aspects of God, He also expressed lovingkindness (v. 12). He cared deeply for David and reached out to him in kindness and love. God's love impelled Him to respond in all those other ways.

David wisely waited on God, and David's God was big enough to be worthy of that expectation. Just as David waited on God alone for deliverance, we can trust in God for deliverance from our troubles. He alone is able to conquer, and He can do so even in the most difficult situation.

"Father, I need help. Thank You that You are big enough and strong enough to give it. I can wait quietly and confidently on You."

Day 320

But if the Spirit of Him who raised Jesus from the dead dwells in you, He who raised Christ Jesus from the dead will also give life to your mortal bodies through His Spirit who dwells in you.
Romans 8:11

One of the most wonderful things that we have to look forward to as Christians is that one day our weak bodies will no longer be marred by imperfection or threatened by death. The day is coming when our bodies will be resurrected just as Christ's body was resurrected.

Christ's resurrection was permanent, and He will never die again. The same is true of us. Once resurrected, we will live forever, and death will no longer have dominion over us.

God will give new life to our bodies that are now so frail. The new bodies will be far superior to the ones we have now. Our current bodies are corruptible and mortal, but our new bodies will be incorruptible and immortal. They will never die, and they will never decay.

Our bodies will be redeemed by God as He adopts us as His children. This wonderful change will take place when Christ returns to the earth to claim His children. We will be raised up and presented before God. We will be equipped to live forever, without the frailty or pain of our current bodies.

Our new bodies will live forever in a place of bountiful comfort and joy. One of the first things God will do for us in heaven will be to wipe away every tear from our eyes. Tears are natural in our current mortal bodies, but they will be banned from our immortal bodies, and we will live forever with God.

"Oh, Father, what a wonderful prospect to look forward to! Help me not to forget this blessed promise. My frail body is for this life only, but one day You will make it so much better."

Day 321

Finally, brethren, whatever is true, whatever is honorable, whatever is right, whatever is pure, whatever is lovely, whatever is of good repute, if there is any excellence and if anything worthy of praise, dwell on these things.
Philippians 4:8

The mind is one of the great battlefields for every Christian, but that reality seems to be increasingly true of someone going through an illness. Sometimes the problem is that you can't think; your brain won't properly process thoughts. Other times the problem is that you think too much; with all the long, empty hours, your brain works overtime. Often, too, your thoughts are a crazy, jumbled mess; they jump rapidly from one thing to another. The direction of your thoughts can be a problem. With so many things happening in your life, and with so much uncertainty, your thoughts naturally want to run to worry, fear, and discouragement. They want to work hard at finding the answers to all the questions you have.

In short, your thoughts are not always very wholesome or helpful. While the task can be very challenging, with God's help you can actively evaluate your thinking. Philippians 4:8 provides a good guide for that. When your thoughts start to go crazy, stop yourself. Ask, "Is this true, or I am inventing something in my mind?" That first question alone is enough to evaluate many of your thoughts, but there are other questions available. "Is it pure, or am I thinking something unwholesome about another person?" "Is it lovely, or am I dwelling only on the negative aspects of my situation?"

If your thoughts don't fit the guidelines, choose to change what you are thinking. Replace the wrong thinking with proper thinking. The Bible has many right thoughts that can counterbalance the wrong ones. If there are particular thoughts that plague you often, find a Biblical substitute. Have that substitute available so that you can quickly redirect your thoughts to what is profitable and good.

"You know, Father, what a struggle this is for me. Help me to replace my natural thoughts with right thoughts from Your Word."

Day 322

I know whom I have believed and I am convinced that He is able to guard what I have entrusted to Him until that day.
II Timothy 1:12b

It is no small God that we serve. We can have a great deal of confidence in simply remembering the one in whom we have believed. He is the creator and sustainer of the universe. He is the one who controls everything – nature, kings, nations, people, and events. He is the one who does miracles and who raises the dead. He is the one who loves us enough to provide salvation at such a great cost to Himself.

This God is worthy of our belief. Because He is such a great God, we can depend on Him to keep what we have entrusted to Him. He is not going to let us down. He is not going to neglect or abandon us. Not only is He entirely trustworthy, but He is also completely capable and sufficiently powerful to keep what we have committed to Him.

What is it that we've entrusted to God? We have entrusted to Him our very souls. We have placed our lives and our entire futures in His hands. We have trusted Him with our eternal destinies. If we can trust Him with those weighty things, should it be any challenge for us to trust Him with our day to day lives?

We can safely trust God with our illness. We can trust Him for the daily symptoms. We can trust Him for the progress or lack thereof. We can trust Him for the strength to go on. We can trust Him for our mental and emotional stability. We can trust Him for encouragement. If God is committed to guarding our souls for eternity, He is certainly committed to keeping us until then.

"Father, You are worthy of my trust. Thank You that I can trust You as much for the day to day aspect of life as I can for eternity. You will keep me."

Day 323

Why are you in despair, O my soul?
And why have you become disturbed within me?
Hope in God, for I shall yet praise him,
The help of my countenance and my God.
Psalm 42:11

God is the Help of my countenance. He is its deliverance and victory. As I go from day to day through an illness, my countenance often needs deliverance. Too often I look like I have just suffered a defeat, and I need victory. When I focus on my problems and my inability to do anything about them, it is easy to feel defeated. This sense of defeat clearly manifests itself in how I look. The burden and strain shows in my face and mannerisms. I look old, weary, and sad. I look like someone who has lost the final battle.

In struggles that so evidently affect me, God is able to help. If I focus on Him instead of on my problems, I realize the battle is not lost. When I look to God, I realize that there is always hope. God is always able to solve my problems and change my circumstances. If He chooses not to do that in an external way, He can still do it internally by giving me grace and strength. No situation is hopeless when God is at work. I can hope in Him, knowing that, at the very least, He will uphold me and help me through the trying time. He will not leave me to fight on my own.

Such a realization changes my whole outlook on life. What was hopeless is now possible. God's help affects what my face looks like, as I draw my comfort from Him and as He encourages me in difficulty. God can take despair, defeat, dismay, and fear, and He can turn them into confidence, victory, assurance, and peace. Those positive outcomes have a powerful impact on my countenance.

"Thank You, Father, that there is always hope with You. Thank You that You can change anything. Thank You that You can turn my defeat into hope."

Day 324

At my first defense no one supported me, but all deserted me; may it not be counted against them. But the Lord stood with me and strengthened me.
II Timothy 4:16-17a

When you are in the midst of trouble, you want to be able to look around and see your friends surrounding you. Paul did not experience that support; when he looked around, all of his companions had fled. Have you found yourself in a similar situation? Perhaps at first your friends rallied around in support, but as time has passed, the helpers have been fewer and fewer. Those who had visited once a week now call once a month. Instead of meals twice a week, you haven't had a meal brought in for two months. People who used to be among your closest friends seem to have totally forgotten you exist. In fact, as you look around for your support network, you can't seem to find a trace of it anywhere.

Sometimes no one else will stand by you. Just like in Paul's situation, it might happen that everyone deserts you. Realizing that none of your friends have remained loyal can be a devastating revelation. Times of trouble reveal who your true friends are, and it is a brutal shock to see the number of faithful friends be very small.

As hurtful as it must have been for Paul to be left alone in his time of need, he did not count the desertion against his friends. He was willing to overlook it even though the friends were clearly in the wrong. Paul goes on to share a much more encouraging thought. You see, it is not your friends that you ought to depend on in times of hardship. They can't give you the level of help you really need.

God is the only one you can truly depend on. God can give you strength. God is always able to rescue, something that people would not be able to do even if they were standing by. Even when all others seem to have deserted you, God is still there. God will always stand with you. His presence and support will not fail.

"Father, when I find myself alone, thank You that You are still by my side to give me strength." $\longrightarrow$

Alone

Alone, abandoned, and neglected souls are sad;
It hurts to be forgotten, isolated, lone.
But there is One who never, never leaves my side;
Though others leave, His presence constantly is had.
Giv'n just one choice, with God I'd choose to be alone;
Though no one else is near, I need Him to abide.

The times I spend alone with God are very good.
In times of sorrowing, He gives His comfort sweet;
In times of hurt, His tender love is well applied.
These times enhance our friendship's depth like naught else could.
He oft prepares and molds me while I'm at His feet;
Instruction wise and teaching come from my good Guide.

The times alone with Him prepare me for the rest;
I need this fellowship to guide me through my day.
Hard times require that I more constantly reside.
To build a firm foundation, time He does invest.
Alone with Him yields preparation for my way,
And in these times He can reserves of strength provide.

And when we stop to think, do we not see it true
That oft God's greatest works come through one lonely man?
No audience exists in whom he can confide,
So God alone receives all praise and thanks that's due.
Perhaps when to the stillness he returns again,
That servant can now hear God's prompting voice inside.

Oh, Father-Friend, alone with You is not so bad,
For You are faithful, loyal, true, and won't neglect.
I need this time in which I can be purified.
So make it count, this time with You, and I'll be glad.
I would not stop Your hand; Your work I won't reject.
As long as You should choose, alone with You I'll hide.

Day 325

Always giving thanks for all things in the name
of our Lord Jesus Christ to God, even the Father.
Ephesians 5:20

As Thanksgiving approached, I anticipated the likelihood of being in a situation in which I would be asked to tell something I was thankful for. I had nothing to share, but to keep from being embarrassed, I made a deliberate effort to come up with a ready answer. My list consisted of two rather obvious and impersonal items – just in case I needed them.

Then my pastor preached on thankfulness. The concept of always giving thanks for all things rebelled against my nature. First Thessalonians 5:18 told me that it was God's will for me to give thanks in everything. I was having a lot of trouble giving thanks for anything. (After all, my life was miserable.) Now was I really supposed to be thankful for everything, including the hard stuff? The idea was so ludicrous that I did the logical thing; I refused. In my battle with God, I told Him not only "I can't," but also "I won't."

Eventually God won the battle, and I'm glad He did. The most striking thing to me about the struggle came from Luke 6:45, which told me that a man's "*mouth speaks from that which fills his heart.*" Words of thanks come from a thankful heart. Not having thankful words to say was a problem. Having an ungrateful heart was a bigger problem. Ungratefulness indicates a heart that places little value on what God is doing. The fact is that what God does always has value and therefore always merits thanks.

I realized that I always need to be thankful. If for no other reason, I can be thankful because God is in control and is using each situation within His plan – for His glory and for my good. I can be thankful for God's provision within the storm. I can be thankful for who God is and that I belong to Him. If my heart is thankful, my list of thankful words will not stop. According to the verse above, thankfulness is not an option; it is a command. Therefore obedience is a choice. Instead of "I can't" or "I won't," my words had to change to "I will."

"Father, give me a thankful heart that spills out into thankful words. Help me to thank You even when my life makes no sense to me."

Day 326

"All the inhabitants of the earth are accounted as nothing,
But He does according to His will in the host of heaven
And among the inhabitants of earth;
And no one can ward off His hand
Or say to Him, 'What have You done?'"
Daniel 4:35

There is no circumstance in the entire world, let alone in your own life, over which God does not have complete control. The speaker of the verse considers the inhabitants of the earth, and he sees that God does His will among them.

God accomplishes His will in regard to individuals, whether they be rich or poor, important or unknown, powerful or helpless. God controls the life of the king as much as He does the life of the slave. God also accomplishes His will among groups and nations. Even when people band together, they create no challenge for God's control. God can move families, defeat armies, and destroy nations. No person or group of people on earth is able to force its will over God's. God's control does not stop even when the situations move beyond the boundaries of earth. God also does exactly what He pleases in the realm of heaven. The heavenly beings yield to His command just as completely as earthly beings do. In heaven or in earth, God is not stopped in doing what He desires.

There are two things that people cannot do toward God. First, they cannot stop His hand. When God puts His hand in motion and begins to do something, man is powerless to deflect His hand or to hold it back. Man cannot exert enough force to keep God's hand from doing what God has decided to do. Secondly, man cannot successfully bring a charge of protest against God. Man might ask the accusing question, but he has no legitimate grounds for demanding an adjustment from God. Man cannot force God into changing what He has done. No one can stop God's hand, because He is completely in control. No one can demand a change, because God is completely right.

"Thank You, Father, than no one and nothing can stop You from accomplishing Your plan. It is comforting to serve a God who always does exactly what He plans to do."

Day 327

Who remembered us in our low estate,
For His lovingkindness is everlasting.
Psalm 136:23

Man is of low estate. The phrase speaks of our very humble condition and of our depressed and sunken state in regards to God. Our state is lower than we would like to consider. We were enemies of God, choosing to sin against His holiness. We were left without any hope of saving ourselves or of reconciling ourselves to Him. In comparison with God, we are extremely weak and foolish, incapable of impressing Him in the least.

Even after salvation we continue to be pitifully weak, due to our body of flesh. We fall over and over again in trying to do the things we want to do. We often fail in our efforts to do right. In addition to those inadequate efforts, there are countless times when we don't even desire the right things. In our own strength we remain helpless and unable to do what we ought to do. Not only in the past, but also in the present, we are very low before God.

It would be logical and justifiable for God to destroy us or, at the very least, to ignore us and simply allow us to be bogged down in our own mire. God does neither; instead, He loves us and looks at us with pity and understanding. He remembers us as we flounder in our pit, and He responds to us. God knows our great need, and He recalls our frail frame. In His everlasting lovingkindness, God delivers us and blesses us. Through Christ He graciously overlooks our multiplied weaknesses and repeated failings, and He accepts us as sons and heirs. Our loving God raises us from our low estate and lifts us up into His family.

"Father, I was nothing, but You saved me. I continue to fail often, but You still love me and meet me in my need. Thank You for Your great love and gracious response."

Day 328

My soul is satisfied as with marrow and fatness,
And my mouth offers praises with joyful lips.
Psalm 63:5

An illness can easily contribute to feelings of dissatisfaction. We can be dissatisfied with our level of pain, our level of energy, and our level of improvement. We can grow dissatisfied with the number of visits from friends, the number of pills to take, and the number of trips to doctors. In the midst of these dissatisfactions, there is one wonderful source of complete satisfaction. God is able to satisfy us with Himself.

At the beginning of Psalm 63, David expressed his earnest desire for God. He desperately and passionately longed for God (v. 1). God marvelously met that longing. God showed His lovingkindness, which was better than life itself (v. 3). He satisfied David's soul to the point that David responded with exuberant praise (v. 4).

David expressed his sweet satisfaction with God in two ways. First, David evidenced his satisfaction by remembering God often. He thought about God and meditated on Him at night (v. 6). He remembered the wonderful ways that God had helped him in the past, and he clung close to His sufficient God (vs. 7-8). Secondly, David showed his satisfaction by trusting in God. In the midst of the difficult situation he faced, he was confident that God would protect him (vs. 9-11).

These two responses are not surprising. They are logical responses to the deep satisfaction of soul that David enjoyed. He had experienced an earnest, soul-rending need, and God had satisfied that need beyond David's expectation. David had found God to be completely enough to meet his every need. It makes sense then that David spent time remembering God. The remembrance of God's sufficiency increased the satisfaction that David already had. It also makes sense that David would trust such a sufficient God. God had met his deepest need, and He certainly could be trusted to meet all other needs. Yes, God can meet every need, and He can completely satisfy our souls.

"Father, there is an emptiness and longing inside me that only You can meet. Show me Your greatness. Help me to be satisfied in You."

Day 329

Help us, O God of our salvation, for the glory of Your name;
And deliver us and forgive our sins for Your name's sake.
Psalm 79:9

In Psalm 79, Asaph describes the destruction of Jerusalem. Dead bodies lie everywhere, the city is in ruins, and the temple is defiled. Understandably, Asaph cries out for God to respond with judgment. A large portion of his prayer is made up of the reasons for which Asaph is asking God to respond. Instead of focusing on himself and his own comfort, Asaph gives five godly reasons as the basis for his request.

First, Asaph prays a humble prayer of repentance (vs. 8-9). He acknowledges the sins of the people and asks for God's compassion in the face of deserved judgment. The people have been brought low before God. Second, Asaph prays based on the reputation of God before the heathen (v. 10). The heathen want to deny the existence of God, but God's action would take the power out of their argument. Third, Asaph prays based on God's compassion (v. 11). He asks God to hear the groaning of those who seem about to die; he wants God to respond kindly to the hurting people. Fourth, Asaph prays for justice on God's enemies (v. 12). He wants right to prevail and wrong to be defeated. Fifth, Asaph prays based on an intention to praise and thank God (v. 13). When God delivers, His people have a reason to give Him the honor He deserves.

Each of these requests is in keeping with God's character. God does forgive sin and restore. God desires to be exalted before the heathen. God is compassionate. God does work justice. God does deserve praise. As we pray for our own needy situations, we can also present reasons based on which we ask God to answer. In order to be effective, these reasons must be accurately based on the nature of God. It is always appropriate to pray humbly. It is always appropriate to desire recognition and praise to be given to God. It is always appropriate to ask God to show His attributes. When we pray in this way, our requests cease to be self-centered, and instead they become God-centered.

"Father, I think an awful lot about myself and my comfort. Help me to focus on You instead. May You receive honor through what You accomplish in my life."

Day 330

And my soul is greatly dismayed;
But You, O LORD – how long?
The LORD has heard my supplication,
The LORD receives my prayer.
Psalm 6:3 & 9

What happens when you become too discouraged to keep fighting and too tired to deal with each new challenge? Life can quickly become overwhelming. Without some way to deflect the repeated assaults, you are left to absorb them. Every disappointment, every letdown, and every burden strikes like a body blow or a knife wound. With each new wound the hurt grows deeper and deeper. Each new pain takes something else out of you until you find yourself an empty shell. There seems to be no end in sight, and you find yourself desperately crying out, "How long? Will this never end?"

David found himself in that condition in Psalm 6. He was suffering physically (v. 2), and his soul was distressed (v. 3). His emotions were distraught, and he cried constantly (v. 6). He was filled with grief and felt as if he were aging prematurely (v. 7). David thought that his situation would never end, and he cried out in anguish to God. He was a man with a very troubled spirit, describing himself as *"greatly dismayed."*

Although David's situation was very bleak, he remembered the lovingkindness of God (v. 4). He took hope in the fact that God knew all about his situation. God heard David's weeping (v. 7). God knew every tear that fell and every pain that caused each tear. David took hope in the fact that God heard his prayer, and his hope was not vainly based. God *was* listening to him as he cried out in anguish. Instead of ignoring David, God received his prayer.

God will do the same for you. You may be hurting deeply. You may be greatly dismayed. You may think your ordeal will never end. Take heart. God knows all about every hurt. He will listen to every prayer, and He will receive each cry for help.

"Thank You, Father, that when I can't go on for another day, I have You to turn to. Thank You for seeing my pain and hearing my cry." $\longrightarrow$

Reflection on Psalm 6 (Anguished Cry for Help)
Do not be harsh with me, O God;
Not wrath, I need Your grace instead.
My flesh is failing in my pain,
And anguished cries go through my head.

O turn to me, my God, my strength;
From such dismay my soul set free.
Look down on me through Your great love
So unto You my praise can be.

I sigh until it wears me out;
My tears are constant and extreme.
My grief has caused me to decline;
I still am young, but old I seem.

O God, You hear; I know You do.
My cries and weeping reach Your ears.
Please answer me, I now implore
And give me vict'ry from my fears.

Day 331

"Are not two sparrows sold for a cent? And yet not one of them will fall to the ground apart
from your Father. But the very hairs of your head are all numbered. So do not fear; you
are more valuable than many sparrows."
Matthew 10:29–31

There are people who care that you are ill. They are concerned for you, and they pray for you. You appreciate that support. Yet there is something missing, a need that is rather difficult to meet. It's hard for you to have someone with whom you can really talk about your illness. You know what I mean. Sometimes you want to talk about the individual symptoms that have affected you that day. You want someone to understand what you mean when you describe those symptoms. You want someone to sit still long enough to give you time to talk it all out. You want someone who will listen day after day to your explanations of constant or recurring challenges without tiring of the repeated details.

Sadly, it seems that most people just want a general "fine" or "not bad today" in answer to their inquiries. They may even take the time to listen once or twice, but they don't want to keep hearing all of those details as the weeks and months drag on. This makes you feel as if people care only in a general way, but not enough to be really meaningful. The deeper level of support is hard for people to give, because they can't really relate to your situation, and the lack of comprehension is uncomfortable for them.

God, on the other hand, does care on a detailed and minute level. You are very important to God, and He illustrates His deep concern in two ways. First, there are millions of tiny sparrows in the world – common, rather nondescript birds – and God keeps track of every one of them. He knows when they fall to the ground. Second, there are thousands of hairs on your head, and the number keeps changing, but God knows how many hairs there are at all times.

If God cares about something as insignificant as a sparrow and as trivial as the number of hairs on your head, don't you think He cares about the details of your life? Jesus Himself said that you are more valuable than the birds. God cares for you to an extreme level. He considers you valuable and worth knowing very well. He cares about all the details.

"Thank You, Father, for caring so carefully for me. Thank You that I can tell you all of the tiny details and You are interested."

Day 332

*Now I want you to know, brethren, that my circumstances have turned out
for the greater progress of the gospel.*
Philippians 1:12

Paul didn't always have such a nice time of it. He spent much time in prison as well as enduring many other sufferings for the cause of Christ. Paul was able to rejoice in his sufferings because He realized that God uses trials for His purposes and that those purposes are far bigger than the lives of individuals.

Paul's imprisonment led to an extensive spreading of the gospel. Many people were exposed to the gospel, both around the prison by Paul's personal influence and around the world by those motivated by Paul's example. Many were given boldness by his testimony; they grew in trusting the Lord, and they increased in courage because of watching Paul. As a result of Paul's suffering, Christ was preached more.

Paul rejoiced not in the trial itself, but in its results. If suffering meant Christ was proclaimed, then he would gladly suffer, and he was determined to praise God for the results (v. 18). Paul made a similar statement in Colossians 1:24. He rejoiced in his sufferings because of the work that was done through the church. Paul's sufferings were specifically used by God for the greater purpose of growth in the church.

As Paul suffered for the benefit of the church, which is the body of Christ, he carried on the continuation of the suffering that started with Christ. Paul rejoiced because of whom He was suffering for. He shared in Christ's sufferings. Likewise, as God does His work both directly and indirectly through our suffering, we are privileged in a small way to be partners with Christ. God is doing something bigger than what we see, something that extends beyond the boundaries of our little world.

"I may not see what You are doing, Father, but if You are able to use my suffering in order to advance Your work, then I submit."

Day 333

Persecutions, and sufferings, such as happened to me at Antioch, at Iconium and at Lystra; what persecutions I endured, and out of them all the Lord rescued me!
II Timothy 3:11

If anyone had a long list of life-time afflictions, it was Paul. In addition to his unnamed physical infirmity, he suffered many abuses. He was put in prison various times. He was beaten so many times he couldn't count them. He was whipped repeatedly. He was stoned and left for dead. In his travels he was often hungry, thirsty, and cold. He spent many sleepless nights. He was shipwrecked multiple times. He spent much of his life traveling in a day when travel was not very convenient or comfortable. All of these things must have taken a tremendous toll on his body.

Beyond the physical strains, Paul was a man under a lot of pressure. He had a weighty responsibility as he cared for the churches and addressed their problems and needs. He invested much of his life in training younger men to serve in the churches. As people opposed his ministry, he was under almost constant threats on his life. He often faced angry and hostile mobs. Paul states that God rescued him out of every one of his numerous persecutions and sufferings.

The afflictions can indeed be many. The good news is that God is always able to deliver. It does not matter how many trials we face. There is no quota with God. It is impossible for us to reach a quantity of afflictions at which God meets His limit, at which He can't or won't help. No matter how many times God has rescued and helped us in the past, He is always able to do it again. It doesn't matter how severe our trials are. None of them is too hard for God to handle. No one else is able to resolve them, but God can. God is able to rescue us from every trial that we must endure.

"Father, it seems that sometimes the problems are piling up. I'm grateful that there will never be too many for You to deliver me from."

Day 334

For we are His workmanship, created in Christ Jesus for good works, which God prepared beforehand so that we would walk in them.
Ephesians 2:10

Your body may be falling apart. You may feel that your life is becoming less and less useful. You may believe that you have decreasing value to others. God has a different evaluation. God looks at you as His workmanship, the labor of His hands. He is carefully and purposefully crafting you into a masterpiece. His hands are forming you and making you into something that is beautiful to Him and that successfully serves His purpose.

What is God's purpose? He wants you to walk in good works. You may not be able to do all of the good works that you have done before, or perhaps not the same kinds of good works that you are used to doing. Being ill, however, does not limit you from doing *any* good works. God is preparing you for the purpose of performing good works; therefore, there must be some good works that He would have you do. Look around and see what tasks may fit your current abilities. Ask God to guide your understanding so that you know what He wants you to do.

Determine to do, to the best of your limited ability, the good works that God has carefully designed you for. His design in the present may be very different from His design for you in the past, but it is what God has chosen for you. In the past you were willing to put forth great quantities of effort in order to do big things for God. Is it any harder to do a small thing? Each Christian works together within God's plan as each person does his part. Every part is important, so give yourself to the little part that God has designed for you. Though it may seem small, it is essential to the completion of the entire task.

"Help me, Father, as Your workmanship, to fulfill the purpose of good works that You intend for me."

Day 335

Behold, God is my helper;
The Lord is the sustainer of my soul.
Psalm 54:4

Here is an idea worth taking note of. God is my Helper. The government is not my helper. My doctor is not my helper. My neighbor is not my helper. My children are not my helpers. My spouse is not my helper. As wonderful and comforting as some of those people are, even the best of them is not able to supply the help I really need. God, on the other hand, is able to provide every bit of help I could ever need.

This word *helper* has the idea of surrounding someone in order to give protection and aid. It is like the picture of a police escort, an armed guard, or a gang of karate experts who encircle the person in need. These defenders form a protective barrier around the one who is being attacked. This surrounding guard comes to the defense and effectively deals with the threat; the person in danger just stands and watches.

I am helpless to defend myself, and I cannot rely on the help of other frail men, but God is always able to deliver me. He is able to help in any situation, no matter how daunting it may seem. Family and friends are able to give help in some areas, but this verse identifies one area in which man is completely unable to help – my soul. God sustains my soul. My soul is so weak and too often falters, but God is able to give it support and hold it up. God can take care of this very fragile, but critically important, aspect of my person. My soul is what most needs to be sustained, and God is able to help in that aspect when no one else can.

"Father, You know the weakness of my body and my soul. I cannot help myself. I need You to be my helper. Protect me, Lord, and keep me from falling."

Day 336

I would have despaired unless I had believed that I would see the goodness of the LORD
In the land of the living.
Wait for the LORD;
Be strong and let your heart take courage;
Yes, wait for the LORD.
Psalm 27:13-14

There is a sense of disappointment that leads to despair when we give up on God's goodness. Sometimes, within the process of suffering and endurance, we believe God's promises and wait on Him for what seems to be a very long time. When the trial continues without our seeing the answers, it is easy for us to give up. After our extended time of faith and patience, we sadly conclude that our hope was poorly based in something empty.

The truth is that there is no such thing as empty hope when it is placed in God's truth. Our hope in Him is never vain. When God says something, it will come true. We can wait for it expectantly. If we will just continue to wait, our hope will be rewarded, because God will do everything that He has said. He will be everything that He has claimed to be.

Because of God's goodness, we can be strengthened, and our hearts can take courage. David's belief in God's goodness within this lifetime was the only thing that kept David from despair. Like David, we don't always see God's goodness expressed within our circumstance or situation. Sometimes we may seem to go for long periods without seeing it displayed clearly; however, we can be sure that God will again show it. God's goodness is not something that we have to wait until heaven to see; God does give it in this lifetime.

This concept gives us hope instead of despair, as we are assured that God will show His goodness to us. If this seems not to be true in reality, the error is in our human patience; we give up too quickly. God's time frame is sometimes longer than our patience. We must not despair, but must take courage. It may not be today, and it may not be tomorrow, but His goodness will come. We just haven't waited long enough yet.

"Help me, Father, not to give up, even when I can't see the answers or even the possibility of answers anytime in the near future. Thank You that my hope in You need never die."

Goodness? (Sonnet 42)

Around me heavy clouds hang low and dark;
I look about and dismal shadows see.
With anguish in my soul I oft remark,
"O God, where is Your goodness unto me?"
(In truth, my memory's weak, my eyes are dim;
His faithful goodness is each moment near.)
Be brave, my heart; be strong and wait on Him.
Have faith; believe His goodness will appear.
It may not be on this day or the next
That sunshine conquers all the clouds in sight,
But sure as that same sun sets in the west,
His goodness will again shine strong and bright.
Without that hope, I'd be left in despair,
But with it, I am certain of His care.

Day 337

O Israel, hope in the LORD;
For with the LORD there is lovingkindness,
And with Him is abundant redemption.
Psalm 130:7

In the midst of affliction, God's lovingkindness is a wonderful topic on which to focus our attention. Lovingkindness is more than simply the idea of love. It is the expression of God's love to those who are beneath Him. It is the faithful and unfailing expression of that love in kindness beyond what we can expect or deserve. It is God's abundant goodness, favor, and mercy graciously bestowed on weak humanity.

One fundamental aspect of God's lovingkindness that the Bible clearly teaches is that it does exist. It is a sure reality. God is a dependable source of lovingkindness. We will find it if we go to Him. Other sources may not provide it and cannot be relied on, but with God there is no doubt. His lovingkindness is evident. It is something that we can readily see because it is displayed in such an obvious manner that is hard to miss (Psalm 26:3).

God's lovingkindness is prolific. All of His ways display lovingkindness. It is not expressed just in some of what He does, but in everything and in every place (Psalm 25:10). God's lovingkindness is widespread. The earth is filled with God's lovingkindness. It abounds to such an extent that it is everywhere we look and is seen in all aspects of the world around us (Psalm 33:5).

God exercises His lovingkindness in the earth; He actively engages in that pursuit. He does so because He wants to (Jeremiah 9:24). God delights in this unchanging expression of His love (Micah 7:18), specifically in the fact that it is always the same. God's lovingkindness is constant; it goes with us all day long because God orders it so (Psalm 42:8).

"Thank You, Father, for Your lovingkindness that is an undeniable aspect of Your character.
Thank You that it is so faithful that I can depend upon it."

Day 338

Blessed be God,
Who has not turned away my prayer
Nor His lovingkindness from me.
Psalm 66:20

God's lovingkindness extends to multitudes of His people. God shows His lovingkindness to His people, to those who belong to Him and whom He has chosen. Several recipients of God's lovingkindness are specifically mentioned in Scripture: Job, Abraham, David, David's descendents, and the nation of Israel. This lovingkindness is displayed to those whom He has claimed as His own. That claim is not restricted merely to these named individuals or even just to people in the Bible. There are also verses indicating that God shows His lovingkindness to His people in general.

God declares that He displays His lovingkindness to those who love Him and keep His commandments (Daniel 9:4). He shows it to those who walk before Him with all their heart (II Chronicles 6:14). As we love and follow God, we become recipients of His divine favor. God's lovingkindness is not limited in its scope or in how many people can receive it. It surrounds those who trust Him, without restriction on how many that may be (Psalm 32:10). It is given to all who call on Him (Psalm 86:5). Multiple times God indicates that His lovingkindness extends to thousands of people (Exodus 34:7). We need not fear that God's lovingkindness will be insufficient to extend to us. We do need to heed His caution, however, that He can remove His lovingkindness from those who rebel against Him and refuse to repent (Jeremiah 16:5).

"Thank You, Father, that Your lovingkindness is sufficient to reach me. Help me to love and follow You so that I can continue to receive it."

Day 339

But You, O GOD, the Lord, deal kindly with me for Your name's sake;
Because Your lovingkindness is good, deliver me.
Psalm 109:21

God's lovingkindness is active. It affects what God does; it causes Him to perform specific actions and to respond to specific situations of need. God gives help to His people because of His lovingkindness (Psalm 109:26). He saves lives because of it (Psalm 6:4). He redeems His people (Psalm 44:26). God's lovingkindness led Him to provide for the building of the temple (Ezra 7:28). It caused Him to give protection to David when he was besieged (Psalm 31:21).

God's lovingkindness has resulted in many great wonders. Some notable examples are the creation, the deliverance of His people from Egypt, His guidance of them in the wilderness, and the victory that He gave them in battle (Psalm 136). God can even magnify His lovingkindness by performing dramatic acts that go beyond the favor He ordinarily displays (Genesis 19:19).

The actions brought on by God's lovingkindness are not limited to people and situations in the Bible. God also works in our lives today because of His lovingkindness. His kind actions toward us are based on His lovingkindness. His lovingkindness causes Him to act on our behalf (Psalm 98:3). God's lovingkindness causes Him to continue to work and continue to lead beyond mere deliverance (Exodus 15:13). He brings events into our lives based on His lovingkindness (Job 37:13). In short, everything that God does for us is based on His lovingkindness.

"Father, thank You for Your interaction and involvement in my life based on Your lovingkindness. Thank You that You don't just stand idly by and watch."

Day 340

Wondrously show Your lovingkindness,
O Savior of those who take refuge at Your right hand
From those who rise up against them.
Psalm 17:7

God's lovingkindness is not hidden. It is apparent throughout our lives, because God displays it to His children in noticeable and practical ways. God's entire relationship with us is based on lovingkindness. It is the means by which He draws us to Himself (Jeremiah 31:3). It is the means by which He binds us to Himself as His bride (Hosea 2:19). It is the basis for God's thoughts and remembrances of us (Psalm 25:7). Without God's lovingkindness, He would not have the motivation for desiring a relationship with us.

God's lovingkindness is key in the area of prayer. It allows us to approach Him in prayer so that we can even bring our requests to Him (Psalm 5:7). It causes Him to hear our prayers rather than carelessly dismissing them (Psalm 119:149). It also causes Him to answer our prayers (Psalm 69:13).

God's lovingkindness is His basis for ministering to our spiritual needs. God gives comfort to His hurting children through His lovingkindness (Psalm 119:76). His lovingkindness brings revival to those who need it (Psalm 119:88).

God's lovingkindness is crucial when we are in trouble. God helps us in times of trouble because of His lovingkindness (Psalm 57:3). It causes Him to meet us in our situations and times of distress (Psalm 59:10). His lovingkindness keeps us from falling when we are unsteady (Psalm 94:18). It keeps us from being shaken when we are uncertain. (Psalm 21:7). God always knows the situation we are in; He keeps His eye on us because we hope in His lovingkindness (Psalm 33:18).

"Father, thank You for the blessings and benefits that are mine because of Your lovingkindness for me. Thank You for Your care and help."

Day 341

For as high as the heavens are above the earth,
So great is His lovingkindness toward those who fear Him.
Psalm 103:11

God's lovingkindness is not like the love of anyone else. The love of everyone else has flaws. We can think of a sweet and gentle grandmother, one who seems to be always smiling with twinkling eyes. She may have the softest voice, the tenderest touch, and the kindest heart that we can imagine. She might be constantly giving of herself in doing special things for others. She is truly a great picture of tender love in action, but even she cannot compare with God.

The Bible uses many descriptions to give us a picture of God's lovingkindness. His lovingkindness is good (Psalm 109:21). There is nothing ugly about it; it is beautiful and pleasant. His lovingkindness is great (Psalm 145:8). It is excessive in its scope, broader than we can comprehend. His lovingkindness is marvelous (Psalm 31:21). It is so outstanding that it distinguishes and separates itself from all others. His lovingkindness is wondrous (Psalm 17:7). It is marvelously beyond what anyone else can do. His lovingkindness is high and lofty (Psalm 36:5). It is described as being as high as the heavens.

God's lovingkindness is worthy of our trust (Psalm 13:5). We can depend on it, and it will not let us down. His lovingkindness is worthy of our hope (Psalm 33:18). We can wait patiently and expectantly for it and assume it will be seen. His lovingkindness is abundant (Psalm 86:5). It is plenteous and overflowing, more than we need. His lovingkindness is precious (Psalm 36:7). It is valuable and costly, not something we would want to give up or be without. His lovingkindness is better than life itself (Psalm 63:3). There is nothing in life that can compare to God's lovingkindness; it is truly amazing.

"Father, the tender love that You show to me is beyond my ability to comprehend.
Help me not to take it for granted."

Day 342

"For the mountains may be removed and the hills may shake,
But My lovingkindness will not be removed from you,
And My covenant of peace will not be shaken,"
Says the LORD who has compassion on you.
Isaiah 54:10

One description of God's lovingkindness stands out above all the rest, being mentioned more frequently in Scripture than any of the other characteristics. This particular aspect is probably the most comforting and encouraging of all the characteristics, and it is that God's lovingkindness lasts forever. This wonderful lovingkindness that God shows to us will never run out. We can never exhaust it.

The simple phrase that His lovingkindness is everlasting is given forty-five times in the Bible. Other Scriptures elaborate on the concept. Not only will it always last, but it always has been (Psalm 25:6). God is diligent to maintain and preserve His lovingkindness (Nehemiah 9:32). He keeps it even to the thousandth generation with those who love Him and keep His commandments (Deuteronomy 7:9). It can be trusted in forever and ever (Psalm 52:8). It will not be removed even if the mountains are removed from the earth (Isaiah 54:10).

God's lovingkindness is constant. He says that His lovingkindness will not depart; it will never leave (II Samuel 7:15). God does not forsake it (Genesis 24:27). He doesn't turn it away (Psalm 66:20). He won't take it away (I Chronicles 17:13). He will not break it off (Psalm 89:33). His lovingkindness endures all day long (Psalm 52:1). It will follow His children all the days of their lives (Psalm 23:6). No one in heaven or on earth is as faithful as God in maintaining His lovingkindness. (I Kings 8:23). All of these statements are different ways of giving reassurance that God's lovingkindness will last forever and that it can never be removed.

"Thank You, Father, for Your everlasting lovingkindness. Thank You that I don't need to fear that I will ever be left without it."

Day 343

I will sing of lovingkindness and justice,
To You, O LORD, I will sing praises.
Psalm 101:1

God's lovingkindness requires a response on our part. We cannot ignore such a great and rich gift that God has bestowed and continues to bestow upon us. Instead, we should be constantly aware of this blessing and continually inclined toward God in an attitude of praise.

First of all, we should focus on God's lovingkindness (Psalm 26:3). We can't give any response to God if we don't first fix our gaze upon the reality of what He is doing for us. In an attitude of worship we should be thinking about God's lovingkindness (Psalm 48:9). We must take the time to consider and ponder God's goodness to us.

Second, we should not treasure the wonder of God's lovingkindness only within ourselves. God deserves glory given to Him because of His lovingkindness (Psalm 115:1). This requires that we interact with others concerning the topic. We are to declare His lovingkindness to others and remind them that it lasts forever (Psalm 88:11). We should encourage one another with these realities. We should tell others about God's lovingkindness (Psalm 40:10). It is good for us to bear testimony of God's goodness and to share with others the wonderful things that God has done in our lives.

Third, we should rejoice in the lovingkindness of God (Psalm 31:7). It should make our hearts glad and give us a cause for rejoicing. This rejoicing should spill over into song as we sing of God's lovingkindness (Psalm 59:16).

Finally, we should thank God for His lovingkindness (Psalm 107:8). Such an unmerited gift should not go without our expressions of gratitude.

"Father, may I not fail to thank and praise You for the wonderful and numerous blessings that You pour on me every day, although I don't deserve one of them."

Day 344

Remember, O LORD, Your compassion and Your lovingkindnesses,
For they have been from of old.
Psalm 25:6

The final topic we will examine regarding God's lovingkindness is the wonderful privilege that we have to be able to pray for it. The psalm-writers offered a number of prayers regarding the lovingkindness of God, and it would certainly be appropriate for us to mimic their prayers and to ask for the same expressions of lovingkindness that these men requested.

We see that it is appropriate to ask God to show His lovingkindness to us (Psalm 143:8). We can ask for God's lovingkindness to be expressed as we hope in Him (Psalm 33:22). We can remind God that we are looking and waiting for it.

It is appropriate to ask God to remember His lovingkindness (Psalm 25:6). It is a key aspect of His character and one that we can claim as His basis for interaction with us. We can ask Him to think on us and remember us based on His lovingkindness (Psalm 25:7). We can ask God to deal with us according to His lovingkindness (Psalm 119:124).

It is appropriate to ask God to continue His lovingkindness (Psalm 36:10). We can ask that His kindness not end, but be shown on a continuing basis.

It is appropriate to ask to be satisfied with God's lovingkindness (Psalm 90:14). We can ask for it to suffice our needs and fill the longing of our hearts.

It is appropriate to pray for His lovingkindness to comfort us in times of sorrow (Psalm 119:76). We can ask God to show it by giving His protection (Psalm 61:7) or by granting deliverance (Psalm 143:12).

Our prayers need not be limited to just ourselves. God's lovingkindness is also an appropriate blessing we should desire for others (II Samuel 2:6). Truly what a privilege we have to be able to ask God to express His lovingkindness in our lives.

"Father, remember Your lovingkindness and act in my life on that basis. May I be encouraged and satisfied with Your expressions of lovingkindness to me."

Day 345

By You I have been sustained from my birth;
You are He who took me from my mother's womb;
My praise is continually of You.
Psalm 71:6

Perhaps the best years of your life have come and gone. As you age, you realize that your health and strength will never be the same again. It is easy to worry about your frailty and your feeble condition. It is natural to wonder how you will be able to keep on going and continue caring for yourself.

Psalm 71 was written by an old man, and this unnamed psalmist has some encouraging truth for you. He begins by recalling that God has always helped him in the past. He has trusted God since his youth, and his trust has always been rewarded. God has cared for him ever since the day of his birth, and the psalmist rejoices in this constant care.

Others around him have taken note of God's past treatment. Now that the psalmist is old, his acquaintances expect God's treatment to change. They cast forth doubts, asserting that God has forgotten him. This man is in trouble again, and those around him expect that God will now forsake him.

The psalmist does not share those doubts. He continues to cry to God for help, just like he always has. He continues to expect God's deliverance, just as God has always given it. He claims God as his continual hope; he will never stop hoping in such a faithful God. His confidence is so great that he prepares to praise God again and share His answer with many people. The psalmist has seen God save him over and over and over again. He knows that God will do the same for him now, even in his old age.

God's faithful and consistent work throughout your life also allows you to be confident in Him. Rather than minimizing God's care, your advanced age actually provides support to prove God's faithfulness. Instead of twenty or thirty or forty years, God has already sustained you for sixty or seventy or even eighty years. He has a long and proven track record. If God were in it only for the short-term and if He were fickle, He would have abandoned you long before now. The fact that He has sustained you for so long is proof that He intends to continue doing so, that He plans to care for you through your whole life. God still cares for you regardless of how old you are. God has never forsaken you yet, and He isn't going to start now.

"When I feel forsaken and alone, thank You, Father, that You have never forsaken me.
Thank You that You will remain faithful through my entire life,
no matter how long that is."

Tomorrow's No Different (Sonnet 47)
I stand upon the scorching desert bare,
While winds drive swirling sand on every side,
And wait for answers to long-standing prayer.
When will God prove to be my faithful Guide?
And then I think about the path behind.
I've not been lost, not buried, nor alone;
He's led no matter how the path did wind.
Through countless storms, protection has been shown.
How could this faithful God desert me here?
His tender, loving care will never change;
He's still all-wise, almighty, and still near.
For Him to let me go would be quite strange.
He's led me safely through so many ways;
He won't abandon in the final days.

Day 346

They drink their fill of the abundance of Your house;
And You give them to drink of the river of Your delights.
Psalm 36:8

Living life with God is like a never-ending Christmas. He fills our lives with continuous bounty. His provisions are abundant, and He never runs out of blessings. There are no shortages or limited rations in God's house. When we try to receive God's unending supply of good gifts, it is like drinking from a fire hose. There is too much for us to be able to take in.

These statements may seem idealistic in the course of an illness, but if we honestly evaluate, we know that they are true. In general, our lives are better than we acknowledge. We do have problems day by day, but we tend to focus too pointedly on them, sometimes making them more significant than they really are. At the same time, we overlook many of the simple blessings that God gives us daily.

Going through a time of difficulty, like a serious illness, allows us to experience sweet joy when better days return. We tend to take our health and other daily blessings for granted, so when they are restored, we experience renewed appreciation. Those fundamental things mean more to us than they did before. It makes us smile just to feel good, just to wake up and be refreshed.

Even in the midst of illness, or if God never gives us restored health, we still have many blessings. We have family, houses, beds, clothing, sufficient food, fresh water, modern conveniences, and qualified medical care; many of these blessings are unheard of in most of the world. Our level of suffering is moderated in comparison with others in the same basic condition.

Even more significant than the routine blessings of practical life is truth about God, His character, and His deeds. If we would take a few minutes to really ponder our salvation, the promise of heaven, God's patience, His love, or any other aspect of God, we would be sobered and silenced at the magnitude of our blessings. We would find ourselves drowning as we try to drink it all in.

"Father, You say that You have abundant blessings, and so it must be true. Help me not to overlook or undervalue those blessings, but to taste them and be satisfied."

Day 347

"I am the good shepherd, and I know My own and My own know Me."
John 10:14

The beginning of John 10 describes Jesus as the Good Shepherd. As a shepherd, He takes care of His children. This shepherd knows His sheep personally. He knows the name of each one, and He calls them by their names. He speaks to them often so that they come to know His voice. His voice is trusted and comforting and encourages the sheep to follow Him.

This shepherd does not send His sheep out blindly or without care. Whenever they must go out, He leads them. He walks in front of them, showing them the way so they will not be lost. As He walks in front, He is able to see all the dangers to avoid and all the paths that are too rough to walk. He also sees the good and pleasant paths, and He guides His sheep to the right ways.

This shepherd cares for each of His sheep. He doesn't leave any behind, but includes them all in His care. He leads His sheep in and out of shelter as they need it. He takes them out and finds pasture for them. His sheep are not left to fend for themselves, nor are they threatened with malnourishment or starvation. The shepherd provides for their needs. He helps them to enjoy an abundant and blessed life that they would not have without Him.

This shepherd does not flee or abandon His sheep in the day of trouble. He is concerned for His sheep, and when attacks come, He stands firm. He remains faithfully with them in the fiercest attacks, and if necessary He gives His own life to protect them. He does this willingly because of His great love for them.

God truly is a good Shepherd. He knows and loves us. He guides us, provides for us, and blesses us. He defends us and saves us, even at the cost of His own life. What a great Shepherd!

"Father, thank You for being my shepherd and for caring for me so thoroughly. Thank You that I can trust You completely. Thank You that You will never forsake me, no matter how bad things get."

Day 348

"If a man dies, will he live again?
All the days of my struggle I will wait
Until my change comes."
Job 14:14

Job was uncertain whether he would live or die, and in that setting he determined to wait on God. He would wait through all the days of his struggle, no matter how many they were. The surrounding context makes it clear that he was waiting on God. He was waiting for when things would change.

Job did not know what that change would be. He knew that he might die from his present illness. He knew that God might choose to heal him. In either case, he knew that God would be faithful to liberate him. Job therefore determined to wait all the days of his life, expecting God to free him either by deliverance from his affliction or by reunion with God in death. Either answer would be a victory given by God. Job placed the choice in God's hands and trusted Him to decide.

Because Job waited on God, he was determined to look to God in spite of his trials and no matter what the outcome. Job realized a very important fact: God is in control of the sustaining of life. God determines each man's years. He decides whether they will be many or few, whether they will be more than average or far fewer. God determines the quality of life for those years. Because God knows precisely what He intends to do through each life, He can determine how to extend or curtail those days. We, like Job, can trust Him to do that correctly. Our life and longevity can be placed in His hands.

"Father, I don't know what the outcome of my illness will be, but I trust You to do what You have determined is best in my life."

Day 349

"Does He not see my ways
And number all my steps?"
Job 31:4

I'm sure you've had it happen. Someone has asked the question, "How long have you been sick now? Six months?" Then you've had to figure out how to graciously respond, "A year and a half." For something as major as the illness you are enduring, it's a bit of a shame when people don't have a better idea of how long it has been going on.

It's hard to keep track of time, especially when the events are in the lives of other people. If the truth be told, there have been times that you have forgotten how long it has been; you've had to stop and figure the timing out yourself. There is then a great reassurance in realizing that God always remembers.

While others may forget some of the hardships you have endured or are enduring, God sees every way that you walk. He is very aware of each journey that you take. Far beyond just remembering each path in a general way, God has intimate knowledge of each of those paths. He knows every step along each of those paths. He knows your paths and the details of them better than you do yourself. He knows precisely where you have stepped and how many steps you have taken on each path.

Some paths are harder than others, and God knows that too. He knows what the terrain is like. On some paths each step requires great effort; maybe you can manage only a small number of steps on those paths. God knows how many steps you can take, and He knows when you have reached that limit. God knows, because He is carefully keeping track of each step, and He will not ask you to walk too far.

"Thank You, Father, that You know my steps. Thank You that I am not walking alone, with no one to remember and no one to care. Thank You for Your close supervision."

Day 350

"These things I have spoken to you so that you may be kept from stumbling."
John 16:1

It is so hard to face the daily temptations. It's hard to know what to do. It's hard to keep from stumbling. With temptations so plentiful and the flesh so weak, how can we keep from falling? The Bible gives us hope. God knows our weakness and our struggle, and He has provided answers and guidance for us. Thousands of years ago He inspired the words of Scripture. In His Word He generously provides help and direction for us.

The Old Testament records the stories of many, many people. Those people faced the same types of temptations that we face. God gave us their stories as examples, so that we would know what to do and what not to do. These stories are intended to instruct us.

Jesus spoke words of guidance when He was here on earth. He spoke over and over again about the way to live and about having victory over sin. He Himself said that His words were given so that we would not fall. God has recorded Jesus' words in the gospels, and we can look to them for guidance.

When we listen to God's words and follow them, we have a firm foundation. We have protection and stability in the face of the assaulting storms. If we do not follow His words, we have no such foundation. Without Christ's words to guide us, we will fall flat and fail miserably. With His words, however, victory is possible. God is able to keep us from stumbling. We can find the guidance we need in His Word. As we look into the Bible, we find the help we need.

"These temptations assault me constantly, Father. I don't know what to do. Help me to seek Your answers and help. Show me from Your Word how to have victory."

Day 351

And His disciples asked Him, "Rabbi, who sinned, this man or his parents, that he would be born blind?" Jesus answered, "It was neither that this man sinned, nor his parents; but it was so that the works of God might be displayed in him."
John 9:2-3

My illness affects me so constantly and is such a major part of my life every day that I easily think of it as being very personal. I think about how my disease affects me. I see its challenges and even its purposes as being primarily focused on me. It is certainly true that I am greatly affected by my disease. It is also true that God has great purposes for my life personally. This personal aspect of the disease does not, however, negate God's greater purposes.

God can use something that is so major in my own life to also work out His great purposes beyond me. God has a much broader scope than a single individual. He can use my illness to do great things in the lives of others also. Though I may seem to be the primary recipient, God desires my illness to bring glory to Himself beyond the limits of my own life.

The ways in which God shows His work and glory through my life are probably more than I can imagine, but I can identify some of His potential purposes. God could be glorified in my life by healing me, showing that He is the great Physician. He could glorify Himself by making my disease mysteriously disappear or by healing me after doctors have given up hope. God could glorify Himself by giving me grace to face impossible days. He could glorify Himself by giving me unexplained strength to carry on. He could glorify Himself by helping me to have a sweet and patient spirit in the midst of pain. He could cause doctors or fellow patients to ask questions. He could cause unsaved friends or family to be amazed and turn to God. He could encourage observers to face their own struggles with His help. He could prepare my children for a career of caring and a lifetime of compassion. Through each of these scenarios, God could cause His works to be displayed. The possibilities are endless, but the bottom line is that God intends to display His work through my situation, thus bringing glory to Himself.

"Father, thank You that my illness goes beyond myself. Thank You that it can be a tool for directing attention to Your works and glory to Your name. Help me not to get in the way."

Day 352

I will cry to God Most High,
To God who accomplishes all things for me.
Psalm 57:2

When I am in trouble and need help, I have an unfailing source to which I can go. I can cry out to the God Most High. He is by no means an insignificant source. He is above all things. He has power and control over every event, every person, every disease, every enemy, and every power or influence on earth. I can cry out to the God who is ultimately in control of everything, and He can help me and work on my behalf. He is the right person to call to because He is the one who plans, controls, and accomplishes all things in my life. My pastor, my family, and my friends cannot do that. Only God can plan all things and then work them out according to His plan.

The word *accomplish* refers to completing a task and guiding its progress from beginning to end. When God accomplishes something, He finishes it according to the way that He designed it. God does that in all things. Everything that works out in my life and everything that happens to me is ultimately done by God. God has control over my life to a level that I don't comprehend.

Every little thing and every big thing in my life is brought about by God. Everything that seems good and everything that seems bad is done by His hand. He does everything that I can understand and everything that leaves me confused. He accomplishes the situations that others support as well as the ones they misunderstand. He brings forward progress, backward slides, and even standstills. God determines whether to allow healing, continued illness, or even death. It is God who provides doctors and treatment and wisdom and finances. God does everything that is humanly viewed as success or failure, but God Himself never fails. He accomplishes exactly what He intends in every situation. He interacts in my life to bring about what He knows is best.

"Father, I don't know what You're doing, but I know that You are the one doing it. I cry out to You to accomplish Your plan and do what is best in my life."

Day 353

So teach us to number our days,
That we may present to You a heart of wisdom.
Psalm 90:12

In Psalm 90, Moses describes how vastly different man and God are in respect to time. God knows no time. He existed before time began. To Him great spans of time pass as if they are nothing. Man, on the other hand, is very much bound by time. Man's days pass so quickly that his lifespan is like fragile grass that withers in the sun. Man's days are brief as a result of sin, and God has purposefully limited the lifespan of man. Even those who reach the upper limits of age have only a very brief window of time in which to live.

In light of God's great holiness and man's brevity, it is essential for man to make his days count. Moses prays in this psalm that God would grant him seriousness about his lifespan. Moses reveals the goal for his life. He wants to be able to present to God a heart of wisdom. He desires to give God a life that matters and a heart that has learned to please Him.

This noble goal is not accomplished easily and never without God's help. Instead of happening naturally, reaching the goal requires a focused heart and mind. A heart that pleases God will not be produced without a keen focus and diligent effort. Even with a life dedicated to God, it takes a lifetime to approach what Moses states as his goal.

With a task requiring so much attention and diligence, there is no time to lose. Man cannot casually waste time or meander half-heartedly toward the goal. He must wisely strive each day to take steps closer and closer to wisdom. He can't afford to take days or weeks off or to let years pass by in which he does not pursue God.

Seasons of illness are not wasted time. God wants to use those days as well. They are an important part of the process if man will soberly recognize them as such. If it is God's intent that illness will shorten the already brief life, then it is even more necessary for man to dedicate himself soberly to striving for wisdom.

"Father, I don't know how many days I have, but I want them to count for You. Help me to respond each day in a way that will make my life a pleasing present for You."

Time (Sonnet 22)
Before a timeless God, the eons drift.
Within eternity a thousand years
Pass like a day or single nightly shift,
But man fades just as soon as he appears.
Almost before he starts, he turns to dust;
His life is shallow and his time so brief.
His sinful nature brings a death that's just;
The paltry years he lasts are full of grief.
For such great sinners, how would You advise?
In such a fleeting time, what can he do?
Teach him to make days count and to be wise,
So he'll present a heart that pleases You.
It's possible if You will work and bless;
'Tis only with Your favor he'll progress.

Day 354

"Call to Me and I will answer you, and I will tell you great and mighty things, which you do not know."
Jeremiah 33:3

When we are in trouble, we need a God who can do great things. We need a God whose knowledge and power surpass that of man. We have such a God, and He appeared to Jeremiah with assurances regarding this topic. God knows what man does not know, and He does what man cannot do. In Jeremiah 33:20-25, God goes on to describe just four examples.

First, man cannot measure the sand of the sea. If he measured it in dump trucks, he would run out of trucks and places to park them long before he dug to the bottom of the sand. Even with modern tools, a man's lifetime would not be long enough to complete such an endeavor. God knows how many grains of sand there are. He knows when a rock crumbles and creates hundreds of new grains.

Second, man cannot count the stars in the sky. Man doesn't even know how many galaxies there are, and he is unable to count the stars in even one of them. God knows how many stars there are. God keeps track of the number even when stars burn out and fall.

Third, man cannot change the schedule of day and night. He can't make the days longer and the nights shorter. He can't even out the long days and nights near the poles. God changes the schedule on a regular cycle throughout the year and He changes it dramatically with eclipses.

Fourth, man cannot change the pattern of the heavenly bodies. He can't rearrange the stars or planets. He can't make the moon closer to the earth. God can hold every heavenly body perfectly in place, or He can send stars hurtling through the sky. He can make the sun stand still or even go backwards.

God can do great and amazing things that man can't even imagine. This incredible God invites us to call to Him, and He offers to show His greatness to us.

"Father, You are a great God. Please show Your greatness to me. Work on my behalf."

Day 355

I know, O LORD, that Your judgments are righteous,
And that in faithfulness You have afflicted me.
Psalm 119:75

Just because something is hard does not mean that it is also wrong. People who carry responsibility often have to make hard choices. They have to decide things or incorporate procedures that they know will be difficult and even misunderstood by those affected. In spite of this, a person of character will make the right decision.

It is an understatement to say that God is a person of character. There is no one else like God. He always does what is right. His character is beyond reproach. His actions and decisions are beyond question. His decrees and declarations are always appropriate and right. Man will not always understand those judgments by God. The results of God's declarations may be very difficult to bear. Nevertheless, God's decisions are right.

Sometimes those decisions include bringing affliction. Even when it is necessary for God to bring affliction, He always remains true to His character. He is true to His character by making the right decisions. He is true to His character by acting in the best interest of all involved. He is true to His character by choosing what will bring glory to His name. He is true to His character by making and carrying out His decisions in love and compassion. He is true to His character by choosing the best and most effective methods for accomplishing His good purposes.

With our limited understanding, we often don't understand how this is true. We need then to allow God to be right; we need to acknowledge Him as right without having the benefit of understanding. Though we lack proper perspective, we can trust God's understanding. There will be situations in which we never understand, but in many cases, some understanding will come with time. As we move into the later stages of the affliction or as we come out on the other side, we are often able to look back and see that, yes, God made the right decision. He did what was best.

"Father, this affliction is hard for me and it is confusing. Help me to trust You to make the right decisions. Help me to realize that You always do the right thing."

Day 356

But now, thus says the LORD, your Creator, O Jacob,
And He who formed you, O Israel,
"Do not fear, for I have redeemed you;
I have called you by name; you are Mine!
When you pass through the waters, I will be with you;
And through the rivers, they will not overflow you.
When you walk through the fire, you will not be scorched,
Nor will the flame burn you."
Isaiah 43:1-2

Parents know that their children must go through hard times. The growing pains are difficult and challenging, but the young people must go through them. While parents don't like to see their children suffer, they are unable to eliminate all of the obstacles. In some cases they wouldn't even if they could, because they know how critical the growth process is. Instead, they give their support and guidance so their children can be protected as much as possible.

This is much like the picture presented in the above verses regarding God and His children. The passage makes it very clear that God loves His children. He created and formed them; He is the one who gave them life. God redeemed them, paying a great price to keep them. He knows them well and calls them by their name. He willingly claims them as belonging to Him. Verses three and four describe the ransom that He paid on their behalf. They tell of God's love for them and of their preciousness in His eyes.

This very loving God realizes that His children must sometimes pass through deep waters and they must at times walk through flames of fire. Because God knows these trials are necessary, He allows them to take place. Because He so deeply loves His children, He also protects them through the trials. He walks through the flood waters with them. He is there every minute to keep them from drowning. No matter how high the waters rise or how swiftly they run, they will not be able to drown His children.

God also protects His children in the fire. Walking through the fire is dangerous and frightening. It would seem to be life-threatening, but God changes that. Not only does He spare the life, but He even keeps His children from being burned by the flames. It is impossible to walk through flooding rivers without drowning and through scorching fires without being burned, but God makes it possible. Because of His love, He tenderly cares for and protects His children in the harshest circumstances.

"When I look around me, Father, I see impossible and destructive trials. Shield me and give me the protection that only You can supply. Thank You for Your great love that impels You to do it."

Day 357

Oh give us help against the adversary,
For deliverance by man is in vain.
Through God we will do valiantly,
And it is He who shall tread down our adversaries.
Psalm 108:12-13

Psalm 108 lets me know that I can be confident in God's deliverance. I can know that God will help. In fact, I can be so certain and convinced He will deliver that I can praise Him before it even happens. I can boldly thank Him, even in the presence of others, for what I know He will do.

God helps me because His love, mercy, and truth are so vast. He is capable of delivering me, because He is more glorious than any other person and even than the creation itself. He is strong enough to control all things. He can do with any nation whatever He wants to do. Surely He can do what He desires in my life. My little problem is a very simple task for Him.

Maybe right now I don't see God's answer. Maybe I can't see His deliverance coming, but it will come. At times I might even doubt that God is on my side, but that doesn't change the facts. God is on my side, and that is a very good thing.

I must have God on my side. There are some people at my side, and they mean well, but they don't really have any power. They want to deliver me, but they are completely incapable. Their attempts to change things just don't work. God, on the other hand, is always successful. God can deliver me from any situation, no matter how great the odds.

In fact, with God I can expect more than just a narrow escape. I can hope to escape with more than just my life and the clothes on my back. God takes an escape and turns it into a glorious victory. With His help, a desperate situation becomes a tremendous triumph. Only God is able to reverse a situation so completely. God's help alone is so amazingly effective.

"Father, I have depended on others for far too long. You are the only one who can really help me. Help me to depend confidently on You instead of relying on mere men."

Day 358

"Though He slay me, I will hope in Him."
Job 13:15a

How far can you trust God? What if you are never healed, having to live with your disease for the rest of your life? What if you become housebound, or even worse, confined to your bed? If this disease ends up taking your life, can you still trust God and hope in Him? Yes, definitely yes. You can trust God no matter what. If the worst happens, God is still the source of hope.

How is it possible to have such faith? You must know that your faith is based not on circumstances or outcomes, but on the unfailing Word of God. You cannot have faith that God will heal or that a cure will be found, because those issues aren't addressed in His Word. You can, however, have complete faith that He will be with you, because He has promised that. You can have faith that He will hear your prayers, that you will be able to do all things by His strength, that nothing will be able to separate you from His love, and that His grace will be sufficient.

In addition to specific promises, God's Word also reveals His character, and God always acts based on His character. God abounds in lovingkindness and is full of compassion. You can have faith that He will act accordingly; therefore you can trust that whatever God chooses is best. If that means life-long suffering or even death, you can still hope in God.

In the face of the worst situation you can imagine, every promise of God will still be true. He will still be with you, never having left your side. He will still have heard every prayer. He will still give sufficient strength. You will still not be separated one millimeter from His love, and His grace will still be sufficient. He will still be loving and compassionate. Even if you reach the threshold of death, it will be okay; you can still hope in Him. Your faith doesn't have to be in whether He heals you or not; it can rest firmly in the promises of His Word.

"Father, thank You that You never change and that I can trust You no matter what. Even if You take my life, I hope in You, confident in Your promise of heaven."

Day 359

"Behold, I am insignificant; what can I reply to You?
I lay my hand on my mouth.
Once I have spoken, and I will not answer;
Even twice, and I will add nothing more."
Job 40:4-5

Your days are not easy. You have to fight through each one, and they seem to be such a heavy burden. Then you look around you, and while others may not share your exact circumstances, you realize that they have burdens too. There's pain everywhere you look – health concerns, financial concerns, family concerns. Many of these situations are quite serious. It doesn't seem right. You and your loved ones try to live for God, and yet life is full of pain, problems, and discouragement that appear never-ending.

Your human weakness asks the age-old questions: "Why would God treat His people this way? Why would He allow those who are trying to live for Him to pass through so much pain? He could prevent these things; why doesn't He?" Sure, you know the answers. God is working things together for good, conforming you to the image of His Son, preparing you for service, and refining you. Still your heart cries out and asks why it is necessary. Why so much pain?

Job asked questions like these, and God responded by reminding Job of who He is. He is the God who was wise enough to design every aspect of the universe. He is the God who was powerful enough to create it. He is the God who is amazing enough to sustain the earth and attentive enough to care for each individual creature. He is the God who sovereignly controls the fiercest weather.

As God rehearsed these amazing truths, Job suddenly saw himself as small and insignificant. What was he in comparison to God? Job could not speak against God. His words and protests were silenced as he placed his hand on his mouth. Job realized that he was so far from knowing as God knows that his human words were worthless. You, too, must recognize who God is. He is so great that you cannot question His actions or wisdom. Simply put your hand on your mouth and be silent.

"I have no grounds, Father, for questioning or speaking against You. Help me to submit to You in each new day and in each new circumstance."

Day 360

"Will you really annul My judgment?
Will you condemn Me that you may be justified?"
Job 40:8

It is natural to want to escape difficult circumstances. It is normal to want the pressure to be relieved. It is a completely understandable response to long for the trial to be over and for life to be easier. God invites us to come to Him with our prayers and burdens, and certainly it is appropriate for us to ask God to deliver us.

In the midst of our asking, however, we must be careful to submit ourselves to God's plan. When our prayers for deliverance don't subordinate themselves to God's will, they take on a whining tone and very quickly cross the line into accusing God. Our prayers become complaints about how wrong our situation is. They become criticisms of God's wisdom and assertions that He should be handling things better. Without intending to or even realizing that we are doing it, we have formulated in our minds a plan that seems better than what God has chosen.

God had to confront Job with that very situation. Job had complained about his situation and had repeatedly declared how unfair it was. The extension of that thought was that God had done the wrong thing. God came to Job with a sobering question. He made Job stop and think about what he was saying. While Job wanted to rant or blow off steam, God asked him to seriously consider the question of whether he would actually change the plan ordained by God.

Would Job really veto God's decision if he were able to? Would he really insist that he was right rather than God? Job responded to God's questions by humbling himself before Almighty God. Job realized that God can do whatever He chooses to do without having to explain it to man. When Job realized who God was and who he was, there was no longer any fighting or insistence on his own opinion.

"Father, you are God. You can do whatever You want. I could not and would not change
my situation – not when it's what You have decided is best."

Day 361

"I have heard of You by the hearing of the ear;
But now my eye sees You."
Job 42:5

There are some interesting surprises in the Christian life. You have heard about God's perfect peace being displayed in the midst of a storm. You have read about endurance and patience through trying circumstances. You know of those who have trusted God in the midst of difficulty. You have seen these things in the Bible, and you've heard about them in the testimonies of others.

When you have heard others describe these seeming paradoxes, you have perhaps envied their sweet experience with God. You may have wondered if those things were really true. You may have wondered if these people really meant what they said. Is it actually possible to experience these aspects of Christianity, or are these people just saying the words that they're supposed to say?

Some things can be fully realized only in the midst of a trial. Although the trial itself is not pleasant, there is tremendous blessing and encouragement when you experience those spiritual victories personally. It is wonderful to realize that these concepts are not just Christian theory; they are reality, and they are possible for you. They aren't just things that happened to people in the Bible or to people that you've heard about. They are, in fact, a first-hand demonstration of the obvious relationship that God has with you personally.

Like Job, you can now admit to having learned about God in a whole new way. What you knew before was a fuzzy and incomplete picture. Now your head knowledge has become experiential knowledge, and the increased comprehension helps your relationship with God to leap forward. You have a new understanding of God. You have now experienced and lived through what previously was largely theory. Having seen these things proven true in your life, it has become easier to believe other things in the Bible and expect them to be true and personal as well. You have increased confidence in God based on your deeper knowledge of Him.

"Father, my view of You in the past has been so limited. Thank You for this opportunity to come to know You like I never have before. Thank You for being so real."

Job's Responses
Oh God, although it hurts, I know You're just;
For each thing taken, You were first the source.
Your work's not wrong, and worship You I must.
I take the good and bad, each in its course.

Oh God, undying trust is due Your hand.
My hope is firm, though You bring me to death.
I know one day I'll see You take Your stand,
Though worms destroy my skin and I've no breath.

Oh God, You are a source of wondrous might;
There's not a man can thwart Your purpose bold.

$\longrightarrow$

321

> *You know my way; You can do all things right.*
> *Your cleansing work can make me shine as gold.*
>
> *Oh God, You are too big for me to know.*
> *I spoke of things so wonderful and vast,*
> *But now I realize that they're really so.*
> *I'm humbled to observe my God at last.*
>
> *Oh God, I realize now that You are God.*
> *I would not dare to change what You decide,*
> *For what am I but just an earthly clod?*
> *I will be mute, and lay all words aside.*

Day 362

> *Now may the God who gives perseverance and encouragement grant you to be of the same*
> *mind with one another according to Christ Jesus.*
> *Romans 15:5*

One of the hardest things about a long illness is precisely that – its length. It's hard to be sick for a week or even a day. When an illness extends to a month, six months, or two years, it takes on an entirely new dimension. It seems like it will never end, and maybe it won't.

How do you handle the permanency of an illness? To some extent you may get used to living with illness, but you never make the mistake of viewing your life as normal. You don't come to the point of enjoying your condition. You don't eventually become oblivious to the pain. No, those things continue day after day. What can you do in the midst of a difficult situation that you know will only continue (and perhaps even get worse)?

What is there to do but endure? You just have to get through one more day, and then one more day. You have to endure. *Endurance* is not really a pleasant word. It's not what you want to focus on when you think about your illness – that you just have to keep going. At the same time, you know that endurance has value. You know that it is admirable and that it brings spiritual fruit. You know that it is what God asks of you. Endurance is a good thing.

Knowing these truths is the easy part. How do you do it? How do you endure? You can't just drum up willpower. You can't dig deep within yourself and find the strength to go on. If you believe you can do that, you haven't been sick enough for long enough. All humans are weak and frail. No, endurance is not in you; it comes from God. Perseverance is one of God's gifts. God is the source of endurance. Rather than trying to produce perseverance on your own, you must depend upon

God for what only He can supply. You must ask Him for it and trust Him to give it to you.

"Father, I can't keep going. Please give me perseverance to meet each new day."

Day 363

For it is God who is at work in you, both to will and to work for His good pleasure.
Philippians 2:13

Do you sometimes feel like a complete failure as a Christian? Do you wonder how you can possibly struggle so much? Does it seem that you will never gain victory? Is your spiritual appetite colder than the ice cubes in your freezer? In spite of all your efforts, do anger and discouragement threaten to take control? These are troubling and frustrating thoughts.

When it seems that you are making no spiritual progress and that you are, in fact, becoming weaker and weaker, you have no valid excuse for giving up. You must remember that there are many related factors going on in your life. For example, your illness itself or the treatment for it can cause very real mental limitations and overwhelming physical fatigue. There is a spiritual aspect to your struggle, but there is also an undeniable physical aspect, and you may not be capable of distinguishing between the two. When you seem incapable of understanding the Bible, or when you find it impossible to pray for more than two minutes, you don't always know why that is. There may be no way for you to know how much of your struggle is spiritual weakness and how much is a limitation of your physical weakness. Instead of torturing yourself about this uncertainty, you simply have to leave it with God and rest in His truth.

God *is* at work in you. He is the one who helps you not only to do the right thing, but also to even want to do it. The truth is that you can never make the results happen by your own efforts. Only God can produce the results. Do what you can; keep fighting and keep trying, but don't demand a certain level of results. Let God take care of that. He knows the reasons for your struggles, and He is the only one who can give results.

It is encouraging to know that God does the work in you for His good pleasure; He does it because He wants to. God derives pleasure from the work He does in you and from the results that He achieves. God likes what happens, so it is reasonable that He will dedicate time, energy, and dedication to the task. In human terms, the process can be compared to a hobby – a project that one throws himself into because he enjoys both the process and the end result. If God enjoys doing the work in you, there is no danger that He will stop.

"Father, I'm so confused. I don't know why I struggle so much. Help me to be faithful and help me to trust You to do Your work and to give the results."

Day 364

Lord, You have been our dwelling place in all generations.
Psalm 90:1

God is our Dwelling Place. A dwelling place is quite simply where someone or something lives. For a bird it is the nest. For an animal it is his den. For a man it is his home. Our dwelling place is where we go to retreat from the strife of the world and to escape the pressures of work and business. It is a place of belonging and acceptance with those who are closest to us. It is a place where everything is familiar. It is a place that is the same day after day in the midst of the changes that surround us. Our dwelling place is where we can relax and lay aside the professionalism that we must present to the world. It is where we can be comfortable, peaceful, and at rest. Our dwelling place is where we are most at home. It is a place of comfort and belonging.

Imagine if we could live constantly with God's presence as our home, our safe and peaceful retreat, and the place that we most long to be. Such surroundings would give us an incredible measure of peace, security, and comfort. Instead of a rare visit, God desires us to reside habitually with Him. With brief periods in God's presence, we receive limited benefit; as our time with Him is extended, the benefits are magnified. God can be our trusted dwelling place. He can be the place that we gladly go back to time after time after facing the challenges of the day. No matter how hard and how crazy things become, we know we have an unfailing retreat.

"Father, what a blessing to forget all the craziness and just rest in You. When I stay in You, I don't have to worry about all the cares and concerns."

Day 365

Put on the full armor of God, so that you will be able to stand firm against the schemes of the devil.
Ephesians 6:11

In the midst of our weakness, Satan sees opportunity. He makes every attempt to try to defeat us, but with God's help, we can stand firm against the attacks. In Ephesians 6, God gives two instructions to help us in the battle. The first, found in verse ten, is to be strong. The instruction is given twice, and both times the strength is identified as being God's strength. We are not and cannot be strong in ourselves.

The second instruction, which fills the next several verses, is to put on the complete armor of God. The armor will help us to withstand the attacks of Satan. In fact, that is God's reason for telling us to wear it: so that we can firmly resist in the spiritual battle. The obvious implication is that we *can* stand firm and that the victory *can* be won. We don't have to be defeated by it or even pushed around or caused to run. We can confidently hold our territory.

The instruction also reveals the nature of the enemy. This is no natural enemy. We are fighting the devil himself. We are fighting against the power and leaders of a worldly system that hates God and against the wickedness of the spirit-world controlled by Satan. This is too daunting a task for mere mortals; God's help is essential.

Standing firm would be impossible without the armor. We need the belt of truth holding everything together; there is no room for doubts or wrong thinking. We need the breastplate of righteousness to protect our most vulnerable spots, and Christ's righteousness is impermeable. We need the shoes of the gospel, which will ultimately end all battles. We need the shield of faith. Our confidence in God's ability to defend us causes the arrows to fall to the ground and even to be extinguished. We need the helmet of salvation, which also protects a very vital spot. Finally we fight back with the sword of the spirit, which is the truth of God's Word. This effective armor is called the armor of God, and it is all God's. It is made up of His truth, His imputed righteousness, His gospel, faith in Him, His salvation, and His Word. Our best efforts would fall far short, but God's armor is up to the task.

"Help me, Father, to use Your truth to combat error and temptation. Give me Your strength to allow me to stand firm against the devil."

Day 366

Now may the Lord of peace Himself continually grant you peace in every circumstance. The Lord be with you all!
II Thessalonians 3:16

A series of questions can help us to examine this verse. First, what is it that we want to receive? Peace. We long for peace both in our troubled world and also in our individual situations. Peace does not come naturally, but it is something that we desire because it makes such a vast difference in facing the chaos of life.

Who gives us peace? God. God is able to give peace because of who He is. He is the Lord of peace. Peace is part of His character; He knows what true peace is. God is able to give peace when no one else can, because He is the source of peace.

How does God give peace? Personally and freely. He Himself gives the peace. He takes a personal interest and He personally interacts with us. He makes sure the job is done. He grants the peace freely. It is not something we have to buy or earn. He gives it because He determines that we need it.

When does God give peace? Now and always. Peace is not something that we want to wait for, and Paul's prayer was that it would be given right away. The giving of peace, however, is not a one-time thing. God doesn't grudgingly give it once and then require us to make it last forever. He gives it continually. God's peace is a gift that keeps giving and keeps being renewed day after day and year after year.

What is the context in which God gives peace? In every circumstance. God is not limited regarding the situations in which He can give peace. In addition to giving it in the "easy" situations, He can also give it in the most challenging situations. Some scenarios are so awful that we would not imagine peace to be possible, but God can give it even then. It doesn't matter how daunting the situation, nor does it matter how many situations there are. God can give peace in every situation we face, even when that list of situations reaches the hundreds or thousands. God is the source of peace, and He can give it effectively at all times and in all places.

"Father, You know I need peace. Even when I have it, it seems to fade so quickly. Please continue to give me peace day after day. Help me to rest in You."

Day 367

Why are you in despair, O my soul?
And why have you become disturbed within me?
Hope in God, for I shall again praise Him
For the help of His presence.
Psalm 42:5

Despair is a common visitor to someone who has a serious or prolonged illness. There seems to be good reason for that despair. The sufferer has lost the life he once knew. He has heard doctors say words like "We don't know what to do next" or "There is no cure." Every time he thinks he is getting better, the improvement disappears. Each time he glimpses a timeline for recovery, it slips further and further away. The new medicines and treatments fail to live up to expectations. The constant assaults of the illness squeeze out every bit of hope.

If the sufferer takes the time to look around him, he will quickly realize he is not alone. Pain is everywhere. Family and friends are hurting and in pain. They are left confused and frustrated by the curve balls of life. Not only does the sick person carry his own burdens, but he also bears the burdens of others. The weight gets heavier and heavier, and it is easy for each new trial he observes to weigh him down even more. It is easy to despair – easy when he sees pain all around him, easy when there seems to be a new challenge around every corner, easy when the same old challenges keep returning to attack again. These constant assaults rob hope.

So if the disease robs man of hope, he cannot put his hope in his health or improvement or prospects. He cannot put his hope in the happiness and peace of others. He must put his hope in something bigger: *"Hope in God."* He must remember that he has a God who is bigger than every challenge. If he is to have stability and hope, his gaze must be fixed on God. No matter how big the mountain is that casts its shadow of despair, God is bigger. God must be remembered in times of despair. His presence is a help, and it gives real hope. Hope in God is well-placed, because there will *always* be another reason to praise God.

"Father, help me to fix my gaze on You rather than on the pain. When everything else is gone, You are still with me. No amount of despair can swallow up the hope found in You."

Day 368

As the deer pants for the water brooks,
So my soul pants for You, O God.
Psalm 42:1

If ever in my life I need You, God, I need You now. I am sensing needs that go deeper than any I have ever experienced before, and they require solutions more profound than any answer I've ever found before. Only You can meet those needs. Only You can meet the deepest longings and desires of my heart. Nothing else will truly satisfy – not a knowledgeable doctor, not caring friends, not faithful family. Not even restored health will meet my deepest level of need. No, God, I need You. You are my source of life. You are my life itself. What is there without You? Just like the deer would die without water, I would have no life without You.

God, You are my dearest friend. Just like with earthly friendships, my friendship with You can grow deeper and sweeter. Often when two people walk through a difficult or challenging experience together, their friendship deepens as a result. So it is with You, God. This time of my life has been and continues to be a tremendous challenge. Because You are with me and because we have gone through this time together, our friendship is deeper than ever. You have walked every step with me. You have listened to the outpouring of my soul's burdens when no one else could understand them.

I love You more than I ever have before. I have a stronger desire to serve You. I have a greater level of confidence in You. I have long desired for You to be my best friend to the extent that I would be assured that it was so, but it took something like this to make that happen. It took this intense situation for me to realize that, yes, You really are my very best friend. No one else, no matter how special, no matter how helpful, can come close to You. I need You.

"Father, keep alive – no, increase my passion for You. May I be thirsty for You so that our friendship can grow yet more and more."

I Seek You, Lord
It's time to seek while You are near.
It's time to call; You'll say, "I'm here."
I seek You, Lord. I seek Your face.
My need is great; I need Your grace.

My sinful soul heads to the grave.
I know that You alone can save.
I seek You, Lord. I seek Your face.
My need is great; I need Your grace.

Upon my knees I humbly fall.
From sin I turn; I yield it all.
I seek You, Lord. I seek Your face.
My need is great; I need Your grace.

My path is dark. What shall I do?
I'll seek Your will, my eyes on You.
I seek You, Lord. I seek Your face.
My need is great; I need Your grace.

I can't go on; my strength is small.
I'll lean on You; You'll do it all.
I seek You, Lord. I seek Your face.
My need is great; I need Your grace.

My spirit pants for such a Friend.
My life with You will never end.
I seek You, Lord. I seek Your face.
My need is great; I need Your grace.

Day 369

But by the grace of God I am what I am, and His grace toward me did not prove vain; but
I labored even more than all of them, yet not I, but the grace of God with me.
I Corinthians 15:10

Have you noticed that God is changing you? Perhaps others have even expressed their observation that you have grown spiritually through your time of illness. There is a sense of excitement when you first realize that God is changing you through your trial. It is encouraging to see that you are not the same as you were before. Whether you notice specific areas of growth or an overall maturity, it is exciting to see that God is doing something in you. Your suffering is not in vain. God's grace and work have not been in vain.

Like Paul, we may give diligent effort to make the most of the opportunities, but it is God who does the work. It is His grace that brings the growth and makes the changes. As you take stock of the growth God has brought, do you realize that you couldn't have bought or earned that growth? You couldn't have read a book that would have showed you how to make the changes. You could not have chosen areas of growth and followed a plan to purposefully learn them. You could not in any way have produced the changes.

The changes came about only because of God's grace within the specific situation He has specially designed for you. He knew the setting that was necessary. You didn't choose that setting; even knowing what you know now, you probably wouldn't choose it. The whole thing happened only because God designed it. Truly His grace has made you what you are.

God is in control of your spiritual growth. You can't perform rituals or routines to achieve growth. There is no magic phrase to pray every day that will bring changes about. Certainly you need to be in a submissive and teachable state before Him, but even that desire comes from Him. In all ways it is God who gives the growth. Should you notice the growth and be thankful? Absolutely. That thankfulness should be directed to the God who worked the changes through His grace.

"Father, thank You, thank You, thank You. You have done for me what I could never have
done for myself, through a situation that I would never have chosen. Thank You."

Day 370

And do not be conformed to this world, but be transformed by the renewing of your
mind, so that you may prove what the will of God is, that which is
good and acceptable and perfect.
Romans 12:2

Oh, how our minds need to be renewed! More than at any other point in our lives, our thoughts are unstable and troubled. Our minds think the craziest things, even things that we know are wrong. Our thoughts are unsteady, changing rapidly, and too many of our thoughts fall into areas where we don't want them to be. It feels like we are in a constant battle that uses up all of our time and energy. We want the battle in our minds to get easier, but the truth is that it is a battle and it is hard.

Our natural thoughts include anger, resentment, bitterness, discouragement, confusion, despair, and similar things. Sadly, we have thought those types of thoughts so often and are so used to thinking them that our thoughts very easily follow those familiar patterns. Very quickly our thinking spirals out of control and always downward.

We need to renew our minds. We need to create new patterns for our thoughts to follow. In order to get a different result, we must change the path. This happens with a focus on Scripture and God's thoughts. We must do less thinking about self and less dwelling on the negative. By contrast, we must do more thinking about God and more thinking about truth and hope. There is a distinct difference between natural thoughts and supernatural thoughts. With a renewed mind, we can think thoughts of submission, hope, trust, faith, and confidence. The result is so much different, and that difference is clearly a result of God's help.

It isn't always easy to think in the right way. Some days are harder than others, but right thinking will gradually get easier as we make a habit of consistently turning our thoughts back to God. We must face the hard times realistically. Sometimes the challenge will increase simply because we are getting tired. We cannot expect a complete change overnight. It takes time to build new habits. There will be continued failures, but we can't focus on the failures. We must confess those and move on, while focusing on the times of victory. With God's help, we can renew our minds and begin to think differently.

"Help me, Father, to establish new patterns of thinking. I want to have new and positive paths for my thoughts to follow. Help me to think Your thoughts."

Day 371

You have taken account of my wanderings;
Put my tears in Your bottle.
Are they not in Your book?
Psalm 56:8

God pays attention to His children. He gives such close observation to their struggles that He knows every step that they take and every tear that they shed. God keeps track of every path that must be walked. He is keeping a careful record. He marks down each weary step. He records every sharp turn and every twisting way. He knows when the path is all uphill. He knows when the footing grows treacherous and when the way is dangerous. God takes meticulous note of every aspect of every path. Not one bit of it is a surprise to Him. His children never have to walk without His attention on them.

God also keeps track of every tear that is shed. He sees when the tears well up in the eyes, threatening to spill over. He sees the quivering chin and the trembling lip. He hears the slightest sniffle. He sees the tears that trickle slowly down the cheeks, and He sees the tears that flow without ceasing. He sees the racking sobs that shake the entire body, and He sees the internal tears that ooze out of a hurting heart. God sees the awkward tears that flow in public as well as the lonely tears that happen in private. He sees the tears that are shed during the long nights and throughout the lengthy days. God takes all of those tears and saves them. He records every one of them in His book, along with His record of the steps that have been taken.

God cares very deeply for His children. He pays careful attention to things that most people don't even know. Is it any wonder that in the next verse David says that he knows God is for him?

"There have been a lot of steps and a lot of tears, Father. Thank You that You know about all of them. Thank You for caring so intimately about my life."

Day 372

But to the degree that you share the sufferings of Christ, keep on rejoicing, so that also at the revelation of His glory you may rejoice with exultation.
I Peter 4:13

Rejoicing is a strange response in the midst of suffering. We would not be able to do so without a good reason. One reason we can rejoice is that we are aware of sharing the sufferings of Christ. Although we are able to share in Christ's sufferings, we do not experience suffering to the same degree that He did. Nevertheless, as we suffer, we are able to experience and understand something of what Christ experienced for us. There is a deeper friendship and special warmth we experience when we share a hardship with someone else. It binds our hearts closer together and gives us a greater appreciation for that person. Having that stronger bond with Christ is a cause for rejoicing. We are able to keep a happy and cheerful spirit as we realize the stronger bond that is being formed with our Savior.

This positive and peaceful response is really just a shadow of the rejoicing to come. We will have a much greater response of rejoicing when we see Christ. If we have ever suffered with someone and borne the burden of his heart over a long distance, haven't we been that much more excited to finally see him in person? First of all, we were thrilled to finally see in person the one to whom we have grown closer. Second, when we are united with Christ in glory, the trial will be over and we will be able to rejoice in the victory. Having suffered with Christ by facing the trial here on earth, we will be able to rejoice with exultation when we reach heaven. This is a stronger rejoicing than what we have now; it refers to exceeding joy that makes us leap in the air. Our rejoicing will be compounded greatly when we see Him.

"Thank You, Father, for the opportunity to share the experience of suffering with Christ.
I long for the day when we can rejoice together."

Day 373

But certainly God has heard:
He has given heed to the voice of my prayer.
Blessed be God,
Who has not turned away my prayer
Nor His lovingkindness from me.
Psalm 66:19-20

God hears your prayers. There is absolutely no doubt at all regarding that fact. God listens when you pray. He pays attention. He never ignores your prayers or tosses them away. Often God answers those prayers dramatically, perhaps in an outstanding way that screams out that only God could have done such a thing. Other times He has answered so quietly and smoothly that the hurdle was barely noticed.

Think back. Hasn't God answered many prayers in the course of your illness? Your list might include a supportive family, a knowledgeable doctor, encouragement to seek treatment, money for medications, an understanding friend, rides to appointments, meals, and cleaning. Those are the kinds of answers that you love to see.

It is probably also true that some of the answers to prayer have not been the answers you anticipated or desired. Perhaps test results were delayed, inconclusive, or positive. Maybe you have experienced ineffective treatment, unsuccessful surgery, or continued pain. Maybe the side effects were worse than you expected. Perhaps your doctor put you off or your insurance denied coverage. Maybe the bills piled up and the friends disappeared.

Those disappointing responses were still God's answers. None of those answers were what you asked for, but they were God's answers just as much as the "successful" answers to the other prayers. The important thing is not that you receive what you want, but rather that God's will be done. As you pray, you can have great confidence in the pending answers to your prayers. God will hear you. Whatever happens will be His answer. No matter what the outcome, you can bless God as the psalmist did and declare to those around you the account of what God has done for your soul (Psalm 66:16). You can tell your friends that God is at work in your life.

"Thank You, Father, for hearing and considering every prayer. Give the answer You choose. Help me to accept all Your good answers and to praise You for them even when they aren't what I choose."

Day 374

On God my salvation and my glory rest;
The rock of my strength, my refuge is in God.
Psalm 62:7

God is the Rock of our strength. When we think of God as our rock, we tend to think of Him as a large, stable, and unmoving boulder upon which we can safely build our foundation. We picture something massive and unshakeable like the Rock of Gibraltar. The book of Psalms uses two Hebrew words for *rock*, and neither of them presents this picture. Instead, both words express the idea of a sharp or ragged rock, or even a cliff.

This type of rock is used as a defensive position or a hiding place. The rock is meant not as a place of stability, but as a refuge and place of protection. Instead of resting on top of the rock, we are hiding behind it, most likely tucked away in one of its crevices. The rock offers many hiding places to those who trust in it, while it presents a great challenge to those trying to attack. The rock is a formidable foe. Anything that reaches us must first conquer the rock, resist the danger inherent in it, and avoid the potential injury that it threatens.

More than just *being* a rock for us, God *gives* us some of the rock. As the rock of our strength, He does something for our human strength. In this situation the word for *strength* probably refers to an internal fortitude that allows us to be strong and able to resist trouble. The term speaks of being stout and hardened. When God gives us that kind of rock-hard strength, we see the possibility for a kind of strength we've never experienced before. It is as if God has gone to a rock quarry, where He has split off a piece of rock and has implanted it in our backbone. The result confirms that any strength we have is clearly from God.

*"Father, You know how weak I am. I need some rock put into me. I also need to hide in
You as my rock. You can help me to face the attacks
and You can also keep them from reaching me."*

Day 375

*"As for you, you meant evil against me, but God meant it for good in order to bring about
this present result, to preserve many people alive."*
Genesis 50:20

Bad things happen. Illness is one of those bad things. It is something that we
would all avoid if we could. We would love to be able to go back in time and change
our genetic predisposition, protect ourselves from the carcinogen, avoid the bacteria,
or, in whatever way necessary, eliminate the trigger for our illness. We can't do that.
We can't go back and change the past. We can't change our current condition. As
hard and as painful as our illness may be, we can't avoid what God has sent.

We don't have to focus on the pain, however. To people without Christ, pain
is precisely that – pain. There is no room for a broader description. As Christians,
we can understand that there is more to it than simply pain. In God's world, bad
things take on a broader meaning. As we understand more of God's perspective,
we can interpret our pain differently. Though we can't change the pain, we can see
a different meaning in it.

Instead of being merely a bruising burden, our pain can become the venue in
which God can do a great work. Even in the hardships of life, God has a plan. God uses
those hardships for His purposes. He uses them to display His glory and to work good
for us. Both of these aspects give meaning and purpose to the difficulties we face.

In Joseph's case God took years of hatred, exile, and undeserved punishment,
and He used them to preserve and prosper His chosen people. God took what was
evil and used it for good. God is so good that He can take even what is bad and
make it into something good. Like Joseph, we may live for years without having
any idea of what God's good purposes are, but we can be assured that God will use
everything, including what is bad in our eyes, to accomplish His good purposes.

*"Help me, Father, to trust You to use my pain for Your purposes. Please take what seems
so bad to me and mold it into something good."*

Not the End
Mistreated Joseph faced his brothers' wrath;
Without remorse they sold him as a slave.
Accused was he and thrown into a jail –

Though helpful, not remembered to the king.
This faithful servant spent long years abroad -
Alone, without reward, with none to care.

Poor doomed Naomi had to flee her land
Because of famine that left her no food.
While far from home, her loving husband died,
Soon followed by the deaths of her two sons.
Once full, returning empty to her home,
She bore a broken heart with bitterness.

Our guiltless Savior faced a hating world;
He wandered, poor, without an earthly home.
In agony He sweat great drops of blood,
And then was beaten, mocked, and crucified.
Rejected by His own and not received,
His gift of love was offered oft in vain.

What profit is there in these stories sad?
Do these dark clouds with any silver shine?
Can any good proceed from such events?
Well, Joseph was prepared to help the king.
Naomi maybe learned about her God,
And Christ's compassion makes Him apt to aid.

Can that be all, or is there something more?
Is all the good found in the trial itself?
Within the context, much is gained, it's true.
We learn of God and are prepared to serve.
We see great growth and gain maturity,
And joy o'erflows to see the victory.

Does profit end with just the vict'ry shout?
Oh, no, my friend, the story is not done.
It's true we see the growth within the test,
But God can do much more than what we've seen.
The trial itself is but a steppingstone;
He has more plans; the best is yet to come.

For Joseph saved his family's lives and then
The preservation of the Jewish race.
Naomi's end was privileged and blessed -
To be included in the line of Christ.
And Christ Himself unlocked the way to God,
Extending free salvation to the world.

→

> *So if maturity is all we see*
> *Or we distinguish just the lessons learned,*
> *Would those rewards alone not be enough?*
> *But praise to God, we can anticipate*
> *That He'll begin to do His finest work.*
> *Just wait – the greatest blessing's yet to be!*

Day 376

> *O God, restore us*
> *And cause Your face to shine upon us, and we will be saved.*
> *Psalm 80:3*

There are several reasons for which we might need restoration to God in the course of an illness. The illness might be God's chastening for past rebellion or sin; God might be trying to get our attention so that we will return to Him. We may have committed sins of wrong responses and rebellion during the illness; if we have grown cold toward God through the time of illness, we need to return to Him. The illness may have so limited our mental capacities that we have been spiritually starved against our desires; we need restoration after the inevitable damage done by the lack of spiritual input. Whichever the reason (or combination thereof), we are in need of revival. Our heart cries out for it. We want God to bring us back to a previous spiritual level, and even to strengthen us beyond where we were before.

This verse from Psalm 80 gives a very appropriate prayer for restoration and for God's favor; the verse is found in a psalm dedicated to the topic of revival. The prayer comes after a time of repentance and tears; the speakers have been broken and are now seeking God (vs. 4-5). God has chosen and cared for these people in the past. They now resolve to follow Him faithfully and depend on Him (v. 18).

The speakers realize, though, that their restoration is totally dependent on God (vs. 3, 7, & 19). As much as they want restoration, it cannot come without God's help. God must restore, and He must show His favor and blessing by causing His face to shine upon them. The restoration can come only as God shows His favor. Without His favor, there can be only failure and frustration. With His favor, there can be no doubt of successful restoration. Interestingly, because the speakers realize so clearly that God is the one who must restore, the resulting restoration causes them to depend on Him even more and look to Him more faithfully than ever (v. 18).

> *"Help me, Father, to be tender to Your touch so that You can do the work of restoration.*
> *Please bring me back to where I ought to be. Cause Your face*
> *to shine on me. I must have Your favor."*

Day 377

Those who sow in tears shall reap with joyful shouting.
Psalm 126:5

There aren't many serious illnesses that do not at some point lead to tears. Some people may have frequent tears, while others may shed them only rarely, but the tears are a normal response to such a weighty trial. There can be tears from emotional strain, from physical weakness, from hopeless news, and from constant challenge. Tears are a natural part of life.

Psalm 126 records the intense crying done by the people of Israel when they were in captivity. It was a bitter and very difficult time for them. They longed for the former blessings and for the bountiful life they had formerly lived.

The psalm reveals that the time of tears was a precursor to a time of joy. God brought Israel back from captivity; He restored them to their land. Their tears and sorrow turned to laughter and joy because God had done great things for them. Not only did Israel itself recognize God's great work, but even the surrounding nations realized that God had done great things for Israel. The sorrow was forgotten and joy abounded. The time of sorrow was necessary first before the intense joy could come. The psalm compares the process to that of sowing seed and then reaping a harvest. When God does great things, He often uses times of great sorrow as the seed for the bountiful harvest that He will give. How does that happen? How can a serious illness be the platform for great rejoicing?

First, God could heal the illness. When He does, the joy of renewed health surpasses and outshines the previous appreciation for life. All involved are able to rejoice at the great things God has done through answered prayer.

Second, God could work in the life through the illness. God could do a transforming work in the life, something that would not have happened apart from the illness. There is rejoicing in the great things God has done in changing and maturing a person.

Third, God could transfer the sick person to heaven. While this does bring sorrow, it also brings great rejoicing in the realization that the person is no longer suffering, but rather enjoying God's presence. In each of these cases, the ill person himself can rejoice, and those around him can also rejoice at the great things God has done.

"Father, my life seems to be filled with tears. If I will only wait, I will see You change the tears to rejoicing. May I trust You to do that, and may I be patient until it happens."

Day 378

But godliness actually is a means of great gain when accompanied by contentment.
I Timothy 6:6

Because it is a life-long area of growth, we logically expect older people to display contentment best. It's easy to think of a sweet elderly Christian who is an excellent display of contentment, perhaps in the face of poor health or loneliness. It's also easy to think of a cranky, sour old Christian who is not a pleasure to be around. Both may have learned much about godliness, but godliness without contentment spoils what otherwise would be a very beautiful person.

Growth in contentment ought to be part of the Christian life, but that growth is not automatic. If we want to mature into sweet older Christians instead of cranky ones, we must grow in contentment. Submission is only the first step. We can submit to something without being content. A two-year old may refuse to eat lima beans; that's neither submission nor contentment. An eight-year old might eat them because he has to; that's submission without contentment. An adult may eat them and be aware of their positive contribution to the meal. Finally, that is submission with contentment.

Contentment is about the depth of our attitude, and that depth should keep increasing. Submitting to God about our illness is the beginning, but it can be incomplete. We may pray things like, "God, I know this is what you have for me, and I know you are going to use it, but I don't like it." We are willing to go through the trial, and we express our willingness to God, but we're also expressing how we feel about it.

Honesty with God is important. We should tell Him the truth and discuss our hearts with Him, but we should also grow. If every time we talk to God about our illness, we insist on telling Him we don't like it, how deeply do we really believe that His will is good? Does it make any sense that we hate the good plan that God has chosen for us? Everything that God does is good. When we habitually express our distaste for God's plan, we may be submitting, but we aren't very content. We are eating the lima beans, but making faces the whole time. If we really believe that what God has chosen is good, than we have to be satisfied to live out His plan. When our contentment grows, our godliness produces greater value.

"Father, it's awfully hard to like this, but I know it is good. Help my contentment to grow so that I can be a more beautiful picture of godliness."

Day 379

After you have suffered for a little while, the God of all grace, who called you to His eternal glory in Christ, will Himself perfect, confirm, strengthen and establish you.
I Peter 5:10

Suffering does not last forever. It is only for a little while, for a limited time. Though that time may seem very long to us, it is comforting to know that God has placed a limit on the suffering. He will end it. It will not last forever, and it will not extend any longer than God has designed.

The fact that our trial will end is in itself a very comforting thought. Even more amazing and encouraging is the way in which it will end. After we have suffered, and when God has determined that our trial should end, God Himself will come to our rescue. The process of suffering definitely involves more than just the pain and breaking down. After the little while required for that part of the process, God will come and do the healing part of the work.

God is paying attention, and He does not leave us bruised and battered by the trial, expecting us to recover on our own. He is the God of all grace, and He is able to impart that grace to us. God knows us; He has called us with the purpose of eternal glory in Christ. A God like this and with these resources and purposes will not forget or neglect us. He will give the deliverance, and He will bring benefits as a result of the trial.

This deliverance, with its accompanying benefits, does come after the trial. Although the benefits may be partially seen during the trial, they are noticed most clearly in the deliverance stage. That's when it all comes together. We have to wait for those blessed results and in faith believe that God will bring them. Wonderfully, our suffering does come to an end; in fact, it comes to a wonderful end as God places His gracious hand on us.

"Father, help me to wait patiently and in faith for the time that You will deliver me and when You will demonstrate the benefits of this trial."

Day 380

After you have suffered for a little while, the God of all grace, who called you to His eternal glory in Christ, will Himself perfect, confirm, strengthen and establish you.
I Peter 5:10

Yes, we will experience pain, but after that little while of pain, God will direct His personal attention to us. He knows the job is not finished. He now has work to do in our lives in order to maximize the profit of the trial. God's personal attention to us is in four parts.

First, He will perfect us. He will make us complete spiritually, giving us the tools we need and equipping us to serve Him. He will make the necessary adjustments to our character. The word also refers to the process of repairing and mending. God will give the necessary healing after our harsh ordeal.

Second, God will confirm us. He will set us steadfastly, establishing our faith very firmly. Because we have seen that we can trust Him in the time of fiercest trial, it becomes incredibly clear that we never again have reason to doubt Him. He will strengthen our faith as we see confirmed for us that everything we have ever believed about God can be confidently depended on.

Third, God will strengthen us. He will give us an increased spiritual strength and vigor beyond what we had before. He will equip us by increasing our spiritual knowledge and teaching us more than we knew before.

Fourth, He will establish us. He will settle us. He will establish a firm basis for our faith. He will deepen and reinforce our foundation so that we are firmly resting upon it. We will now not be able to be easily shaken, because we have firm and deep roots. All of these wonderful benefits come from God's own hand as He accomplishes His purposes in us.

"Father, do Your work in me. May this trial serve as the basis for the spiritual growth and strengthening that You want to do in me."

Day 381

And God is able to make all grace abound to you, so that always having all sufficiency in everything, you may have an abundance for every good deed.
II Corinthians 9:8

In the course of an illness, life is filled with impossibilities. We can no longer do the things we used to do. We can't be as involved in ministry as we used to be. We can't do all the things for our families that we used to do. Sometimes we can't even walk across the room. With such limitations, how can we please God? How can we accomplish anything valuable for Him?

The answer is found in the grace of God. God can give us grace to accomplish what is impossible for us. When we are stretched far beyond our limits and there is no way humanly possible for us to carry on, God pours out His grace on us and enables us to do good things for Him. God knows how much we need grace. He sympathizes with our human weakness, and He therefore gives His grace to make up for our weakness.

If anyone else tried to give us grace, he would fail and be inadequate, but God's stores are so vast that they can never be exhausted. No matter how many people come to draw from them, and regardless of how big the problems of those people are, God's grace is sufficient. It is so abundant that it will never run out. God's grace abounds, and He gives it to us in such abundance that we are able to do everything that He asks us to do. Nothing is so hard that it is beyond the provision of His sufficient grace. How can we think that we could ever use up all of His grace or be left short?

The truth is that God has far more grace than we can even imagine. He can provide strength for the tasks before us, and He can also work in us to bring about heart responses that glorify Him. With God's grace, we *can* do good deeds for Him. What a privilege it is for us to receive so much of God's grace! Though we are small and insignificant, God considers us important enough that He fills us abundantly with His grace. He pours Himself into us and fills us with His blessing.

"Thank You, Father, that Your grace is so abundant to help me. When I am hurting and broken, help me to find strength and comfort in that grace."

Enough Grace (Sonnet 17)
When problems come and challenges attack,
I am incapable to take them on.
I need some help to make up what I lack.
My strength runs out; my own reserves are gone.
Are others able ample help to send?
No, when I look, I find them far away.
And none who's near – not pastor, parent, friend –
Can give enough to get me through one day.
Naught but the grace of God can be enough.
It matters not to Him how many needs,
How many people, or how very tough,
For grace unbounded from His hand proceeds.
His stores of grace are infinitely vast;
They can't run out, but will forever last.

Day 382

Blessed is a man who perseveres under trial; for once he has been approved, he will receive the crown of life which the Lord has promised to those who love Him.
James 1:12

In our human evaluation we would never think so, but God says that a man who perseveres under trial is blessed. That makes no sense to us. How can a person be well off when he is forced to remain under a trial for a length of time? Wouldn't the blessing be to have the trial removed?

God answers by showing us that the blessing comes afterward. The man is blessed because he will receive a crown of life. That crown will be given once he is approved. He must first go through the fire and be found acceptable. He must pass the test. The crown is not given if he falls in the trial. He can't give up.

On the other hand, the requirement is perhaps stated not as strongly as we might expect. God wants His child to stay under the situation and be found acceptable. He doesn't require great leaps of faith, bold acts for Him, or superhuman strength. Essentially, the man must be faithful. Faithfulness is what Christians should exhibit anyway. That is what God requires of His servants. God is giving a crown for something that is really expected of all Christians. The circumstances under which this man must be faithful are just a little harder.

Does this man endure only for the reward? Is his motivation so that he can earn a crown? Oh, no. He faithfully endures because he loves God. God has promised this crown to those who love Him, implying that the reason His children persevere is that they love Him. It is love for God that produces the willingness to suffer. God's reward is given not so much for the faithful endurance, but for the love that motivates it.

> *"Father, may my love for You be deep enough*
> *that I can willingly endure what You place upon me."*

Day 383

> *He brought me up out of the pit of destruction, out of the miry clay,*
> *And He set my feet upon a rock making my footsteps firm.*
> *He put a new song in my mouth, a song of praise to our God;*
> *Many will see and fear*
> *And will trust in the LORD.*
> *Psalm 40:2-3*

Do you feel like you have been cast into a pit of destruction? Do you feel yourself sinking in the miry clay with no possibility of escape? The pit and the clay are, of course, not literal, but they are very real. If you have been sick for very long, you recognize the picture of the swallowing pit. You also realize that the most dangerous pits are not the physical ones, the struggles of your body in the midst of illness. Far more numerous and far more deadly are the pits that threaten to swallow your spirit.

These pits present great danger, but they are not inescapable. You can call out to God. God listens to your desperate cry, and He can deliver you. He can lift you up out of the imprisoning clay that shifts so uneasily beneath your feet, and He can place your feet firmly on a rock that will never move. Instead of constant unsteadiness, you can have a solid footing and restored balance.

God's deliverance is so wonderful that it can put a song of praise in your mouth. Your words can flow forth with admiration to God, the only one who could have given such a dramatic deliverance. The struggles of the soul are so intense that only God could rescue you from them. The rescue itself is so wonderful and dramatic that it begs for a song of praise. Your song of praise not only reflects the joy in your own soul for what God has done, but it also has benefit for others.

Others see your deliverance; they hear your song. They also know how impossible such a rescue of the spirit is. They know that such harsh obstacles cannot be overcome, but that they drown their victims. How then, can you have a song in such a setting? No one expects you to sing, so when you do, your song attracts attention. The only possible answer is that you have a God who is real. You have a God who does what is amazing and even impossible. This realization causes fellow Christians to be blessed and encouraged. It causes the unsaved to stand in awe and to consider the truth of Christianity and the reality of God. Either way, God receives glory.

"Father, deliver me from my pit. Place my feet in a firm place. Fill my lips with praise. May the unexpected song draw attention to You, the deliverer from impossibilities."

Day 384

The LORD will command His lovingkindness in the daytime;
And His song will be with me in the night,
A prayer to the God of my life.
Psalm 42:8

God is *"the God of my life."* He is the very source of life, the one who gave it to me. From my earliest existence, God has controlled and superintended over my life. He was the God of my life at the beginning, and He has been the God of my life every day since.

God is the one who has kept me alive. He is the one who has daily supplied me with breath. He is the one who has sustained every beat of my heart. He is the one who has maintained the systems of my body. God is the one who has spared me from accidents.

God is the God of my life now. I exist today only because God continues to do what He has always done. The God of my life has determined exactly how my body should function. He has controlled every change. While He has allowed weakness, He continues to supply me with life.

God will be the God of my life for as long as I live. I need to depend on Him for every coming day. Each day and week and year that I continue to live will be because of God. He is the one who will give me life for each remaining day. He is the one who will maintain my body.

When the time comes for me to die, this same God will continue to be the God of my life. He was with me at the very beginning, and He will be with me at the very end. As long as I have life, He will be the God of it. When this earthly life finally ceases, the God of my life, having been faithful through every moment, will become the God of my eternity. I will continue to exist because of Him, and I will exist in a wonderful new body that He has prepared for me.

"Father, You are the God of my life – every hour, every day, every year. I exist only because of You and only through Your sustaining."

Day 385

For by these He has granted to us His precious and magnificent promises, so that by them you may become partakers of the divine nature, having escaped the corruption that is in the world by lust.
II Peter 1:4

There is an interesting complication with the promises of people. If people promise something too dramatic, they are unable to keep the promise. If, on the other hand, they promise something they are capable of doing, the promise isn't that exciting. Sometimes people don't even keep those rather mundane promises.

God is quite different from people. God gives promises that are worth something. The promises of God are precious and magnificent. God doesn't offer worthless little things, but promises that are truly incredible. God's promises are worth getting excited about. They are capable of encouraging you. Even though these promises of God are so amazing, He is able to keep every single one. God follows through with what He promises. What are some of these precious and magnificent promises?

God will never leave you and never forsake you. God will be with you wherever you go. God will listen to your prayers. God will give you wisdom when you ask. Christ will pray for you. God will help you against the attacks of Satan. God will provide a way to escape temptation. You will never escape God's love. You will never exhaust God's grace. God will protect you with His peace. God will meet your every need. God will give you strength for every task. God will never let you slip out of His hand. God will give you eternal life. God will take you to heaven when you die. This amazing list contains just a few of God's magnificent promises. Take some time today to ponder these precious promises and maybe even to add some of your favorites to the list.

"Oh, Father, people have failed me many times, but You never will. You will always do what You have promised. Thank You for the amazing promises You have given."

Day 386

Consider it all joy, my brethren, when you encounter various trials.
James 1:2

This is a hard statement. While there are other passages in Scripture that instruct us to rejoice in tribulation, this statement seems to surpass them in its stated requirement. Not only does it refer to multiplied trials, but it also requires a more complete level of joy. According to this verse, we are to consider it to be *all* joy when we are surrounded with trials.

Our response is to be wholly one of cheerfulness and calm delight. This does not allow us to mix the joy together with other reactions; it makes joy our exclusive reaction. While similar passages do not seem to be quite as demanding, perhaps graciously allowing for the weakness of our humanity, we still must consider the claims of this verse. This verse seems to present the ideal of what God desires and the highest benchmark that a mature Christian should long for.

We must recognize that we rejoice not in the trial itself, but in what we know about it. We know that the trial produces endurance, which leads to maturity. A reaction of all joy is therefore possible when we become convinced and persuaded that the most important thing in the world is the development of godly character in us.

When our overwhelming passion is to be like Christ, then we can rejoice in whatever methods God uses to bring that about. We can count it all joy when we no longer focus on God's method, but instead on the progress of our sanctification. We see God do His work as He carefully focuses the trials for the growth and specific lessons that we need. Each new trial is another way for God to build us, and there is joy in realizing that God is deliberately working to produce something with eternal value. We can have anticipation in expecting Him to do so. As we realize that God is preparing us and making us ready for His service, we can rejoice and allow Him to do the molding that we need.

"Father, help me to be so passionate about growing in Christ-likeness that I will be able to rejoice in whatever methods You choose."

Profit (Sonnet 18)
It's hard to face the tests by God decreed;
They often leave me puzzled and in pain.
Yet they're acceptable and meet a need;
Beyond okay, they're good and give great gain.
My eyes are dim, my knowledge incomplete.
Though I can't fully understand or know,
I still can worship thankful at His feet
For skillful work that He's designed just so.
I cannot grasp the profit just for me;
In growth and trust, there's so much I have gained.
Beyond my "now," there's much that I can't see;
To me alone His work is not restrained.
Aware or not, I'll thank Him all my days,
And for His glorious work give Him much praise.

Day 387

How blessed are those who dwell in Your house!
They are ever praising You.
Psalm 84:4

Psalm 84 describes the abundant blessings associated with dwelling in God's house. While the primary application involves God's house, we know that God's house is special because it is associated with God's presence and God's truth. It seems appropriate then, to also associate these abundant blessings with living in the presence of God. The psalm lists three wonderful blessings associated with remaining in God's presence.

First, the person who does so is provided with a sense of belonging (v. 3). Just as the birds find a home where they belong, God's people have a special place of belonging as they dwell with God. They will never be rejected there, but will have the assurance associated with a nurturing home.

Second, the one who dwells with God receives strength from Him (vs. 5-7). The strength is not something man must come up with on his own; rather, it is strength from God. The strength is internal. This man is able to pass through the most difficult and bitter places and find bounty and blessing. Even the desert is like a spring for him. This strength from God does not wear out; it is constantly renewed so that this man can continue on and on. The strength comes from dwelling in God's presence.

Third, dwelling in God's presence provides access to the goodness of God (v. 11). God gives light and protection to His people as they dwell with Him. He gives them grace and glory in His presence. He doesn't hold back any good thing from them as they walk with Him. Dwelling with God is a means to great blessing: a place of belonging, incredible strength, and access to His goodness.

"How I long to abide with You, Father. Hold me close to Your side and keep me from wandering away. I need what Your presence provides."

Day 388

Humble yourselves in the presence of the Lord, and He will exalt you.
James 4:10

There are different ways of explaining humility. One aspect is that humility involves admitting that I am wrong and God is right. I don't like to admit that I am wrong, but it is frequently true. I am wrong in my understanding of what God is doing. I fail to see the big picture or the end result. I am wrong in my response to what God is doing. My heart resists and rebels. I am wrong in my estimation of my ability to handle the trial. I think I can make it through without messing up. I am wrong in how I present myself to God and others. I try to cover over my problems and pretend that I'm pretty good. In each of these scenarios, I must humble myself. I must admit that I am wrong. I must recognize my own weakness. God already knows; I'm not letting Him know anything new.

The wonderful thing is that God responds graciously when I come to Him in this way. He understands my frame and knows that I am dust, and He compassionately wants to help me. I don't need to fear condemnation from God. He has redeemed me and has paid the price of all my sins. He sees me as righteous in Christ. I can freely admit to Him when I am wrong.

The other side of the equation is admitting that God is right. I don't like to accept something that I don't like or can't understand. I don't like to accept something that causes me pain, but when God sent my illness to me, He was right. Who am I to even think that I could talk back or protest or give God advice? I must place myself before Him as lowly, as not qualified to speak. I must humbly accept all that He does and says. He was right in the past when this whole thing started. He is right today in the midst of my current challenges. He will be right forever, regardless of how things turn out. God is right, and I must let Him control my life as He sees best.

"Father, I am too quick to defend myself and paint a pretty picture of myself. In doing so, I cast doubt upon Your truth and Your decisions. Help me to see You as always right."

Day 389

Just as a father has compassion on his children,
So the LORD has compassion on those who fear Him.
For He Himself knows our frame;
He is mindful that we are but dust.
Psalm 103:13-14

A father's heart responds when he sees his children hurting. He may not be able to do anything to help, but he wants to. This caring concern is intensified when we consider God's response to His children. God cares when we are hurting. He has compassion on our humanity. God knows that we are weak and frail mortals. He created us, and He knows very well the feeble components from which we are made. Because God is so aware of our human frailty, He responds with compassion when our weakness breaks through. God filters His thoughts toward us through His compassionate knowledge. What He understands about us affects the way He acts toward us.

God's understanding compassion plays itself out in many practical ways. He gives us an abundance of blessings, many of which are revealed in Psalm 103. He forgives our sins and removes them exceedingly far away. He heals our diseases. He redeems us from destruction. He crowns us with lovingkindness and compassion. He satisfies us with good things. He renews our strength. He acts righteously toward the oppressed. He is compassionate and gracious. He is slow to anger. He abounds in lovingkindness; it exists at excessively high levels. He has not dealt with us as harshly as we deserve.

We may have few friends who understand our illness and its effects. People may look down on us because they fail to understand our struggle. They may act disappointed by our human responses and wish that we could handle things better. These responses are inconsequential. God understands us and responds appropriately. Because He knows our weakness, He does not have unreasonable expectations, nor does He condemn us when we fall short. Instead, He forgives us and helps us to stand back up and keep going. The compassion of people may result only in empty words, but God's compassion is expressed in significant ways that really matter. Our response should be to bless Him and remember His goodness to us.

"May I find comfort, Father, in Your compassionate understanding of my weakness. Help me not to forget your many blessings. May those overwhelming blessings encourage my heart."

Day 390

For this reason, when I could endure it no longer, I also sent to find out about your faith, for fear that the tempter might have tempted you, and our labor would be in vain.
I Thessalonians 3:5

Paul and his companions continually suffered afflictions. They expected this (v. 3) and continued to minister, but the believers in Thessalonica were troubled by the reports of affliction. Paul was concerned that the Thessalonians would be derailed because of his afflictions. He eventually became so burdened about them that he sent Timothy to check on them and encourage them (vs. 1-2). Paul wanted to make sure that the believers weren't being disillusioned or discouraged to turn away from God. He wanted to be sure that their faith was firm.

Affliction, whether it is in our own lives or observed in the lives of those we love, has the potential to lead us from Christ and make us stop following Him. Humans are incredibly fragile and vulnerable. Our flesh is weak because we are only dust and we live in bodies of clay. We must not underestimate the temptation to turn away that a trial brings.

It is so easy to fall. This becomes increasingly true the longer the trial stretches on. It is shockingly easy for someone to fall. In fact, the wonder is not that some people fall away in a trial; the wonder is that everyone does not fall. It is only the grace of God that keeps us from doing what we would assuredly do if we had to depend on our humanity. There is no desire, determination, or effort on our part that can keep us serving God and pleasing Him. The extent to which our lives please Him and are used for Him is due only to His grace. God is the one who keeps us. We must constantly depend on God to hold us firm and to keep us faithful. Only God is able to overcome such a powerful and dangerous temptation.

"Father, on my own I am truly unable to remain faithful. Please keep me close to You lest this trial cause me to fall away."

Day 391

If I should say, "My foot has slipped,"
Your lovingkindness, O LORD, will hold me up.
When my anxious thoughts multiply within me,
Your consolations delight my soul.
Psalm 94:18-19

It is an unpleasant and even frightening situation to feel yourself slipping. There are moments in your illness when that seems to be the only way to describe things. You are too weak to maintain control, and suddenly you are falling. God keeps you steady far more often than you can believe, but there are times when, in spite of everything, you still slip. It can happen unexpectedly when the path seems level and without danger. It also happens on rougher terrain, when every step is a challenge.

How does God respond in those situations? Does He leave you to fall flat on your face? Oh, no. With His gentle and faithful love, He carefully holds you up. The picture is much like that of walking on snowy or icy ground in the winter, as you take someone's arm to help you walk without falling. God offers you His arm to steady you. Your steps might slip and slide, but you have someone who can hold you up and protect you. You may feel unsettled or out of control, but God is there to hold you in your weakness.

Do you not find that some of the most treacherous ground is found in your mind? Your mind is flooded with thoughts that threaten to overwhelm and topple you. Those thoughts can assault you and spiral out of control without warning. You can expect God to hold you steady in those times too. He loves you so much that He can keep you from falling. In the midst of those threatening thoughts, His comfort is available. God can use His love and truth to effectively combat and even reverse your thinking. Take His arm. He can hold you.

"Father, I feel myself slipping so often. My thoughts are especially vulnerable. Hold me up, Father. Stabilize me, and send Your comfort to quiet my thoughts."

Day 392

Therefore, do not throw away your confidence, which has a great reward. For you have need of endurance, so that when you have done the will of God, you may receive what was promised. But we are not of those who shrink back to destruction, but of those who have faith to the preserving of the soul.
Hebrews 10:35–36 & 39

In many ways, it seems that the longer a trial continues, the harder it is to maintain faith. This does not have to be the case, but think about people that you have watched go through hard times. Have you been amazed by their testimony, a testimony that continued to shine brightly even when things got more difficult? Then as the trial reached years instead of months, or decades instead of years, or when another trial was dumped on top of the first two, have you seen Christians who have given up? In the duration of a trial, have you seen people turn away that you never would have expected to do so? It wasn't that they didn't have faith. It wasn't even that their faith was weak. It was simply that their faith did not last long enough. They despaired of ever seeing the answer, and they threw away their confidence.

Instead of throwing your confidence away, you need endurance. You just have to keep waiting and keep believing. Without doubt, there are people who have given up just a short time before God's answer arrived. The answer will arrive. God will respond. There will be a great reward for your faith, and you will receive what was promised. God assures that, and He gives the entire chapter of Hebrews 11 in order to prove it. Some of those people waited many, many years in order to see God's answer. Some of them, in fact, did not live long enough to see God's answer, but it still came. God will do everything He has promised. Maybe you won't live long enough to see God's answer either, but God will always reward faith.

God has not called you so that you can shrink back; He has called you so that you can have faith. The contrast is between an unshakeable belief that refuses to quit and a tentative timidity that easily gives up. These two opposites have very different results, because faith is the way to please God. Is there any reason for you to throw away your confidence in God? None at all. God is faithful. Your confidence in God is well-placed. If you don't see the answers yet, just wait – endure – and those answers will most definitely come. Don't throw away your confidence, because there is something worth having confidence in.

"Father, faith means that I don't see Your answer yet, but I know that it will come. Help me to hold fast to that belief so that I never throw away my confidence in You."

Don't Shrink Back (Sonnet 44)
My child, don't throw away your confidence;
I offer it a rock firm and assured.
Just trust my promises as your defense;
This act of faith I always will reward.
Endurance now to wait is what you need;
Not all deliv'rance happens right away.
As Abram trusted till he saw the deed,
So you must wait; I will do what I say.
You can't shrink back, neglecting faith in Me.
Instead of life, your shrinking will destroy,
But I am pleased whenever faith I see.
Your faith, well-placed in Me, will bring you joy.
Hold fast your confidence day after day.
Endure in faith; don't shrink back or dismay.

Index of Verses

CPSIA information can be obtained at www.ICGtesting.com
Printed in the USA
LVOW041230070812

293268LV00002B/4/P

9 781449 746131